Citizen Coors

Citizen Coors

An
American
Dynasty

DAN BAUM

William Morrow

An Imprint of HarperCollins*Publishers*

HarperCollins books may be purchased for educational, business, or sales promotional use. For information please write: Special Markets Department, HarperCollins Publishers Inc., 10 East 53rd Street, New York, NY 10022.

FIRST EDITION

BOOK DESIGN BY NICOLA FERGUSON

Library of Congress Cataloging-in-Publication Data
Baum, Dan.
Citizen Coors : an American dynasty / Dan Baum.
p. cm.
Includes bibliographical references and index.
ISBN 0-688-15448-4
1. Coors Brewing Company—History.
2. Beer industry—United States—History.
3. Brewing industry—United States—History.
4. Coors family.   I. Title.
HD9397.U54C667   1999
338.7'66342'0973—dc21   99–16830
CIP

00   01   02   03   04   10 9 8 7 6 5 4 3 2 1

For my parents

Contents

[Contents]

Preface

THE GOLDEN FORTRESS

Howdy Folks! read the arch over Washington Street. WELCOME TO GOLDEN. *WHERE THE WEST LIVES*.

Cute slogan, thought Art Stone as he steered his rented car down the main drag of Golden, Colorado, in the summer of 1977. But maybe it should say *WHERE THE WEST STILL LIVES* or *WHERE THE OLD WEST LIVES*. Stone thought a lot about slogans. He was an account executive at one of the nation's premier ad agencies, Leo Burnett and Company of Chicago. Slogans were his business.

Stone fought his city-boy impulse to stomp the accelerator and swerve around the old pickup in front of him. He was in no hurry, after all; he'd arrived early for his appointment to give himself time to check out the town. He cruised slowly past Del's Tonsorial Parlor, with its blue-and-red striped pole. S.C. Western Wear had a lifesize bucking bronco atop its revolving sign. The placard in front of D.J.'s Restaurant promised chicken-fried steak with two vegetables for $1.99. Stone shuddered inside his chalk-striped Savile Row suit.

Golden was more down-at-the-heels than he'd expected, given its romantic name. It looked, really, like any sagging factory town. But what a setting! Undulating above the rooftops was a skyline of pink and tan rock, gleaming with sunshine and rippled with shadow. Just thirty minutes from Denver, Golden felt like a fragment of Hamtramck, Michigan, dropped amid spectacular Rocky Mountain wilderness.

Stone turned right on Twelfth Street and there, just three blocks away, rose the massive Coors brewery, a city unto itself. Great cubes of windowless gray concrete towered above the street, wreathed in steam and topped by the gigantic red Coors logo. The cars and people milling around in front of the plant looked like toys. But even here the works of man were dwarfed by a wall of rock and sagebrush. As Stone waited at a stoplight, his gaze swept up the brewery's mountainous backdrop to a perfect cylinder of red rock that thrust into the diamond-blue sky like a fist.

Knuckles rapped on Stone's window. He rolled it down, and the roasty smell of toasting malt poured into his car. A heavyset man in a BOYCOTT COORS T-shirt thrust a handbill at him. "Brewery Workers Local #366 on Strike for Human Rights," it read. "No Seniority, No Sick Leave, No Dignity." Stone put it on the seat and inched forward. Now he could see a picket line. Several dozen men carrying signs reading UNFAIR paced in front of the gate. What a mess, Stone thought. A company facing competitors like Anheuser-Busch doesn't need labor trouble. He rolled slowly toward the picketers. They gathered around his car, shouting, "Don't cross!" Stone pushed the car gently through the crowd, wincing as palms slapped his hood and trunk. Ahead, he could see a uniformed security officer waving him forward, and as soon as he passed onto company property, the shouting and banging stopped. In his rearview mirror, picketers gave him the finger.

Tell me again, he said to himself. What exactly am I doing here?

Even among family-run corporations, the Adolph Coors Company was an oddball. Bill and Joe Coors, the sixty-two- and sixty-one-year-old brothers who ran the place, spent more than their competitors on their beer and invested a fortune into shipping it cold, owing to what to Stone was a genuine, if anachronistic, obsession with quality. Theirs was a $700 million corporation without a nickel of debt; they refused to borrow money—or to sell voting shares—because they were terrified of outside "control." They fielded only one stodgy product in a complicated marketplace of customer niches. They never paid the kickbacks to retailers and distributors that were standard in the industry. In the increasingly cutthroat brewing business, Coors stood for a time when quality rather than show-manship was rewarded in the marketplace, when a businessman could trust another's handshake, and a craftsman took pride in his product.

But Stone knew that in the Coorses' case, their insistence on refusing to be corrupted by modern times also meant refusing to be educated by them. To Stone, Bill and Joe Coors were an enigma. They made an excellent product, yet made almost no effort to sell it. They seemed deliberately ignorant of the crucial function of marketing. They hired no talent, did no research, shot amateurish ads in-house, and bought cheap TV time. They simply did not play the game.

Yet Coors was the number-one brand in all fourteen western states where it was sold. It was so noticeably superior to its competitors that it inspired devout consumer loyalty; in some places, Coors had three quarters of the market. Coors's potential, Stone had said more than once, was staggering.

If, that is, it could survive the next three years. The modern business world the Coors brothers so disdained had finally kicked in their front door. In 1970, the New York–based Philip Morris Companies had bought the Miller Brewing Company of Milwaukee, giving the genteel community of brewers its first taste of technocratic, cigarette-honed marketing firepower. The industry leader, Anheuser-Busch, had answered the challenge with a jaw-dropping ad budget and a battalion of high-priced marketers hired from the top consumer-products companies in the country. Seven years later A-B and Miller were together spending upward of half a billion dollars a year on ads.

Bill Coors, meanwhile, was still insisting that nobody would "ever choose a beer on the basis of a thirty-second ad." Not surprisingly, Coors's market-share was shrinking everywhere. Bill and Joe appeared ready to ride their principles into the ground.

But maybe not. Coors had just named its first-ever marketing executive. True, the company could have had the best and picked instead a complete unknown from something called American Hospital Supply. But Stone gave the new man credit for being smart enough to call in help from the big leagues.

In fact, that was why Stone was in Golden in the first place: He was getting ready to convince the Coorses that he could build a rip-roaring marketing department from scratch. At a normal company of Coors's size and stature, a thirty-six-year-old account exec like Stone would never have had a shot at such a job. But Coors was hardly your normal American company.

Stone knew, too, that Coors had an additional problem. The family's adherence to handshake-integrity and old-style craftsmanship were coupled with some less universally admired ideals from the nineteenth century: that disparity of wealth is not only inevitable but proper, that efforts to achieve social equality—especially by government—are illegitimate, that the Bible is the rule book for intimate conduct, and that capital must never bow to labor. The Coors brothers, with Joe in the forefront, were dedicating millions to undoing the social, racial, environmental, and sexual revolutions of the late twentieth century. Joe had created the Heritage Foundation and a right-wing TV network, and he was one of Ronald Reagan's first big backers. Moreover, Joe was strikingly public about his politics and philanthropy. He had made himself the poster boy of the conservative movement, and now his company was replacing grapes and lettuce as America's most prominent boycott target. Segments of the left that had either ignored or disparaged each other in the 1960s and '70s— blacks and feminists, unions and gays, greens and migrant workers— were coming together to bash Coors. Through its dedication to the politics of the Right, Coors was ironically becoming the Left's best organizing tool since the Vietnam War.

The Coorses' politics didn't bother Stone personally; he was a Republican who felt the way they did about most issues. But whoever took on the job of marketing Coors beer was going to have his hands full, between the Coorses' contempt for marketing and this organized boycott.

Stone parked and walked inside, giving his name to the receptionist at the front desk. Accustomed to the exquisitely decorated offices of Burnett and its clients, he was struck at once by how colorless the brewery was: gray outside, gray inside. Apparently, hardly a nickel had been spent to adorn the place. A boy in an open-necked short-sleeve shirt and chinos appeared—to take him, Stone assumed, to the vice president of marketing.

But this lad *was* the vice president of marketing. Lee Shelton was a couple of years younger than Stone and dressed like a schoolboy: His clothes appeared to have been pulled from a rack at JCPenney. Stone had his suits made in London, his shirts custom-tailored, and his shoes handmade; he usually wore at least two weeks' pay on his back. As they walked to the Coors family's offices, Stone noticed that people in the hallways raised their eyebrows as he walked past. Some giggled.

Joe Coors and his son, Peter, were dressed exactly like Shelton, as though khaki slacks and tieless sport shirts were the Coors uniform. Joe was a slender giant who wore heavy, black-rimmed glasses. He fidgeted awkwardly, as though his skin didn't quite fit. Peter was equally tall, darkly handsome and, though warmer than his father, also seemed on edge. Stone told them about a recent success he'd had with the Schlitz account at Burnett. He'd repositioned Schlitz Malt Liquor from the black segment of the market, where it was competing unsuccessfully with Colt .45, to the southern white market, where the competition—Country Club—was weaker. Joe, Peter, and Shelton stared; Stone realized his vocabulary—*reposition, segment*—meant nothing to them.

Joe perked up when Stone mentioned that his grandfather had been an independent inventor-entrepreneur, and his father a Nova Scotia farmer—individualists, he added, with no respect for labor unions.

"But business is business," Stone said with a smile. "I had to cross that picket line on my way. I sure hope you can get that cleared up soon."

"We will not be 'clearing that up' at all," Joe said sternly. "It is an unprincipled strike and we are making no effort at all to settle it."

"I'm no fonder of unions than you are," Stone said. "But it would help the company's image not to have pickets outside the brewery."

Joe's frown darkened. "Those pickets, as you call them, have been a part of our family for years," he said, and Stone could see that Joe was struggling to control his emotions. "They have worked hard for us, and we have taken good care of them. This is how they have chosen to express their gratitude. It is not something, frankly, the advertising department need concern itself with."

Peter looked at the floor, visibly embarrassed. Stone was shaken. He wasn't used to topics being off limits. This felt like grammar school.

Some interview, Stone thought, as Shelton walked him back to his car. I didn't even meet Bill, and neither Peter, Joe, nor Shelton know enough about marketing to ask me decent questions. So Stone was floored when the young vice president stuck out his hand in the parking lot and offered him the job. The pay wouldn't be much, but Shelton promised Stone free rein to create a marketing department from the ground up.

As he drove back out through the picket line, Stone wondered what in the world he'd gotten himself into. Having just hired the company's first serious marketer in more than a century of brewing, Bill and Joe Coors might have asked themselves the same question.

I have a feeling you're going to need more than one lesson.
Well, you're going to get more than one lesson.

—*Boss Jim Gettys to Charles Foster Kane*

part
One

1

Sparse Talk

Clear Creek flowed toward Adolph Coors as water and away from him as beer. Born among the frosted peaks of the Continental Divide, it trickles into rivulets atop shoulders of silver plume granite and plunges down twenty-five miles of winding rock canyon into Golden, Colorado—a perfect trove of luscious snowmelt. Adolph Coors founded his brewery here in 1876 with a grubstake of $2,000. Seventeen years later, he was a millionaire. Then Clear Creek rose up and nearly killed him.

It happened on Memorial Day, 1894. A flash flood thundered down the canyon and sheared an expensive new addition off the brewery. Two ice reservoirs—shallow, man-made ponds from which his German workmen cut blocks in winter—vanished under the torrent. The water kept rising. Adolph and his family abandoned their ornate Queen Anne mansion for fear of being swept downriver.

Adolph wasn't religious, so he likely took no comfort from thoughts of God's will as he watched Clear Creek heedlessly tear his handiwork to pieces. Nor was he a devil-may-care who could appreciate the irony of the moment and vow with a laugh to make his second million as easily as he'd made his first. Adolph grimly stood his ground between the foaming cascade and his beloved brewery. Around him, the people of Golden scattered like leaves, grabbing what possessions they could. In front of him, dead sheep, whole trees, and shards of ruined buildings slid past. The river lunged closer and closer to the toes of his boots. The Coors story might well have ended there.

That it didn't is tribute to the double-edged legacy of ingenuity and muleheadedness Adolph bequeathed his family. Even though Adolph Coors died in 1929, he was still effectively running the company more than sixty years later; the company's genius for mechanical invention and vertical integration derived directly from his personality. So did its near-fatal aversion to marketing. The patriarch's portrait glowers every-where—in the boardroom, in the lunchroom, in the annual report. Adolph's signature is the corporate logo. "It's the reason they've had so much trouble doing anything new," one of their former marketing chiefs laments. "They're all afraid old Adolph is going to rise up out of the grave and kick their ass."

Adolph Coors was indeed an ass-kicker: a brooding, taciturn man who demanded uncomplaining performance equally from brewery foreman and youngest grandchild. He wasn't heartless—he lost money keeping his workers on the payroll during Prohibition—but he was all business. Money wasn't his motive, although he did treat himself to finery and displayed instinctively elegant taste. Political power wasn't his mission, either. Adolph Coors believed a man is measured not by wealth or influ-ence but by the quality of his work, and Adolph's work was brewing beer. He had no hobbies, played no sports, sought no learning beyond his craft. He had a wife and six children, whom he carefully arranged around himself for photographs. On Sundays he demanded their atten-dance at extremely formal and virtually silent family dinners. He buried two infants within seven years of each other and left their graves un-marked. Adolph Coors aged into a dark and joyless reticence, unable to take pleasure in his remarkable achievements. He would finally kill him-self, leaving behind $2 million, a unique dedication to quality above profit, and a family tradition of frosty obedience that stifled intellect, thwarted dreams, fostered rebellion, and occasioned a second suicide.

Adolph Coors was born in the central European "patchwork of petty principalities" that would one day become Germany. In 1848, his parents Joseph and Helene moved with baby Adolph from the Prussian country-side into the city of Dortmund so that Joseph could work as a miller. Helene birthed two more children in the home that stood providentially across the street from the Wenker Brewery. When Adolph finished grammar school at fourteen, his father talked to Mr. Wenker and Adolph was awarded an apprenticeship in the brewery's business office.

Within a year, the Coors children were orphans. Tuberculosis killed Adolph's mother in April 1862 and his father eight months later. Adolph, William, and Helene were installed in a Catholic orphanage. Six days a week, fifteen-year-old Adolph trudged to his bookkeeper's stool at the brewery, trying to buy his siblings out of hock.

Two other developments in Adolph's teenage life helped forge the man he grew to be. First was the arrival of the Industrial Revolution to Germany's brewing industry. Young Adolph watched the Wenker Brewery bolt its first steam engines into position and with a clang and a roar multiply its output manyfold. Adolph was entranced. The collar-and-tie front office where he labored over ledgers was all talk and paper. But back in the brewery, men wielded the might of steel and steam against tangible problems. Adolph yearned to be among the men in leather aprons, where sparse talk was valued for its technical content. In a career move that would shape everything to come, Adolph abandoned the business of selling beer for the challenge of brewing it.

The second development was Otto von Bismarck's bloody campaign to unite the German-speaking principalities into a single state by finding common enemies to fight. Conflict was constant and the bloody burden fell upon the nation's young men. Half a million chose to flee to America instead of fighting for the Kaiser. Adolph Coors, twenty-one years old, was among them.

Adolph stowed away on a ship bound for Baltimore, an act that would haunt him the rest of his life. Despite all he achieved, he remained ashamed that he once boarded a ship without paying. Never mind that he later paid the passage. He decreed this never be discussed, and his hold over the family was so strong that they obeyed him long after his death. Family members didn't acknowledge even to each other that their patriarch was a stowaway until after Adolph's son died an old man in 1970. "The idea that our grandfather might have done anything wrong was just too much for us to take," Adolph's grandson, Bill Coors, told television interviewers when he was himself an old man.

With his ocean passage behind him, Adolph found that the East Coast of the United States was no place for him. It boiled with immigrants; German colonies in New York and Baltimore were big enough that a Prussian could pass a lifetime there singing songs of the old country and never learn to speak English. Adolph Coors did not cross the ocean to sit around singing in German. And a job in the industrializing east—if he could find one—was likely to be bleak, dangerous, and low paying. That wouldn't have bothered Adolph if he'd seen such discomfort as a step toward his goal. But how could a man distinguish himself in such a crowd? Moreover, nasty working conditions spawned massive union organizing over such issues as the eight-hour workday. Most workers were either members of a union or under intense and sometimes violent pressure to join. When a strike was called, workers all over town were expected to lay down their tools and take to the streets, facing police truncheons when they did, or the wrath of fellow workers if they didn't. Adolph the loner found unionism repugnant. A man should get ahead on his own initiative, he believed, without asking others to prop him up. In 1869, Adolph followed Horace Greeley's famous advice and walked toward the setting sun, looking to make his fortune on the frontier. He found his first American brewery job in Naperville, Illinois, near Chicago.

During Adolph's three years in Naperville, the Great Fire in Chicago in 1871 destroyed several of the city's breweries and presented an opportunity for those outside the city to increase their business. The Joseph Schlitz Brewing Company, for example, founded in 1850 as an adjunct to a Milwaukee restaurant, seized the opportunity to serve the newly opened Chicago markets and expand beyond its hometown for the first time. Adolph could have helped the Naperville brewery to do likewise, but that would have meant continuing to make someone else's beer, and he'd spent enough time doing that. In 1872, he boarded the new transcontinental railroad for Denver.

The pale blue eyes of Adolph Coors had rarely focused on anything farther away than an approaching streetcar or more colorful than the grimy tenements of Dortmund and Baltimore. Now, through the wavy glass window of the train, twenty-four-year-old Adolph gazed upon amber waves of grain and purple mountains' majesty. It was like a second ocean crossing to yet another land of opportunity. The Battle of the Little Bighorn was still four years away; bison covered the prairie; Indian nations roamed the plains. America west of the Mississippi was wide-open. Here, finally, was the freedom the young immigrant had had in mind.

Colorado was not yet a state and the Denver that Adolph found was only fourteen years old, with all the awkward energy of a teenager. Fifty thousand people lived there, and loans were cheap as bankers nationwide speculated on the frontier. Enough rags-to-riches stories circulated to sustain belief in them. Within a month of arriving in Denver, Adolph used his Illinois savings to buy into a local bottling company, becoming its sole owner before the year was out. Five years after arriving destitute in Baltimore, Adolph was in business for himself.

But "business" as a way of life didn't satisfy Adolph Coors in Denver any more than it had at the Wenker Brewery. There was no craft to running a bottling company. Adolph yearned to perform with his own hands that ancient alchemy that transformed water, grain, and hops into the sparkling, nourishing, and mood-lifting elixir he loved so well. Even though Denver was already served by seven breweries, Adolph wanted to build one of his own.

He spent his weekends during the summer of 1873 scouting the Denver area for a brewery site with ample clean water. He finally found one about fifteen miles up the slope from Denver, an abandoned tannery on the banks of Clear Creek, overlooked by the monumental red-rock knob of Castle Rock. Water, Adolph was convinced, was the most important ingredient in beer and the one most often overlooked. Clear Creek was an ideal resource for a brewery, born two miles high and filtered by twenty-five miles of crystalline metamorphic rock. For capital Adolph went to one of his customers, a fellow German named Jacob Schueler who owned a popular candy store in Denver. Schueler offered to stake the brewery, provided that Adolph did all the work—exactly Adolph's terms. With $18,000 from Schueler and $2,000 of his own, Adolph bought the old tannery, some adjacent land, and enough brewing equipment to get started. As the aspen trees around Golden lit up with yellow autumn foliage, Adolph finally had his hands on a brew kettle again. This time it was his own, albeit with a partner. They called their brewery Schueler and Coors.

At precisely the moment they opened their doors, the nation's economy collapsed in the worst financial crisis in its history. Banks and brokerage houses suddenly deflated, taking their capital-starved business clients with them in a cascading financial calamity. Thousands of companies folded, and hundreds of thousands of people lost their jobs. Denver's distance from the East Coast offered no immunity. The trains on which the city depended rusted in their yards.

Schueler and Coors fared better than most of the local businesses. By the time the aspens leafed again in the spring of 1874, the partners were making eight hundred gallons a day of their Golden Lager. They turned a profit their first year. Beer is said to be recession-proof, but Schueler and Coors was up against eye-gouging competition. They prospered because their beer was good.

Beer had entered Adolph's life at the moment his parents left it, and the minutiae of its manufacture swirled in his brain during the years he had grown from boy to man. Now that he had good water, he applied himself to perfecting his beer's second most important ingredient: malt. Malt is barley that is moistened and allowed to sprout, which brings out its sweetness. The kernels are then roasted to the darkness the brewer wants his beer to have, and then they are ground to a distinctly sweet and roasty flour.

Most breweries, then as now, bought malt from commercial malters. But Adolph wasn't satisfied with either the flavor or the consistency of the available malt, and soon after opening Schueler and Coors he resolved to make his own. He lived on little and put every dollar he could back into the business. Within two years, he had enough reserves to build not only a malthouse but also a steam mill, a bottling plant, and a fifteen-hundred-ton icehouse—all of which he paid for with cash.

Golden's distance from suppliers of malt and bottles helped inspire Adolph to integrate vertically. But control was his real passion. Adolph wanted command over anything that affected the product that bore his name. In time he would add to the brewery a bottle factory, an artificial-ice plant, a cement factory, and machinery to replace corks with the newly invented crimped bottle-cap. He wrote an artless but serviceable motto: "The more we do ourselves, the higher quality we have." In 1879, he married a German immigrant named Louisa Weber and a year later became both the father of a daughter and the sole owner of his brewery. He bought out Jacob Schueler and changed the name of the brewery to the Adolph Coors Company. That year, he sold four thousand barrels of beer. In 1887 he sold seven thousand and by 1890—by which time he and Louisa had six children—he was selling more than seventeen thousand. The money went back into the brewery for kettles, machinery, and ever more land. Castle Rock, a nearly perfect rust-red cylinder overlooking Golden, adorned Adolph's labels.

Though Adolph had shunned unions when he was a laborer, he did not object to his workers joining the United Brewery Workmen of the United States. When they struck briefly demanding the workday be shortened from ten hours to nine with no reduction in pay, Adolph quickly capitulated. He paid his workers well at sixteen dollars a week and threw in a five-minute break every hour during which "beer boys" ran around filling the workers' mugs with free lager. Adolph Coors desired only a smoothly operating brewery that snapped to his command. He hired German immigrants to man it, and they all spoke German together. Treating his workers well came as naturally to Adolph Coors as keeping his machinery properly oiled. He also knew that workingmen made up most of his customers, and Adolph Coors was not about to alienate his customers by squabbling with their unions. His prudence was rewarded. Coors was spared a four-month boycott when the Brewers and Maltsters Union struck Anheuser-Busch and four companies in 1888 over a shorter workday and free beer.

Adolph became a citizen of the United States in 1889. He became a millionaire in 1890. In 1893 his adopted country paid him an even higher honor than riches: His was the only beer from west of the Missouri to win a medal at the Chicago World's Fair. A year later came the Memorial Day flood, when Clear Creek seemed intent on taking back all it had given him.

Adolph Coors stood like Moses at the water's edge and commanded that they recede. He was forty-seven years old. He had survived an orphaned childhood and an illegal ocean crossing. He had hewn his brewery out of a rugged land by dint of backbreaking toil and meticulous craft. He had tamed Clear Creek and given it a sacred purpose. He was not about to let the river change its mind. Before the rising waters could snatch away the core of his plant, Adolph sent an assistant on a perilous trip across Clear Creek with a cash offer for the four families whose houses stood on the opposite bank. Minutes later, an army of workmen followed, tearing down the houses and feverishly digging a new channel for Clear Creek. Adolph bent the river. And bent it remains today.

As it would happen, the force of Rocky Mountain nature was nothing compared with a threat then growing in the flatlands. Adolph first saw a bottle of Anheuser-Busch beer in Colorado in 1876, and most likely he dismissed it as a gimmick. The German immigrant Adolphus Busch had bought an interest in St. Louis's tiny Anheuser brewery in 1865. Beer then was an intensely localized product. Cities the size of New York or Chicago had as many as thirty breweries, each serving an area perhaps no bigger than a neighborhood. (There were more breweries in the United States at that time than at almost any time before or since.)

Adolphus Busch, though, had something else in mind. His philosophy was the direct antithesis of that of Adolph Coors. From the start, Adolphus Busch had looked on his company as a marketing operation rather than a brewery. Busch didn't care if he made the best beer possible; he just wanted to make the most beer possible. He wanted to become the first national brewer in an age when nationwide marketing was unknown. Adolphus Busch was a twentieth-century businessman a century ahead of his time.

Busch didn't even like beer. He preferred wine, and had a nose and a cellar of legendary distinction. Once when he offered a visiting journalist a drink, the fellow ingratiatingly asked for a Busch beer. "Ach," Busch said in his heavy German accent, "that slop?"

A year after Busch bought into the beer business, a scientist in Arbois, France, publicized a method of ridding wine of bacteria by subjecting it to heat. Louis Pasteur had focused on wine instead of beer because he too preferred wine to beer. He wouldn't write about "pasteurizing" beer for another eleven years, but Pasteur's treatise on wine made its way into Busch's hands, and he saw its potential. In its natural state, beer spoiled too quickly to be shipped far. Pasteurized, its market range was without limit. Busch began pasteurizing his beer by immersing the filled bottles in hot water. The first bottles of Busch's pasteurized beer arrived in Colorado in 1876—a year before Louis Pasteur would "discover" the advantages of sterilizing beer with heat.

The very idea of cooking bottles of beer in hot water would have made Adolph Coors shudder. To him, beer was a living thing, which, once bottled, did not improve like wine, but only deteriorated. Heat accelerates its decline, and so does light, which is why beer is almost always bottled in brown glass. Ideally, beer should be drunk as fresh as possible, like milk. Coors invested heavily in making and storing ice because he would not let his beer warm to room temperature, much less scald it. He was content to sell all the beer he could brew in an area reachable by horse and wagon. To a craftsman like Adolph Coors, drinking a Missouri beer in Colorado was like steeping a cup of tea in St. Louis to drink in Denver.

Meanwhile, Adolphus Busch was shipping his beer—then called St. Louis Lager—not only across state lines but, in tiny quantities, across oceans as well, so that he could claim it was drunk "from Lima to London, from Shanghai to Singapore." One can only imagine what a bottle of St. Louis Lager tasted like after a steamship voyage to China, though there's no indication that Busch ever troubled himself with the thought. Adolph Coors surely dismissed Adolphus Busch as a huckster, not a serious beer-maker.

Busch might have agreed. But if he was aware of Adolph Coors at all, he could have gone on to question whether Coors would ever be a serious beer seller.

The movement to ban alcohol was already gathering force when Adolph became sole owner of his brewery in 1880. The Women's Christian Temperance Union and Carrie Nation's Anti-Saloon League were organizing in Colorado "to drive Satanic liquor traffic down to its native hell." In 1893, Colorado's women were among the first in the nation to get the vote and they agitated against alcohol. Many wanted it banned because of its effect on their husbands' paychecks. Others insisted they were "ordained by God" to compel a ban on alcohol. Either way, the temperance movement put beer and liquor in the same category, which infuriated Adolph Coors. In Germany, beer was often drunk at breakfast and mothers considered it nourishing enough to serve to their children. Adolph argued, in fact, that beer itself is a temperance drink because it is so much milder than whiskey. The temperance movement was unswayed. It was bent on taking away Adolph's livelihood and Adolph fought back. Even before becoming an American citizen, he'd helped organize a statewide antiprohibition organization. He was a "wet" activist to the end of his life. Adolph understood the temperance threat earlier than many beer-makers. But neither he nor the rest of the alcohol industry knew how to build a coalition of brewers, distillers, vintners, and imbibers strong enough to counter the prohibition movement. The Coors family was about to get its first lesson in the power of American grassroots politics, manifested in the ability of organized activists to bring them grief.

With an eye on the gathering threat, Adolph began diversifying beyond industries related to beer—into real estate, cement, and, most providentially, a struggling pottery that made pretty dishes from the fine clay around Golden.

Until 1914, every laboratory in the United States used chemical porcelain imported from Germany. Pestles and beakers of chemical porcelain are special; they must withstand caustic chemicals and huge fluctuations of temperature. The outbreak of World War I stopped German exports cold, leaving American science bereft. The U.S. Commerce Department broadcast an emergency appeal to American potteries to fill the need, and Adolph directed his oldest son, Adolph Jr., to do so.

Adolph Jr. wasn't Adolph's oldest child. The first of Adolph's children to live past infancy was his daughter Louise. But since Adolph did not consider girls fit for business, he passed over her and chose Adolph Jr. Unlike her brewery-bound brother, Louise lived a varied, if tragic, life. She married a man from San Francisco and moved there with him, but he killed himself in 1914. Louise then married another California man, and in 1922 he too killed himself. Having buried two suicides, Louise moved back to Colorado, founded the Central City Opera, and worked as a chef in a fancy hotel. Louise and Adolph Jr.'s sister Augusta married the owner of Denver's best hotel, and after divorcing him moved to New York City. The youngest sister, Bertha, likewise lived in New York as the wife of a wealthy mining engineer. While her brother Adolph Jr. was isolating yeast strains and mixing mud in a basement in Golden, Bertha distinguished herself as a record-winning safari huntress in Africa.

Like many first-generation Americans, Adolph Jr. was his family's bridge between the old country and the new. He inherited his father's stiff-backed, tight-lipped devotion to craft, but he was also educated at Cornell in the science of chemical engineering—as almost all future Coors men would be. Unnaturally tall and painfully thin, he spoke little and, like his father, had few interests outside the brewery. He didn't marry until he was almost thirty years old, and was a newlywed when his father called him to the pottery. Combining the modern science he'd learned at Cornell with his inherited obsession with quality, Adolph Jr. worked up such good chemical porcelain that within a year Coors was the sole U.S. supplier of a product that was small in volume but high in value and prestige.

His timing was excellent. Beer, wine, and spirits became contraband in Colorado on January 1, 1916, a full year before the national ban. On December 31, 1915, Adolph Coors, Sr., ordered 561 barrels of beer— almost three months' production—dumped into Clear Creek. Coors was out of the beer business.

Adolph was seventy years old and worth $2 million. His daughters were safely ensconced in comfortable marriages and the business was run day-to-day by his sons Adolph Jr., Grover, and Herman. Adolph could have retired from the field with honor. Another man might have passed his days playing with his grandchildren and swapping stories with friends.

But Adolph's grandchildren were strangers to be judged only by their cleanliness and politeness once a week at Sunday dinner. The closest thing Adolph had to a friend was the family lawyer Cregar Quaintance, but the friendship did neither Adolph nor his progeny much good. Quaintance owned Castle Rock and lent it to the Ku Klux Klan for cross burnings that could be seen all over Denver. The family's relationship with Quaintance and Castle Rock gave it an association with the Klan that it never lived down.

Adolph had sacrificed family and friends on the altar of brewing. Now during Prohibition there was no brewing to be done. Nonetheless, Adolph stayed busy—frantically and unhappily busy. He kept the malthouse open, spending a fortune converting the brewery to a malted milk factory. In another corner of the plant, Adolph's former brewers were turning out a near-beer called Mannah, which Adolph despised. Mannah and malted milk were at best break-even propositions for Adolph Coors, but they meant a paycheck for his employees. Expecting their gratitude, Adolph asked them to take a pay cut to help the business get through Prohibition. Instead, the workers went on strike.

Adolph had always striven for peace with his workers, in part because it was good business and in part because he felt a genuine kinship with them. Adolph Jr., though, coldly advised his father to fire the strikers— some of whom had been working beside old Adolph for a generation— and hire replacements. Nobody, he told his father, should ever tell this family how to run its own business. Adolph acceded, and labor responded by putting Coors on its "unfair" list. Thus was sown the bitterness between Coors and labor that Adolph had worked so hard to avoid.

Old Adolph Coors signed over the business to Adolph Jr. in 1923 and spent the rest of the decade walking the halls of his factory—he couldn't even call it a brewery anymore—watching a children's confection leave the loading dock instead of the healthy, robust brew he loved. Family lore says he never tasted a glass of beer after watching his barrels of foamy brew rejoin Clear Creek on New Year's Eve, 1915. To do so would have broken the law.

Finally, on a warm June night in 1929, Adolph Coors climbed out onto a sixth-story ledge at the Cavalier Hotel in Virginia Beach, Virginia, where he'd gone to recover from the flu. He was eighty-three years old.

In the next room slept his daughter, Augusta, and her daughter, Louise. Standing on the ledge and gripping the window frame, he looked out at the ocean he'd crossed sixty-one years before and saw only a future without beer, a future without meaningful work. Rich and alone, he closed his rheumy eyes and released his grip. In his will was a stipulation that his bill at the Cavalier—$1,876.51—be paid in full.

2

Protected from Human Contact!

As he filed into Alexander Hall at Princeton University on June 19, 1939, young Bill Coors carried a mile's depth more air on his shoulders than he was used to, and he could feel every inch of it. Even after four years at the Phillips Exeter Academy in New Hampshire and five years at Princeton, Bill hadn't grown accustomed to the humidity of the East Coast. Inside his graduation gown, sweat soaked the absurdly formal suit the East Coast demanded. Bill longed to return to the West, where the air was crisp, the vistas unobstructed, and nobody was judged by his clothes.

But that would have to wait.

He scanned the crowd with a familiar mixture of yearning and dread. Somewhere among those faces was that of his father, Adolph Coors, Jr. That grim face had frowned down on Bill Coors since the dawn of memory. Coaxing a smile from it had been Bill's life's mission, but he was rarely successful. No matter how high his grades, precise his piano playing, or diligent his summertime work in the brewery, words of praise seldom passed his father's lips. The A-minus should have been an A. The coda was too hasty. The mop was left standing in the bucket. A good job could always have been done better. A mediocre job was not an option.

Like his own father, Adolph Jr. had little interest in his children beyond a grim insistence that they perform. He kept notes on his children's misdemeanors and on Sundays meted out earned spankings, one child after the next. The dinner table he presided over was as silent as the one at which he'd grown up. Any child of Adolph Jr.'s who had something to say thought long and hard before saying it; if Dad found the comment frivolous, his baleful stare silenced further chatter. Amusing anecdotes from the schoolyard, for example, did not meet Dad's standards. Bill's big brother, Adolph III, suffered from an incapacitating stutter, and Bill's younger brother, Joseph, had inherited his grandfather's silence. But Bill was a talker. He liked jokes and conversation. Day after day, he sat beside his brothers weighing whether his words were worth saying. Usually, around Dad, he decided they weren't.

Bill's life had always been Dad's to rule. It was Dad who decided, after Bill was hurt in a bicycle accident at age six, that Bill should never again play rough sports. Little Bill didn't implore his father to change his mind and he didn't whine about it. He spent years on the sofa, watching his brothers thunder outside to run bases and touchdowns. The doctors who treated Bill's injuries impressed the boy greatly, and he dreamed of becoming a surgeon. Deprived of outdoor play, young Bill began running his fingers over the piano. By the time he finished high school in 1934, the pale and spindly boy played so beautifully his mother urged him to study music. Bill loved the piano and was torn, but ultimately decided he would study medicine. He announced his intention to his father.

Adolph Jr. barely looked up from the brewery output figures he was reading. You are a Coors, he said, and Coors men are brewers. Prohibition has been over for less than a year, he continued, and I will hear no talk of you pursuing another career. You will study chemical engineering as I did. The Adolph Coors Company will be your life—not medicine, and not the piano.

Five years later, Bill was shuffling into Alexander Hall to receive his master's degree in chemical engineering. Surely this would be the day that nod of approval would finally be granted, when his father would look him in the eye and say at last, "I'm proud of you."

Bill hoped so, because no matter what his father said he was finally going to defy him. Bill wasn't going back to Golden. He wasn't going to work at the brewery. With war about to explode in Europe and Asia, the DuPont chemical company was recruiting chemical engineers from the best universities and Bill had accepted a job. He was going to make a career for himself outside his father's shadow. He wanted to succeed where the name Coors would give him no advantage, where he'd be judged on his merits alone.

Bill ran his eye over the throng of parents. It was a sea of high-fashion zephyr-weight checked jackets, polka-dotted foulard ties, "aviary-pink" yoke blouses, and laughing faces. He picked his father out at once. Adolph Coors, Jr., stood like a rock in a river, half a head taller than most of the other men. He was dressed as always in an Edwardian suit of the deepest black. Despite the heat, Dad's three-button jacket was fastened snugly across his bony chest. An archaic starched collar climbed his reedy neck. A prim black bow tie perched on the collar like a charred butterfly. Though Bill couldn't see his father's feet, he knew they were sheathed in black, high-button goat-leather shoes of a type not fashionable since the 1920s. Adolph Jr. might have been acting the role of his own father in a stage play.

But it wasn't the clothes that drew Bill's eye. It was the look on his father's face. There would be no warm smile today, Bill suddenly knew, and no long-awaited hug. The face was worn, the lips pursed, the eyes dull. Quotation marks of worry cleaved the aging man's forehead. He stared straight into Bill's eyes with a gaze as cold and demanding as ever.

Bill knew at once he couldn't abandon the brewery. He couldn't disappoint his father, who had put so much of himself into the family business. Not now, when Prohibition had so recently ended.

Bill had been born when Prohibition started and had gone to college just after Repeal. Prohibition was the family's *Iliad,* a maelstrom of conflicts that defined the world and the Coorses' place within it. Government was the main enemy; with an imperious wave of its too-powerful hand, it had annihilated everything for which the Coors family stood. The workers, too, when push came to shove, had proven themselves greedy and disloyal by striking. The family business had stood in peril every minute of Prohibition. Against government and labor Adolph Jr. had stood barehanded, wielding naught but his genius, integrity, and willingness to toil.

The return of brewing, Bill knew, had not offered his father relief. It had only heaped upon him a whole new mountain of work. Dad's letters to Bill at Princeton told of redesigning and expanding the brewery, and of reactivating seventeen-year-old contracts. Bill had written back with news that a little brewery in Newark was successfully test-marketing beer packed in cans instead of bottles. He'd shipped home a case of Gottfried Krueger canned beer for his father to analyze. It took up half the icebox space as bottles, Bill had written, and steel was even better than brown glass at blocking light from beer. But when Adolph Jr. had delicately sheared apart the cans, he'd found that both the steel and the solder used to hold them together reacted with the beer and tainted its flavor. The trade-off, he'd written Bill, was unacceptable. Cans had their advantages, but nothing was worth compromising the beer.

As if Adolph Jr. didn't have enough to worry about in the years immediately following Repeal, he was plagued by fears of kidnapping. His friend Charles Boettcher, scion of one of Colorado's richest families, was grabbed in February 1933 and held for more than two weeks before being released unharmed. Seven months later, Denver police told Adolph Jr. they had uncovered a plot by two former agents of the hated Federal Bureau of Prohibition to kidnap him as well. The ex-agents had put a ten-day supply of food and water in a remote cabin and were planning to hold Adolph Jr. there for $50,000 ransom. Despite everything else on his plate, Adolph Jr. wrote to Bill at Princeton, he had agreed to serve as bait "if it would help stop this dirty business." Much to Bill's relief, the plot was foiled without Dad having to put himself in harm's way, and both ex-agents were sent to prison.

Finally, there was the matter of Coors being on labor's "unfair" list. Unions were active when Prohibition was repealed—during the depths of the Great Depression—and as Adolph the founder knew, beer was the workingman's beverage. Coors couldn't afford to be considered an enemy of labor. Adolph Jr. didn't want a union, but he held his nose and, following his father's example, invited the Brewery Workers Union to organize Local 366 at the Coors brewery. The union asked for a thirty-six-hour workweek and Adolph Jr. complied. He even threw in a sweetener that wasn't in the contract: an extra month's wages as a Christmas bonus. The "unfair" appellation was removed in 1933, and Coors began enjoying a temporary reprieve from union strife.

By the time Bill accepted his diploma at Princeton, Prohibition had been over for five years and Coors was getting ready for a massive expansion. The brewery had first tested interstate shipping when it began sending beer to Arizona after Repeal. In 1937, Coors had started selling in California. Now, in 1938, Dad's brewery was getting ready to begin shipping to Nevada, Wyoming, New Mexico, Kansas, and Oklahoma, with moves into Idaho and Utah planned for the following year. Dad was swallowing his misgivings about canned beer and building a can line. Bill's big brother, Adolph III, was helping in the business office. But Ad's stutter meant he couldn't serve as the family's front man. Worse, he was allergic to beer. He would be useful in administration, but he would never be a brewer. Bill's younger brother Joe still hadn't earned his master's degree, and everybody knew he didn't really like beer very much. Bill knew that he alone among the sons had inherited a nose and palate that could be trained to recognize and brew great beer. He knew, as his eyes met Dad's grim gaze, that Dad needed him too much. Bill stepped up, took his diploma, and went to dinner with his parents. He didn't even tell his father about the DuPont job. He simply called DuPont the next day and begged off. A few days later, Bill was leaning out the window of a westbound train, straining to catch a first glimpse of his beloved Rocky Mountains.

Long before the name Coors was associated with politics—and decades before Miller Brewing would re-create the brewing industry with Miller Lite—Coors beer was famous for a single unique characteristic: its lightness. Sipped side by side with a Budweiser or Miller, Coors was noticeably milder. "Colorado Kool-Aid," people called it, or, less decorously, "like making love in a canoe (fucking near water)." It got that way, oddly, because Adolph Jr. once ordered Bill to make the strongest beer he could make.

Bill had been back in Golden for a year when his father called him into the bare room at the brewery that he used as an office. Dad sat at his rolltop desk, dressed as ever in black suit, bow tie, and high-button shoes. There was no other chair in the room, so Bill stood. His father had sheets of numbers before him. "Per capita beer consumption is falling," he said. "People are drinking more distilled spirits nowadays. The reason is that they're after the alcohol and don't want to drink so much water to get it. Go brew me a beer as high in alcohol as you can." He turned back to his papers, expecting Bill to see himself out. Instead, Bill spoke.

"Brewer's yeast will produce toxic alcohol if the concentration gets too high," he said.

Dad sent him a look that said, Don't wag your degree at me. Get to work.

Bill walked back to the spare office he shared with his brother Ad. They were dressed identically, as their father dictated, in khaki shirt, chinos, and work shoes. Ad also, as always, wore a baseball cap—a breach of protocol oddly tolerated. Ad was an avid fan and played first base on the company softball team.

Ad was tall and thin, like Bill. But while Bill's facd wore the bony, almost gaunt, look of his father, Ad had inherited his mother's softer features. He also wore glasses, with flesh-colored plastic rims. Ad obediently labored at his gray steel desk day after day, but he often stared out the window. There was a dreaminess about Ad. Though he worked diligently, he maintained a mental distance from the brewery. His disqualifying allergy seemed to free him to think about other things—like baseball, flying, and his dream of owning a ranch—while Bill's brain was chained firmly to the mechanics of brewing, aging, and bottling beer. Ad wore a mysterious whiff of disobedience. He'd quietly refused to get a master's degree in chemical engineering and his father had let him get away with it because he knew Ad could never be a brewer. The baseball cap was another example. No one ever mentioned it, but Dad simply let it go. Finally, the girl Ad was dating, Mary Grant, wasn't their father's sort of girl at all. There was about her none of the quiet obedience Adolph Jr. demanded of his daughters and of the few women he employed as secretaries and switchboard operators. Mary was a city girl who had a quick mind and a willingness to exercise it in conversation. She smoked cigarettes and enjoyed a cocktail. She couldn't have been more different from the homespun Ad, Bill thought. But clearly Ad was crazy about her.

Bill's younger brother Joe had done what Bill could not: taken his chemical engineering degree to DuPont. Joe's letters home, full of news about polymers, plastics, and life in a world bigger than Golden, made Bill wistful. But Bill wasn't a brooder, and he applied himself to the strong-beer problem with characteristic single-mindedness.

Coors had been brewing the same recipe since the days of Bill's grandfather, and Adolph Jr. essentially had proposed to Bill the first addition to the product line since the company's founding. After he had spent a few minutes in his and Ad's office reflecting on the interview with his father, Bill got up from his desk and walked downstairs to the brewery's basement.

The Coors brewery occupied the same piece of ground that Bill's grandfather had selected in 1873, only now it was much larger. Clear Creek still ran through the property from west to east, but its waters were used only for cooling machinery; brewing water now came from wells drilled into the creek's gravel bed. The Queen Anne mansion where Adolph Jr. and his children were raised had been moved to make room for expansion, but remained on the brewery grounds and was still the home of Adolph Jr. and his wife, Alice May. Across the creek, to the north, stood the rose-colored cement buildings of Coors Porcelain. And immediately outside the brewery gates, to the west, sat the town of Golden, home to only about four thousand people. The rich, grainy aroma of roasting malt suffused the entire valley. Luckily, it is not an unpleasant smell, because in Golden, then as now, there was no escaping it.

The hallways Bill walked on his way downstairs were lined in gray tiles made in the family's ceramics plant. As he walked, workers called "Hey, Bill," to him, and he always knew the correct name to call back. The malthouse guys were having trouble calibrating the roaster properly and Bill stopped to puzzle out the problem. In the brewhouse, mechanics struggled with a malfunctioning hop jack and wanted Bill's advice. Bill didn't get his hands dirty; he asked his way through a matrix of questions and took his time counseling a solution. As he continued downstairs, he rolled the problems around in his mind: Was there a way for the roaster to calibrate itself automatically? Could the hop jack be simplified to reduce breakdowns? A thousand such technical issues churned inside his head all the time. Sometimes solutions would occur to him during a meal, while driving to work, or in the middle of the night. Troubleshooting was the aspect of his job Bill loved best.

Bill found an unused room in the brewery basement and moved in a small brew kettle, some tubing, beakers, and flasks. He began that afternoon cooking up batches of beer to experiment with high alcohol content. Whether made in a bathtub or a twenty-million-barrel factory, the recipe for beer is essentially the same: Boil malt flour in water until it looks like hot cereal and its starches are converted to fermentable sugar. Filter the mash to draw out the watery malt extract. Cook the extract again, this time with the bitter leafy buds known as hops. Once the extract is hopped, send it through the hop jack to shake out the hop leaves. Now you have "wort": a hot, sugary, and hop-spiced liquid. Add yeast, and store from five to ten days to let the yeast convert the sugars to alcohol. Once they've done so, the liquid is beer. Let it age to mellow the flavor.

In 1940, when Bill was toiling in his pilot brewery, commercial beer contained 4.5 percent alcohol by weight. By tweaking the balance of yeast, sugar, and time, Bill was able to produce a good-tasting light amber beer with double the alcohol. He had created the industry's first malt liquor decades before anyone would try to market such a thing.

Before presenting it to his father, Bill tried it out on some friends. They liked it, but suffered a peculiar reaction: drenching sweat. That's one hell of a beer you've brewed there, they gasped.

The next morning, Bill went to tell his father what had happened. He found Dad not in his own office, but in the main suite, a vast plain of desks shared by some two dozen executives and secretaries. It was Saturday, so father and son were alone. Dad was on one knee in his black suit and bow tie, sighting along the line of desks. "This one's out of line," he told Bill, nudging it a quarter inch with his hip. "And look." Every desktop was clear except one, on which sat a big black telephone. With a sigh, Adolph Jr. opened the top right-hand drawer and put the phone away as the owner of the desk should have done the night before. At another desk a sweater hung over the back of the chair. Adolph Jr. shook his head, clicked his tongue, and walked into his office. Bill followed, knowing some poor stenographer was going to get a talking-to on Monday morning.

When Bill described the previous evening's sweat bath, his father doubted him, as Bill knew he would. So Bill produced a bottle and poured them each a glass. Halfway through it, Adolph Jr.'s face went slippery with sweat. Primly mopping it with a handkerchief, Dad told Bill to set the high-alcohol-beer project aside.

A week later, Dad summoned Bill again. "We went the wrong way," he said. "We want people to drink more of our beer, not less. This time, take some alcohol out of the beer." He looked at a piece of paper on which he'd written some figures. "Get it down to three-point-six percent."

Many nights, Adolph Jr. would don an apron and stand beside Bill in the makeshift lab, refining strains of yeast, jury-rigging equipment, sniffing, tasting, and jotting careful notes. One way to lighten a beer's flavor and cut costs is to augment the malt flour with neutral starch. Many brewers in the 1930s used dry milled corn, which was inexpensive. Adolph Jr. wouldn't hear of that; he felt the oils and germ in corn spoil a beer's flavor. Instead, he insisted on rice, which was costly. Bill and his father cooked malt and rice together. They cooked them separately. They tried dozens of different yeasts. They tried endless combinations of both pure and aromatic bitterness. Many nights Bill declared himself satisfied with the result, but his father's standards were still not met. Their product was still a little rough, Adoph Jr. concluded; or the aroma was odd; or they had to back off the rice. It took Bill more than a year to produce a lower-alcohol beer to which Adolph Jr. would attach his name. In the process, father and son had developed a beer that was slightly less fattening than others. Nobody had ever before thought of selling a beer on the merits of its health attributes, but Adolph Jr. decided to try it. Ever the scientist, he specified that it be advertised as having exactly 13.8 fewer calories per serving. It went on sale in 1941 and was such a hit the brewery couldn't make it fast enough. They called it Coors Light Beer.

None of the Coors boys served in World War II. Ad was 4-F for nearsightedness. He married Mary Grant and stayed home to manage the brewery. Joe left DuPont to work for the National Dairy Association, which excused him from the draft, too. And in 1941, Bill received a phone call that would lead to a draft deferment for himself as well. The call was from someplace called Radiation Laboratory in Berkeley, California. The war effort required a particular type of ceramic insulator that Coors Porcelain might be able to produce, the caller said.

Bill spent the war making and shipping specialized insulators, crate after secret crate, without knowing what they were for. He lived in Golden with his young bride Geraldine and their firstborn child, whom they named Geraldine but called "Missy." Bill was exempt from the draft for reasons he couldn't explain, knowing the soldiers' moms of Golden wrote him off as a rich-kid shirker. It wasn't until after the war that Bill learned the insulators had gone to the huge Y-12 plant at Oak Ridge, Tennessee, which refined uranium-235 for the Hiroshima atom bomb.

The war years were hectic for Bill as he rushed back and forth across Clear Creek, between Porcelain's mysterious product and the brewery. It was maddening to have wartime materials restrictions imposed upon the brewery by government immediately after the soaring launch of Coors Light Beer in 1941. Grain was rationed and importing hops was impossible. Bill and his father did their best, but their meager government allotments rendered Coors Light Beer and their regular lager into pale, low-alcohol imitations of their former selves. Eventually, they discontinued Coors Light Beer and returned to a single product. Materials were so scarce that Adolph Jr. got into the habit of walking into bars asking for Coors bottle caps so the brewery could reuse them.

In the summer of 1945, the long war was winding down. Germany was licked. Japan was wobbling. Bill and his father could start thinking about proper brewing again. Though they dropped the word "Light" from their labels, the Coorses kept their regular beer at the lower 3.6 percent alcohol so that, as Adolph Jr. put it, people would drink more of it to get the same effect.

Nine days before Hiroshima, Bill's wife Geraldine gave birth to the couple's second child, William Jr. Mary, Ad's wife, was in her eighth month of pregnancy; family tradition being what it was, Ad and Mary were about to be put in the position of naming a baby Adolph in 1945.

When the military had shipped beer overseas to servicemen during the war, it had bought the country's big three brands: Schlitz, Pabst, and Budweiser. Soldiers then brought home a taste for them after victory. People were moving around the country after the war like never before, and the big three breweries were striving to put a glass of their product in front of a beer drinker no matter where that beer drinker happened to move. They were doing, on a grand scale, what Adolphus Busch had only pioneered. Schlitz, Pabst, and Anheuser-Busch were arranging contracts with entrepreneurs in far-flung states who wanted to be distributors, and the term "shipping breweries" entered the industry lexicon. Anheuser-Busch was even building a brewery in Newark, New Jersey, to serve the East Coast—the first American brewer to open a second plant.

The problem for regional brewers like Coors wasn't simply economies of scale. To somebody in Florida, a can of Milwaukee or St. Louis beer was exotic. It could command the higher price necessary to offset shipping. Thus were "premium" beers born—beers fundamentally identical to local brews but wearing a romantic new label. And once the label determined whether a beer drinker bought this or that brand, marketing—not product quality—was fated to rule the industry.

None of this meant a damn to the Coorses. Despite the spread of the "shipping breweries," they were selling all the beer they could make. The tiny amount of advertising Coors did kept the product's name in front of the customer and generated goodwill. The "sales department" was nothing but a regiment of order-takers. Adolph Jr. did the corporate planning on the back of an envelope and kept the books himself in clothbound ledgers. He had functionally achieved his father's boyhood dream: a brewery without a business office.

The central figure in most breweries was the brewmaster, legendarily a gruff old German who by nose and instinct directed manufacturing. Coors had no brewmaster. Adolph Jr. despised the idea. The gruff old

Germans he knew at other breweries were not men of science. They relied on their senses and their experience, both of which Adolph Jr. thought were usually overrated. As he demonstrated when he fired all of his father's longtime workers for going on strike, he would never let anyone outside the family decide how to make Coors beer. He trusted his own taste, but equally his training as a chemical engineer; to him, one was useless without the other. While other breweries advertised their "old world craft," Coors ads emblazoned the words "scientifically controlled" across a tableau of retorts and beakers. "Protected from human contact!" the ads boasted. "Fewer solids!"

Much to the gratification of Bill and his father, American breweries were paying Coors the sincerest form of flattery as they returned to peacetime production. The shipping breweries didn't go back to the 4.5 percent alcohol of yore; they copied Coors and made their beers 3.6 percent alcohol, and with a lighter hand on the hops. The way to draw a man off his local brand, the nationals learned, was by making yours easier to guzzle.

The postwar years started out as happy ones at Coors. Every employee who had gone off to fight came back alive and was given back his old job. Joe left the Dairy Association and returned to Golden with his new wife, a Philadelphia socialite named Holly. Now all three brothers shared an office at the brewery, though Joe's domain was Porcelain across the creek. The company was big enough to be prosperous and small enough to be intimate. Taps were available throughout the brewery, and even the lowliest janitors were free to sip beer all day long, the tradition begun in the days of Adolph the founder being honored. The Coorses also continued to believe that beer was a nutritious food, not a temptation for the reprobate. The first Adolph Coors had trusted his workers not to drink to incapacitation and his son and grandsons carried on the tradition. Few workers abused the privilege. Every Christmas, the Coorses hosted a big party for the employees and served an extra-strong dark beer, called Winterfest, that Bill brewed especially for the occasion.

Everybody who worked at the brewery addressed one another by their first name—except of course, Adolph Jr. He alone was "Mr. Coors," and his word was absolute. But he was a benevolent despot. Old Coors hands like telling the story of Willie Malink. Willie, who had started at the brewery around the same time that Adolph Jr. did, had been a good worker, but as he neared retirement he started to lose control of himself around the free beer. His young foreman fired him, and word got back to Mr. Coors, who called Willie in and asked if he could make good use of a second chance. Willie said that he could, and it turned out he did. He stayed away from the taps from then on until his retirement.

The Coors family was alive with little children right after the war. Ad had three; Bill, two with another coming; and in September 1946, Holly delivered Joe their third son, Peter Coors.

Six days after Pete was born, his fourteen-month-old cousin William Jr. was gnawing on a chicken bone when a piece of it lodged in his windpipe. Bill and Geraldine snatched the gasping baby out of his high-chair and tried to clear his throat as four-year-old Missy watched in terror. Minutes later, the boy was dead. His limp little body lay still on the dining room table.

The next morning, Bill walked down the long gray hallway toward his office, accompanied only by the echo of his heels against the tile. Everybody he passed muttered, "Hey, Bill," and quickly looked away. Bill looked straight ahead, striding briskly, jaw set, trailing a wake of whispers. He walked into the office he shared with his brothers, sat down at his plain steel desk, and went to work.

The boy's death was a tragedy, but the world had seen too many deaths in recent years to stop turning on its axis while Bill grieved. The Coors brewery ran twenty-four hours a day, and Coors men were on duty whenever beer was in the making.

Bill's wife Geraldine had always been a welcome presence among the workers at the brewery—earthy, good-humored, and not above enjoying a beer and a joke in the little tiled bar where workers gathered at shift's end. But after her baby's death, she withdrew and did her drinking alone. Four months after William Jr. died, she delivered another daughter, Margaret, and ten months later she was pregnant again with another girl, May. Almost exactly a year to the day after May was born, Geraldine gave birth to a stillborn daughter. Geraldine sank further into the bottle.

Not only was Bill's once-cheerful wife disappearing into a melancholy fog, she was doing so by means of alcohol. Fear of alcoholism had in-spired Prohibition, and fear of another Prohibition was the Coors family's constant companion. Geraldine's drinking problem made Bill ashamed. But he burdened no one with grief over his son or fears for his wife. Day after day, Bill squared his shoulders and waded into his job. In a plant as big and complicated as the Coors brewery, there was always something that needed Bill's urgent attention. He snapped to his father's direction, listened patiently when a mechanic or pipe fitter had a technical puzzle to unravel, and played piano at retirement parties for his work-men. Anything at the brewery was better than being at home. Geraldine had her drink to console her and the babies hardly knew him anyway. The only one who really needed him at home was Missy, then seven, and she didn't know how to ask.

The strain finally overwhelmed Bill. One day in 1950, he found he could barely pull himself out of bed. He managed to drag himself through the day and then slept like an opium smoker. The lassitude persisted for weeks, but no doctor could find anything wrong. Finally, Bill boarded a flight to Minnesota for a full examination at the Mayo Clinic. He assumed he had contracted some rare and dreadful illness, but the doctors at Mayo were no more successful than the ones in Denver at finding a physical cause of his symptoms.

On the flight home, Bill approached his situation the way he would a jammed barley auger. He made a mental inventory of all the reasons he might be depressed, and decided that he had been taking on too much stress and neglecting his physical health. A better diet and more exercise would fix him. He became a devoted disciple of nutrition guru Adelle Davis and began living on Tiger's Milk shakes, wheat germ, and yogurt. He also started working out—with runs, swims, and long bouts of calisthenics.

All of which took even more time and attention away from his wife and daughters.

Around this time, a shy young man named Lowell Sund applied for a job at the brewery. Sund had spent the war as a fighter pilot in Europe. Decommissioned, he had come to Denver to woo his future wife, Vera, and maybe get a job at United Airlines. Vera was a singer—she'd re-placed Dale Evans on the radio when Evans began her movie career—and was hostess of the weekly *Coors Show* on Denver radio. The station manager advised Sund that he should try to get a job at Coors, because it was the best employer in Colorado.

Sund found Ad Coors at his desk, poring over papers. Ad looked more like a P-39 mechanic—in his khakis and tan baseball cap—than the president of a major corporation. A skinny, serious-looking man whom Ad introduced as his brother Joe sat at an identical steel desk nearby, identically dressed in khakis. The third desk was empty; Bill was out roaming the plant. Ad was in the process of buying a small plane for the company and wanted to hear Sund's war stories. They talked a long time about flying. Ad waxed downright poetic as he described his feelings up among the clouds.

"Are you looking for a permanent job?" Ad finally asked Sund, stuttering over the word "permanent." Sund said he was.

"I mean a career job," Ad pressed. Sund said that's what he wanted.

Ad turned to Ray Frost, the office manager, and said, "He's okay with me."

"Thank you, Mr. Coors," Sund said, astonished at the informality of the proceeding and wondering what he'd been hired to do.

"Call me Ad," Ad said. "My father is 'Mr. Coors.' You'd better meet him, too."

Ad walked him to a doorway at the far end of the office suite, pulling off his cap and shedding his relaxed demeanor as he went. By the time Ad tapped on the doorframe, Sund noticed, he stood as stiff as a second lieutenant calling on a colonel. A pale old man in a black suit sat by himself at a rolltop desk. When he stood, Sund saw he was as comically tall and thin as Ichabod Crane. Adolph Jr. wrapped his long bony hand around Sund's and said with a slight bow, "I am very pleased to make your acquaintance." Thus began Lowell Sund's thirty-seven-year career at Coors, the only civilian job he'd ever know.

The company was brewing 200,000 barrels a year in the early 1950s and was growing fast. Sund became the catchall, manager of whatever wasn't already being handled by someone else. Real estate, water rights, security, and personnel all fell to him. "There are four divisions at Coors," he liked to say, "brewery, finance, sales, and Lowell."

The ex-fighter pilot stuck close to Ad, not only because Ad oversaw administration, but because Ad was the most approachable of the three brothers. The two of them began spending time together outside of work: Lowell Sund, who spoke softly and slowly, and Ad Coors, who had a hard time speaking at all. Yet during long walks through the mountains, Ad would open up to Sund about how he sometimes felt torn. His wife liked the sophisticated life—theater, museums, restaurants, nightclubs—and insisted they live in Denver. Ad didn't mind Denver, but he knew his father disapproved; Dad wanted everyone right there in Golden.

Sometimes Ad would complain about Sundays. They began nicely enough; he and Mary would drop the kids at church and have the morning to themselves. But by noon the whole family had to be dressed up and present itself at the mansion. The children paraded for inspection in front of Adolph Jr. and Alice May and then were allowed to run free until dinnertime. Ad and Mary, though, had to sit on the couch and endure his parents. They never actually said anything about Mary, according to Ad, but he could tell by the pinch of his mother's rouged lips and the arch of his father's eyebrow that they didn't like Mary's wit, her precocious way of answering their questions, the assertive way she would disagree, or the expensive cut of her clothes and hair. Then the dinner was ritualized and endless, the silence broken only by the splashing of fingers in finger bowls and the tinkle of Alice May's silver bell. "It's like something in a wax museum," Ad had once told Sund. "And then listening to Mary all the way back to Denver—hoo boy."

Ad sighed then, and confided that all he really wanted was a ranch. The only place he felt really good was outdoors. "If I had my way," Ad said often, "I'd quit the business and raise quarter horses."

Sund noticed that Ad—so easygoing with him—could be murder on his young son Adolph IV, whom everybody called Spike. When Spike was about eight years old, Sund and Ad took him bird hunting. A grouse jumped up in front of the boy and Spike, awkwardly swinging a big shotgun, missed it. To Sund's horror, Ad tore into him with a sharp scythe of criticism; it was clear to Sund that Ad was offloading onto little Spike his own father's disapproval. Sund took it upon himself, for the rest of the day, to cheer up the little boy.

Coors was doing so well that when Denver's Tivoli brewery showed signs of teetering under the onslaught of the national brands, old Mr. Coors told Lowell Sund not to take advantage. "Don't prey on their draft accounts," he told Sund. "Tivoli has a right to be in business." Blessed with demand that exceeded its capacity, Coors had never had to advertise heavily or give anybody the title "advertising director." But Ad knew Schlitz, Pabst, and Anheuser-Busch wouldn't treat Coors the way Coors had treated Tivoli. He convinced his father and brothers that the brewery needed a person to oversee advertising. "We're brewing a quarter million barrels a year," Ad said. "The time has come."

But Ad didn't conduct a nationwide search for an advertising director. When at a company picnic he met an artistic fellow who had been invited by a friend, Ad hired him on the spot. Bill Moomey had studied art to avoid having to follow his father into the Nebraska cattle business. Slight and handsome, Moomey had the gentle speech of a natural teacher. By

1951 Moomey had a Ph.D. in art history and had started both a little art school that he grandiosely called the Denver Art Academy and a one-man ad agency he called BMF—Bill Moomey's Folly. When Ad Coors offered him a job—at a salary higher than any he'd ever imagined earning—Moomey's mouth fell open.

"Thing is," he told Ad, stalling until he could gather his thoughts, "BMF is actually starting to do pretty well and I'd hate to shut it down."

"You don't have to," Ad said.

"But there'd be a conflict of interest," Moomey said. "I'd be tempted to run Coors business through my own shop."

"I wouldn't care if you did," Ad said. "If you thought that was best."

Moomey was impressed; how could anybody cheat a guy that trusting?

He took the job. Right away, though, he regretted shutting down the Denver Art Academy. His immediate boss, Ev Barnhardt, was amiable, but his only qualifications seemed to be a diploma from Golden High School and the fact that he'd been 4-F—and therefore available—during the war. He knew nothing about advertising.

Worse, there wasn't much chance to shine as ad director for a company selling all the beer it could make. Coors had been using the same image— a bottle of beer standing in a mountain waterfall—since the days of lithographed magazine ads. Moomey wanted to do what every other maker of consumer products did—show attractive people enjoying the product. He approached Ad about it one afternoon as they were filing out of the company auditorium. Bill had begun a series of lectures on the dangers of alcoholism, and attendance was mandatory. As they walked out together, Moomey outlined for Ad his ideas for a people-based ad campaign. Ad cut him off.

"My father wouldn't stand for it," Ad told Moomey. "He'd say, 'We're selling beer, not people.' He worries that if someone doesn't like the look of a person in our ads, they won't buy our beer."

"Then why does every other brewer in the country advertise with pictures of people who are happy with the product?" Moomey asked.

"But which people?" asked Ad. "That's my father's question and I think he's right. If you do a commercial with white people in it, the colored will want one for them, and the Spanish for them. So in order not to show any favoritism, my father says, let's not use any of them."

Moomey could make any commercial he liked, Ad finished, as long as it showed nothing but a bottle of beer in a waterfall.

"Advertising doesn't mean a damn," Bill told Moomey, falling in beside them. "It's the product. We make a good product, buddy, and that's why people buy Coors."

"Bill," Moomey said, "with all due respect, the average guy doesn't know much about beer. He only knows what he's told. We have to tell him."

"You can tell him all day," Bill said, "but nobody is going to decide what beer to drink on the basis of an ad they see in a magazine, or thirty seconds on the radio." Moomey let it drop, shocked at both Bill's ignorance of marketing and at his unfeeling dismissal of Moomey's function within the company.

On one of his first days at work, Moomey encountered Mr. Coors in the washroom. "Come here," Mr. Coors said, washing his hands. "When you're finished using the washroom, you should do this." Mr. Coors reached for a paper towel and carefully wiped out the sink. "The next person doesn't want your mess." And then he walked out, leaving Moomey to wonder why a thirty-year-old Ph.D. needed to be taught how to use a washroom.

Weird as he thought Mr. Coors was, Moomey admired the sense of common purpose he instilled in the company. Mr. Coors had recently issued a handwritten memo assigning himself and his sons corporate titles, but ended the memo warning that the titles "mean nothing and should not be displayed. We all have equal responsibility as individuals and as a group." And in the company it really worked that way. Moomey flew once to their experimental barley farm in southern Colorado and was amazed to see Ad, the company chairman, pulling weeds in the hot sun.

Moomey had spent a lot of years on university campuses among people who read books and were interested in the world. As far as Moomey could see, Bill Coors cared about nothing outside the four walls of his brewery—except maybe lactic acid and free radicals, about which he'd lecture if you gave him half a chance. Ad's mind may have wandered outside the brewery gates, but no further than his dreams of a ranch. Given how expensively the Coorses had been educated, their narrowness surprised Moomey. Joe was the only Coors who came close to having horizons broader than Golden, and Moomey attributed this to Joe having worked elsewhere before coming to Coors. Of the three, Joe was the most up on current events.

Bill worried constantly that his workers weren't sufficiently "loyal" to the family and the company. It was 1951; Senator Joseph McCarthy and the Un-American Activities Committee were rooting out disloyalty in government, and Bill was becoming similarly obsessed within the brewery. Which workers are stealing from us? he wondered aloud. Who is badmouthing the beer? Who isn't part of the team? He laid elaborate traps, such as tools left seemingly unprotected, to catch the sticky-fingered. When security caught a thief, Bill reveled in chastening the miscreant personally and then letting him stay on the payroll with a warning. "Lowell," he told Sund once, "my philosophy is let them win the first one, and if they take advantage of you, that's it." Moomey found Bill's suspicions repugnant, especially in the context of a first-name-basis company.

It pained Moomey to see Ad so dominated by his father, and he was convinced that Ad's stutter was a direct result of years of stifled conversation. As was Ad's frightening temper. Usually the mildest of men, Ad could soar without warning into fits of irrational, violent screaming. His outburst at Spike over the missed bird was just a harbinger. Once Ad was scheduled to pilot his own plane with Mary and two friends for an Arizona vacation. The weather turned bad, and Ad went crazy at the airport; it took Mary and his friends an hour to calm him down and convince him to fly commercial. Another time Mary was out at night with the kids and thought someone was following her in another car. She stopped and called Ad, and when she got home he was out on the lawn in his pajamas, waving a baseball bat and raging into the empty darkness behind her. You'd need some kind of crude release valve, Moomey thought, living under that Victorian anachronism of a father.

Mr. Coors took a liking to Moomey, though, and enjoyed instructing him in the business. Although Coors had by now stopped calling its product Coors Light Beer, Mr. Coors was enthusiastic about a slogan Moomey invented for the label: "America's Fine Light Beer." He also let Moomey paint a lifesize portrait of him for the boardroom. As he was sketching one day, Moomey asked Mr. Coors about the brewery's devotion to making a lighter-tasting brew than its competitors.

"You take a young person," Mr. Coors said. "He wants to drink beer but he really doesn't like the taste very much because of the bitterness of the hops. That can be scientifically measured, by the way, in bitterness units. We strive for lower bitterness units in part to attract that young beer drinker. Because when he then tastes one of our competitors, it will taste too bitter and he'll come back to us."

Moomey looked up from his canvas. "You mean you're trying to get children to drink?" he asked.

Mr. Coors sighed. "Americans can be so puritanical," he said. "Germans think nothing of giving their children beer. But the first taste is unpleasant. We make it less unpleasant, so our beer will be easy to get on and hard to get off."

Yikes, thought Moomey the ad man as he returned to the sketch, don't ever let anybody outside the company hear you say that. But he knew Mr. Coors would indeed say it if the opportunity arose. Mr. Coors was, in Moomey's view, honest to the point of pathology. The portrait was an example. He'd told Moomey to make it as lifelike as possible and Moomey took him at his word. Adolph Coors, Jr., was so agonizingly thin his wife had to send him periodically to a sanitarium to gain weight. In Moomey's painting, bony wrists protrude inches from his sleeves and the long pale hands are skeletal. The eyes, though, make the portrait a startling exception to the usual commissioned work. Gazing out from a gaunt, sagging face, they brim with loneliness and pain. But Mr. Coors pronounced himself pleased; he knew himself well enough to be neither surprised nor offended.

Mr. Coors asked Moomey to redesign the gloomy little workers' bar into a capacious reception area for tourists. Because Coors leaned heavily on its slogan, "Brewed with Rocky Mountain Spring Water," Moomey decided to build an artificial waterfall. The sight and sound of trickling water would reinforce the beer's image, he thought. When the months of renovation work were over, Mr. Coors came downstairs to inspect. He asked if the water in the waterfall was really the spring water with which Coors brewed beer. "No," Moomey explained. "It's just ordinary water. What's the difference?" It was the wrong question to ask the excruciatingly literal Adolph Coors, Jr., for whom the distinction among kinds of water was everything. The old man crisply ordered Moomey to replumb the waterfall with brewery water, even though it meant piping it down two stories. "It is what our guests expect," he said. "It is not right to deceive them."

Several months later, Mr. Coors summoned Moomey into his ascetic office. Finding no second chair, Moomey stood. Mr. Coors was concerned about Anheuser-Busch invading Coors territory. It seemed that every bar and package store in the West suddenly had a neon Budweiser sign on its wall. Coors had never gone in for neon signs; Mr. Coors considered them too flashy. But this was an emergency. Even though Budweiser sales were tiny in the West compared with Coors, Mr. Coors wanted those Bud signs down. He ordered Moomey to have hundreds of neon

Coors signs made at once, regardless of cost, and to get one into the hands of every Coors retailer in the West. The sales force was to tell retailers they weren't allowed to hang both theirs and Budweiser's, Mr. Coors said. They would have to choose. And of course they would rather hang the Coors sign, Mr. Coors continued with a wink, because Coors is the bigger seller.

Moomey flew immediately to Lima, Ohio, home of the biggest neon-sign factory in the United States. Money was no object, he told the foreman. Together, they designed a spectacular multicolored sign, and the factory put aside all other work to rush through the Coors order. Within a month, Moomey was able proudly to report to Mr. Coors that every Budweiser sign in Coors's territory was down, replaced by a brilliant new Coors sign.

The old man frowned. "Leave them there a few weeks," he said as he returned his attention to a ledger book. "Then take them all down and destroy them."

"What?"

"In a few weeks, they will have thrown the Budweiser signs away, and we can take ours down."

"But why?"

Mr. Coors swiveled in his chair and looked into Moomey's eyes. "We mustn't draw too much attention to ourselves," he said. "No brewer should. There are many people out there who would like to bring back Prohibition and we mustn't goad them. That's the reason we don't show people in our ads. We don't want to remind the prohibitionists that people actually drink beer."

Prohibition? Moomey thought as he walked back to his desk. It's 1953. How am I supposed to advertise beer without reminding the public that beer is something people drink? He flopped down into his chair, wondering again about the wisdom of having accepted a job as ad director of a company that already was selling all the product it could make.

Lowell Sund was in the Coors brothers' office one morning when Bill came in waving a newspaper and fuming. John L. Lewis of the United Mine Workers was threatening yet another of his regular coal strikes. The brewery was entirely dependent on coal power and the last two strikes had shut it down. "I will not be shut down again, by anybody! Lowell!" Bill barked. "Our property north of here has coal underneath it. Put a few men and a bulldozer up there and let's start digging our own, goddamn it!"

As Sund nodded, something outside the window caught his eye. Old Mr. Coors was on his hands and knees on the curb in front of the brewery. Passersby glanced at him as he pressed his face to the pavement. The tail of his black suit jacket trailed in the dust. "Uh-oh," Ad said. "We just laid that sidewalk. Dad's checking to be sure it's straight."

It wasn't. The next day, everybody in the office had to shout over the clatter of jackhammers.

Following Bill's orders, Lowell Sund put three men to work on the property north of town and in short order the company was digging all the coal it needed to power the brewery. But in the spring of 1954, barely a year after Coors became energy self-sufficient, three large men in windbreakers appeared in the brothers' office. "We're from the UMW," they said. "We're here to organize your coal mine."

"The hell you are," Bill said. "That mine—if you can call it a mine—exists for one reason only: to keep us running when you monkeys shut the country down."

"You have men digging coal up there," the men in windbreakers said. "That makes it a coal mine. We are not going to have scab mines operating in Colorado. That mine will be UMW, and if there's a UMW strike, that mine will close."

It had happened to Dad and now it was Bill's turn. A union was threatening to turn Bill's workers against him. It was the lowest work Bill could imagine, tricking hardworking men into risking their jobs for John L. Lewis or anybody else. Bill was on a first-name basis with the men digging the coal for him, whereas the UMW men, in his view, cared nothing for them beyond their ability to pay dues. Bill leaned across his desk and spoke through clenched teeth, a nerve twitching in his lean cheek.

"This is our brewery," he growled. "Our grandfather started it and we decide, not you, when and how we operate."

"If you mine coal—" the men in windbreakers began.

Bill cut them off. "We have an alternative to coal and that's gas," he said. "If you shut us down, we'll switch and nobody will be mining coal for Coors."

"Have it your way," the men in windbreakers said smugly, knowing it would cost Coors millions to line up gas contracts and retool the plant. "But if you mine coal your mine is going to be UMW."

The men in windbreakers didn't know that Bill's grandfather had built his own malthouse, his own icehouse, and his own bottle factory to prove his motto "The more we do ourselves, the higher quality we have." Bill surprised them. Coors dug into its reserves and paid cash for a nearby gas field. The company then built a thirty-mile pipeline to carry gas to the plant, and retrofitted the brewery to use gas, all without borrowing. In time, Coors's gas operation grew into Coors Energy Company, a multi-million-dollar subsidiary that owned coal and gas fields all over the Southwest.

Bill's antipathy to unions led him to another ingenious expansion. Back then, Coors bought steel beer cans from the Continental Can Company factory in Denver. An old fraternity brother of Joe's, Bob Hatfield, ran the plant and periodically had to call Bill to say there would be no cans for a while; the union was on strike. Without cans, Coors couldn't brew. Bill called Hatfield and suggested he negotiate each plant's union contract separately so a single strike couldn't shut down the whole company. Better yet, Bill said, lease Coors your Denver plant and let us make our own cans. Hatfield demurred. The union, he said, wouldn't allow either.

"Who manages your company?" Bill asked him. "You or the union?"

Bill told Lowell Sund to advertise for experienced can-makers. He picked an able-looking consortium and awarded it a contract. On the strength of the contract, the consortium was able to borrow enough to build a can plant in Golden to serve a single customer: Coors. This arrangement worked so well with cans that Bill followed the same process to build a bottle factory in Golden. Years later, Coors would absorb both bottles and cans into a massive subsidiary, Coors Container, that no union has ever been able to organize.

3

Hot Slugs
and Cold Beer

Like almost all managers in the years before diversity became a national virtue, the Coorses surrounded themselves with people with whom they were comfortable—people like them. Until relatively late, Coors was a company of white, Protestant men. But more important, they were white, Protestant men who shared certain crucial personal characteristics with the Coorses—first among them a disarming modesty. The Coorses and the people they hired were almost entirely lacking in guile or a desire to brag. They shared a faith that anybody brewing excellent beer doesn't have to trick or beg the public to buy it. And if they mistrusted advertising, they were even more offended by outright sleazy business practices. When the washing-machine heir Fritz Maytag bought the tiny Anchor brewery in San Francisco, he quickly noticed that while retailers and wholesalers asked for all manner of kickbacks, they grudgingly admitted that Coors was the one brewer that never paid them. The Coors culture was one of simple, loyal, western-born men, unclouded by philosophic doubt or the ambiguities of a changing world—much, in fact, like a Rocky Mountain stream: crystal clear and ankle deep.

It is remarkable, therefore, that Bill was led into his greatest engineering triumph by a man so far outside the Coors mold: a Viennese Jew named Lou Bronstein.

Once Bill had assured himself a regular supply of steel cans, he turned his attention to the reasons he disliked them. Canned beer admittedly had many advantages over bottled, especially among Coors's western customers, who often took beer on hikes and picnics. Cans were smaller and lighter than bottles, and they didn't break. They also required no deposit. However popular this was with customers, it worried Bill. As he drove around Colorado, the sight of beer cans along the roadside disgusted him. Not only were they ugly but they were a threat to the company and to the family. Prohibition had taught him how quickly a popular sentiment could mutate into government policy. He reasoned that if beer-can litter bothered him, it probably bothered others too. Sooner or later government would get around to regulating cans to control litter. Government might even require a deposit, which would be disastrous. Unlike bottles, steel cans couldn't be reused. Bill decided the industry had to do something about can litter before government did.

Coors had always seen steel cans as a necessary evil, anyway; the customer wanted canned beer, but the Coorses disliked the effects of steel and solder on their brew. Over time, the can clouded its contents and queered the taste. Bill and his father were striving to keep their beer on the light side of American taste by adding ever more rice and reducing the concentration of hops. The delicate brew they were creating was particularly sensitive to taint. Steel cans required so much solder—around the top, around the bottom, and up the big side seam—that even with tin "keg-lining," they were fundamentally incompatible with good beer.

Bill also dreamed that one day Coors would be able to stop pasteurizing. It pained him to watch containers of his delicious fresh brew sink into a vat of 150-degree water and stew for fifteen minutes. Even if a way could be found to purify beer without heat, steel cans required cooking after filling. There was no way to sterilize them beforehand. Bottles could be sterilized, but by now about 40 percent of Coors beer was sold in cans. As long as canned beer required pasteurization, there was no point in tackling the enormous technical difficulty of cold-sterilizing beer.

Draft beer tasted better than canned or bottled beer because it was not required by law to be pasteurized. The law exempted draft because it was presumed to be used more quickly than canned or bottled, and because the aluminum kegs that held it could be sterilized before filling in a way steel and solder could not.

When Lou Bronstein showed up in Bill's office in 1954 suggesting that beer cans could be made of aluminum, Bill's first impulse was to have him ejected from the brewery. Bronstein was, as Bill later put it, "the antithesis of a Coors, a fly-by-night," a fast-talking operator in a shiny suit. He reeked of the East Coast.

In fact, Bronstein was born in Vienna to a wealthy Jewish family. His father, a physician, wanted his son to follow him into medicine, but young Bronstein was, as a colleague remembered him, "too nervous to be a doctor," the kind of man who is forever remembering what he was going to say a few minutes ago. Instead of wanting to be a doctor, he'd wanted to be a deal-maker and make his millions the easy way. By all accounts, though, Bronstein's father had exerted every bit as much patriarchal authority as had Mr. Coors. Bronstein had trooped off to his premedical training with a heavy heart, knowing he'd been cowed into doing the wrong thing. It took Hitler to set him free.

Whether he was eager to slip his father's leash or was smart enough to see what was in store for Viennese Jews, or both, Bronstein left Europe relatively early—early enough to have become a United States citizen in time to enlist in the U.S. Army after Pearl Harbor. He fought with General George Patton from North Africa all the way up the Italian boot. It was murder, but Bronstein used it as an all-expenses-paid research trip to explore potential products and markets. He came away unwounded and completely devoted to the consumer potential of aluminum.

What had first caught his eye were the clever little drinking cups Italian soldiers carried—so light, so durable, so pleasant in the hand. Bronstein bought thousands of them right after the war and sold out of them immediately in New York. It taught him that people love the feathery gray metal, and that he had the chance to be on the ground floor of a multibillion-dollar aluminum craze. Pots, pans, doorknobs, bicycles, auto frames . . . almost anything made of steel could be made stronger and lighter from aluminum. The giant British aluminum company Alcan apparently thought the market was about to erupt, too; it had just built a behemoth of an aluminum plant in British Columbia that was far too big for current demand. Knowing Alcan would be looking for customers, Bronstein convinced the company to let him act as a kind of broker; if he lined up enough customers for their aluminum,

Alcan would guarantee them a low price. Now Bronstein was traveling the country, supply in hand, looking for demand. He'd already been to a friend of Bill's, who'd sent him to Bill.

"Hiya, Bill," Bronstein said, lowering himself into a chair before being asked. Whatever Viennese elegance Bronstein had once possessed was by this time long gone. He lit a cigarette and looked around for an ashtray, but since smoking was forbidden in the brewery there was none. Cupping his palm under the ash, he tried a few raunchy jokes on Bill and got stony silence in return. Then he plunged into his pitch:

"A couple of little kraut breweries use aluminum beer cans, but their process is clumsy and too expensive for a mass operation," he said, talking about six times faster than Bill was used to. "The Canadians have an interesting process for making aluminum toothpaste tubes. They call it impact extrusion. I can't go into all the details because they're secret, if you know what I mean, but essentially you put a soft aluminum slug in the bottom of a cylinder and wham!" Bronstein punched his palm, showering ash on the floor. "You drive a piston down onto the slug. The aluminum squirts up around the piston and presto, you have a seamless aluminum cylinder with an intact bottom. All it needs is a top. No solder around the bottom. No solder up the side. The whole thing weighs a fraction of what a steel can weighs, and aluminum doesn't react with beer the way steel does."

Bronstein brushed his hands on his trousers. "Hell," he muttered. "If you wanted to go to the trouble, you could even gather up the used ones, melt them down, and use them again. But look at this deal I have from Alcan." He waved some papers at Bill, snatching them away before he could get too close a look. "The aluminum is so cheap you needn't bother reusing the old ones. Why don't you come to Europe with me, hunh, Bill?" Bronstein pressed. "I can show you what's being done over there. You and me, come on."

A swarthy, grasping operator like Bronstein, aswirl with secrets and schemes, was repellent to Bill Coors. What's more, the man knew nothing of engineering, let alone brewing. Lou Bronstein was nothing but a businessman. But he unwittingly struck several of Bill's chords—solder, litter, and the prospect of sterilizing cans before filling. Bill told himself to put aside his dislike of the man's style. He did what checking he could and finally agreed to form a small partnership under the grandiose title Aluminum International. Bill would put up a little money, and Bronstein would be his tour guide through the world of aluminum. Bill insisted on serving as treasurer; he wanted to keep his hand on his wallet.

He consented to go with Bronstein on a five-week research tour through Europe, at Coors's expense. Mr. Coors decreed that Bill and Bronstein travel cheaply, and Bronstein insisted on booking the tickets. When Bill saw the travel arrangements, he noticed how oddly complicated they were. On the airplane east, Bronstein confided that he had several wives after him for alimony that he couldn't afford to pay, so he never entered the country through the same port he exited.

For Bill, the trip was a nightmare of cramped quarters, inadequate exercise, fatty food, and confinement with the windbag Bronstein. But Bronstein delivered. He knew the people to see, the can plants to visit, the laboratories to plumb for information. As they hopped from Frankfurt to Stuttgart to Mainz, Bill grew increasingly excited. Every aluminum can the Germans made cost them twenty-five cents. Bill's mind whirred in tune with the machinery as he calculated costs. Coors could make its own aluminum cans, he thought, and could do it cheaper than the Germans. Bill wrote check after check for used presses, printers, washers, casting lines, and trimmers. He ordered them to be shipped to Golden posthaste, not knowing how all the machinery would fit together. When he got home, he confidently told his family it would take no more than half a year and another $250,000 to begin producing aluminum cans for Coors beer. He approached Alcoa about forming a partnership, but Alcoa told Bill he was dreaming. Nobody can profitably make beverage cans out of aluminum, Alcoa told him, especially not a third-string beer-maker in Colorado. Bill filed away the insult and pushed forward. His grandfather had made malt, ice, and bottles at a time other brewers stuck only to beer. Why shouldn't he make his own cans?

Bill needed an experienced aluminum engineer to launch his grand project. He did not, however, conduct a nationwide search for the best man; instead, he simply opened the Denver yellow pages. Down among the small print he found the name Ruben Hartmeister. Hartmeister was a skinny, balding, and bespectacled man who was slowly going broke in his own small machine shop. Early in his career, Hartmeister had worked in an aluminum rolling mill. He told Bill he'd been raised by a Lutheran minister and would be able to read the German manuals that would accompany the machinery. He also modestly mentioned that his grandfather was the inventor of Beech-Nut chewing tobacco. Machining, aluminum, German, and an experimental nature were all Bill sought. For a shop, Bill gave Hartmeister an unused office at Porcelain.

Hartmeister had no idea what he was doing. He'd been taught church

German; the technical German of the manuals was opaque. But he did indeed have a passion for experimentation. He began bolting machinery together, manufacturing needed parts on his own lathe. He and Bronstein went to Europe together, and loaded up seventeen suitcases with slugs, tools, and bits of machinery. Upon Hartmeister's return, he and Bill spent hours cycling through ideas, sketching for each other on the backs of old brewery invoices. Having served his purpose, Lou Bronstein was paid for his share of Aluminum International and vanished into obscurity. After several months of tinkering, Hartmeister came to Bill's office with a crude aluminum can. Bill carried it around the brewery like the grail of Christ.

Only pure aluminum was soft enough to flow up around the piston. The hated Alcoa was the only source of pure aluminum slugs, and their price was sky-high—in part, Bill suspected, to keep him from going forward. So Bill wheedled more money out of his father and brothers for a slug press of his own, vertically integrating the company yet another step. He and Hartmeister brainstormed constantly, and then it would be up to Hartmeister to wield wrench and cutting torch to give their ideas shape. Making slugs wasn't as easy as Bill had hoped. The equipment frequently jammed, and when the hot aluminum stopped moving it threatened to destroy the machine altogether. When that happened, Hartmeister and his helpers had to grab 900-degree slabs of aluminum with tongs and run, shouting, out into Washington Street, scattering pedestrians in every direction. Once cooled outside, the slugs had to be heated again before they were whacked into shape by the piston. Hartmeister's arms were streaked with burns where the hot aluminum disks had rolled along them. In time, though, Hartmeister became an expert at making slugs. He could produce them at less than half Alcoa's price and pretty soon Coors was selling slugs to General Motors for speedometer tubes, forcing big Alcoa to lower its price and affording Bill a measure of vengeful satisfaction.

Though can-making and slug manufacture were solved, Coors still wasn't ready to sell beer in aluminum cans. The bottleneck now was printing on the labels. The machine Hartmeister had developed could print only 180 cans a minute, far too slow given the river of beer Coors needed to can daily. Late on Thanksgiving Day in 1957, Hartmeister came into the shop, turned on the lights, and began scrounging bits and pieces for a new printer. He worked on his printer—code-named Relentless—all through the winter and spring. On July 7, Hartmeister loaded Relentless with cans and ink and flipped the switch. A hurricane of cans shot through the machine and clattered all over the floor; Hartmeister hadn't yet designed a catcher. He ran the machine for exactly one minute and gathered up the cans. Hartmeister had 513 perfectly printed cans. He ran across the creek to the brothers' office with the good news. "We're off and running!" Bill shouted. Joe, frowning at the can on his desk, said only, "It's not good enough." Both were right.

Coors began pouring beer into aluminum cans on January 22, 1959. Bill convened the first press conference in the company's history to announce the momentous event and was dubbed "the inventor of the aluminum can." *Modern Metals* magazine named him Man of the Year. It had taken five years and $10 million—rather more than the six months and quarter million dollars Bill had predicted. The can wasn't perfect; it was a seven-ounce "pony," and although a supposed advantage of aluminum was its light weight, the walls of the can were so thick that it weighed more than a twelve-ounce steel can. The system was still full of bugs.

But Coors was making aluminum beverage cans for a penny and a half apiece—the first American beverage company to fill aluminum cans, let alone manufacture them. Coors eventually refined the aluminum can into the delicate, featherweight, instantly chilled container it is today. To appreciate what beverage cans were like before Coors's achievement, pick up a can of peas and imagine drinking a beer out of such a heavy, clunky, hard-to-chill hunk of metal. Then consider how many beverage cans are drained in a day and what a mountain of nonrecyclable containers that would create. The work of Bill Coors and Ruben Hartmeister eventually rendered the entire steel beverage-can industry obsolete. American Can Company, Continental Can Company, and all of Coors's beer competitors had to come hat-in-hand to Golden to buy the technology. By 1990, Coors was operating the biggest aluminum can plant in the world—manufacturing four billion cans a year, twenty million a day.

The Adolph Coors Company was a union shop in name only. Local 366 of the Brewery, Flour, Cereal, and Soft Drink Workers International Union was known throughout the Colorado labor community as a lapdog. Wages at Coors were lower than at other Colorado brewers, the benefits more meager. In 1950, the membership objected to its complacent leaders. The annual month's-pay bonus that Mr. Coors instituted in 1934 was nice, they said, but wages should be higher and the bonus shouldn't depend on the whim of the family. It should be spelled out in the contract. When the leadership did nothing, the members voted in a tough new regime.

The local struck briefly in 1953 and the dispute ended amicably, as did the 1955 contract talks. But in 1956, workers at Coors Porcelain—represented by a separate union—went on strike. The Porcelain workers extended their picket line not only around their factory but around the brewery as well, appealing to the brewery workers to stay off the job in support. To the Coors brothers' amazement and fury, all but fifteen members of the newly energized Local 366 stayed home. This was the high-water mark of American union membership and labor solidarity was strong. Managers and Coors family members donned work clothes and manned the machinery, and brewing continued. But Bill and Joe were beside themselves. The brewery workers liked their new contract. They had no argument with the company. Why on earth, Bill and Joe wondered, would they give up their paychecks simply because guys working across the creek had a beef?

Coors settled the Porcelain strike quickly. The brewery workers went back to work; they and Coors agreed to forget the matter. But when Local 366 fined the fifteen men who had crossed the picket line during the strike, Bill and Joe felt betrayed. They had been willing to live with a union in order to have the union label on Coors beer. This business of punishing good workers for nothing more than doing their jobs, though, was too much for Bill and Joe. They decided to see if they could get rid of Local 366 once and for all and have a union-free brewery. The family was producing coal and gas without unions. It was making cans and bottles without unions. It was time for Local 366 to go. Though Ad and Mr. Coors consented, neither took an active role in trying to oust the union.

When the brewery contract came up for negotiation in January 1957, Bill opened the talks. "I want a new clause in the contract," he said. "I want to prevent the union from punishing a member who crosses a picket line."

The union leaders were alarmed. They'd expected a simple wages-and-benefits negotiation. Coors wages were seventy-five cents an hour lower than those at comparable companies in Colorado, and the union wanted only a fifteen-cent raise. And it wanted the annual bonus spelled out in the contract. Bill's proposal was unthinkable. Picket-line discipline was essential to maintaining the threat of a strike.

Joe, seated beside Bill, was unmovable. "We'll meet your wage demands," he said, "but not unless you accept the picket-line clause." When the contract expired on the first of March, the two sides were as far as they'd ever been from reaching agreement.

Four days later, Bill and Joe issued the challenge that assured a strike. They posted notices in the brewery announcing new rules: The union business agent could no longer visit the plant without company permission. The company would no longer help Local 366 collect dues by deducting them from paychecks. Union bulletins would be banned from the brewery. The company would no longer hear union grievances. For Local 366 to accept any of these unilateral changes would be tantamount to folding up. Before the local could call a strike vote, Bill summoned all brewery employees to the company auditorium. The workers filed in, expecting yet another lecture about the perils of alcoholism. Instead, Bill mounted the stage and read a short statement from an index card. "Coors will continue operating in the event of a strike," he said. "If we have to, we will hire replacements." Bill raked a frown over the upturned faces below and then walked offstage without taking questions. The members of Local 366 were speechless; no American brewery had ever replaced striking workers.

To make such a threat was a declaration of war. The Wagner Act of 1934 barred companies from firing workers for union activity, including participation in a strike. But in a complicated 1938 labor case called *NLRB* v. *MacKay Radio and Telegraph Company*, the U.S. Supreme Court ruled it is not "an unfair labor practice to replace the striking employees with others in an effort to carry on the business." The difference between being fired and "replaced"—though imperceptible to a suddenly idled worker—was not trivial wordplay. Flushing one's business clean of strikers with an infusion of permanent nonunion labor was now legal.

For many years, few businesses took advantage of the ruling. To do so was a stronger antiunion declaration than most corporations were willing to make. Even Andrew Carnegie had once advised against hiring replacements. "To expect that one dependent on his daily wage for the necessities of life will stand by peaceably and see a new man employed in his stead is to expect much," Carnegie said. "Calling upon strange men should be the last resort."

But long after Carnegie's time, Congress finished the Supreme Court's job of making the calling upon of "strange men" an easy way to bust a union. Congressional Republicans—enjoying a rare two-year window of controlling the House of Representatives—in 1947 reversed many of the provisions of the Wagner Act by passing, over President Truman's veto, the Taft-Hartley Act. Taft-Hartley, among other things, let replacement workers vote in elections "to decertify," or oust, their union. As Bill and Joe understood it, Coors could now force a strike, replace the strikers, and then call an election in which only strikebreakers voted.

In 1957, the Coors brothers were preparing to be the first American brewer to flex the combined muscle of *MacKay Radio* and Taft-Hartley. They issued a "last, best, and final offer" that raised wages but included all the tough new rules and the picket-line clause. As expected, the members of Local 366 voted seven-to-one to reject it and walked out. Coors began hiring replacements within a week. One hundred twenty crossed the picket line. Punches were thrown, car windows smashed. The Golden City Council hurriedly passed ordinances limiting the number of picketers at the plant gates. (These ordinances were ruled illegal—but long after the strike.) Golden was a small town, and the strike split families and friendships. "Do you think I like the situation that has developed?" Bill asked a *Rocky Mountain News* reporter. "I know every one of those guys out there on the picket line—I worked with them."

As he aged, Bill Coors would develop an appealing candor; like his father, he would say what he thought, regardless of how unpopular it made him. In 1957, though, Bill was only forty-one, living in the shadow of his father and older brother. He was not yet sure enough of himself to speak his mind clearly and take the consequences. So he went on to tell the *Rocky Mountain News* what can only be interpreted—given his actions at the time—as an uncharacteristic lie: "I wouldn't want to try to operate the plant without a union," he told the reporter, "because it is against my principles and that of my father and brothers."

The outcome was mixed. Bill and Joe did not drive out their union, but they did defang it. The strike collapsed after three and a half months and the men went back to work, except for those who had been replaced. The Coorses implemented all the tough new rules they'd earlier posted in the brewery. For good measure, they added to the contract twenty-two reasons for immediate discharge, such as "conduct on company premises which violates the common decency or morality of the community" and "any words or deeds which would discourage any person from drinking Coors beer." Local 366 got its fifteen cents, but was emasculated.

"I've got the big stick," Bill told his workers as they filed back to work, "and I intend to use it."

The other unions still operating at Coors were likewise put on notice. When an out-of-state distributor came to visit the brewery, old Mr. Coors took delight in showing him how he often moved electricians to laborers' jobs, pipe fitters to carpenters' jobs—all in violation of union contracts—just to show the unions he could do it.

Over at Porcelain, Joe Coors broke his union by forcing it to accept an "open-shop" provision that let employees choose individually whether to be union members. Many bolted, and the local collapsed. Joe Coors had beaten Bill to it. At Porcelain, he was finally running a nonunion shop.

Bill's nemesis, Brewery Workers Local 366, hung on. When Bill forced a decertification election, its members voted to stay organized. But after its brief moment of militancy, Local 366 was back to being a company-controlled union. But Bill had tasted blood. And the members, for their part, had been wounded, and were bitter.

Bill Moomey spent a lot of his time looking for ways to promote Coors beer that would avoid reminding people that beer is an alcoholic beverage, or that beer was tasty, romantic, sexy, or fun. Such messages, Mr. Coors continued to insist, might awaken the slumbering dragons of Prohibition. Bill Moomey had a lot of time on his hands.

He was going through the files in the Coors brothers' office one afternoon when he noticed one marked "Charity." What he found inside amazed him. The Coors family was a fountain of philanthropic dollars. Orphanages, schools, hospitals, libraries . . . it seemed any worthy cause could extend a palm and Coors would fill it. Moomey was ecstatic. This could be a wonderful way to boost the image of the company without mentioning beer. Moomey began sketching a strategy: press conferences to announce big donations, the Coors name etched on Coors-financed buildings, print ads extolling the worthiness of this or that cause—with the Coors logo prominently displayed. Finally, Moomey felt he had something creative to do as advertising director. For once, he could stop photographing that bottle of beer on a rock.

Mr. Coors frowned as though profoundly disappointed. "Once we do that, we'll have everybody in the world coming to us," he said. "Besides, we give because it's right. This country has been very good to the Coors family and we owe a debt in return." Moomey sighed and put away the "Charity" file, dreaming of the ads he would never bring to light. Coors philanthropy remained secret. When Holly took her young son Peter to the opening of a hospital that Coors had helped finance, Peter looked at the long list of donors etched into the wall. "Why isn't our name there?" the little boy asked. "Here we are," Holly said cheerfully, pointing to the word "Anonymous."

Bill, meanwhile, had been pondering something he'd seen on his trip through Europe with Lou Bronstein. One small brewery was purifying its beer with something called an Enzinger filter. Basically, an Enzinger was a pad of cotton and asbestos about the size of a manhole cover, sheathed in a stainless-steel case. The beer entered the disk at the edge and traveled the diameter of the pad. Then it went through a second pad. When the beer emerged from filter number two, it was as free of bacteria as pasteurized beer.

Cold-filtering promised problems aplenty, first among them adaptation to the scale of the Coors brewery. In 1957, Coors had passed the million-barrel mark. Though his father thought he was dreaming, Bill was determined to take the brewery up to two million. Such big Midwest and East Coast brewing companies as Anheuser-Busch, Schlitz, and Pabst hadn't yet begun large-scale marketing in the West, and in all eleven western states where Coors was sold, it was far and away the biggest seller. In California, for example, Coors had more than half the market. Cold-filtering a million or two barrels of beer would require acres of Enzinger filters. Moreover, it would mean encasing the entire kegging, canning, and bottling operation in a sterile environment. Without pasteurization as a backstop, one microscopic breach in the long packaging process could force a recall of millions of dollars' worth of beer. Bill shared his ideas about cold-filtering with the plant manager, who shuddered and said, "It isn't something to do if you want to sleep at night."

But the temptation was too great for Bill now that the last big hurdle— the steel can—had been eliminated. Bill began sketching. He decided to stack the stainless-steel cases that held the Enzinger pads like coins, and then lie the stack on its side in rows fifty feet long. Tubes would snake along the stack, directing each mouthful of beer, leapfrog-fashion, through two filters. Each filter case was designed to swivel up out of the stack so the pad could be replaced. A whole separate operation would be designed to mince the used pads and remanufacture them into new ones. Compressors and heat exchangers would keep the filtering apparatus chilled. Beer freezes at 29 degrees Fahrenheit; Bill decided the beer should be held at exactly 32 degrees throughout filtering and packaging.

Filtering, though, was only half the problem. The packaging lines had to be completely rebuilt. Each would have to be as automated as possible to reduce human contact with the product. Those people who absolutely had to work within the sterile area would scrub like surgeons, wear hairnets, and dip their shoes into disinfectant before entering. To be absolutely safe, the whole packaging area would be kept at positive air pressure, so that dust would blow out instead of in when the doors were opened.

Whew, Bill thought, as he looked at his calculations. This will cost millions.

Luckily, Coors had millions. Coors was selling $40 million worth of beer a year. The most serious problem the company faced, as always, was making enough beer to fill its orders. The company was swimming in cash. Part of Lowell Sund's routine every Friday was to call up Coors's bankers and direct them to invest the company's ocean of cash hither and yon until Monday. Put twenty million here, he'd say, and ten million there. The interest piled up, and the receipts rolled in.

The family took little out of the business. Old Mr. Coors lived in the mansion and treated himself to expensive vacations in Hawaii and Nantucket. But his sons lived on modest allowances and had little money of their own. As company chairman, Ad lived in a $16,000 house in Denver and drove an old International Travelall. Mary shopped at the Safeway and did the cooking. Their children went to public school, wore jeans, and had no sense of belonging to a rich family. Their Sunday visits to the brewery and their grandparents' mansion were like trips to another world. The same was true for Bill's and Joe's kids. Well into the '60s, in fact, Joe's kids had to go to friends' houses to see color television.

None of the brothers minded their humble lifestyle. They had all they needed. They were proud to live small. Coorses didn't work for money. They worked to make the best product possible. Their products were beer and ceramics, so that's where the money went.

Mr. Coors was willing to let the boys decide on Bill's cold-filtering idea. He laid out the issues for them over their daily lunch in the mansion. Sitting on so much cash, the family was in a good position to risk cold-filtering. Putting an end to pasteurization had been a shimmering dream for a long time, and now Bill had a clear-cut plan to do so. Joe challenged his big brother on some of the technical points. But Joe wasn't the engineer Bill was. His questions were basic and Bill answered them easily. Having made a face-saving effort to participate, Joe could honorably declare himself convinced. All eyes turned to Ad.

Ad was particularly dreamy in those days. He had finally bought a small ranch about twelve miles south of Golden. Mary, who loved him more than the city, supported the move. With a friend, Ad had bought some cattle and a few quarter horses; not much, but plenty to handle as a hobby. Most days Ad was up well before dawn happily mixing feed or tacking barbed wire to fenceposts. Whenever anybody asked, "Where's Ad?" they usually could find him leaning on his split rail fence, one muddy boot on the lower rail, gazing at his livestock with pure love. As though to compensate for the country life, Ad had recently taken to wearing a tie at work—not a suit or jacket, just a tie. Ad faced the public more than Bill or Joe, as sales and marketing director; and he was, of course, chairman of the company. Ad was also among a handful of investors who thought Colorado might develop a ski industry, and he held his tie in place with a silver ski-shaped clasp engraved AC III.

Dreamy or not, he was still the oldest son, and Bill's cold-filtering idea presented problems his engineering-obsessed younger brother hadn't considered. Cold-filtered beer had to be kept cold to keep from spoiling. Bill had proudly presented a calculation indicating that, handled properly, the beer would gain only one half to one degree on its journey from the brewery to the retailer. Where Bill saw an engineering triumph, Ad saw an enormous burden on his network of distributors. They would have to build refrigerated warehouses and buy refrigerated trucks, all of which were expensive.

It was the wrong argument for Ad to make to Bill. Bill despised the distributors. They were not Coors employees but independent businessmen chosen by the brewery to deliver Coors to particular territories. With Coors the biggest-selling beer everywhere it was sold, the distributors were fabulously rich—many times richer, for example, than Bill Coors. One distributor in Texas had just hosted a wedding party for his daughter, and had filled his mansion's swimming pool with ice and champagne. When Bill—who lived in a modest subdivision house—heard about it, he was livid.

Bill predictably dismissed Ad's concern for the distributors. Handling Coors beer was a privilege, he said. The distributors should be proud to contribute to a vast improvement in the quality of the product.

Then Bill started in on the retailers. It didn't make sense to keep the beer cold, he said, only to have the retailer stock it on the dry shelf and let it return to room temperature. For the customer to taste Coors at its peak, the retailers should be compelled to keep it in the coolbox with the milk.

Ad argued that most beer purchases were made on impulse. If Coors was sealed behind the coolbox door instead of out on the shelf where the customer could see it, they'd scoop up some other brand.

Bill was unmoved. Coors was the best beer in America, he insisted, and they were about to make it better. People would open the coolbox door to get it. The company's salespeople should check every retailer regularly. Any storekeeper caught with Coors on the dry shelf, Bill argued, should lose the right to sell it.

Ad was aghast that Bill essentially wanted to turn his salesmen into a police force.

Why do we need a sales force anyway? Bill wanted to know. Why do we need advertising? We're selling all the beer we can make as it is.

But Ad could see what the shipping breweries were doing in the marketplace. He knew the day was coming when Coors would have to compete seriously with advertising, price promotions, the works. He wanted to make it easier for people to buy Coors beer, not harder.

Mr. Coors sat back and let his sons fight it out. He insisted the company run on consensus, not majority rule. He was willing to wait days, weeks, even months, for the boys to settle their differences. The company would go forward only with everybody in agreement.

In the end, the brothers made the same decision the original Adolph Coors had made when he left Wenker's business office for the brewery: to emphasize the brewing of beer over the selling of it. Ad had to admit to Bill's logic; Coors beer was so popular that no distributor or retailer in his right mind would stop handling it. And Ad did not want to prevent the family from achieving the goal of unpasteurized beer.

At the end of 1959, Coors became the first major brewer in the United States to ship unpasteurized beer in cans and bottles. Coors's salespeople altered their mission. They were no longer in the business of simply selling beer; now they devoted themselves also to policing distributors and retailers. Any caught with a warm Coors got a stern warning. Few needed more than one. Those who didn't measure up lost the franchise. Distributors grumbled at first about the huge new investment they had to make in refrigerated trucks and warehouses. Grocers shuddered when the Coors man came through the door with his clipboard.

But it turned out Bill was right. The public could tell the difference between Coors and other beers. People were willing to open a coolbox door for a beer whose taste was uncompromised by heat. Sales shot up ever higher. In Oklahoma, Coors held 70 percent of the market. If distributors and retailers were bothered by the new rules imposed by Coors, they were too busy counting their money to complain. Coors was a juggernaut. Nothing could touch the Golden boys.

4

Lightning

Bill was flirting with Phyllis Mahaffey again. Her switchboard stood at the entrance to the brewery office suite and she perched there fetchingly on her hard little stool, chirping over and over, "Adolph Coors Company!" Phyllis was twenty-nine years old and a knockout. The less time Bill spent at home with his troubled wife and children, the more he liked to stand over Phyllis's switchboard. She enjoyed the attention. A fourth-generation Coloradan, she'd briefly been engaged to a man from Hawaii, but that hadn't worked out. She was just as glad to be in Golden, working for a fine family. And she was happy to have the boss's son idling at her desk—even if he was married and sixteen years older. Truth be told, she hardly noticed the age difference because Bill was so fit. As she yanked and replugged phone cords, singing, "Just a moment, please!" Bill wedged aluminum cans in the crook of his elbow and crushed them with a flex.

He didn't cut up that way when his father was around, but on this wintry morning—February 9, 1960—his parents were on their annual vacation to Hawaii. Joe even had a radio playing in the office, something their father didn't tolerate. Joe was all worked up over the news, as usual; this time it was the Soviets, defiantly testing missiles in the Pacific. The brothers were supposed to have started a board meeting at ten, but at ten-thirty they were still waiting for Ad. Bill was eager to get started. He'd begun a pilot program among distributors in which Coors was offering to buy back empty aluminum cans for a penny apiece. At that price, it was cheaper to melt down old cans than to buy new aluminum. Collecting cans might also help alleviate litter and forestall government regulation. Nobody had ever tried such a thing. Bill's father and brothers were skeptical that enough cans would come in to make handling them worthwhile. But now Bill had proof; as many as 25 percent of the cans Coors was selling were coming back. Bill wanted to expand the program and require every distributor to open a recycling center. He wanted to take anybody's aluminum cans, even the competition's. He knew that Ad would hit the roof at the idea of heaping yet another burden on his beloved distributors. But that was too bad. Collecting more cans could reduce costs further and would be good for the environment, reducing litter. And Lord knew the distributors could afford it. Their poor-mouthing was ridiculous.

"Where is Ad?" Bill asked, looking at his watch. "He should have been here an hour ago. Phyllis, be a good girl and give Mary a call. Maybe Ad's stuck somewhere." Bill set the crushed cans aside and walked into Bill Moomey's office. If he couldn't start the board meeting he could at least talk about how Coors might publicize its recycling program. In a few minutes Phyllis was at the door.

"Mary says he left at the usual time, Bill. A little after eight. She's worried."

"I know where he is," Moomey said with a laugh. "He's out mooning over that new bull of his."

"Is there a phone out there?" Bill asked.

"Nah," said Moomey. "It's in that far pasture above the house. I imagine he's unwinding, which is just as well after his little, ah . . ." Moomey rolled his eyes. It was common knowledge that Ad had just thrown another legendary fit of temper. He and Mary had gone with another couple for what was supposed to have been a week's vacation in the Bahamas. When they got there and found the hotel didn't have a room for them, Ad went wild in the lobby. He wouldn't go to another hotel, but flew straight home with Mary seething beside him. They'd been home just a day or two.

"You'd better drive out there and get him," Bill said, looking again at his watch. "We've got to get started." He strode out, muttering, ". . . not something he'd do if Dad were here."

"He's so cute," Phyllis said to Moomey as Bill left the room.

"Like a rattlesnake," Moomey said, gathering up his coat. "I'll be back in an hour."

To reach Ad's ranch, Moomey drove south on Highway 285 until he came to Turkey Creek Road. He turned left onto the shoulderless black-top that led to Ad's house. A few miles in, the road dipped into an arroyo and a wooden one-lane bridge crossed the narrow creek. Moomey saw a milk truck parked at the entrance to the bridge. The driver stood beside his truck, leaning in and blowing the horn. Moomey pulled up behind him.

"Hey," Moomey said, burying his hands in his pockets against the cold wind. "What's up?"

"That car's blocking the bridge and the driver's nowhere around," the milkman said. "He's probably off taking a leak, but I've been blowing my horn for five minutes."

Then Moomey noticed that the car blocking the bridge was Ad's green-and-white Travelall. The door was open and the radio was playing. White puffs of exhaust sputtered from the tailpipe. "Wait here a minute," Moomey said.

He reached inside the Travelall and switched off the engine. The sudden silence was unnerving. "Ad?" he called. "Ad!" Only the boom of the wind answered him. Instinctively, Moomey moved to the edge of the low bridge, placed his hands on the rail, and looked down.

In the shallow water was a pair of glasses with flesh-colored rims. A ways downstream, snagged behind a rock, a tan baseball cap fluttered in the shallow current. Near it on the bank, crown up, lay a brown fedora Moomey didn't recognize.

Moomey backed up suddenly as though the bridge rail were hot. His heel slipped and he looked down. He was standing in a two-foot puddle of fresh blood. Now Moomey saw blood splashed on the railing as well.

"Back your truck up and go find a phone," Moomey called to the milkman. "Call the police and say there's been an accident."

Moomey was a member of the sheriff's auxiliary and was sorry he'd touched the bridge rail. He slowly walked the fifty-foot length of the bridge, looking for clues. There was nothing—just the blood and Ad's belongings in the creek. And the brown fedora. Knowing Ad's temper, Moomey guessed what had happened: Two cars approach each other on the one-lane bridge. Neither man is willing to back up. The men leap out of their cars and start swinging at each other, Moomey figured. One of them whacks his head on the railing and the other trundles him off to the hospital. Ad's car was left behind, so he must be the one who is hurt.

It's just like Ad, Moomey thought, to get into a shouting match at eight o'clock in the morning.

Moomey waited on the bridge for the sheriff's deputies to arrive. Then he drove to a phone booth and called all the emergency rooms and clinics in the area. None remembered treating anybody who matched Ad's description. Moomey called the brewery.

"It looks pretty bad, Bill," he said.

"We'd better call Dad," Bill said.

"I'd wait until we know more," Moomey told him. He drove home, loaded his bloodhounds onto his flatbed truck, and hooked up his horse trailer. He buckled on a single-action Colt revolver and drove back to the Turkey Creek bridge. It was crawling with deputies. Moomey's bloodhounds sniffed their way from one end of the bridge to the other and into the surrounding brush, but came up with no scent. Ad never left this bridge, Moomey thought.

The sheriff of Jefferson County, Art Wermuth, was coming to the same conclusion. Wermuth, a survivor of the Bataan death march and seventeen Japanese prison camps, was a tough old cop. He'd won eight combat medals during the war and afterward had served as provost marshal of Manila. Being sheriff of a rural Colorado county was Wermuth's idea of semiretirement. Now he had what looked like a high-profile kidnapping on his hands. "I don't like the look of those glasses in the creek," Wermuth muttered to a state policeman as his search-and-rescue posse gathered around them. "And that blood."

"Bungled?" the state policeman asked.

"Could be," Wermuth said, and he cupped his hands around his mouth.

"Men!" he yelled. "This is a manhunt. We are looking for Ad Coors. He may be dead, or badly injured. Or a prisoner somewhere in these hills. And we're looking for another man—or men—who may have assaulted or abducted him. Let's go!" Horses clopped off in every direction as helicopters clattered overhead.

Back at the brewery, Bill and Joe sat at their desks for a long time without knowing what to say. Ad, Bill, Joe, and their father were the four corners of the living earth. There was no way to comprehend one of them missing.

"What do you think?" Joe asked Bill. "Call Dad?" They balked. Whenever their father was out of town and needed to be called, particularly with bad news, Ad did it. He was the oldest. He was Adolph Coors III. This was, by rights, his brewery.

The implications started to dawn on Bill. He was the oldest brother present. He would have to make the call. Bill didn't let himself think further than that. Ad would turn up. But for the moment, Bill was in charge. He would have to call Dad. He asked Phyllis to book the call to Hawaii.

Waiting for the call to go through was torture. He couldn't roam the plant; at any moment the phone might ring. Bill tried to focus on the papers on his desk. It seemed pretty clear that whatever happened on the bridge was no accident. One of the emergency rooms would have treated Ad by now. But the idea of foul play was too monstrous to grasp. Ad was the nicest man imaginable. He didn't have an enemy in the world. Who would want to harm him?

The union?

Bill could see one of those union bastards taking a shot at him or Joe, but why Ad? The phone rang.

Bill didn't share his thinking about the union with his father. He reported the facts in as dry and flat a voice as he could manage. Suddenly Mr. Coors was living a replay of the early 1930s, when kidnappers had menacingly circled the family. He told Bill to do nothing but wait for his arrival. At Stapleton Airport in Denver, Mr. Coors shouldered past a honking gaggle of reporters, but paused long enough to offer one comment: "I am dealing with crooks who have something I want to buy: my son. The price is secondary."

The price had already been set. The morning after Ad disappeared, Mary received a special delivery envelope with no return address. It had been posted the previous afternoon in Denver. Inside, a single sheet of paper was neatly typed:

Mrs. Coors: You husband has been kidnaped (sic). His car is by Turkey Creek. Call the police or F.B.I.: he dies. Cooperate: he lives. Ransom: $200,000 in tens and $300,000 in twenties.

There will be no negotiating.

Bills: used/non-consecutive/unrecorded/unmarked.

Warning: we will know if you call the police or record the serial numbers.

Directions: Place money & this letter & envelope in one suitcase or bag. Have two men with a car ready to make the delivery.

When all set, advertise a tractor for sale in Denver Post section 69. Sign ad King Ranch, Fort Lupton.

Wait at NA 9 4455 for instructions after ad appears.

Deliver immediately after receiving call. Any delay will be regarded as a stall to set up a stake out.

Understand this: Adolph's life is in your hands. We have no desire to commit murder. All we want is that money. If you follow the instructions, he will be released unharmed within 48 hours after the money is received.

Half a million dollars! Mary had nowhere near that kind of money. She talked to Ad's father and brothers. Of course the brewery would put up the ransom, they said. But they were typically icy, unwilling to show the slightest emotion.

By the second day after the note arrived, Mary was unhinged. What if Ad never came back? What if they were never able to finish all their many conversations? What if they never got over the Bahamas? Mary's house was full of people; all their friends and family gathered as soon as they'd heard the news. Ad had always been the buffer between his wife and the Coors family, and now he wasn't there. Mary could hardly find her children amidst the throng. Daughter Mary was eighteen, Cecily sixteen, Spike fourteen, and Jim ten.

Mary had the presence of mind to persuade the sheriff to pull his men away from the house so the kidnappers would be able to approach her. She insisted on complying with the ransom note. Her ad ran in the *Denver Post* of February 11:

JOHN DEERE. 1957 model 820, 69 h.p. tractor for sale. King Ranch. Fort Lupton, Colo.

No call came. She ran the ad for two weeks and kept the phone line open, but no kidnapper called.

Even with the paucity of evidence, the police and FBI came up with the name of a suspect within eight days. The first clue came from Ad's sixteen-year-old daughter Cecily, who said she remembered seeing a man waiting by that bridge several times in the previous weeks. He wore a hat like the fedora found next to the creek, she said. And glasses. He had a rifle with him, and Cecily had taken him for a deer poacher. She remembered his car was old and yellow.

Two women who lived near the bridge remembered the old yellow car, too. A Mercury, one of them said. Four-door, from the early 1950s. One even had part of the license plate. She was emphatic about it: a Colorado plate, she said, beginning AT-62. She also remembered that on the morning Ad disappeared she heard voices arguing and what sounded like lightning hitting a tree. Twice.

By Saturday—four days after Ad disappeared—the FBI knew that only four Mercury automobiles bore Colorado plates starting AT-62. One of them was a 1951 yellow four-door. It belonged to Walter Osborne, 1435 Pearl Street, Denver. FBI agents hit the building hard but found only an empty apartment and a thoroughly frightened super, Mrs. Viola Merys. "Mr. Osborne was a good tenant," Mrs. Merys said. "He's lived here four years and never gave me any trouble."

"When did he move out?" the agents asked.

"Wednesday," she said. Wednesday was the day after Ad disappeared.

Among the routine police reports the FBI gathered that week was one from Atlantic City. A yellow, 1951 four-door Mercury sedan without license plates appeared to have been deliberately burned. The vehicle number matched the Colorado registration of Walter Osborne. The FBI collected fingerprints from the car, prints that matched those in Osborne's apartment.

They also matched a set on file at FBI headquarters. The man they belonged to wasn't named Walter Osborne after all. His name was Joseph Corbett, Jr.—wanted for escaping from prison four years earlier while serving a sentence for murder.

Corbett had been a student at the University of California at Berkeley in 1950 when police arrested him for killing an Air Force sergeant he'd picked up hitchhiking. Corbett had argued self-defense: The sergeant pulled a gun, he said, and in grappling for it Corbett had shot him. But the shots were oddly placed for a fight—one behind the left ear and one behind the right. The district attorney persuaded Corbett to plead guilty to a lesser charge of second-degree murder, and Corbett received a sentence of five years to life. Psychiatrists at San Quentin found Corbett uncommonly intelligent but "markedly schizoid." They sent him to a psychiatric hospital for three years, and then to a medium-security prison at Chino, California. When five years were up, Corbett decided he'd paid his debt. He went over the fence at Chino and had been missing ever since.

Within two weeks of Ad Coors's disappearance, the FBI had Corbett linked to the crime five different ways. Corbett's fingerprints proved he was Walter Osborne, but that was the least of it. Salespeople at the stores where the ransom-note typewriter and the brown fedora were bought picked Corbett's photos out of a stack. FBI geologists said they could prove the dried mud on the undercarriage of "Walter Osborne's" burned car came from the bed of Turkey Creek. Agents found a set of leg irons at "Walter Osborne's" Denver apartment along with a mail-order receipt for them made out to Walter Osborne. The agents had a great case but for two details: no victim's body and no suspect in custody. Corbett was thirty-one years old. He had a high forehead, straight brown hair, a mild expression, and glasses—the kind of bland, neutral look that made it easy for him to vanish. Some agents suspected he was dead, too, perhaps killed by confederates still unknown. J. Edgar Hoover personally went on television to announce Corbett's placement on the FBI's Ten Most Wanted list.

Thus began nine months of sleepwalking. Ad was neither there nor completely gone, neither alive nor dead. Mary and the Coorses could neither mourn nor act. They couldn't even be sure the blood on the bridge was his. No record of his blood type existed, it turned out—not even at Johns Hopkins Hospital in Baltimore, where Ad had gone for surgery a few years before.

What struck Bill Moomey through that whole dreadful spring and summer was how level the Coors family remained. Moomey knew them well enough not to expect wailing and lamentation. He was the son of a Nebraska rancher himself, and understood western stoicism. He also knew that the Coors brewery ran twenty-four hours a day, and that life had to go on. Still, the icy calm that prevailed at the brewery was creepy. Moomey missed his friend and couldn't help mourning because as days lengthened into weeks and then months, it seemed certain he was dead. The Coorses, however, refused to mourn. Ad wasn't there, and he wasn't dead. He was just gone. Bill and Joe stepped into Ad's tasks, dividing them without rancor. Lowell Sund also took up a lot of the slack. Sund, too, was amazed at how smoothly things ran without Ad. After a while, people stopped talking about the affable if hot-tempered heir apparent— even Bill, Joe, and old Mr. Coors.

Mary spent the first few weeks after Ad's disappearance sedated by the family doctor. Thereafter she sedated herself with alcohol. Longing for one missing man and hatred for another knocked her off-kilter. Her children, meanwhile, were coping not only with the loss of their father, but with their permanent expulsion from the normal life they'd known before. Suddenly, they were rich kids, different from the others, shepherded to school by armed guards and whispered about in the hallways. Dad was missing. Mom was drunk. Their cousins were under orders from Joe and Bill to carry on. The unspoken message from the extended family was, Don't wallow in grief and self-pity. For Ad's children, whatever their ages, 1960 was childhood's end.

The nightmare of uncertainty became the horror of certainty on September 11. A thirty-year-old pizza-truck driver named Edward Greene went looking for a remote place to try out his new secondhand pistol, and stopped his car at a steep gully, some thirty miles south of the Turkey Creek bridge. It was a place illegally used by locals as a dump. Walking downhill, Greene found a pair of trousers. He kicked at the pocket. It jingled. Greene bent down and retrieved forty-three cents and a pocketknife. He turned the pocketknife over and saw the engraving AC III.

The monogrammed ski-shaped tie clasp was there, too, along with Ad's watch, inscribed AC III. The FBI eventually recovered from the dump Ad's blue windbreaker, green-checked shirt, undershirt, shoes full of spiderwebs, right shoulder blade, pelvis with one thighbone attached, and skull with identifiable dental work. Everything else appeared to have been eaten or scattered by animals. Two holes in the back of the windbreaker lined up with holes in the shirt, undershirt, and shoulder blade. Powder burns surrounded the holes in the windbreaker, leading the FBI to conclude that a firearm had been pressed to Ad's back and fired twice.

Mary's seven months of limbo were over. Her first reaction was to sell the ranch house and move back to Denver. If not for the kids, she'd have fled Colorado altogether. Once again, the Coors family appalled her. Joe was traveling on the East Coast when Ad's body was found, and to Mary's amazement he didn't fly straight home. Bill had a business trip planned that he wouldn't delay. Mary thought Bill's sole comment to the press was heartless. "It's obvious the guy was murdered," Bill said. "How it was accomplished is immaterial to me." Mary couldn't believe that neither Bill nor Joe thought to call their father at his vacation home on Nantucket. Adolph Jr. heard the news from a *Denver Post* reporter. "That's news to me," was all he had to say. Mary was forced to make the humiliating admission to the *Denver Post* that she didn't know when a funeral might be arranged.

When Bill Moomey read the details in the paper, he could see the crime unfold before him: Corbett blocks the bridge with his car and refuses to budge when Ad starts blowing his horn. Did Corbett know of Ad's temper and take advantage of it? Moomey wondered. Moomey could picture Ad boiling over and jumping from the Travelall to yell at the obstinate other driver—loud enough that the neighbor hundreds of yards away could hear. Corbett climbs out of his own car, his face partly covered by the snap brim of his fedora. He brandishes a pistol and tells Ad to put his hands up. Momentarily stunned, Ad complies, and Corbett slips around behind him to nudge him toward the yellow Mercury. He jams the muzzle of his gun against Ad's back and shoves. Now Ad's temper erupts and he starts to swing, knocking Corbett's hat off. Corbett, panicking, pulls the trigger once and quickly again. Ad collapses against the bridge rail, spewing blood. Cap and glasses fly into the creek. Corbett doesn't know if Ad's alive or dead as he loads his body into the trunk of the car and speeds away. At a deserted spot on a lonely road Corbett opens the truck and finds he has committed murder. He heaves the body into the underbrush and drives back to Denver. Corbett is at first a man of ice. According to the postmark on the ransom letter, he appears at a post office window that same afternoon and sends Mary the note special delivery, knowing he is demanding ransom on a corpse. By the next day, he's lost the will to go through with it. He clears out his apartment, tells Viola Merys he is heading back to college in Boulder, and drives east toward Atlantic City.

It was Ad's temper that killed him, Moomey reflected sadly. A calmer man would have followed the gunman's orders. A calmer man would have waited for the ransom to be paid. Hell, Moomey thought, Ad would have been in the Bahamas that day if his temper hadn't gotten the best of him. That temper was the legacy of the miserable household he grew up in, Moomey figured. It was the result of bending to his father's will for forty-five years. Moomey thought of Bill and Joe raising their own kids with the same cold insistence on performance, and as Moomey saw it, the same lack of love. He despaired for those lovely children.

Seven weeks after Ad's body was found, a detachment of Royal Canadian Mounted Policemen knocked on a hotel door in Vancouver, British Columbia, at the request of the FBI. "Okay, you got me," was all Joseph Corbett, Jr., said. On Corbett's table were two books, *Teach Yourself*

Spanish and *Teach Yourself Flying*. The policemen found a loaded pistol in his suitcase. Corbett never owned up to the crime, and none of the Coorses attended his trial. He was sent to prison for life.

Unfortunately for Mary and her children, Ad's father had not followed the tradition of inheritance set by Adolph the founder. Old Adolph had still had six years to live in 1923 when he signed over all his stock in the company to his thirty-nine-year-old heir, Adolph Jr. When Ad was murdered at forty-five, Adolph Jr. hadn't yet signed over any brewery stock to his offspring. Ad owned stock in American Cyanamid and a fledgling outfit called Aspen Ski Corporation, but not a single share of Adolph Coors Company. His estate—including the house, the stocks, the Travelall, and $300 in traveler's checks—was valued at about $600,000. Mary was forty and the mother of four children. She asked for and got a widow's allowance from the estate of thirty-five hundred dollars a month. If she thought her children—who included Adolph Coors IV— might someday be heirs to a portion of the family fortune, she was in for a disappointment.

As Adolph the founder demonstrated when he bent Clear Creek, not even nature was immune to the will of Coors. Prohibition hurt, but Prohibition ended. Wartime rationing pinched, but the war ended, too. The war and Prohibition killed off dozens of breweries, but Coors triumphed each time. Labor trouble only strengthened the family's hand against the unions. Anheuser-Busch, Schlitz, and Pabst were abstract competitors; Coors was number one in all eleven of the western states where it was sold. By its single-minded focus on making the best possible beer, Coors licked temperance, world war, organized labor, and the three Goliaths of brewing.

But the death of Ad knocked the earth off its axis. Coors suffered an injury from which, unlike all the others, there was no recovery no matter how good its beer. It was an injury inflicted not by God or government, but by a greedy little psychopath in glasses. Handing the brewery from Adolph to Adolph was the Coors way, and now the Coorses would not get their way.

Old Mr. Coors knew he had only a decade or so more to live. The handoff of the brewery from generation to generation loomed. Adolph the founder had been orderly about it; he delivered the brewery to Adolph Jr. while still around to help out. Now there was no clear line of succession.

Only 15 percent of family businesses survive the transitions from generation one through generation three, and to have lost the namesake in the third generation worsened the odds.

At forty-four, Bill Coors had to adopt a role for which he was unprepared: oldest son. On the day Ad disappeared, and gradually as the facts brought home the tragic finality of it, Bill began his preparation for assuming command of the Adolph Coors Company. He was next in line, and if anything was even more qualified than Ad to run the company. Unlike Ad, Bill was a brewer to his bones, possessed of his father's elegant nose and palate. He had both a gift for engineering and an education in it that Ad had lacked, and this would be essential to the task of growing the Golden brewery tenfold. And he had no stutter; he could serve as the brewery's public face.

Bill had everything it took to lead the Adolph Coors Company, except, of course, the name and the birthright. Bill might be the greatest brewer, the greatest engineer, and the greatest brewing executive in the country, but he could never be Adolph Coors III. His father took pains to make sure everybody knew it. Mr. Coors didn't name Bill chairman, even though Bill was a year older than Ad had been when he was made chairman, and even though Bill was five years older than Mr. Coors had been when he assumed full ownership of the brewery. Instead, when Ad died, Mr. Coors reassumed the title of chairman. He ordered Ad's chair left empty at the board table and a manila envelope placed before it. Inside the envelope was a eulogy the old man had written for his murdered son, and he insisted on reading it aloud like a benediction before every meeting. He always closed the same way: "This company will never be the same." Once that was established, Bill was free to try his best.

As for Joe, his life continued pretty much as before. He ran Porcelain. He was a competent engineer, and he had a phenomenal memory. He remembered offhand comments made in meetings five years earlier. He carried reams of numbers in his head. He could draw machinery he'd glanced at only once. Joe was not, however, the visionary engineer his big brother Bill was. Bill could describe the future; Joe could recount the past. He was quieter than Bill, too, and more awkward in social situations. Most crippling to his career in the family business was the fact that Joe Coors simply didn't like beer very much. He had no gift or inclination for brewing. It was never suggested, by Joe or anybody else, that Joe, not Bill, should lead the Adolph Coors Company. Bill and Joe's sister May Louise—depending on one's point of view—either faded into obscurity or escaped the bondage of the brewery by being born female. May Louise moved east with her husband, and neither she nor her sons were offered leadership positions within the company.

Bill knew that the conviction of Joseph Corbett eliminated any possibility that Local 366 was behind Ad's murder. But the surge of loathing and suspicion that had pulsed through him when Ad disappeared never fully ebbed. Too much mistrust had grown between Bill and Local 366. The ordeal of Ad's murder took its toll on Bill's spirit. He began talking more and more about "loyalty," worrying aloud that his workers weren't sufficiently devoted to the Coors family. They were stealing, plotting some new labor agitation, sabotaging the beer.

One day in 1961, notices appeared in the brewery that the company had hired a team of psychologists to provide counseling for the workers. Bill was always trying some new health fad and the counseling was presented as concern for his employees' well-being. The psychologists would be at the brewery only temporarily—long enough for every employee to have a turn to see one. All therapeutic conversations would be kept in confidence.

These interviews were not optional, the notices said. All employees were required to see a psychologist, and were requested to schedule an appointment.

Bill Moomey had been growing more disillusioned with the company since Ad's disappearance. He missed his friend, and didn't like Bill's brusque, suspicious style. Schlitz had come wooing and Moomey was weighing their offer. The requirement to see a psychologist was a typically paternalistic move by Bill, Moomey thought. How could an employer require his employees to get "help" they might not think they needed?

It was worse than that. From the whispering around the executive suite, Moomey learned that far from being held in confidence, the psychologists' notes were being routed to Bill. The psychologists weren't there to help employees, Moomey realized. They were spies. Fed up, Moomey decided to take the Schlitz job and ended his ten-year career at Coors.

The psychologists were only the beginning of Bill's plan for assuring a loyal workforce. There would be no more offhanded hiring at picnics. Bill established a whole new lap of hurdles that job applicants had to jump before being hired. First was the "Runner Test," a computerized questionnaire that repeatedly asked a series of yes/no questions with various phrasing, looking for inconsistencies that might indicate lies or a guilty conscience. Applicants who made it past the Runner Test were sent to a windowless room for a polygraph.

The technology of electronic lie detection was young in 1960. Few companies used it. But for Bill, electrodes and graph paper promised an appealing opportunity to plumb men's souls with applied science. Bill wouldn't buy barley without subjecting it to scientific testing; why should he buy labor that way? When Local 366's contract came up for renewal, Bill demanded preemployment polygraphs. Local 366 objected weakly but gave in, which reinforced its image, among Colorado unions, as a eunuch.

Bill and Joe Coors used the lie detector to avoid hiring three types: thieves, radicals, and homosexuals. The first wave of questions asked whether the applicant had ever stolen anything and hadn't been caught or ever committed a crime for which he hadn't been convicted. The next wave asked whether the applicant had ever engaged in "revolutionary activity" or knew of anyone engaging in such. The last questions reflected firing-cause H of the 1958 contract; they elicited information about conduct "which violates the common decency or morality of the community." Some men were asked outright if they were homosexuals or had ever had a homosexual experience. Others were asked how often they had sex with their wives, or whether they'd had sex the previous night. Some were asked no questions at all about sex. Word among the employees was that Coors would let homosexuals work at the can plant, but not in the brewery.

All of the new security measures were supposedly justified by Ad's murder. The family was in danger, the Coorses told themselves and others. They had to be more careful about whom they allowed to get close to them. But to the Coorses, Ad's murder wasn't the only disturbing event in the United States at the dawn of the 1960s. Bill and Joe's intensified desire to control their world was as much a reaction to momentous change outside Golden as it was to the murder of their brother.

The Coors family is conservative. Which is not to say they always vote Republican. The Coorses are not uniformly antiabortion. They do not favor ever-higher penalties for drug offenses. Not all of them are born-again Christians. They did not all oppose the Equal Rights Amendment or support laws making English the official language. The Coorses are ideological conservatives in the classic sense. They lent their support to the conservative movement at a crucial moment, when the first books and journals were articulating an alternative ideology to postwar liberalism. Conservatism arguably would not be the ascendant ideology it is today without the timely intervention of the Coors family, Joe Coors in particular.

Unique among the brothers, Joe had spent part of his career working outside Golden. Unlike Bill, Joe was preoccupied with neither learning the role of oldest son nor serving as the essential brewing engineer of the Adolph Coors Company. He therefore enjoyed the luxury of thinking about larger matters than beer and ceramics. What he thought was that the country was going to hell. Gone were the days when a penniless immigrant like his grandfather could, through his own hard work and bold initiative, become a millionaire within seventeen years. Gone was the wide-open freedom to succeed or fail according to one's own abilities. Gone was trust in the natural order of things—that some people will have more and some less, that the sexes and races have their proper roles, that children should obey their parents, that a man has a right to manage his own property as he sees fit. Nowadays, Joe believed, everybody felt entitled. The poor felt entitled to handouts. Women and Negroes felt entitled to "rights" they were never intended to possess. Children felt entitled to expensive college educations that seemed to teach little more than how to deride their parents' values. Workers felt entitled to tell owners how to run their companies. All these people looked to the federal government to deliver their entitlements. And government seemed only too happy to oblige. The more it tried to make people happy, the more power people were willing to give it. In Joe's view, the sacred purpose of the United States was being subverted. Instead of being a proper check on the power of government, an increasingly lazy populace was stoking government's power-greedy maw by mewling for entitlements.

The slide toward socialism, Joe believed, left America vulnerable to the aggressive threat of world communism. In the late 1940s, Britain had elected a Labour government that sang "The Red Flag" in Parliament. Stalin's Soviet Union loomed and China was "lost" to Mao. Senator Joe McCarthy claimed to have proof that the State Department was indifferent—to the point of being sympathetic—to communists within its own ranks.

Joe Coors wasn't alone thinking in this way in the early 1950s, but he could have been forgiven for thinking he was. Though many Americans shared Joe's views, they were scattered. They may have identified themselves individually as "conservative," but there were no journals, think tanks, radio shows, or organizations to help them refine an over-arching conservative vision or provide a sense of common purpose. To the extent that conservatives spoke out at all, it was in the negative—against trends they didn't like. They never seemed to say what they would do if they had power. "In the United States at this time liberalism is not only the dominant but even the sole intellectual tradition," Lionel Trilling wrote in 1950. Each conservative felt he was wandering alone in a liberal wilderness.

When a copy of Russell Kirk's *The Conservative Mind* fell into Joe's hands, he discovered he was not alone. Kirk's book, published in 1953, is the Genesis of conservatives—the first articulation of a coherent American conservative ideology. Joe was fascinated at how Kirk wound all the inchoate strands of conservative dissatisfaction into a clearly stated indict-ment of liberalism's shortcomings. Conservatives weren't just cranky nay-sayers, Kirk argued. They had identified a genuine problem:

"Radicals," as Kirk called them, believed in "the perfectibility of man." With enough planning and money, enough education and law, radicals thought, all poverty and ignorance could be eradicated. Joe agreed with Kirk that the hunger to raise every man to Elysium translated into a passion for political and economic leveling. The way radicals leveled, Kirk wrote, was by taxing the rich to raise up the poor, and by giving inordinate power to labor unions. The right of every man to share the nation's wealth had begun to supersede the right of individuals to control their own property, Kirk wrote. Joe's experience with Local 366 certainly bore out Kirk's words. The welfare state, intrusive regulation of business, flirtations with socialism, and a tolerance of communism all derived from the liberals' *leveling* impulse.

Kirk, a junior member of Michigan State University's history depart-ment, also excoriated the idea of "rights," which he argued were often mere "desires" in disguise. He took particular aim at the Universal Decla-ration of Human Rights that had just been proposed by the young United Nations. Its call for "a reasonable limitation of working hours and peri-odic holidays with pay," for example, was read by Kirk as insistence upon a "right to be idle."

Joe Coors would have been delighted with nothing more than Kirk's identification of the liberal problem. But Kirk went further and outlined "canons of conservative thought" that practically brought Joe to his feet. Economic leveling, Kirk wrote, was not only impossible but downright undesirable. A clear division between haves and have-nots was something to be nurtured, not expunged. "Civilized society requires orders and classes," Kirk wrote. "Unless we call civilization a mistake, any attempt to ignore natural inequality and propertied inequality is sure to cause general unhappiness." Kirk approvingly quoted an earlier conservative who had said that because property ownership was what separated humans from the lower beasts, "the rights of property are more important than the right to life." For government to order property owners to behave a certain way—such as telling them whom they must hire, how much they have to pay in salaries, or how much they could pollute—eroded the right to property. Similarly, progressive taxation—taxing the property of one to raise the economic standing of another—was wrong.

Conservatives also respected social tradition, Kirk insisted. "Innovation," Kirk wrote, "is a devouring conflagration more often than it is a torch of progress." Tradition, "the wisdom of our ancestors," was society's best rulebook. Nobody believed this more deeply than a grandson of Adolph Coors.

To Kirk, though, the most important canon of conservative thought was faith in God and suspicion of the intellectual process. Conservatives accepted that "there are great forces in heaven and earth that man's philosophy cannot plumb or fathom." He declared Darwinism anathema to conservative principles and called the Age of Reason the "Age of Ignorance" because it turned its back on faith. "We do not trust human reason," Kirk wrote. "We do not and we may not. . . . Political problems are religious and moral problems."

Joe Coors was not a particularly religious man when he read *The Conservative Mind*. But Kirk's proposition resonated with him. Raised in an emotionally cold household where conversation was more often forbidden than appreciated, Joe developed no love of debate. Unless the topic was engineering or chemistry, the Coors family had little interest in the intellectual process. The world of literature and the arts was not invited inside because it carried an overabundance of viewpoints. Adolph Jr. brooked no disagreement on matters of importance to the business and the family. "If you had thought this through the way I have," the old man would tell his children, "you'd see it my way." The Sunday spankings Mr. Coors meted out reminded the children of his authority; his success and wealth reminded everybody else. With such a father as role model, Joe built a mental citadel of his own. Joe wasn't by nature a talker, so when confronted with an opposing viewpoint he didn't venture out to do battle; he simply pulled up the drawbridge, folded his arms, and declared himself unconvincable. He couldn't place his faith in God the way Kirk insisted, but Joe Coors did appreciate Kirk's belief in unarguable distinctions between Right and Wrong.

For Joe, it was all right there in Kirk's book: If family tradition had taught Joe anything, it was that progress grew out of the freedom to manage one's own property, that the division between owner and employee was honorable, that nobody was "entitled" to anything he didn't earn himself, and that government efforts to "perfect society"—whether through alcohol prohibition or taxation for social programs—only bred misery.

Soon after Kirk's book appeared, twenty-nine-year-old William F. Buckley began publishing the country's first journal of conservative thought, *National Review*. In the inaugural editorial, Buckley declared: "This magazine stands athwart history, yelling 'Stop!' " Twelve days after the first issue of *National Review* hit the newsstands, Rosa Parks refused to give up her bus seat and the civil rights movement began assembling itself. The civil rights and conservative movements grew in parallel, each drawing energy from opposing the other. To the conservative mind, the civil rights movement was the apotheosis of liberalism. It drew life from an abstract sense of "rights." Its goal was economic and social leveling. It was collectivist, arguing for the advancement of a group—Negroes— regardless of individual merit. It openly reviled the long-standing traditions of the South. And finally, civil rights activists were demanding the federal government wield legislation, court orders, and even troops both to redistribute wealth and to smash tradition. Much of the debate in *National Review* revolved around the proper conservative response to civil rights. Constitutionalists argued states' rights. Traditionalists said imposing the North's attitudes toward Negroes on the South was cultural imperialism. Buckley argued the civil rights movement threatened Western civilization. Whites deserved to rule the South, Buckley editorialized, because "for the time being, [they are] the advanced race." This wasn't ignorant cracker bigotry talking, but a refined argument emanating from educated New England—for this reason all the more terrifying and repugnant to the civil rights movement. Just as conservatives held the civil rights movement anathema, minorities quickly identified conservatives as an enemy—an enemy they would look for opportunities to punish.

The year Ad Coors was murdered, the senior U.S. senator from Arizona, Barry Goldwater, published his own conservative philosophy, alerting the nation that ideological conservatism was ready to begin applying

Kirk's theory legislatively. Because it was written by a U.S. senator and promoted more energetically than Russell Kirk's book, Goldwater's *The Conscience of a Conservative* was most Americans' first contact with a vigorously stated conservative ideology.

"Only a philosophy that takes into account the essential differences between men, and, accordingly, makes provision for developing the different potentialities of each man, can claim to be in accord with Nature," Goldwater insisted. Goldwater would abolish progressive taxation, because "[its] aim is an egalitarian society—an objective that does violence both to the charter of the Republic and the laws of Nature." He would abolish welfare because "such programs are sold to the country precisely on the argument that government has an *obligation* to care for the needs of its citizens" (emphasis Goldwater's). He would ban federal intervention to achieve racial equality and would defy *Brown* v. *Board of Education*, in which the U.S. Supreme Court mandated school integration. "It may be just or wise or expedient for negro [sic] children to attend the same schools as white children," Goldwater wrote, "but they do not have a civil right to do so which is protected by the federal constitution, or which is enforceable by the federal government."

"The time has come," Goldwater also said, "not to abolish unions or deprive them of deserved gains; but to redress the balance—to restore unions to their proper role in a free society." Conservatives, Goldwater wrote, condemned unions precisely because they sought to elevate the economic status of workers beyond that which their "mortal souls" would warrant, and also infringed upon the property rights of company owners.

After the bruising labor battle of 1957, the Coors brothers were delighted to find an intellectual foundation for their instinctive dislike of unions. Labor, though, recognized Goldwater's brand of conservatism as a threat. Unions, like minorities, would look for chances to inflict pain upon Goldwater and his allies.

Despite Kirk, Buckley, and Goldwater, the 1960s were shaping up to be a gloomy decade for conservatives. The election of John F. Kennedy as President was only the beginning. Negroes won every civil rights case they brought to Earl Warren's Supreme Court, each time weakening, according to conservatives, both tradition and the sanctity of the individual. The federal government was stepping in to force restaurant owners in Greensboro, North Carolina, to serve disruptive Negroes and hardly anybody in Congress objected. Even the Republican Senate minority leader, Everett Dirksen, was in on it—authoring legislation to give Washington the power to police elections and accelerate school integration. Washington tried to socialize medicine in 1960, and had to "settle" for a budget-buster of a program to provide medical care to the elderly. In the Senate, only Barry Goldwater refused to vote for the new so-called Medicare. The federal government had no right to tax one group to provide benefits to another, Goldwater argued, and Joe agreed. It wasn't just blacks and the elderly who were clawing apart the social fabric; in April 1960, the Supreme Court gave the whole game to organized labor, too, ruling that railway unions—and by extension others—had the right to strike for a voice in certain company decisions. Nothing could be more menacing to the Coors brothers.

There wasn't much Joe Coors could do to get the country back on track, but he would do what he could. Putting up a brave fight against his own unions was a start, and keeping tabs on revolutionaries inside the plant also made him feel like part of the larger fight. In July 1963, the government devised, in Joe's view, a truly insidious plot to make everybody put numeric codes on their mail. The U.S. Postal Service said the numbers would help it deliver mail more quickly, but Joe thought he saw through that. He saw the numbers as nothing more than another attempt by Washington to keep tabs on citizens' lawful business. He ordered the company's secretaries not to use them. For years, Coors company mail carried no zip codes.

Still Joe wasn't satisfied. There had to be more a concerned American could do.

5

Something for Joe to Do

Murder sheared the oldest son off the top of generation three. Rebellion would do likewise to generation four.

Adolph Coors IV was only fifteen when Joseph Corbett killed his father. He was far too young to step into his father's shoes as heir-in-training. The line of succession therefore jumped laterally, to Bill, which complicated the future order of succession. Bill had no living sons, and grooming a daughter to run the Adolph Coors Company was not an option.

After her cold and lonely childhood, Missy had became a startlingly beautiful woman of eighteen, with short blond hair and, on the rare occasions she deployed it, a dazzling smile. She'd been sent, as her younger sisters would be, to Miss Porter's School in Farmington, Connecticut. At the time of the kidnapping, Missy had just been accepted to Connecticut College for Women. Because girls were considered unsuitable for business, the line of succession would have to jump laterally again when Bill died or retired, to Joe's lineage. All of Joe's five children were boys. So when the family thought beyond Bill and Joe, their eyes turned to Joseph Coors, Jr., then eighteen, three years older than his cousin Adolph IV.

Joe Jr. had inherited his father's extraordinary height, but none of his grim seriousness. His childhood had been free from the shadows of prohibition, war, and the struggle to save the brewery. He grew up instead in the rosy glow of postwar prosperity. Unlike his father and uncle, Joe Jr. had pushed back against the patriarchal rule of his father. No submitting meekly to Sunday spankings for him; if Joe tried to hit him, Joe Jr. hit back. He didn't let his father cut off discussion either, but rather pressed his own opinions—sometimes at top volume. Many a voice was raised during Joe Jr.'s adolescence, and many a door slammed. In school, he goofed off. When it was time for college, he lacked both the grades and the zeal for the family alma mater, Cornell. He went instead to North Carolina State College, where he distinguished himself in basketball. He knew he was in line to inherit and command the family's multimillion-dollar business. As much as anything, Joe Jr.'s rich-kid mentality irritated his father; it was not the way Coorses were supposed to think of themselves.

During his freshman year, Joe Jr. fell in love with a North Carolina woman named Gail Fambrough. Joe Jr. was twenty and halfway through his sophomore year when he announced, in February 1962, that he and Gail intended to marry. They scheduled their wedding for the following month.

From his family's reaction, Joe Jr. might well have said he was taking a job with Anheuser-Busch and intended to devote his spare time to advocating prohibition. Mr. Coors had a rule: Nobody gets married before finishing college. Ad, Bill, and Joe all had obeyed him. Missy had been permitted to break the rule, but she was a girl and emotionally delicate after having watched her little brother choke to death and then growing up with Geraldine's drinking and Bill's indifference. Missy had been eager to start a family of her own—to do it right. She had dropped out of Connecticut College as a freshman and had moved to Tucson with her new husband. Within six months she was pregnant. The family held its tongue.

Joe Jr., on the other hand, was the leadoff batter in the generation-four lineup. Neither his father nor his grandfather, who was seventy-eight at the time, was going to let him get away with marrying early.

Ordinarily, Mr. Coors would have been in Hawaii at that time of year. But he'd received an emergency long-distance call from the plant manager that had nothing to do with Joe Jr.: Bill and Joe were about to borrow money. With all its eager expansion, the brewery faced a short-term cash-flow problem and the brothers were planning to take out a small loan from a Denver bank to tide the business over. Mr. Coors flew home at once, with a different idea of how to ease the cash-flow squeeze. At seven forty-five the morning after his arrival, Mr. Coors gathered around him four hundred men from the company's construction division and told them they were being laid off. They'd be hired back as soon as possible, but for now, they were to go home. Then he chewed out Bill and Joe for even thinking about putting the Adolph Coors Company in debt.

As long as he was in Golden, Mr. Coors decided to have his hair trimmed at his usual barbershop. Frank Leek, the barber, knew the old man wouldn't sit in the chair until the floor was swept, and at the scheduled hour Leek was busy sweeping. When the ever-punctual Mr. Coors didn't show up, Leek walked outside to look for him. Sure enough, there came Mr. Coors, dressed as usual in a black suit, white shirt, black bow tie, and pearl-gray homburg, walking briskly out the plant gate three blocks away. Leek went back into the shop. When Mr. Coors again failed to appear, Leek paced outside again. Mr. Coors was gone. Mildly alarmed, Leek headed toward the brewery. As he passed the alley that bifurcated the block, he glanced in and did a double take. There was Mr. Coors in his finery, sitting on the running board of old Willie Malink's spit-stained 1951 Chevy pickup, sharing a chaw and laughing his head off. "Whew!" said Mr. Coors when he finally settled into the chair. "I took a chew of Willie's Copenhagen and I'm a little dizzy."

"Congratulations," Leek said as he fitted the apron around Mr. Coors's neck. "I hear little Joe's getting married."

Mr. Coors jerked in the chair as though he'd been shot. He whipped his head around and glared at Leek.

"I disapprove," he snapped. "The boy did not get his education. I will not go to the wedding. I will not see him."

Joe Sr. told his son that if he went ahead with the marriage he'd be cut off from the family for good. He would not get a penny of assistance, would not be allowed to work at the brewery—let alone run it—and would not be invited home for holidays. A principle was at stake, Joe said. A son must obey his father.

Go to hell, Joe Jr. told him.

Joe's wife Holly cried herself sick. He couldn't do this, she told Joe.

Joe Jr. was his son. But Joe folded his arms and refused to budge. That boy had been defying him all his life, he growled. This was the last straw. Let him make his choice.

Holly was complicated. She was intelligent, educated, and energetic; before meeting Joe, she'd dreamed of living the footloose life of a freelance photojournalist. But when she'd married Joe in 1941, a change had come over her. Joe and his family demanded retiring obedience from women, and Holly had decided to give it. She'd abandoned all thought of a career and had thrown herself entirely into being Joe's wife and the mother of his five boys. She'd muzzled her intelligence and tethered it behind her husband's authority. She was happy doing so.

In 1961, Holly had become a born-again Christian—the first of many Coorses who would give their lives to Jesus. To become born again is to place control of one's life in the hands of the Lord. After twenty years as Mrs. Joseph Coors, Holly was well suited to surrendering personal authority. But now, a year later, as her oldest boy defied the family rule by getting married early, Holly found she had no power to intervene on his behalf. Joe was not inclined to listen to her and she had no experience or skills in making him listen. Instead, she wept. And she prayed.

As for Joe's brothers, not one of them incurred their father's wrath by standing up for their brother. Thus was Joseph Coors, Jr., thrust out into what he later called "the wilderness." Gail had to quit college to support them. They began having babies—four in all—but were not invited to Golden to show them off. Having never expected to have to prove himself in the wider world outside the family, Joe Jr. wandered from job to job—stockbroker, computer programmer for Frontier Airlines, bureaucrat for the San Diego school system—hauling the family from North Carolina to California to Oregon. Joe Jr.'s search for a satisfying career led Joe Jr. and his family briefly to metropolitan Denver, though not back into the bosom of the family. Their short stay was disastrous. Running into the King Soopers market in Lakewood one September morning in 1967, Gail—seven months pregnant with the couple's second child—dropped their year-old son in the parking lot, snapping his femur. Joe Jr. and Gail spent the following month visiting their tiny son in the hospital, where he lay in traction. It was injury atop insult, and Joe Jr. needed to lash out at somebody. He sued King Soopers, which admitted no wrongdoing but eventually paid him a thousand dollars to drop the suit. Not long after that, the family left for Seattle. Joe Jr. got by. And his resolve didn't crack.

Neither did his father's or his grandfather's. Adolph Jr. lived another six years and never laid eyes on his grandson Joe Jr. again. Just as generation three was decapitated, so was generation four.

Early in the 1960s, Coors Porcelain had a top-secret contract to manufacture part of a missile designed to spray enemy troops with radiation. The Pentagon called the plan Project Pluto, and Coors Porcelain was charged with crafting the ceramic container for the uranium warhead. Max Goodwin was one of the young men hired by Joe Coors to work on the container. When Defense Secretary Robert McNamara killed the project in 1963, Goodwin thought he'd be out of a job. But Goodwin had a polite bookishness about him that Joe liked. So Joe offered him a job as credit manager.

"I only have a year of college," Goodwin protested. "I don't know anything about managing credit."

"I'm not interested in what piece of paper a man has," Joe responded. "I only care about what he can do."

Goodwin accepted, and did a passable job as credit manager of Porcelain. Then Joe promoted him to be controller of the entire Adolph Coors Company.

"What?" Goodwin asked. "That's a job for an accountant. I'm not qualified."

Joe just laughed and patted him on the back. "We don't have accountants working at Coors," he told Goodwin. "And we don't have any lawyers. We don't believe in them." Goodwin went back to his office puzzling over how to do the job of controller of a quarter-billion-dollar industrial corporation that had no lawyers or accountants on its staff. He figured he'd start by looking at the company's financial plans. That way, he'd know what direction Coors was headed. But when he looked around for the financial plans nobody knew what he was talking about.

"We don't make plans," Joe Coors told him. "I don't like plans and I don't like budgets. That's the government's way, not ours. If you have a budget and you don't spend it all, you lose it." That, Max realized, was why Joe didn't care that he was unqualified to be controller—it was a nonjob.

"But Joe," Goodwin said, "you have to have a plan. . . ."

"My father does his figuring on the back of an envelope," Joe said. "That's always worked for us."

When Geraldine Coors quit drinking and her mind cleared, she found she hated being married to Bill.

He often came home after midnight and he sometimes didn't come home at all. Geraldine knew—everybody knew—that Bill was seeing Phyllis Mahaffey. Many of Geraldine's days started with her trying to explain to Margaret and May Louise why their father no longer seemed part of the family. And whenever he was home, he seemed a figure carved of marble. Days passed without so much as a "good morning" passing his lips. Geraldine thought Bill's brother Joe was a creep to banish a son simply because he wanted to marry the woman he loved. When Bill backed up Joe's decision, it was the last straw. Geraldine filed for divorce and Bill didn't try to talk her out of it. He gave her all the money she wanted, paid both of their lawyers, and agreed to put half his net worth in a trust for her and the girls, upon his death. Geraldine appeared alone before a judge the day after filing her papers in September 1962, and, weeping on the witness stand, was granted her divorce. Thirteen months later, Bill took Phyllis Mahaffey on a vacation to Phoenix and married her.

In an expansive mood after his wedding, Bill sat down with the leadership of Local 366 and worked out a pension agreement that had been dividing the union and the company for months. After the turmoil of Joe Jr.'s rebellion, Bill's rapid-fire divorce and remarriage, and the settling of the pension issue, things appeared to be settling down. It was November 1963. The Friday after Thanksgiving, a bullet killed President Kennedy in Dallas.

On Saturday, Coors ran ads in the Denver newspapers announcing that the brewery would be closed on Monday in observance of the national day of mourning. Only "essential production workers" needed to show up for work, the ad said. In reality, Coors had ordered everybody to work on the day of mourning. Local 366's business agent, Richard Roberts, was appalled that Coors was operating on that day. He knew that the Coors brothers reviled JFK, but this was too much, especially since they'd lied about it in the paper. Roberts called the Denver newspapers to blow the whistle. Forty-five minutes later, his own phone rang.

Russ Hargis was calling. Hargis was Coors's personnel manager, a decent guy who was the company's contact with the union.

"Bill's hopping mad," Hargis told Roberts. "He's calling you an 'enemy of the company.'"

"Oh, well, that's just Bill," Roberts said.

"He says he's going to abrogate the pension agreement," Hargis said. "What's more, he wants the union-shop provision out of the contract. He's calling a meeting with your executive board on Friday. He'll explain it all then."

"I'll be there," Roberts said, reaching to mark his calendar.

"No you won't," Hargis said. "Bill says you're barred from the plant."

"That's illegal," Roberts said. "You can't bar the local's business agent from the plant."

Hargis said, "But you're barred anyway. I guess you'll have to take it up with the NLRB."

On Friday, Bill stormed into the meeting and looked around the table. "It's a damn good thing Roberts didn't get in here," he said. "If I'd have seen him, I might have torn him limb from limb." Bill then told the startled board members of Local 366 that he wasn't going to submit the agreed-upon pension plan to the Internal Revenue Service as promised, and that he was going to push to remove the union-shop provision from the contract the next time it came up.

"This meeting is illegal," the board told him. "Under Section Seven of the Labor Relations Act, you are not permitted to negotiate with us without permitting the business agent to be here."

Bill waved away the Section Seven talk. "Any individual who acts to put this company in a bad light is considered an enemy," he said, driving a forefinger into the tabletop. "We're not going to have any enemies on company property." Roberts received a letter to the same effect. He'd always known the Coors brothers were antiunion, but he was astounded by the references to "enemies."

Bill's rash behavior was undone in the end. The National Labor Relations Board found in Roberts' favor and forced Bill to rescind his ban on Roberts. The pension plan was submitted to the IRS as planned. And for a while, Bill dropped talk of getting rid of the union-shop provision.

But the incident ratcheted up tension between the company and the union yet another notch.

That same autumn, Coors hired a nineteen-year-old Coloradan to work on the bottle-washing line. He was a tall, lanky, handsome fellow, a native Coloradan and physically very much the Bill Coors type. But if Bill could go back in time to change one thing, it would probably be to prevent the brewery from hiring David Sickler.

Sickler was raised by a union carpenter in Golden and one of his earliest memories was hanging out at the union hall while the leadership fined "rats"—carpenters crossing picket lines or working below scale. The gavel would come down like a pistol shot with each fine and scare the five-year-old Sickler silly. For all his union upbringing, though, Sickler was not an activist when he joined Coors. He aspired to the solitary life of a horse trainer. He'd worked construction after leaving high school, trying to save enough money to get started. But construction paid too little to launch his horse-training career, too little even to let Sickler party as hard as he wanted on weekends. He should go to Coors, his friends told him. They were the best employer in Colorado. Sickler didn't like the lie detector, and questions about his sex life embarrassed him. But he gave it little thought. Joining the union was a condition of employment and Sickler dutifully paid his dues, but he didn't go to meetings and didn't pay the union much attention, either. Coors put him to work on the soaker, where bottles began their process of sterilization. It was murder. The plant lacked air conditioning in summer and heat in winter. Shifts rotated without warning. Overtime was mandatory. Sickler often worked twelve hours a day, six or seven days a week. Scheduled vacations meant nothing. If the company needed you, you showed up or found another job.

But the pay at the brewery was great, and with all the overtime Sickler was racking up a lot of money. He was young and strong and had no kids, so the trade-offs were worth it.

One roasting June morning in 1964, a coworker named John Gargano asked the shift supervisor to check an adjustment he'd made to the machinery. The supervisor did so, approved it, and a short time later the equipment malfunctioned disastrously. The supervisor chewed out Gargano and hauled him upstairs to the brewery offices for a formal reprimand. Sickler, who had watched the whole incident and knew Gargano was innocent, went along to stick up for him. When he tried to speak, the plant manager pointed a finger between his eyes and snapped, "Shut your mouth or we'll fire you, too." Stung, Sickler backed out the door of the manager's office and was struck by how hot the work floor felt compared with the air-conditioned office. For the first time, he looked hard at the men around him—many twice his age, with wives and children at home. They looked exhausted, like overworked animals.

Sickler found something in his pay envelope one day besides his check. It was a copy of a tract called *News in a Nutshell,* published by the John Birch Society. He glanced up and saw men around him puzzling over their own copies. Sickler flipped through the tract and his hair stood on end. It was vicious, full of crude attacks on blacks and homosexuals. Sickler felt dirty pocketing his paycheck, and dropped the tract in a wastebasket.

When Congress was about to vote on the Civil Rights Act of 1964, Bill called a meeting of brewery workers in the company auditorium and urged them to demand that their senators and congressmen vote against the bill. "If it passes," he told them, "I'm going to have to fire sixty of you and hire sixty blacks." Sickler knew Bill and Joe hated the proposed law because by banning discrimination it would effectively tell business owners how to hire. But Sickler couldn't believe Bill would say such a thing. The act had no quotas in it. Sixty was an arbitrary number. And nothing in it said anything about firing white workers to make room for blacks. When Congress passed the bill and President Lyndon Johnson signed it the same day, Bill summoned his workers for another mandatory lecture.

"The government tells me I have to hire these people," he said with a sad shake of his head. "I just hope you will accept them."

Sickler was disgusted. The biggest employer in Colorado was talking like an Alabama Klansman. A few days later, a big, frizzy-haired union officer named Ken DeBey sidled up to Sickler in the company cafeteria.

"We're looking for someone to run for shop steward in your department," DeBey said as he helped himself to a beer from the free tap.

"Why me?" Sickler asked. "I've never even been to a union meeting."

"You seem pissed off," DeBey said.

They sat and talked. "This could be a better company than it is," DeBey continued. "The pay's fine—"

"The pay's great," Sickler interjected.

"Yeah, but they treat us like dogs," DeBey said. He began counting on his fingers. "You got the lie detector. You got the rotating shifts—"

"There's no air conditioning on the washer line," Sickler interrupted. "Or heat in the winter."

"Right," DeBey said. "I'm in packaging and it's the same." He started counting off again. "They cancel your vacation when they want to. They call you at home and make you come in when you have other plans. . . ."

"They fire your ass for nothing," Sickler said.

"Right again. And," DeBey concluded, "they're racist sons of bitches. You see any Negroes here? Any Mexicans? *Nada.*"

DeBey and Sickler spent the whole lunch break talking. DeBey's rap pricked Sickler's latent union consciousness. By the time they stood to clear their trays, Sickler had agreed to run for shop steward. It was Ken DeBey who formally recruited David Sickler into the union movement, but Sickler always liked to say the person who inspired him to be a trade unionist to begin with was none other than Bill Coors.

If so, Bill created his Frankenstein's monster.

Mary Coors, Ad's widow, kept drinking. It didn't make her jolly. It didn't make her forget. But she drank, coldly, purposefully, intending to drown the coal of hatred smoldering in her chest for the man who'd slaughtered her husband.

With Ad dead, Mary no longer made the Sunday pilgrimage to Golden. After all, Ad's parents had never liked her to begin with. She also knew she shouldn't badmouth her children's grandparents and uncles in front of them, but sometimes she couldn't help it. Mostly she pretended they were no relation, and the brewing wing of the family began receding from her children's lives.

Mary's decline horrified and embarrassed her children. Adolph IV and his little brother Jim were still living at home. The older sisters, Mary Brooke and Cecily, were off at college. Adolph found himself being followed around the schoolyard by security guards, cut off from his friends, and severed from his cousins in Golden for reasons he didn't fully understand. In 1963, he attended Mercer College in Macon, Georgia, but couldn't keep his mind on his studies and dropped out after freshman year. He wanted to hit somebody. He joined the Marines.

While Adolph's cousins in Golden were busy arranging draft deferments for themselves, Adolph decided to be the roughest, toughest leatherneck ever. He punished himself mercilessly during boot camp, adding extra body building and miles of running to the brutal regime. He ate five meals a day and bulked up to 270 pounds. He took up martial arts and became an expert at smashing bricks with his fists and feet and throwing opponents like laundry. He slashed hay bales with bayonet, heaved grenades, butchered targets with storms of bullets—and still had energy to pummel any man who teased him about his name. Pumped on martial aggression, Adolph sat down to write what he considered a long-overdue letter to his grandfather, castigating everything the old man represented. "You remind me of another Adolf," he closed. "Adolf Hitler."

Mr. Coors was unruffled. He'd handled youthful rebellion before. "That boy," he said, setting the letter aside, "will never work at this brewery." He opened his rolltop desk and extracted his will.

When Mr. Coors had a legal document to write, he did it himself with a pen and pad and then asked a secretary to type it because, as Joe had told Max Goodwin, Coors had no lawyers on staff. Mr. Coors assumed he would die before his wife Alice May and that his personal fortune of $20 million would become hers. His will was therefore simple, with only a few specific bequests. Each of his surviving children—William, Joseph, and May Louise—was to receive upon his death exactly $46,244.43. Mary Coors, widow of his oldest son, was to get nothing.

The old man's big money, and the company itself, were in the trust agreement he'd long ago written up for Alice May, since he was so sure she would survive him. In addition, Mr. Coors stipulated that upon her death their estate be divided among the children and held again in trust—the hope being that a trust would be less subject to inheritance tax than a straight bequest. After receiving Adolph's letter, though, Mr. Coors assessed the behavior of Ad's widow and children and inserted the following notation into Alice May's trust agreement: "The settlor excludes the widow and descendants of her deceased son, Adolph Coors III. Her reason in doing so is that the widow of Adolph Coors III, with the full accord of her children, has violently disapproved of and condemned the settlor." It isn't known whether Alice May, in whose name he was writing, ever knew of the change. But that was that. The descendants of Adolph Coors III were severed from the family fortune.

Adolph IV's two-year commitment to the Marines expired in 1966. He was trying to decide whether to reenlist—and go to Vietnam—when he received word that his older sister Mary Brooke had terminal cancer. Adolph returned to Colorado to finish his degree at the University of Denver. When Mary Brooke died at age twenty-six in October 1968 leaving a two-year-old behind, her grandparents Mr. Coors and Alice May refused to attend the funeral.

Cliff Rock had discovered electoral politics in 1964 when a fraternity brother at the University of Colorado lent him a copy of Barry Goldwater's *Conscience of a Conservative*. Rock had been electrified. He'd been raised by conservative parents and was a fan of Ayn Rand, but he'd never seen conservative ideology laid out with such clarity and confidence. He was a big, jolly student and his eagerness to be helpful channeled him into Goldwater's campaign. At several meetings, he noticed a tall, thin man in shop-class glasses sitting quietly by himself. That's Joe Coors, someone whispered. Coors didn't speak often, Rock noticed, and he didn't speak well. He had a halting, awkward style. But it was clear that what little he said came from the heart. Rock liked Joe Coors.

The Goldwater campaign was a disaster in one sense; the candidate lost everywhere but in five southern states and his home of Arizona. But Joe and Rock took heart. Goldwater's was the first national campaign based on a straightforward conservative ideology. For the first time in living memory, conservatives felt like they were on the move. New and promising faces were popping up in the movement, like that handsome General Electric spokesman named Ronald Reagan who'd made all those B-grade movies and starred in *Death Valley Days* on TV. Two weeks before the election, Reagan had given a powerful televised speech that was more a call to conservative ideals than to Goldwater himself. "You and I have a rendezvous with destiny," Reagan had said. "We will preserve for our children this, the last best hope of man on earth, or we will sentence them to take the last step into a thousand years of darkness." No one had known the actor had it in him. Not even Barry Goldwater appealed to American conservatives with such homespun eloquence, or faced the camera lens so naturally. Joe Coors was mesmerized, and he wasn't the only one. Suddenly conservatives from Rhode Island to Catalina Island were talking about the day when Reagan might run for political office.

Joe Coors emerged from the 1964 Goldwater campaign eager to try politics himself. He asked his father to let him run for Jefferson County School Board, but his father was unenthusiastic. The family had never drawn attention to itself, and after Ad's murder he was more obsessed than ever with security. He never left home without recording the serial numbers of the currency in his pocket, believing that doing so might make him easier to trace if he was kidnapped. His chief defense against kidnapping, though, was obscurity. Mr. Coors had a rule: Nobody talks to the press, ever. If a reporter called for any reason, a polite "no comment" was the only sanctioned response. To answer otherwise was a firing offense. Family members did not attend social events where photographers might be present. They drove themselves in ordinary old cars. They lived in unassuming middle-class houses. They ambled around Golden—Meyer Hardware, Foss Drug, and the Fair 5&10 Store—but stayed out of the society pages. Joe ultimately appealed to his father by arguing that a seat on the school board was more civic service than politics. It was clear, too, that Joe, the youngest son, needed a means to distinguish himself within the family. Without an arena of his own in which to shine, Joe might stay in his brother Bill's shadow forever. Reluctantly, Mr. Coors allowed Joe to run for school board.

Bill was not similarly tempted to seek office, though he had more of the outgoing personality that politics demanded. Bill's work was more essential to the company than was Joe's. It was hard for him to be away from the brewery for a two-week vacation, let alone have a second career in politics. Not that he didn't share Joe's views; Bill had always been as economically conservative as his younger brother.

Bill, though, had a harder time than Joe accepting the religious, anti-intellectual nature of conservatism as Kirk and Goldwater defined it. Bill was above all a man of science. He couldn't accept Kirk's notion that some questions are unanswerable, because science rests on a belief that humankind's intellectual potential is limitless. Though many members of Bill's family—including his brother Joe—would become passionately Christian, Bill resisted faith all his life. He couldn't accept the conservatives' faith-based right/wrong dichotomy as easily as Joe. Bill may have been little more open to opposing viewpoints than his father or brother, but he always took more enjoyment than Joe in the debate. Joe was temperamentally suited to be the truer believer. So when the Coors family decided to venture into politics, Joe walked point.

Before Joe could start his campaign for school board, though, he got a call from a political science professor at the University of Colorado, about a half-hour drive north of Golden in Boulder. Ed Rozek was a Polish émigré who, after getting his degree at Harvard, had come to CU in 1956 to teach political science. Like many Eastern Europeans of the day, he was passionately anticommunist. He'd made a name for himself opposing the invitation to campus of such left-leaning speakers as Frank Oppenheimer and Harry Bridges. Rozek, a squat, energetic man with an elfin smile and thick accent, had run into Joe Coors at social occasions a few times since arriving in Colorado and was impressed with the depth of his convictions. In early 1966, a conservative member of the six-person CU board of regents, Dale Atkins, told Rozek a vacancy was opening on the board. Rozek immediately thought of Joe Coors. He called the brewery and asked Joe's secretary for fifteen minutes of Joe's time.

Joe received him in the bleak cement-floored office he shared with

Bill. The University of Colorado, Rozek told him, was a breeding ground for socialists. The head of his department, he told Joe, was an avowed Stalinist and he ran the department that way. Rozek said he'd once tried to object to the department's invitation to a communist lecturer and was persecuted. Rozek believed the "radicals" got the chairmanships and the promotions at CU, whereas conservatives weren't wanted on the faculty. The professors should be emphasizing the strengths of capitalism and the free enterprise system, not woolly-headed socialistic nonsense. It was out of control up there in Boulder, Rozek summed up. It was immoral. They needed Joe.

Joe let Rozek go on for ninety minutes. When Joe wouldn't commit on the spot, Rozek urged him to join him and Dale Atkins for lunch at the Brown Palace hotel in Denver, so he could hear a conservative regent's point of view. Joe accepted the invitation, and Atkins and Rozek drummed on him for two hours this time, and only let him go when he agreed to "ask Dad."

A run for the statewide office of regent was a much bolder step into the public eye than running for the Jefferson County School Board. Mr. Coors was initially opposed, but he couldn't deny the logic of it. The university was the biggest business in Colorado, and he believed that Joe was the kind of level-headed businessman the regents needed. The university was where the state's best minds were trained, and the company was going to need well-educated workers in the future. And Mr. Coors had no less desire than Joe to correct the nation's woeful liberalism. He had been giving generously to conservative causes—as well as hospitals and libraries—for years. There was no denying that in the mid-1960s, college campuses were the hottest ideological battlefield a conservative could choose. The old man finally agreed to let Joe run for regent.

Joe barely mentioned academic excellence in his campaign. "I believe that the University of Colorado should be dedicated to preserving and strengthening the cause of freedom in America," his campaign literature said. "There is nothing that I want more than for your children and mine to be able to look forward to a bright tomorrow in a free America . . . unfettered by excessive government control." He took a stand on only one specific controversial issue: the loyalty oath. Two years earlier, Justice Byron White of the U.S. Supreme Court—a CU alumnus—had written a decision striking down the State of Washington's loyalty oath for state employees as vague and unconstitutional. In March 1966—in the midst of Joe's campaign—the CU faculty asked the regents to do away with CU's loyalty oath, and the issue wasn't yet settled. Joe Coors was firmly in favor of keeping the oath. "Shouldn't every citizen in these United States be willing to express his or her loyalty to our country, to respect our flag and to uphold our government?" his brochure asked. "I believe so. I certainly am."

As the campaign progressed, campus liberals became increasingly appalled at the prospect of Joe Coors becoming a regent. The Coors name was well known in Colorado, of course, and Joe was known to be conservative. But not until his campaign did Coloradans gauge the heat of Joe's beliefs. Even by the standards of Goldwater supporters, Joe Coors was a fire-breather. University president Joseph Smiley went abroad for a UNESCO meeting in October and expected to be away for the vote. "If Coors is elected," he told his assistant, "send me a cablegram saying 'Don't come home.'"

Coors was elected, and Smiley came home in time to hear him accept the office of regent in January 1967. Joe quickly made it clear he intended to prevent "the sixties" from infecting the CU campus—single-handedly, if necessary. The nation, as seen through the eyes of Joe Coors, was coming unglued. In February, the federal government showed that the Civil Rights Act of 1964 was no empty gesture. Private industry beware: the Justice Department filed its first discrimination suit against a private company, Dillon Supply Company of Raleigh, North Carolina. Meanwhile, the Negroes, in Joe's view, were waging outright rebellion. Stokely Carmichael, an open advocate of overthrowing the capitalist system, said "If we don't get changes, we're going to tear this country apart." Buffalo, Tampa, and Newark went up in flames in June; Detroit and Boston in July. Even before the ashes cooled, Martin Luther King, Jr., was threatening "major disruptions" if Congress didn't give every American a guaranteed annual income. Campus after campus was shut down by marijuana-smoking antiwar demonstrators, and it seemed to Joe that university administrators were letting it happen.

Glimmers of hope flickered in California, where voters resisted the civil rights juggernaut by amending their state constitution to give property owners "absolute discretion" in selling or renting their property. But almost at once, Earl Warren's Supreme Court took it upon itself to declare the Californians' wishes unconstitutional. As if things weren't bad enough on the Court, President Johnson appointed Thurgood Marshall— architect of the *Brown* v. *Board of Education* case—to be the Court's first black justice. Within months the Court turned several murderers loose because the killers hadn't been read their "rights" properly or didn't have the kind of jury they liked. All this permissiveness, conservatives believed, was responsible for a 12 percent increase in crime in a single year.

Another businessman might have viewed the current of change and asked, "How can I adapt so I don't get hurt?" But Joe Coors's family had bent a river. Joe was not a man to adapt. The changes happening in America were wrong, he felt, and he was determined to fight them. Joe was heartened by the new governor of California, elected the same day as Joe and equally disgusted by the universities' capitulation to radicals. Governor Ronald Reagan cut the University of California budget almost 30 percent. Why should the taxpayers, conservatives wanted to know, finance the kind of rebellious atmosphere prevailing at Berkeley and other campuses? When ten thousand California students and faculty turned out to jeer Reagan, the governor gave as good as he got. Joe flew to the annual conference of Republican governors in Palm Springs just to shake Reagan's hand. He resolved to do all he could as regent to show solidarity.

Joe plunged into the job with appetite. He fought hard for the loyalty oath. "It's about time we get back to being willing to show a little patriotism," Joe said, and he saved a slightly watered-down version of the oath and made sure every professor in Boulder was compelled to sign it. He unsuccessfully opposed tenure for the professor who served as campus adviser to the Students for a Democratic Society and for another who put Jerry Rubin's *Do It* on his required-reading list. Unable to purge the political science department of leftists, Joe tried unsuccessfully to create a whole new "government" department alongside it, with Ed Rozek as chair. Professors, he said, "should zealously support the nation's authority and interests. . . . It is the duty of every one of us to love our country and to be patriotic, notwithstanding academic freedom or any other freedom." When the Student Assembly criticized Joe for belittling academic freedom, Joe shot back that the regents must obey the wishes of the Coloradans who elected them, "even if, in so doing, so-called 'academic freedom' must be somewhat restrained."

Joe's longest-running battle was with SDS, which he described as "hating almost every aspect of American life." He passed around copies of a *Look* magazine article on SDS, which said the organization supported draft resistance in opposition to the Vietnam War and wanted China admitted to the United Nations. Joe told the regents, "You just don't let the enemy into your camp, give them all the privileges and courtesies they ask, and then let them plot your destruction." When an SDS-led action blocked access to a group of Central Intelligence Agency recruiters on campus, Joe was apoplectic. He called his young friend Cliff Rock and arranged to have the beefiest football players and fraternity brothers on campus escort students past the demonstrators. "There's glory in getting beaten up by a policeman," Rock told Joe with a laugh, "but there's no glory in getting beaten up by a football player."

CU expelled four students for leading the demonstration. But as activists planned a massive protest of the expulsions, the university quickly readmitted the four. Exasperated, Joe wagged his finger at the regents. "College administrators who condone, capitulate, and make concessions to student insubordination under threat of reprisal ask for chains on their doors," he fumed. In November 1968, Joe was able to engineer a vote of the regents to ban the SDS from campus, but three weeks later the regents reversed themselves, with President Smiley breaking the tie.

Students and liberal faculty members criticized Joe for injecting politics into the business of the regents. Joe denied that his actions were politically motivated, adding, "I am not running for office and have no intention of running for office." To Joe Coors, "politics" meant elections and the quest for personal power, and under that definition Joe was telling the truth. He never sought another elective office.

He was, of course, injecting *something* into the business of the regents besides a concern for academic excellence and the fiscal affairs of the university. But it wasn't strictly politics. It was ideology. Joe Coors was that rare public figure: a true believer. When he drew attention to himself through strong statements, it wasn't for personal aggrandizement. It was in defense of a worldview he held as strongly as his wife Holly held her faith in Christ. Joe Coors could no more tolerate noisy dissent about U.S. foreign policy than Holly could accept atheism. Conservative principles were Joe Coors's dogma, and they gave him tremendous strength. He would not begin to suffer crippling defeat, in fact, until he faced opponents whose ideological fervor matched his own.

The high point of Joe's tenure as a regent was securing California Governor Ronald Reagan's promise to speak on campus in May 1968. Reagan had been governor little more than a year, but conservatives already were pushing him to run for president. He showed up with his press secretary, a round little man named Lyn Nofziger, and addressed a packed house at CU. Afterward, Joe Coors and Ed Rozek accompanied Reagan and Nofziger in the limousine to the airport. Rozek, sitting in the middle, urged Reagan to run for the Republican nomination for president. "Neither Nixon nor [New York Governor Nelson] Rockefeller have enough delegates to win on the first ballot," Reagan said with a wink. "I may be better off waiting to break a convention deadlock."

"Governor," Joe Coors said, and Reagan leaned across Rozek to hear him. "If you become president, can I be secretary of the treasury?"

Reagan laughed and said, "Sure, Joe." Rozek and Nofziger laughed, too. The only one not laughing was Joe Coors. He gazed out the window with a proud little smile; Rozek was sure he was taking the oath of office in his mind. Joe wangled himself a spot on the Colorado delegation to the Republican convention in Miami, and distinguished himself as the sole Colorado delegate to resist the pressure to vote for Richard Nixon on the first ballot. Reagan garnered only seventy-eight votes, but Joe Coors's was one of them. With an eye toward a run next time, Reagan launched a weekly radio program to espouse and refine his conservative philosophy. He needed sponsors, and he remembered Joe Coors. On the strength of a single phone call from Reagan, Joe agreed to put the Adolph Coors Company behind Reagan's radio shows. The Coors-sponsored shows turned out to be vastly important to Reagan's political maturity. He coined the phrase "welfare queen" on the show, for example, and used it to devastating effect later.*

Joe Coors did not keep the 1960s from reaching the University of Colorado. CU adopted coed dorms, professors as well as students wore long hair and beads, antiwar marches were frequent, and the SDS held a national convention on campus.

But Joe was proud of his service. Without his presence on the board, he felt, the university would have lurched even further left. Somebody had to speak for traditional American values at this trying moment in history, and Joe Coors believed that fate had chosen him.

He didn't know it, but standing as the flamboyantly quotable voice of the right, Joe had begun a ten-year job of painting a bull's-eye on his nose. Around the time Joe was elected regent, California's Mexican-American grape pickers elected Cesar Chavez's United Farm Workers their sole bargaining agent. While Joe was pushing for the loyalty oath, the UFW was drumming up support for a national boycott of table grapes. They wanted to pressure vineyards to treat their workers better

---

*As late as 1999, neither the tapes nor transcripts of Reagan's early radio addresses have been made public. Harry O'Connor, Reagan's former producer and holder of the tapes, says Reagan has consistently refused all requests for access.

and publicize the plight of migrant workers in the West. But the UFW also had the broader aim of organizing Hispanics nationwide into launching their own civil rights movement. In downtown Denver, a Mexican American named Rudolfo "Corky" Gonzalez was scrambling to mobilize Denver's growing Hispanic population. Almost a tenth of Denver's people were Hispanic. As in most of the West, Denver Hispanics were largely relegated to dangerous, unpleasant, and low-paying jobs. Few Denver corporations employed Hispanics or blacks above the most menial level. Corky Gonzalez was looking for a hook, something to inspire Denver's Hispanics to begin thinking of themselves as a unified community with a grievance.

Joe Coors's campaign for regent in 1966 had been covered by Denver's newspapers more heavily than most because the Coors name was famous in Colorado and Joe's campaign rhetoric was eccentric. Gonzalez took notice. Joe Coors frequently made good copy during his tenure as regent, too. The guy was way out there, Gonzalez thought. He was a raving conservative nut and wanted everyone to know it.

Gonzalez examined hiring practices at the Coors brewery and found that Coors was about as bad as most industrial employers in Denver. Out of forty-five hundred Coors workers, only nine had Spanish surnames. None of the nine held a position of authority. Moreover, Joe Coors was going out of his way to identify himself with the same conservative movement that every Hispanic knew was opposed to antidiscrimination laws. To Gonzalez it seemed that Joe Coors was in the paper once a week with yet another outrageous comment. You couldn't miss him.

Because of all the excitement over the UFW's grape campaign, boycott was the first tool that jumped to Gonzalez's mind. The more he pondered it, the better the idea seemed. To begin with, Joe's name was on every can of Coors beer; the association between Joe and the product was easy to make. Then, Gonzalez thought, beer was a perfect product to boycott. It was inexpensive enough that everybody could participate, and there were plenty of other beers to buy that tasted pretty much the same. To participate in the boycott, Gonzalez concluded, a Hispanic had only to move his hand six inches along the shelf or call out a different name in a bar.

Gonzalez launched the boycott with big ads publicizing Coors's poor record of hiring and promoting Hispanics. He filed a complaint with the Equal Employment Opportunity Commission. Gonzalez's genius was in breaking off one tiny piece of the huge, abstract conservative enemy, putting a human face on it, and then vilifying the product that carried that face's name. Any Hispanic who wanted to hit back at the conservatives could do so by ordering a Budweiser.

In May of 1969, Joe addressed the Colorado School of Mines commencement in Golden—his most prominent speech to date. He was aboil not only with ideological fervor but with personal anger; his own fourth son, Grover, had joined the hippies. Long hair, drugs, posters of Ho Chi Minh on his University of Denver dorm-room wall, playing guitar in a rock-and-roll band—Grover had even turned in his draft card. In a rage over how the 1960s had invaded his own family, Joe unloaded on the School of Mines graduates a forty-five-minute syntactically breathless jeremiad against society's "pleasure-loving parasites." Welfare recipients and "hippies," Joe said, "are satisfied living off the state dole and handouts in a carefree existence." There was none of the traditional future-gazing in Joe's commencement address. He looked backward. "Our generation," he said of his own, "has not created a sick and decadent society—far from it. . . . [Now] a vocal minority among the youth, the educators, and the news media—which are making the loudest accusations about our 'sick society'—are the very ones who are promoting obscenity, drug use, atheism, and unrestricted freedom from any kind of control or order." Gonzalez read the account in the *Rocky Mountain News*, and, chuckling over Joe's racially loaded comments about welfare recipients as "pleasure-loving parasites," reached for his scissors.

The Hispanic Coors boycott germinated, nourished by Joe's increasingly intemperate comments and spread, in part, by rumor. Around this time, the Denver Police Department bought a couple of clapped-out Korean War-vintage helicopters and began flying patrols. Simultaneously, Coors Porcelain won a contract to make bulletproof ceramic shields for the bellies of Vietnam-bound helicopters. Somehow the two stories merged into a devastating calumny: Coors had bought the Denver PD helicopters to spy on Hispanic neighborhoods. Hispanics furious at Joe Coors's far-right politics readily believed the tale. The American G.I. Forum, an organization of Hispanic veterans, announced that it was joining the boycott.

The Coors brothers were oblivious. Demand still exceeded supply. Every bottle of beer the Hispanics didn't buy would be happily snapped up by someone else.

6

Something Even Better for Joe to Do

On a business trip to Seattle in 1966, Bill Coors decided to kill some time at a local science exhibit. The fair hummed with optimistic new technologies, and amidst the oscilloscopes and double-helix models, Bill came upon two cages, side by side. In one, a baby spider monkey cuddled with its mother, while in the other, a second baby spider monkey morosely clutched a stuffed doll.

The experiment had something to do with animal imprinting, but—as Bill would explain years later in a startlingly self-reflective speech—the sight of that lonely spider monkey gripping the inert doll for warmth triggered a wave of ugly memories. That wretched monkey, he reflected, was himself as a child. He never had had a real hug from his parents, he thought. They never had told him they loved him. Bill was fifty years old. He commanded a multimillion-dollar business and the number-one beer market share throughout the western United States. He was the inventor of the aluminum beverage can, the tamer of unions. As he stood staring at the baby monkey, his blue eyes streamed tears.

On his way home from Seattle, Bill decided to visit his nutrition guru, Adelle Davis, at her home in California. He wanted to sit at his mentor's feet and glean her insights. To his horror, he found Davis shockingly overweight and a chain smoker—the poor woman could hardly finish a sentence without coughing. Davis was deep into Freudian analysis and wanted only to talk about long-suppressed desires to kill her mother. We have secrets locked in our minds, Davis told her abashed acolyte. We will never be happy until we unlock them. Bill pondered Davis's rantings the rest of the way home and became a convert. He arrived in Golden as determined to unlock the secrets of his mind as he had been to manufacture an aluminum beverage can. He found a psychiatrist and began going several times a week to lie on the couch. Within a month Bill was insisting that all the members of the Coors board, and all the company's key executives, try it. The company would pay for it, he said. Go unlock the secrets of your minds! The stoic men Bill had spent a lifetime assembling around himself rolled their eyes at each other. Bill was always trumpeting some new health kick but this was ridiculous. Everybody tried it once or twice and then dropped it. Bill, though, continued analysis with his customary zeal.

In March 1967, Phyllis delivered Bill a son. William Kistler Coors, Jr., had died on the dining room table in 1946; this baby, born twenty-one years later, was given the name William Scott Coors. Everybody would come to call him Scott. Bill at age fifty-one had enough distance from his own childhood—and enough months of analysis under his belt—to see how harsh and distant a father he had been to his three daughters. He couldn't remember a single time he'd said, "I love you." He couldn't remember ever hugging his daughters, or spending quiet time with them, or listening to what they had to say. He reflected, with ashamed horror, that he'd inflicted upon his daughters the same icy upbringing his father had inflicted upon him. He'd hated it, and he knew his daughters had hated it. Joe, Bill realized, was rearing his sons in the same painful, destructive way. That couldn't be helped, nor could Bill go back and change things with his daughters. But he could be a different kind of father to Scott. He lifted the sleeping baby into his arms and whispered in his downy ear, "I love you."

Brewery Workers Local 366 was the biggest union at Coors, but at one time many others had represented workers there, too. Every time the Coors brothers had a chance they broke another union. They would force a strike and replace the strikers. Or they would force open-shop elections and use a combination of stick and carrot to get the men to surrender union membership voluntarily. Or they would simply offer higher wages as an enticement to decertify.

Often it wasn't hard to do. Labor was beginning its decline—membership fell from almost a third of the U.S. workforce in 1960 to little more than a quarter in 1970. The Coors unions were part of a trend. One by one they fell: Asbestos Workers Local 28, Boilermakers Local Union 101, Brick Layers Local 1, Cement Masons Local 577, Electricians Local 68, Glaziers Local 930, Iron Workers Local 24, Lathers Local 68, Linoleum Layers Local 419, Millwrights Local 2834, Painters Local 79, Pipe Fitters Local 208, Plumbers Local 3, Roofers Local 41, Sheet Metal Local 9, and Tile, Marble and Terrazzo Helpers Local 85. The Coors brothers rid their plant of fifteen building-trade locals in the 1960s. Every report of labor defeat at Coors made the small print of the nation's union newsletters, and added another brushstroke to the company's increasingly vivid antiunion reputation.

That reputation was eminently deserved, David Sickler believed. The longer Sickler served as a shop steward of Local 366, the angrier he got. Many of the complaints workers brought to him were over petty insults by the company—men's shifts jerked around, men docked a day's pay for being a minute late to work, lockers and lunchboxes searched by Coors Security, that sort of thing. It was the contemptuous attitude of the company toward its workers, as much as the substantive insults, that irritated Sickler. A fitness freak—like Bill Coors—Sickler woke every day at three-thirty to stretch and take a long run. As he loped through the dark streets of Golden, throwing shadow punches, he came to think of employment at Coors as well-paid slavery. They've bought us with high wages, he'd think, and now they think they can treat us like property. That's why they're driving out their unions—so the workers can't fight back.

Ever since the brewery workers had struck in support of the porcelain workers in 1956, Bill and Joe had feared and resented gestures of cross-craft solidarity. For years they wouldn't even allow their workers to form a credit union because it might give them too much of a sense of unity. In the late 1960s and early '70s, Local 366 had manned picket lines in Denver to help the United Farm Workers publicize their grape boycott, and when Bill Coors heard about it he was furious. "I have a whole damn cellar full of grapes," he told Sickler, "and I'll break that boycott single-handedly." Sickler believed him because a Coors truck returning from California—supposedly empty—had recently overturned near Grand Junction, spilling nonunion lettuce all over Interstate 70.

The grape and lettuce boycotts fascinated Sickler. Strikes, he knew, often failed. Once the workers vacate a plant, only the conscience of the employer prevents all the strikers being locked out and replacements hired. Ceding that much control to the company seemed crazy to Sickler.

A boycott, though, truly had the potential to punish a corporation. Much better to withhold customers than labor; customers could not be replaced. A boycott provided the public with a relatively painless way to feel involved in a struggle. Already, Sickler knew, there were big segments of the public who wouldn't be caught dead with a bunch of grapes or a head of iceberg lettuce in their shopping carts. The problem was, too many boycotts were halfhearted; they were declared, publicized once, and forgotten. Also, not every product could be easily boycotted. In general, the less expensive and less essential the product, the easier the boycott. Grapes and lettuce, therefore, were great targets.

But more than that, the UFW was conducting itself beautifully. It wasn't just broadcasting a shotgun appeal to the national public; it was breaking off markets. UFW activists picketed supermarkets, neighborhood by neighborhood. They appealed to restaurants. They approached the churches. They networked with other minority organizations. Sickler took notes.

Sooner or later, Sickler knew, Coors and Local 366 were going to come to blows again. The company seemed to be trying to provoke the union. Colorado had ratified the Equal Rights Amendment in 1970 and Coors grudgingly hired its first women as production workers. Bill and Joe Coors knew it was good business to honor the ERA, but the thought of being forced to adjust their hiring practices infuriated them. As a shop steward, Sickler watched the company do all it could to drive the women out. The brewery had no women's restrooms, and rather than build some, the company made the women brewery workers walk all the way to the secretaries' restrooms, and then counted the time against their breaks. At one point, a Coors foreman ordered a woman worker to move crates of broken glass, each weighing about as much as the woman herself. Sickler confronted the foreman, who laughed and said, "We have to hire women but we don't have to keep them."

Coors was the fourth largest brewer in the United States as the 1960s ended, with $160 million in sales and annual profit of $10 million. The beer was still sold in only eleven states. But it was the biggest seller in

California and all ten others as well. Beer drinkers from the states east of Oklahoma found it exciting when visiting Coors territory that the biggest beer around wasn't even sold back home. To someone in one of the thirty-nine states where Coors wasn't sold, the beer was a novelty. A six-pack fit easily in a suitcase, and many a can traveled east surreptitiously. Coors appealed to a rising "small is beautiful" ethic whose adherents were repelled by the idea of national, standardized brews. Lots of Americans liked the idea that the Coors brewery was owned by a single family whose name was on the can. Also, Mr. Coors and his sons disliked ring-pull litter, so until late in the decade, Coors was the only canned beverage in the country without a ring-pull top. Beer drinkers needed an old-fashioned churchkey to punch two triangular holes in the lid, and that was exotic as well. What's more, many found the beer delicious—crisp and light. It was easy to drink a second or third Coors. Bill enjoyed gathering the employees in the sixth-floor auditorium to announce another increase in market share, another boost in sales or profit.

DeBey and Sickler noticed that the employees received these reports with a mixture of pride and anger. They liked working for a brewery that cared about its product. Coors beer was the best in America, the workers felt. None doubted that the family would spare no expense improving its beer. But they asked each other, With the company doing so well, why can't it treat us better? Bill often greeted his employees with a handshake as they filed into the auditorium. He was good at matching faces with names. And he ran meetings in an avuncular, good-humored way that made him personally popular among the workers. But Bill could rarely resist the temptation to stray from company business into whatever was on his mind. At one meeting in 1970, for example, he explained to his four-dollar-an-hour employees that the right to vote should be based on how much a person pays in taxes. "Those who pay the highest taxes should have stronger votes than those who pay little. And if you pay no taxes, you should get no vote," Bill said, shrugging his bony, khaki-clad shoulders in that neighbor-over-the-fence style of his. "Doesn't that make sense?" The employees filed back to work shaking their heads and muttering.

Adolph Coors, Jr., worked his last day at the brewery on Monday, May 25, 1970. He was eighty-six years old. He walked home as usual, but the next morning felt poorly and checked himself into St. Joseph's Hospital in Denver. By Thursday night he was dead. On Friday, work at the brewery continued as usual. Mr. Coors wanted no pauses, no memorials, no funeral. He does not lie beside his parents at Denver's Crown Hill Cemetery, although his sisters do, nor beside his murdered son across town at Fairmount Cemetery. Mr. Coors's body was cremated and the ashes scattered. Six months later, Alice May followed him into death and she too was cremated without a funeral. Bill Coors finally assumed the post of chairman. The second era of Coors brewing—in which Mr. Coors transformed his father's tiny, Prohibition-stifled brewery into an innovative national giant—was over. It would soon be remembered around Golden as the good old days.

Coors's attitude toward planning—that the company didn't believe in it—placed the brewery at one end of the corporate spectrum. At the other end was another consumer-products company, Philip Morris Companies, which had an appetite for planning that was downright visionary. Even before the Surgeon General issued his devastating report in 1966 officially linking cigarettes with cancer for the first time, the giant tobacco company could see that Americans were going to smoke less in the future and might even demand that government restrict the industry. For its long-term survival, Philip Morris had to diversify. In so doing, Philip Morris came straight at Coors's throat.

Philip Morris Chief Executive Officer Joseph Cullman started shopping around in the 1950s for companies to buy whose products were compatible with cigarettes. In 1960, he bought American Safety Razor on the theory that razor blades, like cigarettes, were inexpensive, were used daily, and needed constant replacement. But Philip Morris never found a "unique selling proposition"—that is, a distinctive reason consumers should buy the product—to rival that of Gillette and Schick. American Safety Razor fizzled.

Cullman tried gum, which was likewise inexpensive and used up quickly, and which was distributed by the same wholesaler network that handled cigarettes. Philip Morris bought Clark Chewing Gum in 1963 but again couldn't engineer the magic combination of product and marketing to entice chewers off Wrigley, Beech-Nut, and Dentyne.

Pressure built in Congress in the late 1960s to ban cigarette advertising on television. Like all cigarette companies, Philip Morris became frantic to diversify. The company knew the ocean of cash now spent annually on TV ads would soon be freed by the ban to invest in new products. Cullman thought that beer might do for Philip Morris what razor blades and chewing gum couldn't. Like both, beer was inexpensive and consumed rapidly. But it also was a vice product, which made it much more like cigarettes than either razors or chewing gum. Philip Morris had a certifiable genius for marketing vice products.

Like cigarettes, mass-produced beers are "commodity products." No matter how the Coors brothers might protest to the contrary, modern marketing theory holds that each brand is pretty much the same. The trick to marketing commodity products is building an image around a brand, so that the consumer believes he is saying something appealing about himself when he reaches for your product. Different types of people respond to different images; for example, young male athletes won't buy products marketed to elderly women, and vice versa. It's a wise company that has many brands afield in the marketplace, each "positioned" to appeal to as many different groups as possible. Identifying market segments and creating product images to lure them is the essential art of marketing. Advertising—specific appeals to the disparate market segments—follows.

Philip Morris long had multiple cigarette brands in the marketplace, and was sophisticated at analyzing market segments and tailoring products to them. Marlboro, for example, was a minor Philip Morris brand in the 1950s, barely breaking even. It was considered a "woman's brand," the kiss of death because fewer women than men smoked. Philip Morris hired the Chicago marketing firm of Leo Burnett to help it reposition Marlboro as a man's brand. Striving for the manliest of images, Burnett and Philip Morris chose cowboys, backed up by the rousing theme music from the 1960 western film *The Magnificent Seven*. The public response was instantaneous; Marlboro started growing faster than any other cigarette. In 1977, it zoomed past Winston to become number one. Four decades after its repositioning, Marlboro is still using cowboy imagery.

In 1965, Philip Morris did it again, only this time in the opposite direction. It created a new brand called Virginia Slims, and then—almost perversely—positioned it as a cigarette just for women. Cullman privately thought eliminating more than half the smoking market was lunatic, but he agreed to try it. On the strength of the Virginia Slims slogan—"You've Come a Long Way, Baby"—the cigarette was a hit. Women remained in the minority of the smoking public, but Virginia Slims had enough of them to be hugely profitable.

With the TV ad ban looming, Cullman was itching to bring the marketing wizardry of Philip Morris into the brewing business for the first time. He tried to buy into the Canadian Carling brewery, which made Black Label and other beers. But another cigarette-maker—Rothmann's, of England—already owned a piece of Carling and wouldn't let Philip Morris in. Then one Sunday afternoon in 1969, Cullman's home phone rang. The shipping magnate Peter Grace was calling to offer Philip Morris his 53 percent stake in the Miller Brewing Company of Milwaukee.

Cullman instantly understood the implications. Unlike Coors, Philip Morris enlisted an army of planners who had already run the numbers on Miller. Miller was the number-seven brewer in the country and going nowhere. It fielded one product: Miller High Life. Its slogan—"The Champagne of Bottled Beers"—was a good-news-bad-news joke, lending it a reputation for quality, but also pushing it to the margins, because most beer drinkers were workingmen who viewed champagne as sissy stuff. Miller was limping along at less than half of its production capacity, a sitting duck for takeover. The 47 percent of Miller not owned by Grace was, oddly, owned by a charitable foundation devoted to supporting Catholic clerics. This meant there weren't a lot of minority owners out there that Philip Morris would need to buy out.

"It's an interesting idea," Cullman told Grace. "When do you need an answer?"

"Tomorrow," Grace said.

Cullman, loaded with data, was able to jump at the opportunity. He paid Grace $127 million, and he paid the clerics' foundation an additional $100 million. Philip Morris was now $227 million into the beer business, with a moribund brand and a lousy slogan.

Cullman turned Miller over to his number-two man, John Murphy— a loud, flamboyant career marketer. Murphy immediately fired almost all the old Miller management. He spent two years and another quarter-billion dollars correcting what he thought was an inferior product. Miller High Life was too heavy, too bitter, and sat on store shelves too long. He ordered the beer lightened and the hops toned down—in other words, he wanted it to taste more like Coors. Then he copied Coors' practice of having a "pull date" stamped on every label, and of ordering the Miller sales force to cancel the franchise of any wholesaler or retailer who stocked stale beer. Finally, Murphy "discovered" that many people can't finish a twelve-ounce beer and ordered up a line of seven-ounce ponies— again imitating Coors.

But what Murphy did next was nothing at all like Coors. He analyzed the market. He found that 30 percent of the beer drinkers—blue-collar men—drank 80 percent of the nation's beer. He and his ad agency—McCann-Erickson—intuited that these workingmen didn't really want to hear about beer. They wanted to hear about themselves. They didn't just want a passably drinkable beer from a brewery; they also wanted thirty-second movies with themselves as the star. So in 1972, Murphy ordered a series of upbeat ads depicting ordinary Joes—welders, cowboys, factory hands—coming off a hard day's work and heading for the corner bar. "If you've got the time," the ads offered, "we've got the beer." The beer drinker, not the beer, was the centerpiece of the ads, and beer drinkers lapped it up. Miller High Life, repositioned from "champagne" to friend of the workingman, sat up in its coffin. Beer marketing would never be the same again.

National Review published a poll in 1971 stating that three fifths of the nation's college students identified themselves as liberals. Half favored the socialization of all basic industries, half believed organized religion harmful, and half preferred surrender to nuclear war with Russia. After five years of fighting those attitudes on the CU campus, Joe Coors was appalled. Thank God, anyway, young Grover no longer numbered among the hippies. After the Kent State shootings in May 1970, Grover realized, as he later put it, that "protesters sometimes get hurt." He took down the Ho Chi Minh posters, cut his hair, and went to work at Porcelain. Joe welcomed Grover back. He did not, however, extend an olive branch to Joe Jr., then doing mid-level administrative work for the San Diego School Board.

Although Joe had spoken often of running for a second six-year term as regent, he faced a hard decision as his term was expiring. Joe enjoyed being part of the struggle to keep the nation from sliding ever leftward. The movement needed him and his commitment.

But Joe was beginning to doubt whether he was personally suited for politics. He disliked forcing smiles and knew they'd never come naturally for him as they did for the pros. He felt awkward making the effort at small talk and knew he came across as stiff and formal. And he realized after five years on the board of regents that politics was a game of never-ending compromise. He now understood that a politician needed to be able to give ground, without regret, when the situation demanded. He also knew he wasn't one to give ground. He believed too deeply. Finally,

Joe understood he was neither a theoretician nor a strategist nor a generator of new political ideas. So when Joe sat back in 1971 to reflect upon what a man of his convictions could bring to the conservative movement, he came up with a simple and earthshaking answer: money.

Joe Coors had lots of money, little desire for luxuries, and tremendous conservative faith. At the time, though, no model existed as to how a conservative millionaire could use his money to the best political advantage. The huge foundations that would later finance so much of the conservative revolution—Scaife, Bradley, Olin—either didn't yet exist or hadn't begun large-scale political funding. Shortly after his father died, Joe had his assistant, Jack Wilson, write a letter to a friend, U.S. Senator Gordon Allott, Republican of Colorado. Allott, Joe thought, might have some good ideas about how best to inject money into the conservative movement.

Allott wasn't in when Wilson's letter arrived, so it was routed to Allott's press secretary, a baby-faced young Wisconsin named Paul Weyrich. Weyrich, a conservative since high school, had gotten an early lesson in the power of committed organizations to affect policy. At age fifteen, he'd helped organize a grass-roots campaign to save the Chicago, North Shore and Milwaukee Railroad that succeeded in delaying its dissolution. "Mr. Coors," Wilson's letter read, "is looking to invest in conservative causes." Weyrich first thought Wilson's letter was a practical joke—to offer unsolicited money to a D.C. political operative is to dangle a very fat worm before a very hungry fish. Weyrich scooped up the phone and invited Wilson to Washington. Then he called his friend Jim Lucier in Senator Strom Thurmond's office.

Although Lucier had grown up in one of the most heavily unionized and Democratic cities in the country—Detroit—he hadn't met a Democrat until he'd left high school. His family was so sheltered that when they heard someone on the radio describe himself as a liberal in 1956 they were shocked that anyone would publicly admit such a thing. Lucier and Weyrich came to Washington the same year—1967—and it hadn't taken them long to find each other. Genuine conservatives were rare on Capitol Hill then, even in the offices of Republican legislators.

Weyrich and Lucier had quickly noticed a glaring problem: conservative members of Congress had no reliable source of information. The Library of Congress, in their view, was practically useless. Its staff consisted of academic liberals who could cough up bare facts but were worthless on analysis. The few times Lucier called them they didn't understand his questions, let alone provide helpful answers. Besides the Library of Congress, the liberals had the vast and powerful Brookings Institution. A liberal legislator or professor had only to muse about some new expansion of government—often on the Op-Ed page of *The New York Times*—and Brookings would go into action. Brookings scholars would assemble the supporting research, Brookings writers would package the data into a digestible report, and Brookings officials would brief members of Congress and their staffs on how to implement the new policy. The conservatives had nothing like it . . . unless you counted the American Enterprise Institute, and Lucier didn't. AEI was run by eastern big-business managers. True conservatives, Lucier and Weyrich believed, were as hostile to big business as they were to big labor or big government.

Lucier and Weyrich dreamed of creating a counterweight to Brookings, a place where conservative legislators could obtain not only reliable numbers but sophisticated analysis, accurate political projections, large-sample polling data—the slings and arrows of Washington politics. They knew it would take money. And so they waited four years. When Wilson's letter arrived, Weyrich almost took an infarction.

When Joe Coors himself finally came to Washington, Weyrich found him touchingly unschooled in the ways of power. "I do believe I've never met a man as politically naive as Joe Coors," he chuckled to Lucier after the meeting. "Coors is the kind of guy," Weyrich said, "who thinks you can write to your congressman and get something done."

Joe, in turn, was dazzled by Weyrich's sophistication. Weyrich was the first Washington operative he'd ever met. "We are engaged in a war," Weyrich told Joe. "A war to preserve the freedom this country was built on. Think of what we need as combat intelligence."

"I like your idea," Joe said. "But I'm also thinking of investing in the American Enterprise Institute."

Alarmed, Weyrich sent Joe to speak with Lyn Nofziger, Ronald Reagan's former press secretary whom Joe knew from Reagan's CU visit, now working as President Nixon's deputy assistant for congressional relations. "AEI?" Nofziger asked Joe with a sneer. He picked up an AEI study and blew dust off it. "That's what they're good for—collecting dust." Largely on the strength of Nofziger's remark, Joe decided to fund Weyrich and Lucier's project. The two young men quit their staff jobs and created Analysis and Research Corporation It was hardly the counterweight to Brookings Weyrich envisioned. It occupied a musty basement office and was plagued by both internal squabbling and an inability to gather more donors. Analysis and Research was small and obscure, but it was a step in a new direction. Joe Coors had midwifed the first truly conservative think tank in Washington, D.C.

Soon after, Defense Secretary Melvin Laird invited Joe to an intimate luncheon. Weyrich wasn't the only one lamenting the unchecked power of Brookings. Laird was trying to found a big conservative think tank of his own and would be presenting his plan to a select group of about a dozen wealthy potential contributors. National Security Advisor Henry Kissinger was to be the featured speaker. Joe mentioned this to his friend Ed Rozek at CU and Rozek lit up. "I know Kissinger," Rozek said. "We were undergraduates together at Harvard. He's a snake." Rozek gave Joe an article from *The New York Times* in which Kissinger was quoted as saying right-wing Republicans were a bigger danger to American freedom than communism. Joe put the article in his pocket.

At the luncheon, Kissinger delivered a stridently conservative speech— Joe Coors-style fire and brimstone. When he finished, Joe raised his hand. "I'd like to read a quote by you in *The New York Times*," Joe said, unfolding the article. He asked Kissinger if the quote was accurate and Kissinger said nothing. "Your silence speaks louder than words," Joe Coors told Henry Kissinger. "You say you're on the right with us, but apparently you think otherwise." Disgusted, Joe returned to Colorado with all his money in his pocket. Then Paul Weyrich called again.

Analysis and Research is okay, Weyrich said, but the time has come to go all the way. What conservatives really needed in Washington, D.C., is a *headquarters*. From where Weyrich sat, it appeared that the liberals had addresses all over town. Besides Brookings, they had the AFL-CIO building, the civil rights organizations, and every union headquarters in Washington. One could even have said that they had the White House; conservatives were quick to notice that they were never invited there, while George Meany and civil rights leaders were there often.

The need for a prominent headquarters had been a lively topic among conservatives for months. One activist was fond of phrasing the need in grand historical terms. "All the great movements of the world were nothing but hot air until they had territory," Richard Viguerie was fond of saying. "The Jews were the world's whipping boys until Israel. The communists were a bunch of pamphleteers until they took Russia in 1917. The Mormons were irrelevant wanderers until they had Utah." Weyrich told Joe Coors that what conservatives really needed was some prime Washington real estate. "We need someplace to gather, someplace for reporters to call for a reliable conservative viewpoint," he said. "We need a home of our own."

Weyrich caught Joe at a good moment. Not only had he been softened up by Laird, Washington was personally harassing him. The Federal Trade Commission had just ruled that Coors illegally restrained trade by forbidding its distributors from handling any other brand of draft beer. "It's typical of what American industry gets," Bill fumed to the Denver press when he and Joe appealed their case to the U.S. Supreme Court. "[Government bureaucrats] seem to think there is something evil about success."

It was Joe, though, who added bite to Bill's bark. He told Weyrich he'd stand behind a full-blown conservative institute on Capitol Hill. He gave Weyrich a quarter of a million dollars, plus an additional $300,000 for a building plus a commitment for millions more down the road. It was a breathtaking amount of money in 1973. It gave the new institute instant legitimacy and the power to attract further donations.

"Institutions such as the Ford Foundation and the Brookings Institute [sic] have had a disproportionate influence upon policy decisions at the Federal level and that influence has been consistently liberal," the prospectus for Joe's new organization said. "This has been a case of the viper of socialism in the bosom of the free enterprise system." A new conservative foundation was needed, the prospectus argued, to provide research and analysis "in behalf of traditional values," and to serve members of Congress "who struggle to cope with the initiatives of the liberal-socialist 'think tanks.'" The name Joe and Weyrich chose for the organization was the Heritage Foundation.

Heritage was fun. At the end of every workday, Weyrich bundled up the day's internal memos and sent them to Joe Coors in Golden. Joe enjoyed watching the conservative movement gel in an institute of his own creation. Among the conservatives he revered, Joe was becoming an honored player. And all he had to do was write checks. No more suffering through dreary regents' meetings, no more getting booed by unruly college students, no more public comments taken out of context by the press. He liked jetting back and forth between Golden and Washington. He liked striding a stage larger than Coors Porcelain and larger than CU.

Since he was flying back and forth anyway, Joe got into the habit of attending Cornell's annual commencement ceremonies. Holly and his friends thought it marvelous that with all his other important responsibilities, Joe was finding time to be a devoted alumnus. In time, his commitment to attending Cornell's commencements would become all-consuming—much to the later regret of his wife and children.

Joe Jr. had been unmoored from the family for ten years. In whispered phone conversations, his mother Holly had been imploring him to accept Jesus Christ as his personal savior. Turn control of your life over to the Lord and accept his love, Holly urged. Joe struggled. One afternoon in the spring of 1972 he was on the sixteenth hole of a San Diego golf course when he heard God speaking to him. "Go home," the voice told him, as clearly as if the caddie were speaking. "Go home."

Joe Jr. did, and as Holly prayed nervously, Joe Jr. walked into his father and uncle's shared brewery office. Though as extraordinarily tall as his father, Joe Jr. was heavier, with a padded softness about him that the pastel golf clothes he preferred seemed to accentuate. "I am ready to rejoin the family," he told Bill and Joe. "The Lord has spoken to me, and he's told me it's time to take up my responsibilities here."

Bill and Joe hoisted their eyebrows at each other. They knew Holly talked this way; it was a little odd to hear it from Joe Jr. "Thank you for coming," Joe told his son. "We will take your words under advisement." Eyes wet, jaw set, Joe Jr. stood and walked out. He took the next plane back to San Diego as Holly wept.

Joe Jr.'s cousin, the ex-Marine Adolph IV, was similarly adrift. He graduated the University of Denver at twenty-six and told his bride, B.J., that he intended to be a millionaire by the time he turned thirty. He would prove he could do it without his brewery family's help, he said. He would make his alcoholic, outcast mother proud.

Adolph tried selling commodities and wiped out within a couple of months. He turned to real estate and did no better. All he got out of his next couple of attempts at starting a business were lawsuits. Within a year of graduation, Adolph was doing what he swore he'd never do: knocking on the brewery door for a job.

Bill and Joe received him more warmly than they had Joe Jr. Adolph IV had never disobeyed either Bill or Joe. As for the "Adolf Hitler" letter to his grandfather, well, they figured, the boy had suffered a lot. Sure you can have a job at the brewery, Bill and Joe said. Scrub the fermenting tank. That's where all of us started.

Adolph squeezed his bulk into overalls and did what he was told. A few months later he was back at the office door, asking for a spot in sales and marketing—his dad's old department. "I don't have any chemistry or engineering," he said. "I studied business at DU." Bill, though, believed Coors men needed a solid foundation in the science of brewing. He put Adolph in research and development. When Adolph predictably failed there, he was packed off to the can plant. Undaunted, he struggled to acquit himself and earn a rightful spot in management. He went in early, stayed late, spent his spare hours figuring innovative ways to improve the can operation. He was like the Little Engine That Could, panting "I think I can, I think I can" while feverishly chugging uphill to where he thought he belonged—the apex of the Coors empire. Adolph's first son was born during this period, and though he'd always hated his name and what it represented, Adolph now insisted the baby be named Adolph V. Fed up with her husband's long hours and erratic attitude toward his family, Adolph's wife, B.J., started keeping a written list of all the reasons she wanted to leave him.

In October 1973, twenty-eight-year-old Adolph left the brewery at eight-fifteen after a fourteen-hour day. The Yom Kippur War had started that morning and Adolph listened intently to the radio. Halfway home, his Volkswagen convertible drifted across the line and plowed head-on into an oncoming car. Luckily, neither Adolph nor the man in the other car were badly hurt. Adolph spent several days staring at a hospital-room ceiling, thinking. When he returned to work, he insisted that his uncle Bill give him a job in administration. Bill asked Lowell Sund, then fifty-one, to look after him.

Sund recognized his old self in Adolph IV's unhappiness. Sund had reached his fiftieth birthday the year before in a funk of midlife blues. Once the most easygoing of men, he'd grown grumpy, dissatisfied, and bored. The evident contentment of his wife Vera, the former radio singer, drove him nuts. She seemed to Sund perfectly at peace, humming through the day, sleeping soundly at night. Though he hated to admit it, he began to believe that her serenity grew from a commitment she'd made seven years earlier. Vera had become a born-again Christian. Sund had berated her at the time: "You're a loony," he'd said, "a freak." But as his life grew increasingly empty, Vera's seemed to grow fuller. Finally, Lowell said, "Vera, I want what you have." Vera opened the Bible and led him in the Sinner's Prayer. "I accept Christ as my personal savior," he said, and as though he'd thrown a switch, Sund felt a warm glow inside. He woke the next morning feeling younger, more alert, and calmer than he had in years. His life was no longer his own to control; it belonged to

Jesus Christ. Colleagues noticed the change. "Something's different about you, Lowell," they told him.

Sund's conversion delighted Holly Coors. Though the Lord was making headway with her sons, old Joe and Bill resisted consistently. "I wish I was smart enough to understand all that politics Joe does," Holly would tell the women in her Bible studies class, though they knew Holly was smart enough to understand anything she wanted. That's Holly, they said to each other. Such a *good* wife. So self-effacing. So willing to stand by her husband.

About a year after Adolph returned to work, Sund traveled to Arkansas for a meeting with Coors's rice growers. It was duck season, so he stayed afterward to hunt and came back with about twenty ducks. Sund invited Adolph and B.J. to help eat them. Sund and Adolph had remained close since the day Adolph—then called "Spike"—missed the grouse with his shotgun. Sund watched the young couple as he carved the ducks. They looked a wreck. They sniped at each other and barely made eye contact. As they were finishing dinner, B.J. turned to Vera. "I know you don't work," B.J. said. "What do you do with yourself, Vera? What keeps you busy?"

"Well," Vera said, "if you really want to know, I'll tell you." The two couples sat up until the small hours of the morning, talking about Jesus Christ. Not long after that, B.J. read the Sinner's Prayer with Vera and came home humming. In front of Adolph's astonished eyes she tore up her list of his failings. Her dissatisfaction melted away; she was a changed woman. Adolph thought it was plain weird. He moved out.

Sund felt terrible that he and Vera had helped instigate the split. But they prayed for Adolph, hoping he too would find salvation. In the meantime, Sund became a kind of informal company chaplain. He was a member of the board by this time, and Bill let him say a short benediction before each meeting. He also let Sund edit his Christmas message to the workers; Sund could never tell if Bill was just trying to vex him with such assertions as "Jesus was one of the sons of God."

Bill would not be budged in the direction of the Lord. Whenever Sund tried to ease him toward the Bible, Bill got crabby. "I have to do this on my own," he'd say. But Bill did feel a spiritual need. His enthusiasm for psychoanalysis was waning. Four sessions a week, lying on his back and jawing about himself, didn't seem right anymore. The whole business was starting to feel self-indulgent. Bill's passion for the teachings of Adelle Davis was ebbing, too. He'd just been to see her again, and found her lounging in a womb-shaped, body-temperature swimming pool jabbering about "rebirth." Bill decided she was a nut and left her teachings for good. Continuing his search for the perfect path to health, Bill discovered the book *The Stress of Life* by Hans Selye and began "supersaturating" his body with fistfuls of vitamins. Then Bill found transcendental meditation.

The early seventies were the height of TM's popularity. Bill ordered Phyllis to arrange a week for them both to take the training. Their social schedule was so busy it took her two months to find the time, but they took the training together and sat cross-legged through a mystical incense-soaked initiation ceremony involving three pieces of fruit, six flowers, and a linen handkerchief. Bill began meditating twenty minutes a day and couldn't praise it enough. He invited TM teachers to the brewery and ordered all his executives to take their classes.

David Sickler was flummoxed by this latest health obsession of Bill's. Sickler was no longer a Coors employee; he now was Local 366's business manager, his salary paid by the union. Sickler enjoyed fighting grievances, and went into meetings with company managers pumped up for combat. His adversary was often Jack Bramble, a beefy, broad-shouldered mid-level manager who equally enjoyed a fight. In 1973, they met to argue an employee's grievance, and as the meeting heated up, Bramble—instead of pounding the table and yelling the way he usually did—suddenly folded his hands, closed his eyes, and started humming. Sickler was rattled, and the meeting ended inconclusively. About a year later Sickler and Bramble met again on another matter, and this time the old Bramble was back—waving his arms and screaming obscenities. Sickler smiled. "Looks like Bill's off his TM kick," he said.

"Yeah," Bramble said, "and not a goddamn minute too soon."

Bramble wasn't quite right. Though Bill stopped imposing TM on his employees, his personal enthusiasm fledged. He even called the *Denver Post*—something he wouldn't have dreamed of doing when his father was alive—and gave a long interview, saying meditation improved his short-term memory, his sleep, and his moods. "I think TM has a tremendous potential for solving all kinds of problems for our society," he told the *Post*. "Anything I can do to lend it credibility and responsibility, I will."

The image of Bill Coors wreathed in incense smoke and chanting a mantra clashed with another image of him carried in the Denver papers. Bill was at the same time playing the tyrant in the San Luis Valley of

Colorado—in a way so undemocratic even the usually laudatory *Denver Post* was implicitly critical. Most of Coors's barley—some $8 million worth a year—was grown in the valley by farmers holding coveted Coors contracts. Bill was as hard on his farmers as he was on his distributors; any who didn't deliver barley with the proper starch-to-germ balance lost the lucrative franchise. Quality he could control; price was another matter. The farmers' prices to Coors fluctuated wildly as rain interrupted the harvest or hailstorms blew through the valley, leveling acres of barley.

Hail and untimely rain were no more obstacles to the Adolph Coors Company than flood had been; Bill ordered the hail suppressed and the rain regulated. His pilots salted the clouds above the valley with silver iodide pellets, which timed the rain to the farmers' liking. Though good news for the farmers, it was bad news for the ranchers, who made up the vast majority of the valley's population. They rose in fury, voting thirty-two to one in favor of a resolution demanding Coors stop the salting. Bill wrote to each county commission in the valley, refusing to stop. Sixty percent of Coors's barley grew in the San Luis Valley, he wrote, and "ten percent is the maximum amount we are prepared to place at the mercy of the natural elements." The Denver papers had never editorialized against Coors, and this was no exception. But the tone of their coverage was decidedly—and uncharacteristically—negative. The stories made Bill Coors appear arrogant, and contemptuous of the democratic process—not to mention of Mother Nature.

7

The Bull's-Eye

Robert Pauley, an investment banker in Boston, had an idea. Like many conservatives, Pauley thought the news media exhibited a disgraceful liberal bias. He wanted to restore some balance by having the conservative movement start its own television news service. The service Pauley envisioned would sell fully produced video packages to independent local stations to broadcast.

The idea of waging ideological warfare on the airwaves was decades ahead of its time. In the days before the Internet and widespread use of cable or satellite transmission, it was especially ambitious. United Press International was the only independent news film service at the time, and it delivered features and sports reels to TV stations by truck. Pauley wanted to use the same telephone-line transmission technology the networks used for breaking news, so that client stations could get up-to-the-minute reports. Creating such an agency from scratch would take piles of money. In the early 1970s, when conservatives needed money, the man they called was Joe Coors.

Joe put up a million dollars to create Television News, Inc., headquartered in swank twenty-seventh-floor offices in midtown Manhattan. He committed an additional $2.5 million a year to TVN because, as he put it to the *Rocky Mountain News,* "network news is slanted to the liberal-left side of the spectrum and does not give a balanced view to the American public." Joe hired seven experienced print and broadcast journalists to man TVN. Dick Graf, most recently news director of WNBC television in New York, was put in charge. "There will be days when I'll put pieces on the air that will make your flesh crawl because of your personal beliefs," Graf told Coors when he accepted the job. "But I'll be doing it because of my professional news judgment, and I'll play them down the middle."

"That's what we want you to do," Coors replied. "As long as it's down the middle, okay."

But it was clear to Graf the first month that Joe's idea of "the middle" was different from his own. Joe assigned his political assistant, Jack Wilson, to monitor TVN's content for him. Wilson went further. In the weeks before TVN went on the air in May 1973, Wilson walked around Capitol Hill gathering story ideas from conservative legislators. Some days, the bureau received as many as six story suggestions from Wilson. Graf resisted, and three weeks into the experiment Wilson and Coors wrote him that TVN's coverage "requires a more balanced presentation of the news than the service has thus far exhibited." Wilson's critiques of TVN's coverage read as follows:

To: Joe Coors
From: Jack Wilson June 7, 1973
Subject: Critique of Daily News Feed
Elderly. This matter of the elderly is obviously a problem, but why was only Hubert Humphrey given a chance to voice his socialist viewpoints. . . . This was a chance to damn those who made it the welfare state it is today.

To: Joe Coors
From: Jack Wilson July 12, 1973
Subject: Critique of Daily News Feed
The American Civil Liberties Union is generally recognized as the legal arm of the extreme left if not the Communist Party in the United States. They held, as our reporter said, "a well-attended press conference" and TVN—just like everyone else—set cameras alongside each other and gave them a full uncontested exposure for their line. . . .

To: Joe Coors
From: Jack Wilson July 26, 1973
Subject: Critique of Daily News Feed
Martin Luther King was an avowed communist revolutionary. It is not

necessary for us to cover him or any of his subordinates (Abernathy) just because the other networks do so. . . .

Joe named Wilson president of TVN, and Wilson immediately fired Graf and four others of the original news staff. All new job applicants, he decreed, must be vetted first by Heritage Foundation staff. Wilson told his new news director, Tom Turley, that the "middle" was no longer welcome at TVN. "I hate Dan Rather," he said. "I hate all those network people. They're destroying the country. We have to unify the country. TVN is the moral cement." Wilson still wanted a sophisticated image, however. "See that tugboat out there?" Wilson asked Turley, pointing out the office window. "Did you ever see the way a tugboat turns an ocean liner around? It doesn't do it in one swift motion. It pushes and nudges the liner slowly. That's the way we want to put our philosophy in the news: gradually, subtly, slowly. It must be subtle."

Turley was apparently too subtle and Wilson soon fired him, too— after getting into a fistfight with him in the office. Wilson and Joe Coors then decided they weren't going to break the liberal network-news mentality if they kept hiring network-news people. So they went outside journalism to hire their next news director, a young public relations specialist named Roger Ailes. Ailes had never worked as a journalist. He'd produced staged TV "confrontations" between President Nixon and selected citizens, and trained Republican legislators in the art of television appearance.

Ailes was more to Joe Coors's ideological liking, but he wasn't able to keep TVN alive. Only about forty stations signed up. By the time Joe Coors's experiment shut down in October 1975, it was losing more than half a million dollars a month. All told, the TVN experiment cost Joe about $8 million.

The Miller Brewing Company, once the embodiment of stodginess, was now, in the early 1970s, the industry's smart-aleck upstart. John Murphy built on the popular "If You've Got the Time" ads with an even more successful campaign trumpeting "Miller Time." Sales shot upward.

Bill Coors paid Miller no mind. To him, Miller was nothing but a big puff of braggadocio with a mediocre beer at its core. He had something more immediate on his mind—inventing the culture of recycling.

When Bill first suggested to the U.S. Brewers Association the idea of recycling aluminum cans, Anheuser-Busch presented a $30,000 study showing that consumers would never go for it. That was in 1960, and the entire brewing industry had sided with Anheuser-Busch. But Coors went its own way. Not only was every Coors distributor required to take cans back, Coors designed an automated "Can Bank" for vendors of canned beverages. The machines ingested aluminum cans and gave coins in return. A decade later, Coors's "Cash for Cans" program—which paid ten cents a pound—was getting back eighty-five out of every hundred cans Coors produced. Now every other brewer in the country was scrambling to create recycling programs of their own to save money, and—in the wake of the first Earth Day—to be environmental heroes.

Bill was eager for another packaging breakthrough. He'd reluctantly adopted the ring-pull can, but was no happier with it than he had been with the steel beer can. Environmentalists were making an issue of ring-pulls because they were scattered everywhere, were plainly ugly, cut people's bare feet, and hurt the animals that ate them. Bill agreed, and worried again about beer-industry litter attracting unwelcome government attention. Also, ring-pulls were a waste of aluminum because they weren't returned. Bill directed his engineers to find an alternative, and ultimately held the company's second press conference in its ninety-eight-year history to unveil "Press Tab," a new can top that generated no litter. (The company's first press conference was to announce the aluminum can in 1959.) Press Tab consisted of two raised buttons. The consumer pressed both; they broke away but remained attached to the can. It was Coors engineering at its best: elegant, cost-effective, and environmentally sensitive.

Unfortunately, nobody could open the can. If the beer was cold, held on a table, and in Golden, Colorado—at more than a mile above sea level—an easy seven to nine pounds of pressure was required to press the two buttons. At sea level, or if the beer was warm, or held in the hands, opening it required far more pressure than many people could achieve. A market-oriented company would have tested the cans in isolated locations, held focus groups, refined the design, and evaluated whether the cost savings were worth the effort. To Bill, focus groups were folderol. He was the inventor of the aluminum can, and he knew Press Tab was mechanically and environmentally superior to the ring-pull. The better product should be distributed everywhere at once, he decreed. All across Coors's territory, women, senior citizens, and those who simply couldn't be bothered struggling to open a beer can moved their hands six inches along the shelf and made another selection. Bartenders stopped stocking the cans, too; struggling with the buttons slowed them down. Although Coors distributors weren't Coors employees, they had contracts that said they could handle only Coors beer. They took the heat from angry retailers. A distributor in Los Angeles had a six-pack thrown through his plate-glass window. Sales slid. The distributors begged Bill to reverse his decision and restore the ring-pull.

He refused. Distributors who complained got angry letters in return. Startled brewery workers would occasionally find Bill tapping them on the shoulder. "Here," he'd say, thrusting a can at them. "Open this." Woe be unto the brewery worker who couldn't make Press Tab pop on the first try. Bill convened an employees' meeting in the sixth-floor auditorium and held up a can of beer. "Here's how this damned thing works," he snapped, and rolled his knuckle across the buttons, opening both. "There," he said to the embarrassed crowd. "What's so damned hard about that?" Then he stormed back to his office, and rather than fix the problem, picked another fight with organized labor.

In 1973, the independent beer distributors in San Francisco were banding together to throw off Teamsters Local 888, which represented every beer driver in the city. The Coors distributor was only one of many who joined the effort. Acting in unison, the distributors violated their contracts by imposing new work rules, which forced the drivers to strike. The distributors hired replacements and put an armed guard in the cab of every truck. A car full of armed security men followed each truck on its rounds. The Teamsters picketed as many supermarkets, restaurants, and liquor stores as they could and after two months forced the distributors to sign letters of agreement with the Teamsters and take the drivers back.

All except the Coors distributor.

The beer distributors in the East Bay tried the same thing, forcing the Teamsters there to strike, too. The distributors were clever this time. They learned that of the entire twelve-hundred-member Teamsters local, only three beer drivers were black. So the distributors hired a security firm that, though owned by whites, hired all black guards. They made an issue of the Teamsters' apparent racism. Guns were drawn, knives pulled, and it was considered a miracle nobody was killed. But the Teamsters prevailed again. All the East Bay distributors renewed their union contracts.

Except, again, Coors's.

Though Allan Baird was business representative of Teamsters Local 921 in San Francisco, which represented newspaper drivers, he didn't look or talk like a central-casting Teamster. He was slight and intellectual, with a high, tentative voice. When the beer strikes began, Baird was reassigned from the newspaper drivers to the beer drivers, and when the East Bay strikes ended with Coors holding out again, he took a long look at the brewery's record. Until recently, Baird had never thought of the company one way or the other, except that he liked its beer. Then he discovered the list of unions the company had broken in the past twelve years.

Baird learned that Corky Gonzalez's organized Hispanics in Denver were boycotting the company over hiring practices and that at their urging, the EEOC was filing discrimination charges against Coors on the basis of both Hispanic and black hiring. He learned from gay acquaintances about the sexual-preference questions on Coors's lie detector test. He found clippings about Coors's fights with ranchers and meddling with the weather in Colorado. Gays, greens, and minorities as well as labor had a beef with Coors, Baird mused. In California, that presented an opportunity.

Baird traveled around the Bay Area asking minority organizations to boycott Coors beer. He got Gene Upshaw, president of the National Football League players' union and owner of a bar popular with blacks, to pass the word to other black bar owners. He appealed to the Black Panthers. He made a deal with Cesar Chavez's United Farm Workers; Baird's men would picket Safeway stores in support of the UFW's Gallo wine boycott, and the UFW would talk up the Coors boycott among Hispanics. Baird learned that Arab storekeepers had recently run a successful boycott of an egg distributor they thought discriminated against them. He knew activist organizations liked battles—they kept the membership motivated—so he told the Arabs of Coors's discrimination record. They joined wholeheartedly. By the middle of 1974, pickets of every conceivable hue stood in front of liquor stores and bars, asking arriving patrons not to buy Coors beer. Baird watched his efforts snowball. Somebody in San Francisco started a rumor that Coors had given a million dollars to the gun-control lobby. Hunters soon announced they were boycotting Coors, too. The company denied the gun-control rumor, and that caught the attention of the San Francisco-based Sierra Club. Annoyed at Coors's "pro-gun" stance and goaded by the cloud-seeding, the Sierra Club urged its members not to drink Coors beer. Suddenly, for reasons they couldn't begin to fathom, Bill and Joe Coors had enemies all over California.

The boycott was in full swing when Baird went to see the movie *Fun with Dick and Jane* starring George Segal and Jane Fonda. It was a light comedy and Baird enjoyed it until . . . there on the screen was Jane Fonda—leftism incarnate—drinking a Coors beer. Baird wrote a letter to Fonda's new husband, antiwar activist Tom Hayden, asking why on earth a woman with solid liberal credentials could drink a racist, union-busting beer on screen.

About a week later, Baird was working in the boycott office when his phone rang. "This is Jane Fonda," the unmistakable voice said angrily. "If you have a problem with me, you write to me. You don't go running to my husband like I'm some kind of milquetoast housewife. Do you understand?"

Baird apologized. He was hip to labor, minority, and gay struggles, but he still sometimes trod accidentally on the toes of the feminists. Fonda accepted the apology, and asked about the Coors boycott. Baird gave her a thumbnail account and asked, "How could you turn your back on the cause that way?"

"I feel terrible about it," Fonda said. "It was a prop they handed me. I didn't even look at the label. What can we do now?"

Baird knew Fonda was about to begin filming *The Electric Horseman* with Robert Redford. "I'm going to send you a BOYCOTT COORS T-shirt," he said. "Will you wear it in the movie?"

"If I can," Fonda said, "I absolutely will." (She didn't.)

Baird showed up for work at the boycott office one morning and learned Bill would be speaking that day to the Rotary Club in Sacramento, about two hours away. He looked at his watch, and quickly rounded up a score of Teamsters. They raced east and set up a picket line outside the hotel where Bill was scheduled to speak. Baird had a bullhorn, and they put on a loud show on the sidewalk. Suddenly, a tall, thin man with a balding pate and sky-blue eyes pushed through the crowd. "Is one of you Allan Baird?" he barked.

"That's me," Baird said.

The man looked him up and down, then jammed a forefinger into his chest. "You're a son of a bitch," the man said. Then he turned and walked into the hotel. Baird was speechless.

"You know who that was?" one of the drivers said. "That was Bill Coors."

"He came out here alone," another said. "That's pretty brave."

About an hour later, the hotel door opened again and Bill Coors appeared. He wasn't fuming this time. He just ambled down the line of picketers. "Allan," Bill said, "I want to talk to you. I apologize for my words before. That wasn't right. Listen," he went on, "I'd like to invite you to meet me at my brewery in Golden, Colorado. Will you come?"

"Sure," Baird said. He found himself shaking Bill Coors's hand.

The Teamster leadership in the Bay Area was thrilled. The boycott must really be hurting Coors for Bill to invite Allan Baird to Golden. Baird flew to Colorado with several top union officials on the Teamsters jet. When they were shown into the Coors conference room, Bill was sitting at the table with a black man beside him.

"I just wanted you to see that yes, I do hire black people," Bill said as he shook the Teamsters' hand. He didn't introduce the black man, and the black man neither moved nor spoke during the meeting. Bill offered the Teamsters "a nice cold Coors beer." The Teamsters refused.

"Oh, my," Bill said, shaking his head sadly as he looked over the stack of boycott leaflets, in English and Spanish, that Baird brought with him. "What's this all about?"

"We don't think the Coors distributors should work nonunion when every other beer distributor in the Bay Area is organized by the Teamsters," Baird said. He told about the violated contracts, the armed guards, and the threats against strikers.

"Whoa," Bill said, holding up his hands. "I don't control the distributorships. I just make the beer."

Baird didn't believe him. "You award the distributorships," he said. "You could cut off their beer."

"I won't interfere in another man's business," Bill said coldly.

"Mr. Coors," Baird said, "you don't realize what's going to happen. We're going to the next phase of this boycott. We're going to meet with leaders of the gay community."

For the first time during the meeting, Bill seemed genuinely not to know what Baird was talking about.

"Gay community?" he asked. "What's a gay community?"

"You don't know?" Baird asked. Bill shook his head. "Well," Baird said, "you're about to find out."

It had been hard, as a Teamster, for Baird to ask the Black Panthers and Arab storekeepers to support a Teamster-led boycott. As the beer distributors rightly pointed out, the Teamsters was an openly racist union. These were the Teamsters' dark days. Jimmy Hoffa was in prison. The union's name was synonymous with corruption. Baird had had to talk long and hard about common cause to move the Panthers. But that, he figured, was easy compared with his next task. Because if the Teamsters were rough on minorities, they were murder on gays. The burly men in windbreakers may have been sufficiently sensitized not to say "nigger" in public, but they hadn't yet learned not to say "faggot." If the Coors boycott was going to work in San Francisco, Baird felt, the Teamsters needed the gays.

The man to see, Baird knew, was Harvey Milk, owner of a camera shop on Castro Street. He'd run for the city Board of Supervisors the year before, and though he'd lost, Milk's strong run as an openly gay candidate was a first. His campaign had become a rallying point for the city's gays.

Castro Camera looked nothing like a camera store to Allan Baird. A barber chair dominated the storefront, which seemed more like a living room—with couches and easy chairs—than like a place of business. Milk was tall and thin, with a craggy charismatic face. He had been an investment banker in New York—and a Goldwater supporter—before moving west, coming out, and involving himself in the fight to end discrimination against gays. His camera shop was his political headquarters.

Milk installed Baird in the barber chair, pulled a stool up beside him, and bade him speak.

Baird laid out the Teamsters' beef with Coors. He described how he'd brought minority groups into the boycott. Milk let him talk for a while and then put up a hand; he knew all that. And he knew Coors's record on gays, of course. It seemed to Baird that Milk had been awaiting his visit. Milk explained that he was always looking for ways to ally homosexuals with other oppressed minorities. He wanted them valued as partners in a wider struggle. It was hard, because the oppressed minorities— Hispanics, blacks, and Asians—all had special hangups about gays. "And organized labor," Milk said, "forget it."

Then he leaned forward. "What do you need?" Milk asked. Baird took a breath, knowing he was about to lay a tall order on someone who owed nothing to the Teamsters.

"I need Coors beer out of every gay bar in San Francisco and the East Bay," Baird said.

Milk snorted. "When the Teamsters asked us to support Cesar Chavez, your leadership didn't want to be up front about it," he said. "They didn't want anybody to know the Teamsters had made an alliance with the queers."

"I know," Baird said. "This time it's different. This time we want to acknowledge your support, proudly. At a joint press conference if you like."

Milk nodded. It was what he wanted to hear.

"Coors out of every gay bar in San Francisco," he laughed. "I like it." Baird shuddered with relief. "But," Milk continued, "you've got to do something for us."

"Name it," Baird said.

"I want the Teamsters to put gays on union beer trucks," Milk said. "I'll send some people around to the hiring hall." Baird had figured this was coming; it was the standard quid pro quo. His mind began racing to find a way to convince the stodgy and homophobic Teamster leadership to accept it. He prayed the gays Milk chose would be discreet. Maybe the Teamsters would never even know. . . .

"That's not all," Milk went on, breaking Baird's reverie. "When the guys show up, they have to say, 'I'm gay.' If they don't say 'I'm gay' you don't hire them. Got it?"

Baird nodded and shook Milk's hand, dumbstruck at the man's integrity. Milk wasn't just some ward heeler arranging favors for his people. And he didn't stop at getting homophobes to quit mistreating gays. Milk knew his constituency was never going to win power in the city until every lesbian and gay man was out of the closet and proudly identified with the movement. It was as much about transforming gays' attitudes about themselves as it was about changing the mainstream's attitudes toward gays. Baird never forgot the lesson.

Howard Wallace was one of Harvey Milk's troops. Wallace was tall, handsome, and broad-shouldered. When Milk needed gay men to announce their homosexuality inside a Teamsters hiring hall, he thought first of Howard Wallace. Wallace had come out of the closet only three years earlier, but already was a well-known activist in San Francisco. In the spring of 1971, Wallace had been a union organizer, keeping his homosexuality secret and helping put together a huge antiwar march. The march organizers had assembled contingents of blacks, Hispanics, labor, Indians, and women. Wallace was in the room one night when the labor people objected loudly to including a gay contingent. "What are you going to have next?" a union man asked. "Midgets?" Wallace decided soon after to come out, but he didn't give up on labor. When the TV show *Marcus Welby, M.D.* ran an insulting episode about a gay teacher, Wallace organized a joint petition drive by Gay Liberation and the American Federation of Teachers.

"I'm looking for a job as a beer driver," Wallace said loudly when he appeared before Baird in the Teamsters office. He looked around the room to make sure all the windbreakers were listening. *"And I'm gay."* Baird put him to work on a Falstaff truck. Within two weeks, there wasn't a gay bar in the Bay Area selling Coors beer.

Then internal Teamsters politics wrecked everything. Baird got a call from headquarters ordering him to stop supporting the UFW Gallo boycott and to sever all contacts with Chavez's people. The Teamsters were trying to organize the farm workers themselves. Baird told the Teamsters leadership that he wasn't going to break a useful relationship just so the Teamsters could improperly raid a brother union's membership. A few days later, Baird looked up from his desk at the boycott office to see a band of meat-faced giants in windbreakers storming through the door. "Out, out," the windbreakers said, physically pushing Baird and his staff out the door. In a twinkling, Baird and his people found themselves standing on the street, listening to the click of the door locking from inside. The Teamsters' Coors boycott was over.

But Harvey Milk, Howard Wallace, and the Bay Area's black, Hispanic, and Arab communities had discovered the Coors boycott as an organizing tool. Their beef with the Colorado brewer was only beginning.

It turned out that Joe Coors's dalliance with being a media baron cost him a lot more than $8 million. The day before Richard Nixon resigned the presidency in August 1974, he nominated Joe to sit on the board of the Corporation for Public Broadcasting, an agency Joe wanted badly to reform. CPB nominations require Senate confirmation, and congressional Democrats decided to make an issue of Joe Coors's ownership of TVN. Installing Joe Coors on the CPB board, one Democrat said, "is like putting Yasir Arafat on the Israeli cabinet."

When Senate Democrats faced Joe during his CPB confirmation hearings, they got him to admit that he supported "the thoughts and ideas" of the John Birch Society and had given the controversial organization $6,000. The confirmation fight dragged on for fourteen excruciating months. The National Council of Hispanic Citizens and the American G.I. Forum took the opportunity of the hearings to tell the nation about their Coors boycott. The Black Media Coalition weighed in as well with a plea that the Senate reject Joe for the CPB board. To make matters worse, the EEOC chose the summer of Joe's hearings to file the discrimination charges it began investigating when Corky Gonzalez first started boycotting Coors in 1966. Coors had "intentionally engaged in unlawful employment practices" for ten years against blacks, women, and Hispanics, the EEOC said.

Paul Weyrich wisely chose this moment to appear before Joe with his hand out again. Wouldn't you love to see some of those liberal senators thrown out of Washington? Weyrich asked Joe. Heritage is great, Weyrich said, but it can only do so much. We conservatives can't just suck our thumbs and dream up policy analyses. Watergate is going to make it extra tough next November. We need an *operational* outfit in Washington. We need a street-fighting army to get conservatives elected and send this bunch of liberals packing.

Once again, Joe eagerly dug into his pocket . He also walked around the Coors brewery and asked for contributions. His son Jeffrey gave him $500, as did Lowell Sund and several other Coors executives. A group of Coors employees' wives bundled up $5,000 in contributions. Thus was launched Committee for the Survival of a Free Congress. In April 1975, Weyrich mailed a letter—signed by Republican Senator James McClure of Idaho—to fifty thousand targeted Americans. "I am writing to you today to ask for help in defeating one hundred of the most liberal, anti-business, and pro-welfare congressmen on Capitol Hill," the letter said. "If we can gear up in one hundred congressional races we will deal the liberals a staggering defeat and turn this country away from socialism and prevent a communist defeat of America." More than $400,000 came in response. The effort did not endear Joe to the Senate Democrats still deciding his fate on the CPB board. (Among the conservatives the Committee for the Survival of a Free Congress helped elect in 1976 were Senator Richard Lugar and Congressman Dan Quayle of Indiana, and Senator Orrin Hatch of Utah. Incumbents who held their seats with CSFC support were, in the Senate, Barry Goldwater of Arizona, Bob Dole of Kansas, Peter Domenici of New Mexico, Jesse Helms of North Carolina, Bob Packwood of Oregon, and Strom Thurmond of South

Carolina; in the House, Trent Lott of Mississippi and Jack Kemp of New York.)

Joe made his own confirmation troubles worse. In the midst of the process, CPB prepared to air a documentary about the funeral industry based on Jessica Mitford's critique, *The American Way of Death*. At the request of a friend who owned a Denver mortuary, Joe wrote Henry Loomis, president of CPB, lamenting that the service might air a film that "wrongly attacks this industry." Joe promised Loomis he would "pay close attention" to such attacks "if I ever become confirmed on your fine board." Loomis made the letter public; between it and Joe's ownership of the dying TVN, the Senate rejected his nomination. Joe was crestfallen.

During the creation of Heritage and TVN, Joe had remained in the background, little known outside Colorado. With the fight over his CPB appointment, Joe acquired a national reputation. During the Senate hearings, in May 1975, *The Washington Post* ran a two-part page-one series on Joe's political life in Washington. The story was reprinted in newspapers across the country. Full of names, dates, and figures, and reprinted from one of the country's most prestigious newspapers—the story confirmed many people's vague sense that Coors was a right-wing company. *Newsweek* and *The New York Times Magazine* followed *The Washington Post* with their own long profiles of Joe, adding information about the Hispanic boycott, the EEOC charges, and Coors busting the building-trades unions out of the brewery. Around the same time, the U.S. Tax Court ruled that Coors had "made payments to influence legislation" and then claimed them as tax deductions; Coors owed more than $5 million dollars in tax, interest, and penalties. The bull's-eye on Joe Coors's nose grew more prominent.

Sensing they'd drawn more attention to themselves than was healthy for the company, Joe and Bill created the Adolph Coors Foundation to manage donations, distancing themselves, at least a little, from their political philanthropy. Joe even asked Ev Barnhardt, the brewery's sales director, if he should "back off the heavy political stuff" to avoid alienating customers.

"Nah," Barnhardt told him with a slap on the shoulder. "Nothing can hurt our sales."

The nightmare envisioned by Coors's brewery manager in 1959 came to pass in 1974. Cold-filtering had rendered better-tasting beer than pasteurizing, but the risk of contamination circled above the plant for years like a vulture. Finally, in June—just when the beer-drinking season was starting in earnest and Press Tab was driving Coors's customers crazy— the vulture struck. Bacteria lurking in a lubricant somehow came in contact with the fresh beer as it squirted into the cans at blinding speed. Because of the brewery's passion for freshness, the contaminated cans— like all others—were hurried out of the plant and onto railcars, most of them to California. Lactobacillus wasn't dangerous, but it was disgusting; the bacteria grew mucuslike strands in the beer. By the time the company knew something was amiss, retail customers were furiously returning six-packs of slimy beer.

The Internal Revenue Service chose this moment to decide that the trust agreement Mr. Coors had written up by hand was prepared "in expectation of death" and could not legally shield the family from an enormous inheritance-tax liability. Bill wrote a check to the state of Colorado for more than $400,000 to cover state liability. The federal bill came to about $15 million. As Coors was in the process of expanding into eastern and southern Texas at the time, the company suddenly didn't have the cash available. It faced two choices: borrowing from a bank or going public by selling shares.

Borrowing was out of the question. Adolph the founder had repeatedly said "never." But going public sounded like fun to Bill and Joe. Even with the California boycott and the product recall, Coors's annual sales were up to around $500 million. The brewery realized a $9 return on every barrel it shipped, almost twice that of Anheuser-Busch. Bill and Joe were proud to be offering shares in such a company.

It seemed to Lowell Sund that given their aversion to both taxes and outside influence, Joe and Bill were remarkably sanguine about going public. "Don't do it," Lowell urged them. "You'll be living in a fishbowl." But Bill and Joe argued that going public would accentuate the positive aspects of Coors's reputation—the mystique of the beer—and deemphasize the negatives: Joe's politics. As for ceding control of the company to outsiders, Bill and Joe had a solution; they'd offer only 10 percent of the company's shares, and nothing but Class B nonvoting stock. All the voting stock would remain in the family's hands.

The only question was what price to ask for the shares. Bill, Joe, and Lowell Sund thought $16.00, or maybe $16.50. The investment bank Dillon Read, though, convinced the Coors brothers to ask twice that. Bill, Joe, Lowell Sund, and the rest of the board gathered at Joe's house at five-thirty on the morning of the offering to await news. The sale was a huge success: All the shares sold in a single day at $32.00 apiece. Lowell Sund flew to New York to collect the proceeds, and was driven, mysteriously, to a dingy warehouse district in New Jersey. It turned out Dillon Read kept an office there just to close deals because the taxes in New Jersey were lower than in New York. Sund was taken to an elegant office incongruously situated atop a grimy industrial block and handed a check for $120 million—more than enough to pay the inheritance tax and finance a planned expansion into eastern and southern Texas. Sund turned and handed the check to a banker, who snapped it into a briefcase.

Within a week the "Coors mystique" was lost on Wall Street. The reality of investing in an archaic, parochial company and not having any say in its management eclipsed the company's Rocky Mountain glitter. The stock price fell ten points, leaving many investors feeling burned. Securities analysts, whose job is to recommend stocks to investors, summoned Bill Coors to New York for a grilling, and Bill, his prestige and financial security newly dependent on these money-minded strangers, was obliged to go. The analysts wanted to know how Coors, with only 8 percent of the national market, was planning to compete with giants like Anheuser-Busch, which held 25 percent. Was Coors thinking of a bigger expansion? they asked him. "Perhaps," Bill said, "if we can guarantee the quality of our product."

What about marketing? they asked. How will Coors compete with Anheuser-Busch—and comers like Miller—if it wasn't willing to spend more on marketing? Bill gave a folksy chuckle and delivered a line that would make him infamous in investors' circles during the coming dark years. "We make the best beer in the world," Bill told Wall Street, "we don't need marketing."

[
part
Two
]

8

Baby Steps

Peter Coors grew up easily. As a boy, he bathed in stories of travail his grandfather and immigrant great-grandfather had faced. The early orphaning of Adolph Coors, his intrepid ocean crossing and venture into the wild West, the hewing of the brewery from great vision and toil, the sacrifices to keep workers employed during Prohibition and World War II—these were Genesis and Exodus, *The Iliad* and *The Odyssey* for the Coors family. Still, for Peter, they were just stories. Born in 1946, he arrived as the fat years were dawning. The home his parents kept in Golden wasn't opulent; in keeping with Coors tradition, it did reflect the middle-class comforts of Golden's better neighborhood. More important, the tone of Peter's childhood was unfailingly optimistic. Well into his adulthood, the biggest problem for the Adolph Coors Company seemed to be making enough beer to meet an insatiable demand. While Peter was learning to climb trees and ride a bike, to fish and to hunt in the mountains around Golden, the company was pioneering the aluminum can, mastering cold-filtering, and expanding into new territories. The family's beer was stylish and of peerless quality. The Coorses didn't need to flaunt their accomplishments; to carry the name Coors meant to possess not only personal wealth but the dedication and work ethic to make visionary dreams come true.

Peter entered the Phillips Exeter Academy at age fourteen, a year after his Uncle Adolph was killed. He suffered with his family in Golden the shock of the kidnapping and murder, but was spared the dismal, loyalty-obsessed years following the tragedy, when the newly widowed Aunt Mary declined into alcoholism and Uncle Bill and Aunt Geraldine divorced. The timing of Peter's departure to Exeter was emblematic of the boy; it put him at a half-step's remove.

Peter distanced himself from the family's next trauma, too; the Pyrrhic rebellion of his older brother, Joe Jr. To Joe Jr.'s amazement, Peter, then sixteen, stood back in cool neutrality during this first real mutiny. "It's between Dad and Joe," Peter said blithely, standing clear. Not that seventeen-year-old Jeff rose to his brother's side, either. But Peter was so *cool* about it. No open soul-searching, no abject apologies, no audible speeches to the shaving mirror. Eleven-year-old Grover and six-year-old John were held below the fray. But Joe made no secret of his belief that he'd thrown himself on a grenade for Jeff and Peter and was therefore surprised to find their bayonets in his back.

Peter followed family tradition from Exeter to Cornell, and there walked the same careful line on the Vietnam War and civil rights—two issues it was hard to stay neutral about on college campuses in the mid-1960s. To the extent he could, Peter behaved as though the sixties weren't happening. He studied hard at industrial engineering. He managed the Psi Upsilon fraternity house, and joined the crew and ski teams. He was an easygoing, kindhearted presence around campus, good for a pickup basketball game or a round of cards. Six feet five inches tall with a Sunday-school haircut and brightly shaven cheeks, Peter ambled around Cornell in his letter sweater and creased chinos while shouting demonstrators blockaded the ROTC building and hippies lounged in the quad smoking reefer. He lent his cheerful nature to newcomers, volunteering to help show freshmen around campus during orientation week. He returned from vacations with cases of his family's coveted beer and was generous with them. But when the talk turned to politics, as it inevitably did in those days, Peter withdrew. He was neither for the war nor against it, neither a civil rights activist nor a redneck. "Sure it's a bad war," he'd say, "but don't we have to stop the communists somewhere?" Or: "The Negroes deserve full equality, but that Stokely Carmichael is going a little too far." He participated in no antiwar marches or sit-ins, but neither did he join the kind of conservative counterdemonstrations his father championed. Like the row between Dad and Joe Jr., Peter kept the antiwar and civil rights movements at a distance. While armed black students took over the Cornell student union the spring Peter graduated, he plowed on toward a useful diploma and a quieter life.

His father's controversial war on liberals was painful to him. Everyone around him was excited about the sixties' social changes, and yet his own father was trying to turn back the tide—and in far more public a fashion than was customary for the family. Home on a break, Peter drove up to Boulder to attend a Psi Upsilon party on the CU campus. He charged through the front door smiling widely, expecting a good time, but instead was confronted in the vestibule by a longhair yelling about Peter's "fascist" father. Peter's eyes grew wide and his face went as crimson as the C on his sweater. Then he turned and left the party.

Like all Coors men, Peter escaped the draft. Though the draft lottery gave him number 63 at the height of the fighting in Vietnam, he was classified 1-Y—available in time of war—and was never called.

Peter prudently waited until the August after graduation to marry his girlfriend, a premed Cornell student from upstate New York named Marilyn Gross. Their formal wedding took place the same week that 400,000 of their contemporaries were wallowing in mud and music in another corner of rural New York. For Mr. and Mrs. Peter Coors, Woodstock might as well have been happening on another planet.

Though a competent engineering student, Peter was the first of his family since Uncle Ad to relish the intangible, personality-dependent world of business. In this respect Peter was more like his voluble mother than his taciturn father. He was too sociable to bend his mind forever to slide rules and numbers, and looked forward to a career in marketing or advertising—anywhere but at the Coors brewery.

Like his father and uncle, Peter dreamed of making it on his own. And like his father and uncle, he would not. Peter and Marilyn enrolled at the University of Denver graduate school, Marilyn to study cellular biology en route to medical school and Peter to become the first Coors to earn a master's of business administration. By the time he achieved his one-year M.B.A., Pete and Marilyn both had reversed course. Peter bowed to what he later called "the inevitable." He crawled into the fermentation tank in 1970, the year his grandfather died. "I'll end up there anyway," he told Marilyn when he received his M.B.A. "Why waste time?" Marilyn traded a career in medicine for one as a Coors wife. While Peter worked at the brewery, she decorated their home and worked as a substitute teacher. In April 1971, the former premed student began noticing odd symptoms in herself and became convinced she was dying of cancer. The correct diagnosis was pregnancy. The first of Peter and Marilyn's six children, a girl named Melissa, was born the following January.

Though Peter began his career at Coors on the same lowly rung as his cousin Adolph did, he was given a business-office job when he asked for one. Max Goodwin, the bookish ceramics worker thrust years earlier into being controller, was now, in his prim middle age, the company's chief financial officer. Bill and Joe put the twenty-five-year-old Peter under Goodwin's wing and gave him the grand title "director of financial planning." Making Peter director of financial planning of a company that did no financial planning might have been his father's and uncle's idea of a sinecure, but Peter took the job seriously.

He was amazed, after earning an M.B.A., to find that the Adolph Coors Company—a $350 million industrial corporation—still kept its records by hand in ledger books, using the antiquated double-entry accounting method. Coors still had no accountants or lawyers on staff. The company's "advertising department" consisted entirely of old Harris Hamlin, an amiable dinosaur who'd started during World War II as a production worker and had inherited advertising after Bill Moomey left. About all Hamlin did was send a photographer into the hills once a year with a sleeping bag and a Jeep to shoot footage of bubbling brooks.

The sprawling industrial plant with its thousands of workers was essentially being run like a mom-and-pop grocery store. Five years after becoming controller, Goodwin still hadn't produced the thing he noticed his very first day that the brewery lacked: a proper financial plan. He assigned the task to Peter.

"They'll fight you over there," Goodwin said. "Financial planning isn't something your grandfather or great-grandfather did, so nobody thinks they need it. Your uncle Bill included. He's a genius when it comes to engineering, but he doesn't think anything else means a damn."

Goodwin went on, wanting Peter to have every advantage.

"Let me give you some advice," he said. "Your father is the business brain. When it comes to business, your father is more decisive, more forceful, and more insightful than Bill. If you need something, go to him."

Peter started walking around the brewery with a notebook, asking questions. How much does this cost? How much do we spend on that? What's your budget? What's your accounts receivable? In the malthouse and in finishing, in the brewhouse and on the bottle line, Coors workers and managers often didn't understand Peter's questions. They'd never thought in terms of "income forecasting" or "sources and uses of funds"—two elements of a financial plan Peter had been taught in business school to compile. In truth, money wasn't something people talked a lot about at Coors. It was a by-product of the brewery's real work— making good beer—rather than an end in itself. Success was measured by quality and barrelage, not earnings. The money came in, the money went out, it was distributed generously to the workers, and nobody thought much more about it. So Peter was, to many at the brewery, a pest—a college boy asking a lot of fancy questions about money. On the other hand, nobody wanted to tell Joe's boy to get lost. They complied, if grudgingly. When they didn't have the number Peter needed, they spent a couple of days getting it for him. Slowly, Peter's questions began to accomplish two tasks: They helped him assemble the brewery's first real financial plan, and they got everybody at the brewery thinking more the way an M.B.A. is trained to think—about money.

Bill and Joe gave twenty-seven-year-old Peter a seat on the board in 1973, alongside themselves, Peter's older brother Jeffrey, Ev Barnhardt, Max Goodwin, Lowell Sund, and half a dozen crusty old engineers from Mr. Coors's day. Unique among them, Peter read the marketing press and was following John Murphy's successful repositioning of Miller High Life. What he saw both excited and frightened him. With the portrait of Adolph Coors, Jr., scowling down at him, Peter argued for an additional job: director of market research. Bill flapped a hand at him. What's to research? he wanted to know. People drink beer because they like it. The better the beer, the more they'll drink.

Max Goodwin nudged Peter with his elbow and motioned with his chin toward Joe. Peter turned to his father, who had flown west for the meeting. Between TVN and the startup of the Heritage Foundation, Pete's dad was spending more and more time back east. This was a rare chance for Peter to appeal to his dad in person.

"The beer industry is changing," Peter said. "If you look at the demographics—"

"Our sales have doubled in five years," Bill interrupted. "Doubled!"

"But we have to look *forward*," Peter urged. "The baby boom is aging, which suggests, net-net, a shrinking of the beer-drinking cohort in the mid-near term."

"Beer drinking what?" Bill asked.

Bill and Joe had no idea what Peter was talking about and no discernible interest in learning. But Peter pleaded. It wouldn't hurt to know more about the market, he said. Think of it as combat intelligence. Joe listened, nodded, and approved Peter's plan—provided Peter didn't act on this intelligence before checking with the board. Bill, somewhat more warily, gave his consent, too. The other board members quickly signed on.

Peter began visiting Coors distributors around the West in 1974, partly to gather information about their customers and partly to smooth feathers ruffled by Press Tab, the bacteria contamination, and the Bay Area boycott. The distributors also had something new to gripe to Peter about: his father.

The Democratic party had called for wage and price controls and Joe, secure in his newfound political sophistication, had acted on the rhetoric as though it were a done deal. He'd advised Bill to raise prices before the "new government controls" could go into effect. Bill, a bit dazzled by Joe's political connections, took his brother's advice. Coors raised prices 9 percent in the summer of 1974, and its competitors didn't. Price controls were never imposed, leaving Coors 9 percent more expensive than Bud and Miller during the crucial season. The Coors distributors, already coping with a product recall and the California boycott, threw up their hands.

Peter didn't share the family view that distributors were ungrateful parasites. They were his link to the people who drank Coors beer. He took them out to dinner, to professional basketball games, and on hunting and skiing trips. He toured their warehouses and took notes on their suggestions. Long-neck bottles are popular in bars, distributors told him. How come Coors doesn't offer one? We need more advertising, they said. You can watch TV all night and not see a Coors commercial, but you'll see a Bud or Miller spot every ten minutes. While he traveled, Peter drank a lot of beer in a lot of bars, handing out his business card and buying rounds for the house.

Peter loved his job. He knew there wasn't another member of the family who could do what he did—chat people up, make small talk, engage in the windy pleasantries Coorses had disdained since his great-grandfather first sought a transfer from the front office to the brewhouse in Dortmund. As Peter chatted, a whole new frontier opened before his eyes, a frontier in which the brewery could profit by handling its distributors and its customers with as much care and respect as it handled its beer. Peter became legendary among bartenders. One morning he walked into a Mexican restaurant in Denver, took off his jacket, and helped the manager install new taps. In a blue-collar bar in Spokane, he beat everybody at pool and still paid for the beers. At a roadside inn in California, it was Peter Coors himself who hung the Coors neon in the window.

One afternoon in Boise, Peter and the local distributor were walking bar to bar, randomly questioning bartenders, when the distributor led him straight past one that had a Coors sign in the window. Peter stopped.

"Aren't we going in here?" he asked.

"Nah," the distributor said. "You don't want to go in there."

"Why not?"

The man laughed mirthlessly, fidgeted, and looked side to side. "It's a, uh, gay bar."

"So what?" Peter said. He pointed to the sign in the window. "They're our customers. Let's go in and have a beer."

In they marched, Peter in the lead. Boise had a small gay community in those days and the patrons at the bar recoiled from the strangers, expecting trouble. Peter extended a long arm to the bartender and illuminated him with a beaming smile. "Pete Coors," he said.

"You're kidding," the bartender said. Peter gave him a card, and ordered a round of Coors draft for everybody in the bar.

Until that night, the Bay Area gay boycott had been to Peter Coors an abstract nuisance. Now Peter learned for the first time the reasons behind it. He listened as the Boise men explained to him, in heartfelt terms, how offensive the lie detector was.

The men weren't just homosexuals; they were also serious beer drinkers. One, wielding a pint of syrupy black Guinness, said he wished Coors made a heavier beer as well as its lightweight one. Another said he liked Coors the way it was, but wished it came in quart bottles. The bartender chimed in with the news that Coors draft, packed at higher pressure than other beers, caused problems with his taps. Peter took it all in, turning his full attention to each man, repeating back criticisms and suggestions, jotting notes on a cocktail napkin.

As market research, Peter's effort was sporadic, unscientific, and laughably understaffed. But for the first time in the company's century-long history, a member of the Coors family was listening to beer drinkers and trying to figure out what they wanted. Seven decades into the twentieth century, the Adolph Coors Company was taking its first baby steps toward joining it.

In the midst of the drubbing Joe took at the hands of Senate Democrats during the CPB board hearings, a Coors sales executive asked, "Why are you putting yourself through this, Joe?"

"If we don't get involved in our government," Joe told him earnestly, "things like this brewery won't exist anymore."

To Joe it was all of a piece: The free enterprise system and unfettered economic freedom were the foundation of the family business. He applied himself to their defense with a zeal to match Holly's faith in Christ, and at times Joe's political rhetoric seemed borrowed from a Pentecostal revival. He warned of dire consequences for inaction and expected total commitment from those who shared his interests. How can you stand by "inept and unorganized," he asked a group of Denver financiers, "while the environmentalists and radicals walk all over us?" Beware the "tentacles of bureaucracy," he warned. "One half of the public today believes big business is the source of all our troubles."

The Republican party, in Joe's view, was barely better than the Democrats. Joe met with twenty-seven other bedrock conservatives to try to deny Gerald Ford and the relatively liberal Nelson Rockefeller the 1976 nomination. The man who could "lead us back," they decided, was the former governor of California, Ronald Reagan. Joe helped organize a meeting at the Madison Hotel in Washington to convince Reagan to form a new party to the right of the Republicans. Reagan laughed off the suggestion, knowing that bolting the Republican party was political suicide, but he managed to hold the loyalty of Joe's highly ideological wing of the party. Reagan knew there was nobody in the party to his own right.

And that gave him room to woo the center by announcing his running mate in 1976 would be Pennsylvania Senator Richard Schweiker. To Joe Coors-style conservatives, Schweiker—a school-prayer advocate who opposed gun control, abortion, welfare, and busing—was a liberal. The telephone of Reagan's public relations chief Michael Deaver almost melted with the heat of the calls he got. "I'm sending you and your friend Ronny Reagan thirty pieces of silver," one longtime supporter said. Another told Deaver, "I'd rather my doctor called and said my wife had the clap." Joe Coors didn't have to talk to Mike Deaver, though. He picked up the phone and called Reagan personally. "Ron," he said, "you really disappointed your conservative supporters, including me."

But Joe hung on, not only because he had no other horse in the race but also because he genuinely adored Ronald Reagan. He swallowed his disappointment over the ticket and went to the convention as an energetic

Reagan-Schweiker delegate. He introduced a platform resolution against busing. He pushed a plank to phase out federal aid to public schools and day care centers because they "hand education in [children's] early years over to the government." He introduced a resolution opposing "federally sponsored" books which "undermine and deride the values of our society and the Judeo-Christian ethic . . . with the pseudo-religion of secular humanism." He fought a plank affirming GOP support of the Equal Rights Amendment. He was on the losing side of every battle, with the sole exception of striking platform language that criticized oil companies for profiteering from the energy crisis.

Joe was at his most flamboyant when he had manufactured 2,259 plastic records of the speech Walter Mondale had just delivered to the Democratic National Convention accepting the vice presidential nomination. Both Mondale and presidential candidate Jimmy Carter had pledged not to make Ford's pardon of Nixon a campaign issue, but Mondale mentioned the pardon in his speech. To Joe, the low blow highlighted the Democrats' perfidy and showed they were running scared. Every delegate at the convention found one slipped under his or her door.

Joe had long ago stopped putting John Birch Society literature in his workers' pay envelopes, but he still liked to preach conservatism to them. He thought of a clever way to teach his workers that taxes were too high. He ordered the Coors payroll department to stop deducting taxes from paychecks for a few weeks—and then to withhold all the accumulated taxes from a single check, all but wiping it out. It was a headache for payroll, and all it taught the workers was that Joe didn't mind screwing around with their paychecks to make a political point. Joe's nemesis, the IRS, eventually ordered Coors to stop it. Between his political organizations and the Cornell commencements, Joe was spending less time at the brewery and, in the view of some of his people, losing touch. Perhaps his father had been right to let Joe enter the bigger arena of politics, which seemed better suited to his either-or personality than running the Porcelain plant. Joe was wielding a lot of influence on the national scene and he wasn't doing the brewery any harm. Or so it seemed in the mid-1970s.

John Murphy, the new president of Miller Brewing Company, was pleased with the revival of Miller High Life. But Murphy had spent too many years marketing cigarettes to be satisfied with having only one product in the marketplace. He ordered new formulas brewed and campaigns built around them—Miller Malt, Miller Ale, and an economy beer called Milwaukee Extra. None caught on. Murphy kept at it, though. Philip Morris wasn't going to recoup its half-billion-dollar investment in Miller with just one brand on the shelves.

Among the properties Philip Morris had bought with Miller was a little Chicago brewery called Meisterbrau. Meisterbrau was a low-calorie beer, and Murphy had paid it no attention because the history of low-calorie beers was bleak. Early in the 1960s, New York's Rheingold brewery had pushed a low-calorie beer called Gablinger's, and it flopped. Beer drinking and health consciousness didn't go together, it seemed. But it wasn't the beer Meisterbrau made that interested John Murphy. The little brewery had trademark-registered a cute misspelling of the word "light"—"Lite"—in a distinctive script. That, Murphy decided, had potential as a unique selling proposition. It wasn't the early sixties anymore; jogging was in vogue in 1972, as was decaffeinated coffee and "spritzers"—white wine diluted with soda water. Baby boomers were trying to delay the slide toward middle age by being more active and health-conscious. A low-calorie beer might work better in the mid-1970s than it had in the early 1960s, especially if it tasted good.

Rheingold had made Gablinger's low-calorie simply by pouring water into it. But Murphy learned that what packs calories into beer is the sugars that remain in the beer after fermenting. Murphy ordered Meisterbrau to ferment its beer longer, and to add a newly discovered enzyme that converted those sugars to alcohol. Then he had the extra alcohol drawn off to bring the brew down to 3.6 percent. The result was a reasonably good-tasting beer with only 96 calories per can instead of the usual 140. The process was more expensive than simply adding water, but Murphy deemed it worthwhile.

Murphy chose Anderson, Indiana, for the first test marketing of the reformulated Meisterbrau Lite because it was a blue-collar town of traditional male beer drinkers. The beer was locally advertised as having a third fewer calories and its success surprised Murphy. He ordered national blind taste tests in 1973 and got the same encouraging result. The taste was fine, and the idea of a low-calorie beer appealed to a broad segment of the public. But much to Murphy's surprise, if the beer's calorie count was stressed too heavily, it had the opposite effect: It repelled people. Too heavy a hand on the low-calorie theme could make the beer seem wimpy to Joe Six-pack. The last thing Murphy wanted was to end up with a "woman's beer."

Once he had a satisfactory product, Murphy moved it from Meisterbrau to Miller. He peeled the "Lite" trademark off Meisterbrau and pasted it to the flagship brand. Miller Lite—and an entirely new category of beer—was born.

McCann-Erickson decided that the way to avoid Miller Lite being relegated to the category of "woman's beer" was to advertise it with manly locker-room humor. They lined up a string of current and former athletes and had them argue in a locker room about whether Miller Lite tastes great or is less filling. Calories were mentioned only once per ad, almost as an aside. The ads began in 1975 and were hilarious. In one, the gigantic Bubba Smith praised the "easy-open cans" and tore the entire top off one—no way, after that, would Miller Lite be a "woman's beer." All the ads ended with the same memorable slogan: "Everything you ever wanted in a beer . . . and less."

The ads weren't just good, they were everywhere. Philip Morris had never put much marketing muscle behind its nontobacco products, but this time Cullman sensed a winner and took the plunge. Suddenly, obscure little Miller was spending three dollars a barrel on advertising—twice the industry average. It was hard to watch fifteen minutes of television without seeing a Miller Lite ad. Within a single year, Miller's profits soared from $6 million to $29 million. From a standing start, Miller had 9 percent of the beer market, and was climbing.

All eyes turned to Coors, which was, after all, "America's Fine Light Beer." How would Coors respond?

Bill Coors poured a Miller Lite and held the glass up to eye level. The color was a flat, weak yellow. He sniffed—hardly any aroma at all. Bill tilted the glass and noted the scant foam disintegrating against the side. Finally, he took a mouthful, and knew at once the nonfermentable sugars—the complex carbohydrates that give beer its texture, aftertaste, and mouthfeel—had been boiled out of the beer. He set down the glass, declared the beer inferior, and refused to think any more about it.

He had good reason to feel optimistic. In none of the eleven states his brewery served was Coors's market share below 35 percent, and in some it was as much as twice that. The "Coors mystique" was now a nationally recognized phenomenon. In what turned into a minor scandal, President Gerald Ford's Secret Service detail got caught on a Denver stopover loading Air Force One with crates of Coors. The President owned up that the beer was for him; Wednesday was Mexican-food day at the White House, he said, and he'd become enamored of Coors while skiing at Vail. Paul Newman was photographed holding a can of Coors and called it "the best American beer, bar none." John Denver had released his hit "Rocky Mountain High" in 1972, lending the Coorses' state a rosy glow. (Coors briefly considered hiring John Denver to sing Coors ads. But Denver was caught hoarding gasoline in a huge underground tank during the 1973 energy crisis, and Coors backed away.) East Coast college students helped finance their educations by driving west during vacations and loading up their cars with Coors to sell at usurious profit back home. Bill was ambivalent about presidents and college students hightailing Coors beer east. It pleased him that Coors had such a great reputation even where it wasn't sold, but the thought of all that beer traveling unrefrigerated pained him. The beer wouldn't taste as good as it should when it arrived. He worried that beer drinkers would taste substandard Coors and think it the genuine article. Bill even went so far as to run full-page newspaper ads in East Coast papers with the heading: "Please Don't Drink Coors Beer," and it was no gimmick. He really didn't want Coors beer traveling warm back east. Emblazoned with the Coors logo, the ads only heightened the beer's mysterious appeal. So rigid was Bill's mania for delivering refrigerated beer only through authorized dealers that he refused a dying movie star's wish. The actor Steve McQueen, who had made laetrile famous, was in the last months of cancer in a Chicago hospital when he heard that Coors was lower in carcinogens than other beers. He called Golden personally to order several cases. But because Illinois was outside Coors territory, Bill refused to send him any. His sales director had to ship it on the sly.

Despite the "Coors mystique," the Coors's distributors were distraught. Until recently, they'd been easy millionaires. Boycotts, a product recall, and a hard-to-open can were one thing; now the competition was coming at them with a whole new weapon—light beer—and they stood unarmed in the marketplace.

"Relax," Bill told them in his characteristic engineer-speak. "Miller Lite is nothing but alcohol and water. It's almost utterly lacking in complex carbohydrates!"

"But it's gobbling market share!" the distributors cried.

"Miller Lite is bad beer," Bill said. "Coors doesn't need to respond to bad beer."

Miller, meanwhile, crept up and snatched from Coors the coveted number-four spot behind Anheuser-Busch, Schlitz, and Pabst. One of Bill's executives—new to the company—sent him a memo suggesting that "Coors consider an entry into this new market." He got a terse memo in return. "Coors already makes the best light beer in America. We will not make a 'light beer' and I consider it heresy to suggest it.—W. K. Coors." Bill assured his horrified distributors that people would soon tire of drinking Miller Lite. He promised that as long as Coors continued making the best beer in the country, its dominance would be assured. When someone suggested boosting the ad budget—Coors was spending only sixty cents a barrel on ads, one third of the industry average and one fifth of Miller Lite's ad budget—Bill said he wouldn't hear of diverting money from brewing to make ads. He repeated his favorite mantra: "Nobody is going to decide what beer to drink on the strength of a thirty-second commercial."

Bill Coors was so unruffled by Miller Lite that he extended a limited olive branch to Local 366. His timing was good. Momentous events far from Golden were knocking the institutional legs out from under the Coors local and leaving it even weaker than ever.

First, AFL-CIO general secretary George Meany decided in early 1972 that his federation would take the unusual step of remaining neutral in the upcoming presidential election. The president of the Colorado AFL-CIO, though, defiantly declared his chapter's support for Senator George McGovern, the Democrats' candidate. Meany retaliated by placing the Colorado AFL-CIO in trusteeship—he took it over, in other words—because he believed maintaining organizational discipline was crucial to keeping the respect of industry.

A year later, Local 366's parent union—the Brewery, Flour, Cereal, and Soft Drink Workers International Union, based in Cincinnati—decided to leave the AFL-CIO and to affiliate with the Teamsters. The members of Local 366 didn't want any part of the change. During the grape boycott, when they had helped the United Farm Workers picket stores, the Teamsters had been their sworn enemy. The local decided to break with the departing International and become a DALU—a directly affiliated local union of the AFL-CIO.

Suddenly, Local 366 had no parent union, and was an afterthought of a labor federation both hostile to Colorado and ill suited for managing affairs on a local level. Already feeble, the local now was on its own.

When the brewery workers' contract came up for renegotiation in 1974, Bill was in an expansive mood. Neither the bacteria breakout nor the Bay Area boycott had yet occurred. Despite the drop in California sales owing to the other boycotts, the brewery was doing fabulously well—growing by at least 10 percent a year for more than a decade. Bill still thought that the Press Tab issue was a case of distributors bellyaching rather than a serious problem. Also, he was deeply into transcendental meditation and simply wasn't in a fighting mood. So he told Russ Hargis, who handled union matters for him, to be generous.

David Sickler led the talks on behalf of Local 366. Everything Sickler asked for, he got: strengthened seniority provisions, workers' input on setting shifts, a statute of limitations on reprimands, and a generous pay increase. Sickler's fellow union members thought the 1974 talks indicated a change of attitude on the part of Bill and Joe Coors toward the union. Sickler, though, was wary. He was a newshound and followed national politics more closely than most of the brewery workers. Joe Coors had become such a prominent conservative that Sickler knew he must have been embarrassed in front of his fellow right-wing industrialists to have a union operating in his brewery. "They broke eighteen unions in eight years," he reminded his friends. "Sooner or later they're going to come for us."

Adolph IV was miserable. Living alone in a rented apartment, he ventured to his job in the can plant daily, determined to make it up the Coors corporate ladder. But it was hard to watch Peter ascend as though fated for the things Adolph struggled fruitlessly to achieve. And if work life was tough, private life was worse. Adolph hated being separated from three-year-old Adolph V, whom everybody called Shane. The lawsuits from his failed real-estate career continued to sap his money and his energy. He was lonely and adrift, so he finally went home.

The B.J. he found was not the B.J. he remembered. She was thoroughly immersed in Christianity: praying constantly, evangelizing, referring every tiny detail of her day to her relationship to the Lord. Adolph had to admit she seemed calm and content, and very loving toward him. A Christian friend of his pressed a thin paperback into his hands: *Do*

Yourself a Favor: Love Your Wife, by H. Page Williams. It was a call for all men to be the "good king" of their households, the way God commanded. "A woman wants to be ruled," Williams wrote. "Her great desire is to be subject to her husband because God has ordained it so." Men who belittled, ridiculed, cheated on, or otherwise mistreated their wives were succumbing to Satan's tricks, Williams wrote, quoting the book of Ephesians: "For since a man and his wife are now one, a man is really doing himself a favor and loving himself when he loves his wife" (5:28). As Adolph read, he believed he felt his vision clearing.

One Sunday morning in early 1975, he accompanied B.J. and the Sunds to Cherry Hills Community Church and read with them the Sinner's Prayer. His Christian rebirth struck him in a fit of uncontrollable weeping. Kneeling beside his wife, tears streaming down his cheeks, Adolph delivered his life to the Lord and found the emptiness in his soul "instantly filled." He went back to work at the can plant, but without self-aggrandizing ambition. Now Adolph felt he had something genuine to share. In a brewing class he took, Adolph spent coffee breaks pressing his love of God upon his classmates.

That summer, Adolph and B.J. visited his fifty-five-year-old mother, Mary, and tried to talk her into accepting Jesus as her personal savior. Mary had gambled the city life she loved on the country life with Ad, and it had been paying off—until an instant of greed and savagery on the Turkey Creek bridge destroyed everything. Now, with her husband slaughtered, her firstborn dead of cancer, and her life sodden with alcohol, Mary listened to Spike explain her misfortune in terms of Jesus. In inspirational speeches, Adolph would later describe this conversation as "brief and meaningful." But she didn't commit; she was leaving that day for a vacation at a friend's home in Aspen.

The next evening, Mary tumbled down the stairs of the Aspen chalet and was rushed to the hospital with head injuries. By dawn she was dead. Adolph publicly remembers her death as "a massive stroke." Either way, Adolph knew the real cause of death was her consuming hatred for Joseph Corbett, a hatred that burned in Adolph's own chest. The sight of where that hatred had taken his mother moved Adolph. Jesus had not hated even those who nailed him to the cross, and with his dying breath asked God to forgive them. Should not Adolph Coors IV forgive the murderer of his father? Adolph struggled. He prayed. He wanted to see Corbett face-to-face, to confront the man who had destroyed his family. One morning when the aspens were turning gold on the hillsides,

Adolph made the four-hour drive south to the penitentiary at Canon City. Corbett, who'd never admitted to the crime, wouldn't see him. Adolph drove home. He tried again a few months later, and again Corbett refused to see him. Again, Adolph drove home to Golden, praying. He was searching for the power within himself to forgive and when he felt he'd found it, he drove to Canon City one more time. As he expected, Joseph Corbett refused to walk from his cell to the visitors room. But this time Adolph was ready. He handed the guard a Bible for Corbett, into which he'd inserted a note. "I want to forgive you for what you did to my family," the note read. "And I ask for your forgiveness for the hatred we've had for you all these years." Adolph got back in his car feeling as though a cinder block had been lifted off his chest. For the first time in seventeen years, he felt free of his father's murder.

A few years later, on the anniversary of his father's death, he left the Adolph Coors Company forever in order to found Denver Outreach, "to reach out to Denver's executive and professional people with the word of God." He hosted a series of Christian dinner parties at the Cherry Hills Country Club "to make sure they're getting fed the word of God," he said. The Apostle Matthew, who spoke of such things, might have viewed Adolph's new job as stuffing camels through the eye of a needle. But First Corinthians says, "Let each one remain in the same calling in which he was called" (7:20). Adolph was called while a hustling suburban entrepreneur, so that was the flock he served. "I feel a need," the thirty-three-year-old Adolph said, "to spread the word of God to professional people."

Philip Morris was transforming the Miller Brewing Company, but that was only the center attraction of what was fast becoming, in the mid-1970s, a brewing-industry three-ring circus.

Stage left, Schlitz—the nation's onetime leader and still number two—was destroying itself with breathtaking speed.

Stage right, Anheuser-Busch was performing a full-blown Gothic opera, complete with a hundred-day strike, a patricidal coup, and the massacre of most of its executive corps.

Peter Coors watched it all happen, but couldn't get his father and uncle to pay attention—until it was almost too late.

The Joseph Schlitz Brewing Company, founded by August Uihlein in 1850, had expanded out of Milwaukee for the first time to capitalize on

Chicago's Great Fire of 1871, and had become the nation's biggest-selling beer eighty years later. But even during their decade of dominance after World War II, the Uihleins failed to maximize the brewery's potential. "A big lion dozing in the sun" was the way one Schlitz executive described the company. Schlitz had roused itself to invent the ring-pull can when it slipped to number two in the early 1960s. The company had also produced two highly praised ad campaigns: one that declared, "When you're out of Schlitz, you're out of beer," and the other built around the appealing word "gusto." In the fifties and early sixties, Schlitz was no longer number one, but appeared to be a solid number two.

Then the company lost its rudder. Its fifty-nine-year-old chairman, Robert Uihlein, squandered millions on a string of foolish acquisitions that diverted the company's attention from beer. He shuffled his top managers too often, leaving the company without consistent leadership. But Uihlein's biggest blunder was to do exactly what Bill Coors abhorred: Uihlein compromised quality for short-term profit. Schlitz cut its brewing time from twelve days to four in 1974 and replaced a lot of the beer's barley malt with corn syrup. Earnings shot up as costs plummeted, and Uihlein was ecstatic. The customer, he insisted, would never taste the difference.

He was wrong. Beer drinkers noticed at once that the beer was both sweeter and more prone to the off-taste of spoiling. For those who hadn't noticed, Schlitz's competitors made an issue of the recipe change. Schlitz tried a new foam stabilizer to extend shelf-life, but it left vile-looking flakes in the beer. The company secretly destroyed ten million bottles and cans of the flaky brew, but word got out and the sneak trashing only made things worse. If Schlitz was dumping its own beer on the sly, who wanted to drink it? Market share tailspun from 16 to 14 to 12 percent in three years. Standing amid the self-made wreckage of his family's century-old company, Robert Uihlein discovered in October 1976 he had acute leukemia. Two weeks later he was dead.

Schlitz's own brewers had dealt Schlitz its mortal wound, but its marketers helped dig the grave. After Uihlein died, ad men at Leo Burnett and Company tried to rescue the company with a series of commercials in which burly hard-hats shouted into the camera, "You want to take away my gusto?" The ads were more scary than inviting. Advertising wits— a particularly brutal group when judging each others' work—dubbed the campaign "Drink Schlitz or I'll Kill You." The onetime industry leader became a walking corpse. A $50 million profit in 1974 was a $50 million loss five years later. By the end of the decade, the once-mighty Schlitz was all but gone from barrooms and stores, its stock price deflated from $69 to $5.

The Schlitz tragedy only confirmed Bill Coors's deepest-held beliefs. He'd have cut his own throat before cheapening beer to save money. And unlike Uihlein, he was a hands-on manager. What happened to Schlitz couldn't happen in Golden.

As for Anheuser-Busch, Bill had nothing but sympathy. They made a good product, Bill thought. Not a great beer—pasteurized and all that—but nothing to be ashamed of. Old Gussie Busch, a contemporary of Bill's and a longtime acquaintance in the fraternity of German-descended brewers, had his hands full. Despite ever-climbing sales, Gussie couldn't make the brewery earn a profit. His stock price slowly sank in the early 1970s to half its late-1960s value. In 1971, Gussie named the first non-Busch as company president, but that didn't do the trick.

Bill Coors knew Gussie had panicked when Schlitz cut costs and admired him for refusing to tamper with his own product. Instead, Gussie guillotined his management staff. When the non-Busch president resigned in 1975 over the extent of the bloodletting, Gussie installed his son, August Busch III. That turned out to be a brilliant move for the company but a bad one for old Gussie.

August Busch III was thirty-seven years old when he became president of Anheuser-Busch. He and Peter Coors, six years his junior, were both generation-four sons of German-descended brewing families. But the two men could hardly have been more different. August Busch III was stocky, steely-eyed, and utterly lacking in Peter Coors's gollygosh charm. Peter was liked by colleagues—even such bested relatives as Adolph IV—for his humble ambivalence. He was in no hurry to become president. August Busch III, on the other hand, had from his youth possessed a blunt-to-the-point-of-rude ambition to command his family's business. While Peter was getting his one-year M.B.A. from the easygoing University of Denver, August Busch III was becoming a brewmaster at Chicago's Siebel Institute of Technology and then, rather than earn an M.B.A. himself, he had simply hired as a consultant the legendary professor Russell Ackoff from the high-powered Wharton School. While Peter liked to take distributors fishing, August Busch III liked to analyze financial data. Peter was deferential to his elders; August Busch III was a hard-charging workaholic who was unafraid of his father and perfectly willing to play the mean SOB.

As president, August Busch III filled the vacuum left by the purge with bright young Wharton M.B.A.s. Then he picked off the few top managers Gussie had left standing, installing his own loyalists in their stead. Finally, within a year of becoming president, he arm-twisted board members—some of whose laps he'd sat in as a boy—to unseat his weakened father and give him, August Busch III, chairmanship and total control of Anheuser-Busch.

As maximum commander of the Anheuser-Busch empire, August Busch III made his priorities known at once. He eschewed his father's grand two-room office suite for a small cubicle more fit for directing combat, but he bought back the corporate helicopter his father had sold to save money and used it to commute daily to the brewery because it gave him extra time in the office. Anheuser-Busch executives arriving at the parking lot knew they were dangerously late if they saw the chopper already on the roof. When a trade magazine published an unflattering story about the brewery, Busch went crazy with anger, launching a witch-hunt for the leaker that eventually led to an interrogation of a St. Louis dentist believed to have filled a brewery executive's teeth.

Bill and Joe Coors disliked August Busch III's personal style, but they admired his grit. In his first year as CEO, Busch faced a hundred-day strike by the Teamsters. As Busch saw it, the union wanted a say over changes in the company's production methods. Gussie had always given in to keep peace with the unions, but his son wasn't going to let the Teamsters tell him how to run his brewery. Busch paid a price for his principles. Budweiser production dropped to half when the Teamsters walked out. Market share dropped from almost a quarter to less than a fifth. The stock price sank to a nine-year low—a quarter of its 1972 price. The strike ended up costing Anheuser-Busch $30 million.

It might have been worse, but Bill and Joe Coors sent an explicit directive to their distributors and sales force: Do not take advantage of the Anheuser-Busch strike. Do not prey on Budweiser customers. Busch was battling the same union that was boycotting Coors in California, but more than that, a principle was involved. Labor must never tell management how to run the business. Young August deserved professional courtesy, Bill and Joe insisted. Surely someday he would return the favor.

The Coors men overlooked a crucial detail of Busch's behavior toward the union. As the strike dragged on, August Busch might have cajoled impatient workers to vote to abandon the Teamsters, but he'd learned enough from Gussie that he did not seek the union's annihilation. Furthermore, when the strike was over, it was over. In this regard, Busch was like Bill and Joe's father and grandfather. He did not petition the government to hold a decert election. Instead, he traveled around the country holding banquets for his unionized workforce, explaining his plans for the company.

Once he'd consolidated power within the company and coped with the union, Busch was ready to turn his full attention to the challenge from Miller. He took the cigarette-sharpened genius of John Murphy as a personal challenge. Busch may not have agreed with his great-grandfather that the family's beer was "slop" in comparison with wine, but he was proud of a familial vision that had dared market "St. Louis Lager" from Lima to London a hundred years ago. Adolphus Busch had founded the brewery as a marketing operation and his great-grandson would not be bested in that arena. "Tell Miller to come right along," August Busch told *Business Week*. "But tell them to bring lots of money." Titans were about to collide.

Coors was oblivious. Even Peter had only the faintest sense of what was about to occur, and it didn't matter what he knew. Bill and Joe ran the brewery and all they noticed was that they'd been expanding at double-digit rates every year for a decade. They earned nine dollars for every barrel of beer they made—twice as much as Anheuser-Busch—in large part because they spent so little on advertising. To Bill and Joe Coors, the turmoil descending on their industry only reinforced their belief that their way was the right way.

9

Spitting Out Teeth

Although beer can be made from any grain, and some fine wheat and rye beers are made in Europe and the United States, brewers' overwhelming favorite is barley. It is a hardy plant, resistant to blowing over in the field, and its kernels store well. The kernel is low in oil and high in a distinctive enzyme that helps convert the seed's starches to fermentable sugar. When ground for brewing, it is less sticky than other grains, which makes it easy to use. And its outer husk imparts a pleasant flavor to beer. Barley was far too important to the making of good beer for the Coorses to trust it to the vagaries of other people's work. They'd developed their own strain in the 1950s and contracted farmers all over Colorado and the West to grow it. Coors scientists roamed the farms constantly, measuring starch and oil content against strict brewery standards.

For some reason, the 1975 barley was slightly "off." Bill spent days in the lab, squinting under fluorescent lights, sniffing and tasting, contemplating color and puzzling over the inferior barley. He adjusted the malt, the hops, and the yeast of his brews. But without good barley, it was hopeless. He never got that year's beer quite right.

It was the worst possible time to produce substandard beer. Miller Lite had appeared the same year. Press Tab was driving away customers. The summer was unusually cold and wet, which discouraged beer drinking. Those who'd had the misfortune of buying the previous year's slimy, bacteria-tainted Coors were reluctant to try the brand again. Joe's price-raising blunder—expecting price controls that never materialized—left Coors more expensive during a summer when the pivotal southern California market was deep in recession. As for northern California, the ever-expanding Teamster-led boycott was beginning to pinch. TVN went bust in 1975, the EEOC filed its discrimination charges against Coors, and the U.S. Supreme Court ruled against Coors in the suit over whether Coors could prevent its distributors from handling competitors' brands. Then came the share offering with its disappointing price plunge. In 1975, it seemed that everything that could go wrong did go wrong.

When Peter and Max Goodwin presented the year-end numbers to the board early the following year, jaws fell open. After reliably growing by double digits for as long as anyone could remember, sales had fallen 4 percent. After zooming from number twelve to number four in the industry, Coors had slipped backward to sixth place. Anheuser-Busch, Stroh's, Pabst, Miller, and Heilman all had sold more beer than Coors in 1975. After years of allocating beer to a demand that exceeded its capacity, Coors finished the year with a warehouse full of unsold beer. Bill and Joe asked to see the data again, and then again. They couldn't believe it. For the first time since Prohibition, the Adolph Coors Company was losing ground.

Peter took advantage of the stunned silence to press his oft-repeated theme: Coors had to begin thinking as hard about selling beer as about making it. "There's no shame in saying we need help," Peter said. "I would like to hire an experienced marketer to help us get a winning campaign on track."

"Waste of money," Bill said.

"Do you know what Miller spends on advertising per barrel, net-net?" Peter asked. "Three dollars. Do you know what we spend? Sixty cents."

Because of that, Bill said, Coors beer was better.

Peter tried another tack. Since the energy crisis, fuel and transportation were the brewery's biggest expense. Miller and A-B were building breweries all over the country to lower their transportation costs to market. Peter argued that Coors should do likewise to increase the breweries' "efficiencies."

Bill found himself having to explain to his own nephew that Coors was a Rocky Mountain brewery, "Brewed with Rocky Mountain Spring Water." Not only wouldn't he trade away the company's identity, Bill said furiously, he wouldn't sell beer out of a brewery he didn't run himself.

Peter's father and uncle had grown the company into a Goliath and

Peter had always seen them as the brewery's greatest assets. But now they were becoming obstacles in the path Peter knew the company had to take. *Business Week* knew it, too. In a big, fawning piece on Miller, the magazine had just counted as one of Miller's strengths the fact that "unlike many family-owned breweries, Miller is run by managers who were not raised in the brewing business." Four generations of experience and heritage were now liabilities in the beer business, not assets. Peter knew he wasn't going to be able to shove his father and uncle aside the way August Busch III had done to his father. Indeed, he had no desire to do so. Their combined experience was still the core of what made Coors great. Their obstinacy toward marketing was their one tragic flaw. Peter would have to talk them through it.

Peter had spent a lifetime sidestepping trouble, backing away from confrontations like that between his father and big brother, keeping his head low. Now, though, he was a director of the Adolph Coors Company, watched over in the boardroom by the stern images of his grandfather and great-grandfather. They had not been men to sidestep trouble, particularly when the health of the brewery was at stake.

He stepped in trouble's path.

He criticized the Press Tab.

The room grew quiet. Everybody in the company knew the Press Tab was a loser kept alive by Joe's intransigence. What's more, Joe had made it clear he didn't want it discussed—any more than Bill would hear of a light beer.

"A dollar a thousand we save," Joe finally said. "A dollar a thousand."

"And it's ecologically sound," Bill added.

Peter didn't withdraw. He requested a vote of the board on whether to keep Press Tab.

Everybody at the big table looked at one another. A vote? There had never really been formal votes in Coors board meetings. The senior family members—Bill and Joe, and their father before them—had always decided what they wanted to do and expected everybody else to lend their support.

But Bill couldn't very well refuse. "All those in favor of retaining the Press Tab," he said, "raise your hand." He raised his, as did Joe. Jeff raised his, too. So did Al Babb, Lowell Sund, Max Goodwin, Ev Barnhardt, Ed Edlund, Ray Frost, Russ Hargis, Bob Mornin, Myron Nelson, Elmer Werth, and Jim Wildman: the entire board. Peter sat with his hands folded in front of him.

Bill called for those opposed, and Peter raised his hand. "Never before," Joe growled.

Never in the history of the company had there been a dissenting vote at a board meeting, Joe said, and knowing Joe's memory nobody doubted him. Joe was fuming.

Peter refused to cower. Instead, he escalated the fight. Coors needed to make a light beer, he said. Light was the only growing beer category. Anheuser-Busch was on the verge of releasing one. Coors had to respond in kind.

"No," Bill and Joe said in unison.

"We already make 'America's Fine Light Beer,'" Joe snapped. "What are we supposed to do, make 'America's Fine *Lighter* Beer'?"

Bill even posited that Miller Lite was doing Coors a favor. When people tired of drinking beer utterly lacking in complex carbohydrates, he said, they would rediscover the truly fine light beer on the market: Coors. Peter would continue trying—with increasing desperation—to convince his father and uncle to make a light beer. But the conversation stayed stalled on such a note for almost three years.

With the disastrous 1975 results hanging over him, Bill did what he always did when faced with adversity; he prepared to pick a fight with Local 366. He'd done it after the Porcelain plant strike in 1957. He'd done it after his brother Ad was murdered and after President Kennedy was shot. He'd done it when customers and distributors were complaining about the Press Tab. It was as though the union were an old sore that Bill couldn't help picking when he felt edgy or blue.

Now he moved Bob Mornin from the can plant to the brewery. Mornin was a brilliant hands-on engineer. He had improved the aluminum-can-making operation and ironed out its bugs. Like a charismatic infantry sergeant, he both drove his subordinates hard and inspired loyalty.

But he was also both ardently antiunion and skilled at fighting off organizers. Bringing him from the can plant to the brewery was like lining up artillery for an assault.

Bob Mornin had always kept the can plant nonunion by keeping his workers in the golden handcuffs. The work might be hard and the company imperious, but the pay was so good nobody wanted to complain. When he felt it necessary, he also used what union people call strong-arm tactics. In the period when Mornin was preparing to move to the brewery, he got a chance to show Bill his stuff. Can plant employees petitioned the NLRB to hold a union election in 1976 and Mornin waged a war of memos that threatened and lied. The memos broke NLRB rules—but they were rules that were virtually unenforceable. In one memo, Mornin warned that failing to vote "is the same as a vote for the union" when in fact union votes were decided by a simple majority of those who voted. In another, Mornin said a union, once elected, couldn't be dissolved "because you will have already given away your right to make your own decisions," when in truth workers could decertify a union they no longer wanted. Finally, Mornin threatened that the company would hire replacements in the event of a strike and would not hire back strikers.

Mornin won. The can plant narrowly rejected the Aluminum Workers International Union. Mornin came to the brewery flush with victory and freshly educated in beating a union.

Now the Adolph Coors Company turned its attention to Local 366.

Among the people working on the 1976 Reagan-Schweiker campaign in Colorado was young Cliff Rock, the big, jolly student who had admired Joe ever since working on his campaign for CU regent. Rock was astounded at the difference Joe's Heritage Foundation was already making. A group of conservative U.S. senators had managed to get an hour of floor time, for example, to present a Heritage alternative to the 1975 federal budget. Such deference to conservatives would have been unthinkable a few years ago, Rock thought. Never had a presidential campaign season begun with the public so well prepped in conservative ideals.

Rock viewed Joe Coors as the ideology guru of the 1976 Reagan campaign. Whenever Rock's enthusiasm flagged, all it took was a few minutes on the phone with Joe to recharge Rock's zeal. Joe also could find short-term money faster than any man alive, Rock knew. He either made a few phone calls to raise it, or simply wrote a check.

Bill Coors's behavior struck Rock as odd. The two brothers still shared an office, their desks just a few feet apart. But Bill never joined political discussions; he would hardly look up from his work as Joe and Rock planned fund-raising and organized rallies. Rock sensed a tremendous ambivalence. He knew Bill was every bit as conservative as Joe. Bill had just given a rousing interview to *Forbes* magazine in which he stood behind his brother's political activism. "The survival of our company is locked into the survival of the free enterprise system," Bill said. "And hell, somebody has to defend it." But Rock sensed that Bill didn't want the family too far out front. Bill might even wish Joe would throttle back a little. It was funny, Rock mused. Bill was the older brother and the chairman of the brewery. He could have muzzled Joe if he wanted to. It was lucky for the country he was torn.

After the 1976 election, Rock went to work for Joe as a kind of all-around political operative. By title, he was an outside consultant, but he had an office in the brewery and received an Adolph Coors Company check. Joe assigned him to Jack Wilson, Joe's personal lobbyist since the demise of TVN. A few months after Rock started work, Wilson called him down the hall to his office and said, "We have a job for you."

Wilson explained that Joe was impressed by an organization in California run by a group of conservative lawyers calling themselves the Pacific Legal Foundation. They were turning Ralph Nader-style tactics against the left, Wilson said. While Nader filed lawsuits to push around General Motors and General Electric's nuclear division, Pacific Legal Foundation sued to block affirmative action, to limit the tactics of environmentalists, and to help car companies fend off regulations.

Joe wanted to start a conservative law center of his own that would do in the Rocky Mountains what Pacific Legal Foundation was doing in California. "This project is dear to Joe's heart," Wilson told Rock as he dispatched him to Washington to raise money. Rock set up a card table in a bare K Street office and started making phone calls on behalf of Joe Coors. The response was overwhelming. On the strength of Joe's name, Rock raised a million and a half dollars almost instantly. He arranged tax-exempt status and named the new organization Mountain States Legal Foundation. All that remained was to find a lead attorney to command the new organization. "We want someone who shares our values," Wilson told Rock, "but we also want someone who knows the political game."

An oil-industry lobbyist told Rock, "I know just the guy."

"He used to work on the Hill," the lobbyist said. "By the time he was thirty-two, he was an assistant secretary of the interior. Then Ford assigned him to the Federal Power Commission."

"Where's he now?" Rock asked.

"Still there," the lobbyist said. "But Carter's folding the commission into the Department of Energy, so this guy's looking for work. He's a hard-core conservative, and a born-again Christian to boot."

"What's his name?" Rock asked.

"James Watt."

Peter's older brother Jeff was quiet, studious, and, like all the Coors boys, unfailingly polite. Perhaps because Joe Jr., the oldest brother, was a rebel, Jeff was achingly obedient and restrained, happiest when alone in the lab with his retorts and beakers. Jeff, like Peter and their father, had received an undergraduate engineering degree at Cornell. He'd pulled number 216 in the draft lottery so hadn't worried about Vietnam. Instead, after graduating, Jeff had traveled to Denmark to continue his education in chemical engineering at the Alfred Jorgensen Laboratories. At a social club in Copenhagen, he'd met a pretty young Danish woman named Lis Nielsen, who was raised as a Lutheran and, like Jeff's mother, was fiercely religious. They'd dated briefly, but Jeff had returned home when the year was up to work at his family's brewery.

Lowell Sund remembered picking him up at the airport. Lowell had always liked Jeff; he was a bit of a propeller-head, sure, but quiet and modest.

"Uncle Lowell," Jeff said as they drove toward Golden. "I'm really concerned about going to work out here. I'm not sure I can cut the mustard."

Lowell was used to confessions by the Coors boys, who, unable to share their feelings with their father, tended to unburden on him. "You'll do fine," Lowell said.

One day during his first year at the brewery, Jeff was walking from his lab to the far end of the plant when he passed a tour group coming the other way. There, among the visitors, was Lis Nielsen. They began dating again, and in time Jeff embraced her fundamentalist Christian faith. When he and Lis were married in Denmark, a select group of Coorses flew across the ocean with the plane's hold full of Coors beer. Joe Jr. was forbidden by his father to attend, as was Grover. "You can go if you get a haircut," Joe told Grover. But at that time Grover still felt more hippie than Coors.

Peter went to the wedding, though he and Jeff had never been great pals. Their personalities were too different—Peter so outgoing and impatient with engineering details, Jeffrey so shy and technical. As time went by after Jeff's wedding, the intensity of his faith divided the boys as well. Peter's wife, Marilyn, was a charismatic Catholic who studied the Bible with friends, and Peter attended church with her, but like his uncle and father, Peter couldn't quite fathom faith. He would remain the only of Joe's five sons not to be born again. Still, Pete and Jeff respected each other. Each knew his fortune depended on the other.

After Dad and Uncle Bill disparaged advertising and light beer at the board meeting, Peter invited Jeff to lunch. He needed his big brother now more than ever.

Jeff, Peter knew, was quite possibly even more oriented toward engineering and product than was Uncle Bill. When Jeff had voted to keep the Press Tab, it wasn't just to be safe; it was because Jeff believed Press Tab to be better engineered than the ring-pull. That's all that mattered to him. There was no way that Peter could convert Jeff with marketing talk. Instead, he presented his most important idea as an engineering challenge.

Peter appealed to Jeff's pride as a brewer. People obviously wanted light beer, he said, but those cigarette-makers had no idea how to make one. Miller Lite was big because it was first, but nobody's beer could hold a candle to Coors.

Jeff, ever the engineer, brought up the problem of complex carbohydrates. Without them, beer didn't have the mouthfeel or aftertaste.

Peter raised family pride. Coors was the company that figured out the aluminum can, he said. They were the one who had figured out cold-filtering. If anybody could brew a good-tasting light beer, it was Coors.

Jeff kept coming back to the unfermentable sugars. And ninety-six calories was an awfully tough benchmark, he said.

Peter hammered away, stroking Jeff's engineering ego until his older brother allowed that yes, he probably could come up with a good-tasting low-calorie beer if he had to. But the point was moot, Jeff argued, because Dad and Uncle Bill were set against it.

Peter was ready for him. He said he would handle the elders. He began sketching a plan on a cocktail napkin.

He would start running taste tests on Miller Lite, Budweiser, and Coors, and try to get a sense of what consumers liked and didn't like about each. He'd gather data on who exactly was buying Miller Lite. Was it really jocks, like in the ads? Or was it women, too? Or young people? Old? Coors didn't have a clue. He would do it all, he told Jeff, without telling their father and uncle, squeezing the money out of here and there.

Jeff raised his eyebrows. Peter plunged ahead.

In the meantime, he said, Jeff should be brewing a light beer, secretly. At night, if necessary. He should make up some story to tell Dad and Uncle Bill to explain his extra hours at the lab. Anything to keep the elders away until he had a great-tasting light beer. Peter wanted to present Dad and Uncle Bill with a complete, unassailable package: a great beer, thorough market research, and a full-fledged advertising plan. He wanted to do it as soon as possible.

"We're getting kicked in the teeth out there in the market," Peter told his big brother as he called for the lunch check, "and I'm tired of spitting out teeth."

When David Sickler heard that Bob Mornin was moving from the can plant to the brewery, he took a mental inventory of the union men around him and said, "Uh-oh." He had a sense of what made tough trade unionists. And the men around him, he knew, didn't have it.

Sickler had been business agent of Local 366 for three years and was already a minor star within the AFL-CIO. His energy was boundless; it was clear to those who worked alongside him that being business agent of a minor Colorado local was more than just a job for David Sickler. He never missed a regional or national conference the way the porkchoppers did. He read labor history and followed labor news. He motivated the men of his local to spend their spare hours picketing stores in support of the United Farm Workers' grape and lettuce boycotts. Lots of other business agents did likewise, but few spent their vacations in the dusty outback of Delano, California, working alongside Cesar Chavez and Dolores Huerta, the way Sickler did. Sickler had found a kind of religion as strong as any Coors's in his thirties and that religion was a workingman's fury—fury at the way Coors treated its employees, fury at how the drive for corporate profit chewed up ordinary people's lives, fury at the labor movement's ossification. Every worker's fight was his fight.

Sickler loved the UFW boycott in particular. The cause was highminded—dignity for migrant workers—not simply a question of dollars and cents. Sickler learned from Chavez that a successful boycott isn't just a blanket appeal to avoid a certain product. It is a finely targeted attack on as many segments of the product's market as the boycotters can reach. Sickler was impressed at how effectively the UFW shopped its cause not only to other unions but to churches, students, consumer groups, minorities, and environmentalists. Its broad appeal was what made it work while so many other boycotts faded away. The AFL-CIO had boycotts running against Ringling Brothers Circus, Croft Metals, Home Building Products, R. J. Reynolds Tobacco, Kingsport Press Books, and Dal-Tex Optical Glasses, but none was laying a glove on its target company and Sickler could see why. Their issues were too narrow and the boycott organizers too lazy.

Lazy wasn't the problem at Local 366; lack of experience and union commitment was. The president of Local 366, James Silverthorn, was a tall, slow-moving, fifty-eight-year-old brewery worker who had backed into the presidency because he was too nice to say no when asked to assume union tasks. Raised in Denver, Silverthorn had had little to do with unions before joining Coors. Sickler liked Silverthorn and admired his dedication to the local. But Silverthorn had no fire in the belly for the cause of unionism, the way Bob Mornin had against unions. Silverthorn cheerfully admitted to Sickler that he was locked in the golden handcuffs. The company forced him to work overtime, violated his vacations, jerked his schedule around, and made him take a lie detector test. It timed his breaks and reprimanded him when he took a minute too long. It left him sweltering in summer and shivering in winter. It ordered him to cut his hair when it got long, and told him how to vote at election time. "But hell," Silverthorn would invariably add, "they pay me well, take care of my children when they're sick, and are going to give me a pension." As long as Coors kept the pay raises coming, Silverthorn had little complaint.

Ken DeBey, the broad-shouldered and frizzy-haired vice president who had first recruited Sickler to be a shop steward, was equally peaceable. "Sure the company treats me like a piece of machinery," he'd say. "But man, the pay is great." The health plan, DeBey would argue, was the best imaginable. The company was self-insured; workers could see any doctor and simply send the bill to Coors. Winning a little more money, contract to contract, was all Silverthorn and DeBey imagined a union should do. And by those standards, the latest contract talks, in 1974, had gone better than ever. Silverthorn and DeBey were much like the rest of organized labor in the 1970s—pinched by double-digit inflation and increasingly focused on the narrow goal of boosting wages.

Unions had changed a lot since the days when young Adolph Coors first fled the crowded and heavily organized East Coast for the wide-open spaces of Colorado. And the way they'd changed was about to prove fateful for Local 366. Back in the mid to late nineteenth century, American unions thought of themselves less as wage-bargainers for individual shops than as battalions in a "working-class army" fighting the "capitalists." The bald nomenclature is their own; union leaders spoke of their struggles in grandiose ideological terms that today sound embarrassingly overwrought. "Capital has changed liberty into serfdom," a railroad striker said in 1877 in rhetoric typical of the day, "and we must fight or die." The kind of cross-craft solidarity Bill and Joe abhorred was the norm back then. When a tiny shop of upstate New York laundresses struck in 1869, seven thousand people marched in support. A hundred thousand workers from dozens of trades were able to organize a three-month general strike in 1872 around the eight-hour workday. The owner-employers were no less explicit about class conflict in the old days. The megabanker Jay Gould had once boasted, "I can hire one half of the working class to kill the other half."

It's hard to imagine today that airline baggage handlers might try to convince teachers to walk off their jobs by railing against "aristocratic vagabonds and exploiters." Labor made a conscious choice in the late nineteenth century to abandon such class-based ideology. As the century waned, unions narrowed their goals from workers' revolution to "business unionism." Instead of violent general strikes, they opted for collective bargaining, company by company, to gain higher wages and shorter hours. The standard bearer of this new pragmatism was the American Federation of Labor, founded in 1886. "We are practical men," a founding officer of the AFL assured the U.S. Senate. "We have no ultimate ends. . . . We are fighting only for immediate objects—objects that can be realized in a few years."

Fast-forward ninety years, and the idea of working-class solidarity was as archaic as spats. Far from linking arms with their class brethren, non-union workers in the 1970s increasingly told pollsters they resented the "inefficiency" unions created, and partly as a result, union membership was dwindling. Unionized workers—the "hard hats"—had voted Republican in 1968 and 1972 and, in an astounding reversal of the norm, were now polling more conservative than wealthier Americans. The AFL-CIO itself had been unable to choose between George McGovern and Richard Nixon—the first time in twenty years labor didn't endorse the Democrat. By the time the Coors brothers were fixing Local 366 in their sights, the American union movement had fully abandoned the "ultimate ends" of class justice and was focused only on the "immediate objects" of higher wages and benefits. No overarching philosophy or ideology guided labor; it was every union—often every local—for itself. Class warfare was the farthest thing from labor's mind.

Unfortunately for Local 366, class warfare was very much on the minds of Bill and Joe Coors. The Coors brothers wanted to bust their union not so they could pay their workers less, and not because the workers were threatening their control of the brewery. The Coors brothers wanted to bust Local 366 because they had an ideological commitment to doing so. By 1976, Bill and Joe Coors had spent a quarter century honing their inherited dislike for unions into an informed, articulate antiunion dogma. Unions disregarded the individual, the Coors brothers believed. Unions advanced lazy workers and held back good ones. Unions denied company owners the right to manage their property as they saw fit. The brothers, as devotees of Russell Kirk, also believed in "orders and classes" and understood unions as instruments for blurring them. Since reading Kirk, Joe had collected under his own institutional roof in Washington—at Heritage—the finest conservative thinkers in the country. Joe had been parleying with the likes of William Buckley and Lewis Lehrman in grand terms—about freedom and morals, God and country—while the leaders of Local 366 fretted over fifteen-cent shift differentials. Bill and Joe understood class conflict with an explicitness the members of Local 366 couldn't begin to match. Mentally, they were back in the 1870s, girding to battle a "working class" that had long since forgotten how to wage class warfare. The amiable men of Local 366 were about to find themselves on a strange battlefield, unarmed.

It was one of those warm January days in Colorado when it's almost possible to forget about winter. David Sickler's eyes popped open at 3:30 A.M. as usual, his head already churning with details of a meeting planned for later that day. Careful not to wake his wife, Sickler crept out the back door for his long morning run. After an hour of pounding along Golden's darkened streets, he started for home. But the rusty knob of Castle Rock was so appealing in the dawn light that he turned toward it and, barely breaking stride, ran straight to the top.

During Prohibition, Cregar Quaintance had realized it was more profitable to lease the knob to local entrepreneurs for a speakeasy site than it was to lend it to the Klan for cross burnings. A lively little bar operated on top of Castle Rock for several years, complete with narrow-gauge railroad to ferry passengers up the hillside. Sickler followed the old railbed, then mounted the cement stairs poured five decades earlier. The hour-long run and dash up Castle Rock still hadn't burned off Sickler's nervous energy and he paced the old foundation of the speakeasy, digging a pack of cigarettes from the waistband of his sweatpants.

Below him, Golden and the brewery gleamed in the daybreak sun. Even up here the roasty smell of malt was strong.

From atop Castle Rock, the massiveness of the Coors brewery seemed physically to dwarf the tumbledown little village of Golden just as it did politically. Sickler was friendly with the few Democrats on the city council and county commission, and they regaled him with stories of how thoroughly Coors controlled the valley. Outlawing the pickets during the 1957 strike was the least of it. If the brewery wanted land rezoned, it got it. If it wanted water rights rewritten, it got that, too. Never with threats or outright bribery; Coors was the biggest employer and taxpayer around, and was generous with donations of fire engines, libraries, and parks. Golden was happy to be a company town.

Brewery land started right in downtown Golden and stretched for miles down the Clear Creek valley. All the old charming buildings of the brewery were gone, except for the mansion, which was still used for meetings and the daily 1:20 P.M. lunch of Bill, Joe, Peter, and Jeff. Everything else was stark gray concrete, adorned only by rolling clouds of steam and the towering red Coors sign. The story went that old Mr. Coors had once made some poor steeplejack repaint the sign three times—a weeklong job each time—until he got the shade of red exactly right. Sickler shook his head as he wolfed cigarette smoke. The Coorses needed a lesson in how to treat their people.

Sickler lit another cigarette. Today he was to start a wage reopener—a mid-contract adjustment of wages. President Ford's WIN buttons notwithstanding, inflation was running at almost 10 percent and Sickler wanted at least that big an increase to keep the men abreast of the cost of living. He didn't expect trouble today; Coors was a terrible company to work for in a lot of ways, but an area in which they generally showed decency was wages. Coors paid well in order to "buy" lousy contracts from the workers, but so be it. Wage reopeners usually went smoothly, and Sickler figured today's would, too.

When he opened the door on the small negotiating room five hours later, though, Sickler felt the tension squeeze down his expansive mood like a vise. Russ Hargis, the company negotiator who'd always treated the union as a respected opponent, was sitting off to one side. In his place at the center of the table was a pale, cold-eyed young technocrat from Joe's staff at Porcelain: Gerry Kaveny. Next to Kaveny sat a man wearing a silk suit and an urban sneer. Sickler had never seen the man before and thought he looked as out of place in down-home Golden as

French cuffs at a barn dance. Sickler looked him up and down and thought, Union buster.

"My name is Erwin Lerten," the man said by way of opening. "I'm from Beverly Hills and have been hired by the Adolph Coors Company to supervise these negotiations." Lerten sat back and folded his arms.

"Well," Sickler said, "let's talk about pay."

"Here," Lerten said loudly, tossing a packet of peanuts across the table. "I brought you these from the airplane."

The gesture rattled Sickler. Coors could be high-handed and even abusive to its workers, but its negotiators had always maintained a polite decorum in talks. Something was up.

Kaveny picked up a sheet of paper and, reading from it, offered the workers a 5.5 percent raise—about half what Sickler expected. Kaveny set down the paper and stared blankly across the table.

Sickler looked to his left at Silverthorn, and to his right at Jay Dee Patrick, the AFL-CIO's regional representative, who'd flown in for the talks. Both shrugged.

"Uh, guys," Sickler told the Coors negotiators, "you know we can't accept that. That puts us below the rate of inflation."

"You want an open shop?" Lerten snapped, leaning forward and slapping the tabletop. "That's what you'll get if you're not careful, an open shop!" An open shop—a workplace in which union membership is not required—is a clause a company can push for in any contract adjustment. Open shops kill unions, and it was the last thing Sickler wanted on the table.

"All I'm trying to say," Sickler said, "is that the membership isn't going to accept what amounts to a pay cut."

"Go ahead and strike," Lerten said. "We don't give a shit."

The three union men physically recoiled. The word "strike" was explosive. Coupled with Lerten's crude obscenity, it was shocking, and way out of character for the Adolph Coors Company.

The union men withdrew.

"I remember that Lerten guy," Silverthorn said as they left the building. "He was around in 1957."

"We should have expected this," Jay Dee Patrick said. Patrick, a short broad man with a hard round belly, a thick head of black hair, and an Irish lust for struggle, had been sent west in 1972, when George Meany took over the Colorado AFL-CIO. He was a longtime veteran of union fights and something of a mentor to Sickler. "You guys ought to be ashamed of yourselves, working under that lousy contract of yours," he continued. "I've got to tell you, you're a laughingstock in the AFL-CIO."

"What do you suggest we do?" Sickler asked him.

"It's a wage offer," Patrick said, spreading his hands. "We've got no choice but to take it to the membership." He paused a moment and snapped his fingers. "When we do, we should take a strike vote at the same time. Not that we'd strike, mind you, but if the men vote to strike we can use it at the bargaining table." Under union rules, a strike vote by the membership gave the local's executive board authority to call one at any time.

"You heard Lerten," Sickler said. "They're hoping we'll strike."

"All companies say that," Patrick told him. "But no company really wants a strike."

Sickler doubted the members of Local 366 could be mobilized to pass a strike vote. For one thing, they liked the Adolph Coors Company too damn much for Sickler's comfort. They were proud of the quality of the beer they helped make and shared the family's pride in the "Coors mystique." Many still remembered old "Mr. Coors" walking through the plant in his black suit, nodding in greeting. And almost everyone in the plant had a soft spot for Bill. "Why," Sickler heard more than once, "Bill remembers every worker's name; remembers their wives' names, too!" Whenever Sickler tried to bring up some of the racist or antiunion comments Bill made in his mandatory employee meetings, he'd get a shrug in response. "That's just Bill," Sickler's fellow union members would tell him. "Doesn't mean a thing."

Sickler had his doubts, but Jay Dee Patrick was an old AFL-CIO warhorse whereas Sickler was still a greenhorn and knew it. He deferred to Patrick's experience. By the time the membership could be gathered at the union hall on Independence Avenue that evening, a leaden lid of clouds had moved in over Golden and a sharp wind sliced across the parking lot. "Remember, we've got to frighten the company," Patrick told him as they rushed inside with upturned collars. "A strong strike vote will do that."

Sickler took the podium. For the occasion, he'd thrown a sports jacket over his Qiana bodyshirt; its lapels flared in either direction like the wings of an F-111. His glasses, tinted along the lens tops as was then the fashion, made it hard to see the crowd unless he tipped his head back. Tall and wiry, he gripped the sides of the podium and leaned into the microphone.

Sickler talked about the lie detector. He talked about forced overtime and missed vacations. His voice rising, Sickler talked about the lack of heat and air-conditioning, the company's disrespect for seniority, the arrogance of foremen, the compulsory rotating shifts. Sickler had heard enough union-hall speeches as a boy to understand their rhythm and dynamics. What's more, the longer he talked, the angrier he got. The company had been buying contracts for years—increasingly lousy contracts, from the union's point of view. Sickler said he was unwilling to sell away his dignity any longer, especially for an insultingly low price. "We make the Coors family rich," he shouted, "and this is how they treat us!"

The members of Local 366 began to stir. Individually, none of the little indignities Sickler mentioned amounted to much. But hearing them passionately enumerated, one after the other, gave them weight—especially when the customary counterweight of high wages wasn't there. "We let them treat us like property because the pay was good!" Sickler yelled. "Now they want us to accept inadequate pay!" He brandished his fist and pounded the lectern. Heads in the audience began to nod. Shouts of "Damn right" echoed back. The men of Local 366 may have lacked a nineteenth-century sense of class. And they may certainly have held some affection for the Coors family and the company. But they also knew when they were being insulted. Sickler reminded the workers again about the John Birch Society literature in the pay envelopes, about Bill's prevaricating about the Civil Rights Act, and about Joe's meddling with their paychecks to make a political point. "The time has come," Sickler shouted, "to say 'Enough is *enough*!'" Fourteen hundred brewery workers leapt to their feet.

"Strike!" they yelled. "Strike! Strike!"

Whoa, Sickler thought as he backed away from the podium mopping his face with a handkerchief. Now what have I done?

The vote was called and came in overwhelmingly in favor of giving the executive board the authority to call a strike. "Good work," Patrick said to Sickler, pounding him on the back.

"I hope you're right," Sickler said into his ear as the men around them cheered and gave each other high-fives. "You realize we have fourteen hundred guys ready to strike over four and a half percent? It's crazy, Jay Dee."

"These guys know it's just for show," Patrick said, looking around. "I think."

At the next negotiating session, Kaveny and Lerten sat across the table like mandarins, expressionless and immovable. "You know about our strike vote?" Sickler asked.

"We're quaking in our boots," Lerten snorted.

On a coffee break, Sickler cornered Russ Hargis next to the water cooler. "You haven't said a thing since these talks began," Sickler said.

"You're up against the family's beliefs," Hargis said, dropping his voice to a whisper. "They're ready to go down the drain over this."

"But it's just a wage reopener!" Sickler cried.

Hargis rolled his eyes, shook his head sadly, and walked back into the meeting. The wage reopener deadlocked. Coors had successfully called the union's bluff. Jay Dee Patrick mumbled something about a crisis in New Mexico and hotfooted out of town.

Sickler knew a strike was suicide. The union only represented fourteen hundred of the company's ten thousand employees. The company would simply move people around and then replace the strikers to be rid of the union. Silverthorn and DeBey agreed. They now had to go back to the union hall and talk the membership out of the strike mentality they themselves had inspired.

"You don't strike a brewery in January," Silverthorn told the agitated crowd. "Let's wait until summer, when they really need us."

Sickler reminded the men that a full contract negotiation was coming up next year. If they really wanted to strike, that would be a better time to do it.

There was silence in the hall for a moment after they spoke. Then someone yelled from the back, "Sellouts!"

Up front, a man in a Cubs hat jumped to his feet and shouted, "Cowards!" A hulking Vietnam vet from the bottle line pointed a finger pistol-fashion at Sickler's face. "Don't be fucking with my head, man," he roared. "First you tell me one thing, now you tell me another!"

A few days later, a handful of rank-and-file members filed a lawsuit against Sickler and the rest of the leadership. With Local 366 divided, events began unfolding fast.

Joe, Bill, and Bob Mornin—advised by Erwin Lerten—devised a clever way to use jujitsu against both the union and the federal government. The government, through the EEOC, was accusing Coors of discriminating against women and minorities. The Coorses came up with a plan to satisfy the EEOC and wound the union at the same time.

For years, the brewery's hundred-odd foremen, called "leadmen," had been the highest-paid members of Local 366. Now Coors demoted them all to general brewery workers and eliminated the leadman classification altogether. Instead of leadmen, Coors created a new layer of management, outside the bargaining unit. Coors cunningly gave most of the new positions to Hispanics and women. Because so few worked at the brewery—that had been the basis of the EEOC complaint—the company had to go outside to find them. Instantly, Coors appeared to be an earnest affirmative-action hirer and promoter.

What Coors had done—unilaterally eliminating union positions—violated the contract. But it was effective. Local 366 ran to the National Labor Relations Board, which cranked up its ponderous bureaucracy to investigate, but in the meantime the old leadmen—7 percent of the local and its most senior members—suffered the demotions. Sickler, Silverthorn, and DeBey felt the new management positions were just for show; many of the people hired to fill them knew nothing about brewing or management. They simply had the right color face or were the right sex. But now the union was in the position of having to oppose the company's hiring of Hispanics and women. Sickler put his head in his hands.

The AFL-CIO chose this moment to move him to Helena, Montana. The field office there needed a director, and Sickler, by now the best-trained and most politicized official of Local 366, was tapped. When he met Silverthorn and DeBey for a last beer at the Ace High Tavern, Sickler offered a final piece of advice. "Whatever you do," he told them, "don't strike."

After throwing the jab of the leadmen demotions, Coors followed up with a roundhouse punch at the union's viability. Union security—requiring new hires at the company to join the union—is crucial for a local's survival. "Right-to-work" states ban it, but in most of the country, union security is a matter of negotiation between a company and its union. Colorado was somewhere in between. An obscure 1943 law—euphemistically titled the Colorado Labor Peace Act—threw an additional high hurdle in front of unions. It let companies require that their unionized workers hold a special election to decide whether new hires had to join. The law required an astounding 75 percent of a union's eligible workers to ratify a "union shop" before the local could even begin negotiating union security with the employer. Most Colorado companies—Coors included—didn't require the vote and simply negotiated union security directly with their unions. Now, though, Erwin Lerten told Silverthorn the workers would have to hold a Labor Peace election if they wanted to try to keep their union shop. To make matters worse, the NLRB scheduled the election for Christmas week, a time of vacations and blizzards that would be disastrous for turnout. This time, a no-show really would equal a "no" vote.

Local 366, energized by the wage reopener strike vote and provoked by such heavy fire, finally started acting like a real union. Silverthorn and DeBey cracked the whip over their shop stewards to lobby members. Though no longer officially in charge of the Coors local, Sickler flew back and forth from Helena to help in the last weeks before the election. The leadership formed committees to call on as many brewery workers' homes as possible. They established phone trees and called every member. They found the Coorses had inadvertently done them a favor over the years by refusing to deduct union dues from paychecks. The leaders had been forced to approach each man face-to-face for his monthly dues, thus forming real friendships. Members quickly caught the spirit of the Christmas-week election.

This isn't such a bad local after all, Sickler thought, as he canvassed his old Golden neighborhoods in the snow.

Bill Coors fought back. When he gathered his workers in the sixth-floor auditorium for the annual Christmas address, he departed from the usual holiday themes. "If you've seen one union, you've seen them all," Bill said. He scanned the crowd but couldn't read a reaction, which irked him. "My father wanted a union but now the company philosophy is different. If there is a strike, we'll close the damned place down." Bill thought for a minute and added a piece of history dear to his heart. "We can take it. The 1957 strike didn't hurt us one damned bit."

In the end, Bill's bellicose talk backfired, sending workers into the Labor Peace election angrier than ever. Organizers had to pull several members out of hospital beds to get them to the brewery to vote, but the union won the Labor Peace election with more than 92 percent.

What a transformation, Sickler thought as he boarded the plane back to Helena. Local 366 was now, he thought, as solid as a rock.

10

Union Shit

The Coors workers milled around Local 366 headquarters giving each other mail-fist salutes. Right after the Labor Peace election, Coors opened the new contract talks with a cross to the jaw. Not only wouldn't the company give up the lie detector, it was demanding the right to fire workers without warning, require urinalyses and blood tests on the spot, eliminate entire job classifications without union approval, and move workers' shifts without regard to seniority. Moreover, Erwin Lerten said, the company was unwilling to negotiate. It was take the contract or leave it. The union men were stunned. Coors stood over them with its dukes up, daring them to hit back.

Let's finally have that strike, the workers told each other. That'll get 'em! We won't make their beer!

They were pumped up in Golden, all right, but Sickler—kept abreast in Helena by Silverthorn's phone calls—was nervous. The workers' switch from complacent affection to righteous anger was too sudden for his liking. Once they'd discovered ire, they'd taken to it like drunks on the wagon. Sickler wasn't sure it would last.

The modern record of strikes wasn't encouraging, either; the tactic seemed more and more a relic of the 1940s. It had been a long time since a union had flat-out won a strike against a big company. A strike could work if workers were highly specialized and hard to replace, or if the company feared acquiring an antiunion public image. Neither was the case at Coors. Anybody could be trained quickly to make beer, and the Coorses didn't shy from appearing conservative. Furthermore, Sickler reminded himself, Local 366 was inherently weak. It was a poor stepchild of the AFL-CIO instead of belonging to a proper union. And the AFL-CIO was both preoccupied with bigger problems and suspicious of Colorado since the state AFL-CIO disobeyed George Meany over the McGovern endorsement.

The hotter the situation in Golden got, the more time Jay Dee Patrick spent there and the angrier he became. This, too, worried Sickler. Strike fever is a powerful condition, and as a local veers in the direction of a walkout, it needs at least one cool head to be saying, "Slow down." Sickler liked and admired Patrick—Patrick had been his first mentor—but he began to suspect Patrick was catching strike fever himself.

Sickler found himself thinking about boycotts. It would be much better to deprive Coors of beer drinkers than to deprive Coors of beer-makers, he thought; unlike brewery workers, customers can't easily be replaced. And a boycott doesn't put workers' jobs at risk the way a strike does.

But lots of boycotts failed, too. The Amalgamated Clothing and Textile Workers Union, for example, had recently launched what it was calling "the most beautiful boycott in history" against the textile giant J. P. Stevens. But the boycott wasn't touching Stevens and Sickler could see why. J. P. Stevens products don't carry the company name; its sheets are "Mohawk," its blankets "Utica," its carpets "Gulistan." It was hard for even the most sympathetic consumer to remember which products to boycott. In any case, how often did a person buy blankets and carpet?

We wouldn't have that problem if we boycotted Coors, Sickler thought. The name was right on the can, and people bought beer every day.

Like grapes and lettuce.

Another problem at Stevens was the conflict itself. The company was using what the Clothing Workers called unfair tactics to keep the union from organizing its mills. But the Clothing Workers hadn't done a good job of publicizing the dehumanizing conditions the nonunion Stevens workers endured. The dispute looked like nothing more than a big company versus a big union. It hadn't been spun properly to groups of potential supporters the way Chavez and Huerta had done.

Sickler was determined not to make the Clothing Workers' mistake if it came to blows in Golden. The Coors workers were suffering, he told himself, and he would make damn sure everybody knew it. A light bulb went on above his head. Local 366 could call a boycott *instead* of going on strike. He called Local 366 headquarters and got DeBey.

"Let's do a one-day strike as a show of force," Sickler said, "then go back to work and institute the boycott."

"Nah," DeBey said. "People won't support a boycott if the workers aren't on strike."

"What do you mean?" Sickler asked. "The grape and lettuce boycotts were the most successful ever and there was no strike in the fields."

"Farmworkers are different," DeBey said.

Sickler called Silverthorn.

"I'm with Ken," Silverthorn said. "We might go out for a day and get *locked* out. If it comes to that, we might as well have a real strike."

Silverthorn, DeBey, and Jay Dee Patrick held round after round of stony talks with Kaveny and Erwin Lerten. "You know what Bill Coors told me when I said you might strike?" Lerten said in one session. "He said, 'We buy our labor like we buy our barley.' " Hearing about this on the phone, Sickler took Lerten at his word that the company would just as soon the union struck. "They want a strike," Sickler told Silverthorn again and again. "Don't give them what they want."

But the contract expired on December 31 without agreement, and three weeks later the members of Local 366 gathered for another strike vote. Jay Dee Patrick, caught up in the emotion of the moment, recommended to Silverthorn an odd departure from standard practice. Instead of a secret ballot, he urged, there should be an open show of hands. A rousing shout of "Yea," Patrick felt, would inspire the workers and stiffen their resolve. Patrick got his shout. Only eight men voted "No." But he also got a lopsided view of the local's mentality. Few in the union hall that night wanted to appear chicken. Silverthorn and Patrick ended up thinking strike sentiment was a lot stronger than it was.

Big, ponderous Jim Silverthorn turned out to be the cool head, but he spoke too quietly and too late.

"We're going to get creamed," he muttered to a member of the executive committee named Don Jorgenson. It was late at night and both men were exhausted, leaning against the union hall vending machines, drinking Cokes.

"I know," Jorgenson said. "But if we accept what the company wants, we won't really be a union anymore anyway."

Silverthorn took a sip and gazed around the union hall—at the uneven rows of folding chairs, the florid AFL-CIO charter on the wall, the limp American flag.

Silverthorn felt a wash of sadness. Either way, he thought, Local 366 was finished.

George Meany, general secretary of the AFL-CIO, summoned Sickler and Jay Dee Patrick to Washington. Also there were Larry Gold, the AFL-CIO's chief counsel, and Nick Kurko, the federation's mountain-states regional director.

"Where are you getting them?" the diminutive Meany asked Kistler when Sickler was introduced. "From the Celtics?"

Meany had a cold and imperious image in the press, but Sickler found him charming, witty, and smart. Sickler had come prepared to brief Meany, but the squat, jowly president knew as much about Coors as Sickler did, down to the tiniest detail of the latest events.

Meany nodded first at Jay Dee Patrick, who argued passionately for a strike and made his pitch that the federation should grant strike authorization and promise strike benefits. "Then," Patrick said, "the AFL-CIO should declare a boycott."

Kurko snorted. "A boycott can be a weapon, nothing more," he said. "The local has to be ready to carry its own water."

"This local's ready," Patrick insisted.

"I don't know," Kurko said. "Weeks ago I suggested you send men out to win over the distributors. You haven't done that. You haven't told your guys that they shouldn't make any big purchases or borrow money." Kurko looked squarely at Meany. "I don't think these men are ready for a strike," he said slowly. "They don't have a clue what it takes."

"They voted!" Patrick cried. "They're practically unanimous!"

Kurko shrugged. "The open ballot worries me."

Meany pointed his smoking cigar at Sickler.

"With due respect to Jay Dee," he said, "Nick's right; the workers are going to get slaughtered if there's a strike. It's what Coors wants. My idea is the AFL-CIO declare a nationwide boycott, and we simultaneously hold a one-day strike to show we mean business."

"Can't do it," AFL-CIO chief counsel Larry Gold interjected. "Federation rules preclude a boycott without a strike."

"What are you talking about?" Sickler asked, incredulous. "The UFW wasn't on strike. There's no strike at J. P. Stevens."

"Well . . ." Gold said.

"Check that, will you?" Meany told Gold. He leaned back in his chair and peered at the men through curls of cigar smoke.

"The strike's gonna be a loser," he grunted finally, and Sickler's heart soared. Maybe Meany would stop it. Maybe there wouldn't be a bloodbath. "But," Meany went on, "Jay Dee is right. The workers have voted. They're adults. We have to assume they mean what they say."

"The AFL-CIO will authorize?" Patrick pressed. "Pay strike benefits?

"Yes," Meany said. "And you're right. It's going to take a boycott."

"But what about boycott with *no* strike?" Sickler pressed. "That way we don't lose a lot of good men their jobs."

"Larry's going to check on that," Meany said distractedly. "In the meantime, we go forward."

"And the AFL-CIO will boycott?" Sickler asked, hoping at least to salvage a promise.

"Yes," Meany said. But he said nothing about how much support he'd give.

Sickler was gathering his papers to fly back to Montana when Tom Donahue, the AFL-CIO's number-three man, stuck his head in the door. Sickler was a big fan of Donahue's and started to unload his worries about the Coors situation. He was hoping for a pep talk but Donahue waved him off.

"I know all about it," Donahue said gloomily. "You're in for a long fight. The Coorses are true believers."

Silverthorn tried taking the contract issues to a federal mediator, but came away more dispirited than ever. The company wouldn't budge. "I'm beginning to think you're right," he told Sickler on the phone. "They want us to strike."

In February, the company cranked higher the pressure on the union to walk out. As in 1957, Coors posted notices around the plant announcing the company was unilaterally implementing all its contract initiatives as though the union didn't exist. What's more, the company suddenly was offering a 7 percent wage increase. Not just offering, either; the increase would be in the next paycheck. To reject the contract, the workers would have to refuse to cash their checks. Fat chance, thought Sickler.

As Sickler saw it, the Coorses won either way. If there was a strike, they busted the union, and if there wasn't, the Coorses had a workforce that was more malleable than before. He pushed his tinted glasses up onto his forehead and rubbed his eyes.

He kept calling Larry Gold's office for a ruling on whether the AFL-CIO could boycott without a strike. But the AFL-CIO was preoccupied. George Meany was busy crossing swords with the new President, Jimmy Carter, over the minimum wage—an uncharacteristic conflict between labor and a Democrat. No one at AFL-CIO headquarters had the time or the inclination to referee a dispute in Golden. Meanwhile, both Nick Kurko and Jay Dee Patrick were promising the workers an instantaneous AFL-CIO boycott in the event of a strike, which in Sickler's view only fanned the flames.

Sickler watched in despair as momentum gathered for a strike. He flew down to Golden and began giving boycott classes at the union hall, so the local would at least understand that option. You don't just put out a blanket appeal to boycott the beer and leave it at that, he urged. You have to break off pieces of their market one by one. Sickler's hopes lifted briefly when a federal arbitrator ordered Coors to reinstate the demoted leadmen within thirty days. Maybe they'd beat Coors back, complaint by complaint, Sickler thought, and avoid a strike that way.

Coors simply ignored the arbitrator's order.

"Joe says he's had enough of the federal government telling him how to run his business," Gerry Kaveny told Sickler the next time Sickler was in town for contract talks. The company was on a rampage against "meddling" by "intrusive" federal agencies—the EEOC, the NLRB, and even OSHA, Kaveny explained. "We're making OSHA inspectors get search warrants before they come in the plant," Erwin Lerten boasted. "You think we're afraid of your arbitrator?"

Sickler feverishly went through the mechanics of a boycott for any brewery worker who wanted to attend his classes. The brewery ran twenty-four hours a day, so Sickler was giving classes around the clock, often sleeping in his chair. He also argued again and again that the local shouldn't conduct a full-blown strike. "One day, max," he told anybody who would listen. "Go out for one day and go right back inside before they can hire replacements." Nobody was listening. The more high-handed the company behaved, the more the workers remembered their Labor Peace victory and became convinced they could win a strike. "It's not about money," they told each other and the Denver reporters who by now were hanging around waiting for the story to break. "It's about dignity issues."

On April 5, 1977, Jay Dee Patrick walked out of the negotiating session and told Silverthorn and DeBey the talks were hopelessly stalled. "What about the pension stuff?" Silverthorn asked. "Did you get to the pension stuff?"

"It's deadlocked, Jim," Patrick said. "We didn't even get that far. They're not budging." Kaveny reported the same news to the Coors family.

"We don't really know how the members feel about striking," Local 366 executive board member Don Jorgenson told the board when it met that night to vote on whether to call the strike. "That open ballot worries me. I don't think all those who voted to strike will really do it."

"I vote no," said Frank Bruno, another member.

"Me too," said Dennis Capps.

"Well I vote aye," Ken DeBey said. "This local's been pushed around long enough."

"Aw, hell," Don Jorgenson said. "I guess we have to make a stand somewhere. Aye." All but Capps and Bruno voted to strike. Silverthorn didn't vote because he wasn't needed to break a tie.

Word spread at once that the executive board had finally called the strike the members had voted for weeks earlier. "No violence!" Silverthorn shouted above the din as men poured into the hall to grab picket signs. "No violence on the picket line!" Knots of cheering men gathered at each of the plant's twenty-two gates, huddled in islands of halogen light in the night's chilly darkness. "It's about time!" they chanted to the Denver television cameras. "It's about time! It's about time!"

Silverthorn hustled from gate to gate. "No violence," he kept saying as phalanxes of Golden police officers, Jefferson County sheriff's deputies, and Coors security men faced the picketers, tapping riot sticks against their palms. "No violence. No violence." A tall man trooped across the parking lot, shouldered through the picket line, and headed through the gate to the plant. A bushy-bearded guy from packaging followed close behind. "Scabs!" the picketers shouted at their backs. "Scabs!"

My God, Silverthorn thought. An hour into the strike and already they're crossing.

His heart sank further. One of Local 366's own executive board members was already scabbing.

"Hey, Jim!" DeBey yelled merrily. He handed him a cup of coffee, looked side to side, and let the smile drain from his face. "Six have crossed at the main gate," he whispered.

They stood quietly a moment, watching the thin line of men shouting at the huge, floodlit, concrete brewery.

"The AFL-CIO should have someone in here running this thing," Silverthorn said. "Because I don't know shit about it."

DeBey brought copies of the *Denver Post* to the picket lines at dawn. Silverthorn worked the paper like a bellows with half-frozen fingers, looking for what he dreaded to find. "Here it is," he grunted: a half-page Coors ad, advertising for replacements at seven dollars an hour. "The very first goddamn day," Silverthorn said. "Jesus Christ." It was unseemly. He'd never heard of a company advertising for replacements before talking to the strikers.

"Jim!" a voice called. A short man from the malthouse, a friend of Silverthorn's, ran up, looking worried. "They've pulled our health coverage," he panted, puffing clouds of steam.

"What?"

"We don't have any health insurance!" the man wailed. "I just talked to my wife. My daughter's got the flu, and when she tried to take her to the doc the doc said Coors wasn't paying benefits for any strikers."

Silverthorn and DeBey looked at each other. How could they not have thought of this? Being self-insured, Coors could turn off the tap at will.

"Jim," the little malthouse man said, "I gotta cross. I don't have any choice. My kid's got a hundred and two fever." Silverthorn could see the man's chin quivering. He looked away.

"I can't help you," Silverthorn said softly.

"Say what, Jim?" the man asked urgently.

"I said I can't help you!" Silverthorn shouted, suddenly furious. "We all got kids! We're all gonna get sick! Do what you have to do!"

The man patted Silverthorn on the arm, ducked his head, and pushed through the line. A chorus of "Scab!" went up. The little man kept walking. "Scab!" the picketers cried. "Scab!" Silverthorn watched for a moment, then cupped his hands around his mouth and yelled "Scab!" at his friend's back.

Two questions dominated conversation on the picket lines the first day: When would the AFL-CIO begin paying strike benefits? and: When would the much-promised boycott be declared? Silverthorn kept running back and forth between the line and the union hall looking for messages, but none came.

By the morning of the third day, it seemed to Silverthorn that the Denver and Golden papers were completely on Coors's side. The com-

pany had opened a hiring center at a disused Chevrolet dealership and
the papers carried a picture of the queue, with applicants lined up single-
file to stretch the appearance of their numbers. STRIKE DRAWS JOB SEEK-
ERS TO COORS, a headline said. It was practically an advertisement for
strikebreakers, Silverthorn thought.

Every now and then a fresh volley of "Scab!" pulled Silverthorn's attention away from the paper, and he'd look to see another union member
striding briskly toward the plant, head down, as though into a stiff wind.

Silverthorn spotted a buddy from his neighborhood getting ready to
cross. "What are you doing?" Silverthorn asked him.

"Hey, man," his friend said. "They gave us seven percent. What more
do you want?"

"But you voted to strike," Silverthorn said, taking hold of the man's
sleeve. "I saw you." And maybe that's precisely the problem, Silverthorn
thought. Maybe if the vote had been secret you would have voted no.

"I don't have a problem with this company," the man said, pulling
his arm free.

"Seniority?" Silverthorn asked in disbelief. "Getting rid of job classifications? Firing guys without procedure?"

"That's union shit," the man said. "You guys care about that stuff. I
don't." He turned and walked through the line, head up. When the
catcalls started, he didn't look back. He just raised his middle finger and
kept walking.

All day, men ran up to Silverthorn, aghast at the cancellation of their
health insurance. "I know," Silverthorn kept saying. "I know." They
asked about the strike benefits and the boycott. "I don't know," Silverthorn said time and again. "I don't know." He withdrew some money
from his own bank account and began handing it around, in tens and
twenties, to men who really needed it.

Five days into the strike, Bill Coors gave a terse statement to the
press, saying the strikers had one last chance to return to work before
he started hiring as replacements the people who'd been flooding the
employment center. By day nine, Coors was claiming that half the strikers—some 715 workers—had crossed the picket line and returned to
work. DeBey told the *Denver Post* that "only" 308 had done so. Even by
DeBey's count a fifth of the membership was already helping to break
the strike, and the end of the month hadn't yet arrived. Nobody had yet
had to face a house or car payment without a paycheck.

Adolph Coors of Dortmund, Prussia, was fourteen when in the span of months he was both apprenticed to his first brewery and orphaned. When he fled the Kaiser's conscription in 1868, it was not to the comfortable German colonies of New York but to the Wild West, so he could build his brewery near the continent's highest-born water. *Courtesy of Colorado Historical Society*

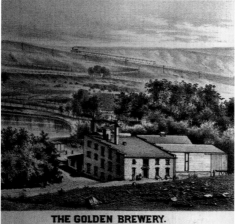

THE GOLDEN BREWERY.
GOLDEN, COLORADO.

Adolph found this site, an abandoned tannery on the banks of Clear Creek near Golden, in 1873, and opened his brewery with a partner that fall. *Courtesy of Golden Pioneer Museum*

Adolph Coors was a millionaire by 1894, when, on Memorial Day, a flash flood tore a piece off his brewery (*right*) and threatened his new Queen Anne mansion (*background*). Adolph quickly bought out the homeowners on the opposite bank, had their houses demolished and a new channel for the creek dug through their property. *Courtesy of Denver Public Library Western History Department*

Adolph Coors and his ornamental family, circa 1893. The future Mr. Coors, Adolph Jr., is the resolute lad standing at right. *Courtesy of Colorado Historical Society*

Prohibition took away Adolph Coors's beloved livelihood as a brewer. He endured thirteen beerless years before throwing himself off a hotel balcony. Here, Adolph and Louisa Coors vacation in the Bahamas a few months before his suicide. *Courtesy of Colorado Historical Society*

Adolph Coors launched the company, but Adolph Jr. made it great. By 1955, when this picture of the brewery was taken, Coors was sold in nine western states and its biggest problem was brewing enough beer to meet demand. *Courtesy of Golden Pioneer Museum*

In 1959, Bill Coors invented the first mass-produced aluminum beverage can. (*From left*) a slug of pure aluminum, which was whacked by a piston inside a cylinder to become a one-piece seamless can; (*right*) the painted 7-ounce "pony" can and the lid. *Cans courtesy of Ruben Hartmeister*

The line of succession was severed with the kidnap and murder of "Ad" Coors III (*standing right*) in 1960. Standing with him are the second son, Bill (*left*), and Joe. Their father sits to the right beside his brothers Grover and Herman, who were only peripherally involved in the company. *Courtesy of Colorado Historical Society*

The portrait of Adolph Jr., painted by ad director Bill Moomey, that hangs in the Coors boardroom. Until his death in 1970 "Mr. Coors" was rarely seen in anything but a nineteenth-century-style black suit, black bow tie, and high button shoes. *Courtesy of Bill Moomey*

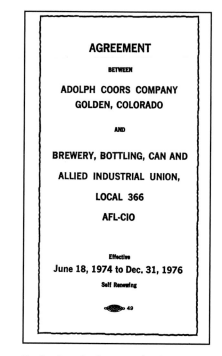

By the time the Coors workers' contract expired on December 31, 1976, Bill and Joe had become prominent conservatives. Within four months of the contract's expiration, they maneuvered Local 366 into the strike that destroyed it, and Coors has been uniquely non-union ever since. *Courtesy of Colorado AFL-CIO*

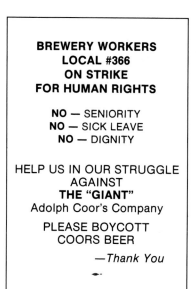

Outsmarted and overwhelmed by the Coors brothers' ideological anti-unionism, Local 366 folded quickly. Pickets distributed these handbills, but shareholders, suppliers, tourists—and union members—freely crossed the picket lines. *Courtesy of Colorado AFL-CIO*

Jim Silverthorn had assumed the presidency of Local 366 largely because he was too nice to say no when asked. Though he knew within hours of the walkout that the strike—and the local—were doomed, he kept the local alive for twenty months. *Courtesy of Colorado AFL-CIO*

David Sickler, Local 366's combative business agent, was given the job of organizing the AFL-CIO's boycott when the strike folded. His goal was not to pressure the company but to destroy it. *Courtesy of Colorado AFL-CIO*

David Sickler was as ideologically committed to the cause of unionism as Bill and Joe were committed to the ideal of a union-free workplace, and he considered no weapon off limits. These bright orange stickers warned customers that Coors was unpasteurized. *Courtesy of Colorado AFL-CIO*

As national organizer of the boycott, David Sickler tried to unite labor with minorities, women, gays, and environmentalists by presenting Coors as a stand-in for Reaganism. This anti-Coors comic book (below) equated the Coors boycott with the United Farm Workers' grapes-and-lettuce boycott and linked it to other causes of the left. *Courtesy of Colorado AFL-CIO*

Although the lie detector was a minor contract issue, it took on huge emotional importance to the strikers and boycotters, as this detail from the boycott comic book illustrates. *Courtesy of Colorado AFL-CIO*

Boycott bumper stickers. *Courtesy of Colorado AFL-CIO*

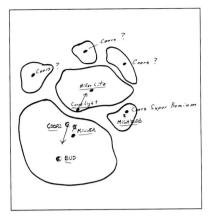

John Nichols doodled this map of the beer market to demonstrate to the Coors brothers that the images of Coors and Coors Light were dangerously similar. Nichols's arrows showed his intention of challenging the leaders in the premium and light-beer markets—Budweiser and Miller Lite. The smaller circles represented essential markets— import, super-premium, economy-priced—in which Coors had no products. *Courtesy of John Nichols*

Though Nichols's campaigns arrested the company's slide, the brash Texan—who hung a sign in his office promising "Nothing in Moderation"—never got the culture of Coors to accept either him or the need for aggressive marketing. *Courtesy of John Nichols*

John Nichols revived Coors's Banquet brand beer with a catchy slogan differentiating it from the "downstream," "flat land," and "city" beers of its major competitors, St. Louis-based Anheuser-Busch and Milwaukee-based Miller. As usual, David Sickler's boycott committee co-opted Coors's best efforts by using the slogan in this boycott leaflet. Morever, soon after the AFL-CIO began publicizing the presence of asbestos in Coors's Enzinger filters, the company switched to all cotton. *Courtesy of Colorado AFL-CIO*

IT'S NOT FLAT LAND BEER

IT'S NOT CITY BEER

IT'S JUST ANOTHER **COORS BEER** IN DISGUISE

BOYCOTT

"HERMAN JOSEPH'S" 1868

ALL COORS BEERS ARE ASBESTOS FILTERED

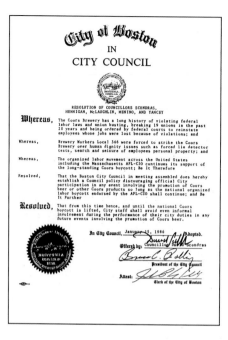

Nine years after the strike and two thousand miles away from Golden, the boycott was as strong as ever. On January 15, 1986, the Boston City Council passed a resolution directing the city staff to "avoid even informal involvement . . . in any future events involving the promotion of Coors beer." *Courtesy of Colorado AFL-CIO*

Joe Coors (*right*) had spent two decades and millions of brewery dollars promoting a stridently right-wing political agenda. Finally, in 1980, Joe could enjoy the election of a truly conservative president, his longtime personal friend, Ronald Wilson Reagan. *Courtesy of Ronald Reagan Library*

"I still think we can win it," DeBey said to Silverthorn as they sat at the union hall late one night.

"Of course we can win it," Silverthorn said. But inside, he was counting the mistakes they'd made so far: Letting the company drive a wedge between the union and both women and minorities with its replacement of the leadmen. The open strike vote. Forgetting that the strikers would lose health benefits. Letting the workers get used to the 7 percent raise before striking.

"There's a principle involved here, right?" DeBey asked. "We have dignity issues."

Silverthorn lifted his head tiredly and said, "Dignity issues don't mean shit."

On day ten of the strike, strange cars began appearing in the employee lot, some with out-of-state license plates. Replacements. The picketers heckled them mercilessly and got the finger in return. But Silverthorn's "no violence" rule held. Palms were beaten on car hoods, but no punches were thrown. Watching exhaustedly from the line, Silverthorn ruefully reflected that he had enough authority to prevent violence, but not enough to prevent scabbing. The Denver papers reported that more than half the strikers had gone back to work.

"What about the strike benefits, Jim?" asked men still on the line.

"What about the boycott?"

"Did you hear they took away our health insurance?"

Bill Coors walked to the lectern in the big sixth-floor auditorium, smoothing the unaccustomed tie against his chest. He tried not to look at the television cameras lining the wall. This was only his second annual shareholders' meeting since going public, and he wasn't used to it. Strangers in the brewery were supposed to be smiling tourists, not this mob of petulant busybodies. The whole idea of having to explain his management of the brewery to outsiders was repellent. Now, with the strike, this year's Adolph Coors Company shareholders' meeting was the whole world's business. Bill had wanted to bar the cameras but was advised against it; Wall Street didn't like stock-exchange companies trying to limit access to their public functions. So there they were, a line of leering Cyclopses, following him along the stage.

Bill faced his shareholders. About 150 were present, spread thinly around the auditorium. They looked surly. Bill and Joe had insisted on holding the meeting at the brewery instead of elsewhere. That meant the shareholders had been forced to cross the picket line to attend, and each had taken a terrible razzing on the way in.

"Nineteen seventy-six was a record year for the Adolph Coors Company," Bill began. The shareholders stared back at him. "As you know, our first year as a public company had been disappointing. But we came back strong. Our net income in 1976 was our highest ever."

He took a sip of water.

"Now it's true our first-quarter sales this year are down some." A wave of fidgeting went around the vast room. First-quarter earnings were down more than "some": They were down 70 percent. The AFL-CIO boycott had been declared a couple of weeks earlier and the shareholders were hoping Bill would announce a conciliatory gesture to forestall catastrophe. In typically modest fashion, Coors had never advertised the virtues of cold-filtering over pasteurization; it had simply let the taste speak for itself. Now customers were learning for the first time from the AFL-CIO that Coors beer was unpasteurized; the labor federation was telling people it was unsafe to drink. The beer's best selling point had thus been turned into a crippling negative. "Beer consumption generally has taken an unexplained drop," Bill said, "which has led to the kind of discounting we'd hoped to avoid." An anticipatory silence answered him.

"Also," he said, "our Press Tab, which we introduced out of a sense of environmental responsibility, has had a depressing effect on sales. We have been inundated with calls about it."

Silence.

"But I assure you I am fielding all complaints about Press Tab personally," Bill said with a nervous, monosyllabic laugh.

More silence.

"And I don't need to tell you that California is a marketing zoo."

"Uh, Bill," a voice came from the back. "If I may call you Bill."

"Please do."

"What about the strike? And the boycott?"

Bill sighed. Peter was in the front row, watching him.

"This strike," Bill began, raising his gaze to the crowd, "is the most irresponsible strike ever perpetuated on a brewery. Those monkeys out on the picket line think only about what they can do to destroy this company."

Joe was in the front row, too.

"It's business as usual at the Adolph Coors Company," Bill went on, warming to his topic. "Now I believe unions have a rightful place in our society. But it is incumbent on a company to maintain a proper balance of power. In the Coors case, power has swung way over to the side of the union."

A woman's voice reached his ears from beyond the glare of the TV lights. "What have you done to settle the strike?"

"Absolutely nothing," Bill said. "Nor will we. Oh"—he gave another barking laugh—"I did have one meeting with a group of them, and one delightful lady took exception to our rules requiring company loyalty." He pinched his voice into a taunting whine. " 'We made seventy-six million dollars last year,' she said, 'and you owe us more consideration.' " Bill laughed again and returned his voice to normal. "I told her she and some of her friends should set up their own brewery and see how things turn out."

Jeff sat up front with Peter and Joe.

"They admit we pay higher wages than almost anybody else in Colorado," Bill continued. "They admit that! They say this strike is about 'dignity issues.' Well, I'm here to tell you this union has no dignity left to preserve."

Someone asked how many workers had so far crossed the picket line. "Nine hundred of fourteen hundred," Bill shot back, an astounding figure to be able to boast only a month into the strike. Bill went on to describe one man who'd gone back to work and then walked out again because his wife's father and brother were striking and she'd threatened to divorce her husband if he didn't rejoin the picket line. Bill called the man "chicken."

"My name is Harry Methner," a stubby man in a maroon jacket said, rising. "My wife Ruth owns stock in your fine company, and on her behalf I object to your calling your employees 'monkeys' or 'chicken' or whatever."

Bill stopped and blinked into the lights. *So this is what it means to be a public company. Strangers telling you how to talk about your own people.*

"Well, I'm sorry," he said graciously. "You're right. I should not have said that and I ask the secretary to strike my comments from the record."

The reporters in the room felt no such obligation. Peter levered open the *Rocky Mountain News* business section next morning. WILLIAM K. COORS TERMS STRIKERS "MONKEYS" read the headline.

Sickler felt like an infantryman pulled straight from the mud into the colonel's elegant office behind the lines. Donald MacDonald, lawyer for Local 366, sat behind his grand desk in a finely cut suit. Sickler, damp and rumpled from long days and nights on the picket line, leaned tiredly against a wall gulping coffee. Jay Dee Patrick was there, as well as Jim Silverthorn and Ken DeBey.

"We have a loser here," MacDonald said.

"Bullshit," DeBey said.

"You've lost!" MacDonald cried. "More than half your guys are back inside the plant. The rest of you are being replaced. The drivers are crossing your picket lines. The strike's over."

"We stopped a train this morning," DeBey said. "It was coming in for a load of beer. We got up on top of the Fifty-eighth Street viaduct in Arvada and dropped a strike sign right in front of it." He laughed and sat forward. "You should have heard the brakes screech!"

"That doesn't change the fact that more than half your guys are back inside," MacDonald said.

"We're hurting them," DeBey said. "We're hurting them bad."

"Oh, please," the lawyer said with a dismissive flap of his hand. "They beat you. Take my advice: Accept the company offer and go back to work."

This was exactly what Sickler had expected would happen if the union struck. It was the reason he'd argued so strongly against it.

But now that the men were out, they should stay out, he thought. Otherwise it would be pure victory for the Coorses.

"No way," Sickler said. "We're not crawling back."

"Listen to Mr. Strike," Silverthorn said with a snort. "You never wanted us to walk out in the first place."

"That's right," Sickler said. "But now that we're out we shouldn't go back."

"I don't want to go back inside, either," Silverthorn said. "But I think we're making a mistake with this." He held out a sheet of bright orange stickers that announced, WARNING. COORS BEER IS UNPASTEURIZED AND UNSAFE TO DRINK. They were designed to stick on Coors cans in stores. "You don't put the bad mouth on the product," Silverthorn continued. "Someday we're going to go back inside that plant, and it's going to be embarrassing to make beer we've said is unsafe."

Sickler pushed himself away from the wall and squared his shoulders. "This is war," he said. "We have to hurt them any way we can."

"I don't understand the AFL-CIO," Jay Dee Patrick said, half to himself. "They didn't launch the boycott for almost two weeks. They didn't start strike benefits for three weeks. I can't understand why they're not fully behind us." Sickler wanted to pull Patrick out of his chair and slap him.

"Don't blame the AFL-CIO," he said angrily. "They're doing all they can. This was our mistake. It was *your* mistake, Jay Dee. You knew better than to take this local into a strike."

"Guys," MacDonald said, holding up a hand. "This isn't the place."

But Silverthorn was now on his feet and shouting—Silverthorn, usually the mildest of men. "You're the one who told us there'd be a boycott 'the minute' the strike started!" he barked at Patrick. "Your words: 'the minute' the strike starts."

"You have a lawyer here who wants to throw in the towel," Patrick shot back. "And you can't maintain discipline on your own picket line!"

"Gentlemen . . ." MacDonald said.

Silverthorn advanced on Patrick. "I won't be responsible for violence!" he shouted. "I'd rather lose the strike."

"Well, you're going to get your wish," Patrick snarled.

"Gentlemen," MacDonald said again. "Let's concentrate. You've got men hurting on the picket line, for nothing. It's time to call it off."

The union men spoke in unison: "No."

Jim Silverthorn kept looking over his shoulder, expecting a platoon of cops to descend on them at any moment. He, Ken DeBey, and Jay Dee Patrick were here because Russ Hargis had bearded Silverthorn in Foss's Drug Store one day and whispered an alarming suggestion: Talk to Bill. Now, after a flurry of furtive phone calls, the three union men were walking up the long driveway of the big boss himself.

They looked left and right as they rang the bell. No security people were in sight. The door opened and there stood Bill. He smiled and stepped out onto the path.

"Hey, Bill," Silverthorn said.

"You men all right?" Bill asked.

"Well, we'd like to end this strike," Silverthorn said.

"So would I," Bill said with a cock of his head. "I don't mind telling you, the boycott isn't doing the company any good. I'm amazed at you people, saying our beer is unsafe to drink. You know better than that, Jim."

Silverthorn's face grew hot. He fought an impulse to apologize to Bill, and said nothing.

"Are you men ready to go back to work?" Bill asked.

"Can't do it," DeBey said. "Not with that contract."

"I can't do anything about that," Bill said. "My brother Joe won't hear of it. He's coming over to the brewery from Porcelain, you know. He's going to be co-president."

The three union men were silent. They hadn't known. First Mornin, now Joe—Coors was grouping its antiunion firepower.

"What about the lie detector?" Patrick asked. "If we could just get rid of the lie detector, the men might decide they'd won enough."

Bill shook his head and looked down at his feet. "Joe says no," he said. He looked up at Silverthorn. "You remember what happened to Ad. And now California."

Silverthorn nodded. A group calling itself the New World Liberation Front had just set off a small bomb at a Coors distributorship in San Jose. Nobody had been hurt, but it scared everybody, not least Silverthorn. "Joe's afraid of a bomber in the brewery," Silverthorn suggested.

"It isn't just that," Bill said, looking up. "We've had threats, sure. But Joe and I believe there is a principle involved here. This is our brewery, and we're not going to let anybody tell us how to run it."

"I've worked here twenty years . . ." Silverthorn began.

"And you've been paid well for your work, haven't you?" Bill asked. He stepped in close to Silverthorn, his friendliness gone. "We've kept our share of the bargain, and up until now you've kept yours," he said sharply. "But you don't own this brewery, Jim. You don't share the risk, you don't share the headaches, you don't share the responsibility. And therefore, you don't share the say in how this brewery will be run. You mention the lie detector. If we say it stays, it stays. If you don't want to live with that, you're free to leave."

"So that's how it is then," Silverthorn said derisively.

"We stand for something, Jim," Bill said. "We have beliefs and we're not going to abandon them. What do you people stand for, besides gimme gimme gimme? What principle are you trying to prove?"

"Bill," Silverthorn said, suddenly tired. "We're hurting. We want to go back to work. But we have to give the membership something, some reason to think this was worthwhile. Can't you throw us a bone?"

"I can't do it," Bill said. "My brother won't allow it."

"*I want* a transfer," Jay Dee Patrick said.

Five men sat in a Denver hotel room: Patrick, Sickler, DeBey, Silverthorn, and, from AFL-CIO headquarters, Nick Kurko.

"The strike's a loser," Patrick continued, without looking at Silverthorn, DeBey, or Sickler. "I'd like to move over to legislative affairs."

"You bastard," Sickler said. "You're the one who pushed this strike."

"With a *boycott,*" Patrick said. "I always said it would take a boycott. I didn't know the AFL-CIO was going to punk out on us."

"Watch your mouth," Kurko said. "I always worried that you were so hot for a boycott. I should have realized it meant you didn't think this local could carry off its own strike."

"The membership is committed, which is more than I can say for you," Patrick shot back. "Making us meet secretly down here, so the membership doesn't know about it, is disgusting."

"Just as well," Sickler interjected. "If the workers could see you turning tail, they'd kill you."

"Well, it's finished," Patrick said. "It might have worked with a proper boycott, but . . ."

"A weapon!" shouted Kurko. "I always told you a boycott is a weapon, nothing more."

"Well, it hasn't been much of a weapon," Patrick said. "You waited two weeks into the strike before declaring it. And three weeks before paying strike benefits. Even now you're slow with them."

"The AFL-CIO is a big organization," Kurko said. "We have more going on than this strike."

"He's right," Sickler told Patrick. "You can't fault the AFL-CIO. This strike was a loser before it started, and you should have known that. The question is, What should we do now?"

"I have a message from Mr. Meany," Kurko said. "Dave, he wants you to take over the boycott. You'll have a budget. Not a big budget, but a budget."

"I already have a job," Sickler said. "Up in Helena."

"Well," Kurko said, "Mr. Meany wants you to do this, too. As of now, you're the director of the Coors boycott. If anything can be salvaged from this, it's up to you."

11

A Pride Thing

Since the Press Tab vote, Peter had retreated into his usual avoidance of conflict. He watched Bill and Joe prepare to annihilate Local 366 and knew in his gut it was a mistake. The Adolph Coors Company didn't need to start a war with a union at precisely the moment Anheuser-Busch and Miller were launching aggressive western campaigns to grab Coors territory. Peter was no more fond of unions than Bill or Joe but he had a more vivid sense of external threats. The union demands seemed about as damaging as BB guns when lined up alongside the marketing howitzers deployed by Coors's competitors. The union might take a nibble out of Coors profits but Bud could devour them. That, however, was a money argument, and at heart his father and uncle were unreceptive. They cared about quality. They cared about principle. And while on one level they naturally cared about their business's financial health, on another level it was, quite literally, the least of their concerns. Peter prayed his father and uncle would make peace with the one adversary who would accept an olive branch. But he wasn't going to fight them over it. The Press Tab vote had retaught him the central lesson of his childhood: Head-on confrontation is a mistake, especially with Dad.

Lowell Sund—who'd been with the company since Peter was in diapers—had begged Bill and Joe to settle the strike and they'd told him it was none of his business and warned him not to mention it again. The sales director, Fred Vierra, had pressed the point at a board meeting and nearly ended up in a fistfight.

"Bill. Joe. I'm begging you," Vierra had said. "Please make peace with the unions."

Bob Mornin had leapt from his seat. "I've warned you never to say that!" Mornin had barked, bringing up his beefy forearms. "Do not say that again, ever!"

Peter had watched Sund and Vierra fall on their swords, and kept silent. The fight with the union, he decided, would be painful and distracting. It would cost Coors more than would making peace. But it would not threaten the company's survival. Peter knew his best bet was to bide his time, husband his credibility, and keep his eye on the real menace: Miller and above all the beast Miller had energized, Anheuser-Busch.

It had taken August Busch III unnaturally long to figure out how dangerous John Murphy and Miller Lite were going to be. Busch had had a lot on his plate at the time Miller Lite appeared. He was unseating his father, reorganizing the executive corps, and settling the hundred-day Teamsters strike. When he'd finally turned his full attention to the Miller challenge, he'd made two crucial mistakes.

First, he misread Miller Lite. Busch wasn't sure light beer would remain popular and didn't think it would catch on at all in Texas, an enormous Budweiser market. Busch didn't want to risk diluting the Budweiser name with something called "Budweiser Light," if it was just a passing fad. A highly trained brewer, Busch was offended by Miller's use of artificial ingredients and tried to make an issue of it in his advertising. Those two concerns led him to call his light beer—when he finally got around to making one—Anheuser-Busch Natural Light Beer, an awkward mouthful. The public didn't share Busch's interest in "natural" beer and continued buying Miller Lite in terrifying quantities, even in Texas.

Busch's second big mistake was letting John Murphy buy up all the best sports advertising in the country: the World Series, the Indianapolis 500, the college football game of the week, and the most-watched weekly television event, *Monday Night Football.* Busch at first thought Murphy was making a colossal mistake. He viewed such high-priced advertising in terms of raw dollars and couldn't fathom Miller's strategy of calculating dollars-per-thousand-viewers. By the time Busch and his marketing people caught on to the wisdom of wedding beer to sports advertising, it was too late. There were no big-time sporting spots left to buy.

But Busch wouldn't be bested. He tripled his advertising budget overnight to $100 million. He hired a hundred experienced brand marketers from Pepsi, Coca-Cola, Procter & Gamble, and the other heavy hitters of consumer-products marketing. He sat down one afternoon with his beefed-up troops and a directory of colleges thick as a Manhattan phone directory. They started with A and plowed through to Z, looking for intercollegiate teams. When they found a college fielding any sort of sports team, Busch barked, "Buy 'em!"

Budweiser's bow-tie-shaped logo, big and white against a field of patriotic red and blue, was suddenly prominent everywhere two colleges played anything: football, tennis, crew, curling. Outside the college arena, Anheuser-Busch sponsored speedboat races, polo matches, hot-air ballooning—any sporting event where a television camera might pan across the Budweiser logo. Busch went so far as to create such advertising events as the Budweiser Iron Man Triathlon World Championship and the Michelob Night Riders cycling circuit. The company ultimately produced a thousand of these Budweiser sporting extravaganzas. You could channel-surf late at night in some parts of the country in the late 1970s and come upon a rubber duck race in a creek and sure enough, the Budweiser logo would be waving above the finish line.

Peter Coors, the only one at the Golden brewery who was reading the marketing press, fought a swell of panic. The most he'd been able to wring out of his father and uncle for advertising was $12 million a year. His hands were tied creatively, too. While Miller Lite's people-centered ads were proving supereffective, Peter was allowed no more than a bottle of beer on a rock. He knew that waving his arms and screaming, "Miller! Bud! Look out!" would only harden his father's and uncle's resolve to ignore them. The marketers running A-B and Miller represented everything Bill and Joe Coors disdained. They were Visigoths, Peter's elders believed, beholden to the bottom line and brewing beer as an afterthought. In early 1977, Bill and Joe were no more focused on Bud and Miller than they were on the rings of Saturn. They were concentrating avidly on destroying Local 366. The months ticked by. Budweiser's and Miller's market share inched upward. Coors's earnings slid.

Peter might have panicked but for his hole card: the light beer with which Jeff was secretly tinkering. Little by little, Jeff had expanded the tiny cubby of a lab Bill had created in 1939. Now it was a high-tech "pilot brewery" where Jeff could reproduce in miniature the functions of a full-scale brewery, testing and tweaking various beers before sending them into mass production. Peter called into his office Jeff and Chuck Hahn, one of Jeff's small cadre of brewing specialists. How was the secret light beer project going? Peter wanted to know.

"Well," Jeff said, furrowing his brow. "Basically what we're doing is making a beer with a little less alcohol. As you know, when we say three-point-two percent alcohol, that's not by volume. It's by weight. By volume, our beer is four percent alcohol."

Peter tapped his foot under the desk, knowing not to rush his big brother.

"Alcohol gives six point nine calories per gram," Jeff went on. "Fat gives twelve. A can of beer is three hundred and sixty grams, so—"

"Can you get it done for ninety-six calories or less?" Peter couldn't help interrupting.

"We can," Jeff said, pressing his fingertips together and frowning at them. "But not if you want the beer to taste good. What Miller's done to keep the alcohol up is precipitate out the complex carbohydrates that give the beer its texture and mouthfeel."

"But they're under a hundred calories," Peter said. He put his hand on a stack of research materials he'd compiled since their golf-club lunch. "Everything I'm hearing tells me that's their selling point."

"That may be," Chuck Hahn interjected. "But our strength is that we make beer that tastes good."

Jeff stared at his fingers for a long moment. Peter waited. Finally, Jeff lifted his head.

"A hundred and five," he said.

"Pardon?" Peter asked.

"A hundred and five calories. If you can give us a hundred and five calories, I can brew a good-tasting light beer."

Peter drummed his fingers on the desktop. Under a hundred calories was the holy grail, the bar that Miller Lite had set and Anheuser-Busch had met. On the other hand, all of Peter's research so far showed that people didn't really like the taste of Miller Lite. Wives bought it for their overweight husbands and the men dutifully drank it, but not with enthusiasm. Women suggested that its poor taste was part of the reason they bought it; every unpleasant sip reminded them they were watching their weight. People liked ordering Miller Lite because it announced they were conscious about their health. But when the barman set it before them, few really enjoyed the drink.

There was, after all, no law saying a beer could only be called "light" when it's under a hundred calories. A hundred and five would make Coors Light a quarter fewer calories than Coors regular. Miller's is a third fewer, but who really registers the math?

"Okay," Peter said. "A hundred and five calories. But do it fast, please. I want to get this into blind market testing as soon as possible. In the meantime, I'll keep working on Dad and Uncle Bill."

Dad and Uncle Bill had a series of surprises for Peter. The good news was they were scrapping the Press Tab. The bad news was they were replacing it with Press Tab Two. Instead of two little buttons to press, Press Tab Two had one big tear-shaped button. Peter made a training video for the distributors to introduce it, but was unable to open the can on camera. When he finally figured it out, he realized opening a can of Coors now meant the customer—or, worse, the bartender—had to stick his finger in the beer.

"Dad," he said. "Uncle Bill. This is no better. If anything, it's worse. The distributors are up in arms. The customers don't like it. Please, we have enough trouble without making extra."

"I like Press Tab Two," Joe said. He swiveled his head and looked at Bill.

"I like it, too," Bill said.

Discussion closed.

The next surprise Joe sprung on Peter was a vice president of marketing.

Peter was amazed. He had been arguing for months that the family needed to bring an experienced marketer on board. If Dad and Uncle Bill ever came around to agreeing, Peter had expected, he would be told to conduct a nationwide search, maybe hire a high-priced headhunter to find the best person. Coors, after all, was a $400 million corporation with considerable cachet. It could attract the best. Peter asked his father where the new man was coming from, hoping Joe would say Procter & Gamble, Philip Morris, or some other giant of brand marketing. Or if not that, Leo Burnett, Ogilvy & Mather, or another of the great ad agencies.

Instead, Joe said the new marketer was coming from something called American Hospital Supply.

[A Pride Thing]

It didn't take Lee Shelton long to realize he needed serious help, and Art Stone's phone rang at Leo Burnett and Company in Chicago soon after. When Stone heard about the opportunity at Coors, his first thought was, Colorado? Denver was a marketing wasteland. It housed few consumer-products companies, so there was no cross-fertilization of marketing talent like there was in Atlanta, New York, Chicago, and Los Angeles. You could count on two hands the Denver companies who spent twenty million a year on marketing. Coors wasn't among them.

But at age thirty-six, Stone felt like he was being pushed into retirement at Burnett. Internal politics had relegated him to the United Airlines account, which was slow death. He wanted back into the rock-and-roll world of consumer-products marketing. He called Lee Shelton, who invited him out.

On the reception-area coffee table at Coors, Stone found a recent copy of *Denver* magazine with a cover story on Coors. Wow, Stone thought as he flipped through it. May every company I ever work for get such positive press. The story was so upbeat it didn't even mention the strike or Coors's plummeting market share. The magazine even let go unchallenged Bill's assertion that "the one thing we avoid at all costs is nepotism. Anyone who bears the family name has a tougher time getting ahead than anyone else."

Joe was awkward to the point of mute as Stone told his marketing war stories. He didn't ask a single relevant question. Peter, at least, seemed interested, if little more knowledgeable. At one point he offered Stone a beer, and since Coors wasn't yet sold in Illinois and was a treat, Stone accepted. Peter handed him a can from the little refrigerator behind his desk.

Most beer companies were still using ring-pulls, but when Stone reached for the ring it wasn't there. Instead, a large, tear-shaped bubble looked back at him like an eye.

"This is our own design," Peter said mechanically. "It's superior because the tab stays attached to the can. You don't throw away valuable aluminum, and there's less litter."

Impressive, Stone thought. Another Coors engineering feat. He pressed the bubble and nothing happened.

"Harder," Peter said. Stone pressed harder, but couldn't make it pop.

"Put it on the desk," Peter said. Stone did so and finally pressed hard enough to break through. His finger plunged unappetizingly into the beer. When he pulled it out, the hole's edge sliced his finger.

"Uh . . ." he began, wrapping his bloody finger in a handkerchief.

"It needs work," Peter said sheepishly.

Stone was so eager to escape Burnett and run his own marketing department that he didn't object to Coors's absurdly low salary offer—about a third less than he was making at Burnett. More important, though, he ignored his own instincts. From his brief, vague interview with Joe—and the fact that Bill didn't even bother to meet him—Stone could tell that neither knew the first thing about marketing. Worse, they weren't interested. In Stone's experience, successful consumer-products companies have CEOs who understand and enjoy the rough-and-tumble world of finding market niches and creating attractive products for them. Clearly, the Coors brothers did not. In his eagerness, Stone buried his doubts.

During his first week on the job, Harris Hamlin—the man Stone was replacing as ad director—said he was ready to hand over his company car. Would Stone please give him a ride home? Hamlin was a nice man of about sixty, thickly built, with a crew cut and wearing on this night, as usual, a polyester sports shirt and shop glasses. Stone, half his age, stood stiffly in his slick suit as Hamlin emptied the contents of his desk into a cardboard box. "Nothing personal," Hamlin said sadly, "but the old gent wouldn't have given guys like you the time of day. Professional chess players he called you, with no sense of loyalty."

"Well . . ." Stone said.

"Here today and gone tomorrow," Hamlin said as he hoisted the box and led Stone to the parking lot. Hamlin opened the door of the car he was bequeathing to Stone, a block-long black Electra 225 with a red plush interior. Stone gasped. He drove a BMW and wouldn't be caught dead driving such a garishly tricked-out behemoth.

"You're the only one who gets a company car," Hamlin said with a rueful smile. "Not even Peter has one."

They started driving toward Hamlin's house.

"All Peter's interested in is the eighteen-to-twenty-nine age group," Hamlin lamented. "He just sees the market from his own age's viewpoint."

You bet, Stone thought. They're the ones who drink the most beer.

"I told him, 'Your granddad didn't feel that way about it,'" Hamlin went on. "I guess that cooked my goose."

Stone left Hamlin standing on the curb in front of his house, hugging the cardboard box to his chest. Stone felt terrible. He drove home, parked the Electra 225, and didn't touch it again.

Stone was invited soon after to sit in on a board meeting, and was appalled at what he learned. The entire beer industry was in an uproar, Coors's market share was falling out of the sky like a poisoned bird, and the board did nothing but listen to Bill pontificate about how great Coors beer was. It was like a meeting of Idi Amin's cabinet: Nobody dared raise a different subject or opposing viewpoint. "We prevail," Bill said loftily, "because we alone have a commitment to *quality*."

Jesus Christ, Stone thought. What have I gotten myself into?

He worked fast. He sent a flurry of memos to Lee Shelton but never heard back on any of them. So he went ahead on his own, developing a print ad depicting a lone horseman in the snow. He rushed it into production. A couple of weeks later, Joe bearded him in the hallway.

"You just made Coors history," he said, looking down grimly at Stone. "How so?"

"You put a person in an ad," Joe said. "We'd never done that before." He walked away leaving Stone nonplussed.

Next, Stone rounded up his Nashville connections, who dashed off a cute country jingle:

Taste the wide open sky
Taste the Rocky Mountain high
Make it Coors
Make it Coors
Make it yours

It wasn't exactly Gershwin, Stone had to admit, but it would do. He took it to Lee Shelton, who frowned and said he'd better call a board meeting. Coors had never used a jingle before, let alone country music. As Stone was ushered into the inner sanctum, he felt like he was entering a medieval star chamber. But he bravely set a cassette player on the table and played the tune.

Silence.

Jeff Coors spoke first. "I don't know," he said. "I don't like country music."

Stone opened his mouth to point out that the personal tastes of Jeff Coors were irrelevant. Country music was big at the moment, and popular with Coors's target age group. But he closed his mouth without speaking. He was just a director. Directors spoke only to vice presidents. Vice presidents spoke to Coorses.

After a long silence, Joe spoke.

"It's nice," he said. Shelton nodded to Stone, and they left. For the first time in its hundred-and-eleven-year history, Coors would have a radio jingle for its beer. It was a start.

Stone's phone rang one afternoon and it was Peter, asking if Stone had a minute to come up to his office. You own the damn company, Stone wanted to answer. Of course I have a minute. When he arrived, he was met by a semicircle of glum-looking men facing the door like a firing squad. Peter was seated beside them. Bill and Joe stood by the window, with Bob Mornin.

"Okay," Bill said derisively as Stone walked in the door. "Now we'll hear from advertising, the *modern* way." He folded his arms and turned to stare out the window.

"Hello," Stone said.

Joe smiled at Stone and gave him a slight, bemused flick of the eyebrows, as though to say, Don't worry about Bill. Go ahead and do your stuff.

"These are our California distributors," Mornin said. "They're, uh, a little upset. I thought maybe you could explain how we're going to turn this company around with a new ad campaign."

Oh, great, Stone thought. Set me up to fail.

But he talked. He explained how markets are segmented and products created for them. He talked about target television and radio shows, about billboards, about price promotions, about in-store displays. Not that he had the authority to implement any of it, he thought. This was more an exercise in out-loud wishful thinking.

When he finished, he went back to his office and forgot about it. But a few hours later Peter called again, asking him to ascend to the sixth floor in a hurry.

"I want to spend a million dollars in California right away," Peter said when Stone walked into his office.

"What?"

"I want to spend a million dollars in California right now," Peter said. "We have to do something."

"Well, this isn't the way you do things," Stone said. "You develop a plan and then you see how much it costs. You don't go in waving money or the ad people will take it off you before you can blink, and you'll end up with a lot of uncoordinated junk. What's your strategy?"

"I don't care about that," Peter said. "I want to spend a million dollars in California. Right now."

Peter didn't care what Art Stone did in California as long as he did it fast and big. Stone chose billboards because it was something Peter could see with his own eyes right away, and he knew it would make an impression. He got the heads of two billboard companies together and demanded their best locations. "I'll know the difference," he told them, "and if either of you tries to slip lousy spots past me I'll give all my business to the other guy." The campaign came off well, and Stone returned to Golden determined to shake things up at Coors.

It was heavy going, because the company seemed determined to shoot itself in the foot at every opportunity. Stone had some sympathy for his immediate boss, Lee Shelton. The job was obviously over his head. But he'd known enough to hire Stone, giving his department some experience and connections. Stone was friendly with Bill Phillips, chairman of Ogilvy & Mather advertising, and they spoke occasionally on the phone.

"Who is this guy Shelton?" Phillips asked. "I never heard of him. *Nobody's* ever heard of him. How did they pick him?"

"Don't ask me," Stone said.

"You know, I'm friends with Bill and Joe Coors," Phillips told Stone. "But they never call to pick my brains. I figured they'd at least ask me whom to hire. "

"It's a pride thing," Stone said.

Stone did eventually convince the Coorses, through Shelton, that a company their size needed to retain an ad agency.

But when it came time to choose, Shelton seemed intimidated by the big names Coors could have garnered—Ogilvy & Mather, Ted Bates, or Leo Burnett. Instead, he chose a tiny outfit neither Stone nor any of his friends knew. Worse, the agency started off by killing Stone's best spot. Stone had used his Nashville connections to line up the country singer Kenny Rogers. He managed it at the perfect moment, right after Rogers's song "Lucille" was released and just before "The Gambler," which made him a superstar. Stone paid Rogers a mere $25,000 to sing a nice little ditty that included the words "it's right for you and me." At the end of the spot, someone off camera threw Rogers a can of Coors and he caught it with the logo facing the camera. It was beautiful. But the agency refused to air it.

The government wouldn't allow it, they said. Kenny Rogers doesn't drink, and the song had him saying "it's right for you and me."

Stone wondered what government agency policed the drinking habits of actors in commercials. The real reson the agency killed the spot, he figured, was that they hadn't come up with it themselves. Two weeks later, Rogers won the country music performer-of-the-year award and his fee shot to a quarter-million dollars. Stone decided it was time to go around Shelton with strategy ideas. He wrote Peter Coors a memo about the company image, but he never heard back.

The longer Stone stayed at Coors, the more he felt like he'd fallen into a time warp. At a sales conference near Telluride, Stone was sitting at a table with Joe, Peter, Jeff, and some other executives, and tried to start a conversation about music. Who, he asked, are the greatest influences on contemporary music?

"The two greatest influences in *my* life," Peter said, "are my uncle Bill and Jesse Helms."

"No, *music,*" Stone said. "Who do you think the greatest influences on modern music are? Elvis Presley, maybe? The Beatles?"

"Glenn Miller," said Joe.

Stone coughed into his napkin.

"Tell us a little about what you're trying to do for us," Joe said to Stone.

Stone perked up, overjoyed that a Coors—and of that generation!— was showing an interest in marketing. He launched a detailed explanation.

Stone said he was looking for a "branding element," he said, a tune that would become popular and evoke the company's product the way the *Magnificent Seven* theme did for Marlboro and "Fly the Friendly Skies" did for United Airlines. Stone wanted to record the tune in a number of different styles to appeal to key market segments. "I'd do a Natalie Cole kinda thing for the black ethnic market," Stone said, "and a Waylon Jennings kinda thing for the country market. . . ."

"Country music again!" Jeff interjected. "I *hate* country music."

"But it appeals to a big segment of our target market," Stone explained. "We run spots on a lot of different stations, and you want your ad to sound like the station."

"I just don't like it," Jeff said irritably.

"So what are you saying?" Stone asked.

"I'm saying it seems stupid to use country music," Jeff said. "It's awful, that twangy stuff."

Stone turned to Joe, but the elder Coors was getting up from his chair, stretching a long arm to greet a distributor from New Mexico.

Stone felt a flush of anger. The bad choices and silly mistakes seemed deliberate. It's as though the Coors family, having decided marketing is worthless and unseemly, wants to sabotage its own efforts to prove the point. Stone didn't know how much more of it he could take.

A few days later, Joe called Stone into his office.

"We have to do something about this strike," Joe said.

Thank God, Stone thought. Finally.

"I want you to write us a full-page ad to run in all the major newspapers in the West," Joe said. "I want it to explain why we're not giving in."

Stone sighed.

"I want the headline to say, WE ARE CONSERVATIVE," Joe said, spreading his hands across an imaginary page and gazing into space. " 'Our politics are based in historical American values. Our business is to make good products and take care of our people, and we do that.' " Joe returned his gaze to Stone. "That kind of thing. Can you do that?"

"I can . . ."

"Then go to it. Show it to me when you're done."

Stone knew better than to argue. He returned to his office, put aside what he was doing, and wrote a humdinger of an ad. Joe loved it.

"I strongly advise you not to use it," Stone said.

"Why not?"

"It will just make everything worse. If you want to live by your personal politics, do so and take the consequences. If you'd rather sell more beer, settle the strike. But this"—he gestured at the ad—"is trying to have it both ways. You're going to make the unions madder."

Joe chewed on the advice, and ultimately accepted it. But to Stone's disappointment, he chose Option A: to live by his personal politics and take the consequences of the strike and boycott. The consequences, of course, were a spiraling market share that Stone's best efforts couldn't arrest.

Stone's tenure ended shortly thereafter. One gray November day, he was pulled out of a meeting by Coors Security officers who were furious that he'd entered the brewery through the wrong gate. "Okay," he said, eager to get back to his meeting. "I won't do it again. May I go back to work?" But the officers declared the matter "very serious" and berated him in the hallway for another ten minutes. They finally stalked off muttering dark warnings about putting a "letter" in his "file."

Then Lee Shelton reprimanded Stone because one of the writers he'd hired often came to work later than eight-thirty in the morning.

"She's here late at night," Stone said. "Creative people are like that."

"Not here they're not," Shelton said. "Eight-thirty."

Stone went to Peter. "Can I talk to you a minute?" he asked, pushing his head into Peter's office. Peter looked up with a pained expression.

"Uh, no actually," Peter said. "I'd rather you took your concerns up with Lee Shelton."

"My concerns *are* Lee Shelton," Stone said. "That's what I want to talk to you about."

"Well, we have a hierarchy here," Peter said. "This isn't appropriate."

"I've been sending you memos," Stone said. "Have you seen them?"

"No."

"Are you aware of my concerns?"

"No."

"And I can't talk to you about them," Stone said.

"No," Peter answered, looking back down at his desk.

Not long after, Shelton called Stone to his office and pushed two pieces of paper across his desk. One was a dismissal, the other a resignation. "Sign one," Shelton said.

"I'll have a new job tomorrow," Stone said bitterly, signing the dismissal. "You'll never have another job."

Stone had lasted six months. Coors's first experiment with a real marketing man was over.

Every time Peter had a chance, he raised the need for a Coors light beer. Every time, his father and uncle rejected the idea. "We *are* 'America's Fine Light Beer'," Bill argued. "Let's advertise ourselves as a light and be done with it."

"Then where would that leave the heavy-beer drinkers?" Peter asked. "The whole point is to have *two* beers on the market."

"But our one beer is the best!" Bill shouted. "Make a good product, sell it at reasonable cost, and the people will buy!"

"That's not true anymore, Uncle Bill," Peter said, his voice rising, despite himself. "Philip Morris changed all that!"

"I'm not going to turn my back on the way my father and grandfather did business just because a bunch of cigarette people decided to make beer," Bill said.

Bill and Peter had this argument with mounting regularity as Coors's market share continued to slide. Joe, on the other hand, grew increasingly silent during the light-beer disputes; a sense went through the brewery that Joe was softening.

Jeff continued tinkering with his illicit light beer while Peter and Lee Shelton ran secret taste tests. All the results were promising. "A company is thinking of entering the light-beer market," they would say, and the subjects often responded, "I hope it's Coors." Almost half of those identifying themselves as Miller Lite drinkers had switched from Coors, Peter learned, and most of them pronounced themselves eager to go back once Coors offered a low-calorie beer. To hide its identity in the taste tests, Coors packed its light beer in unpainted cans. The Coors employees running the taste tests started calling the cans "silver bullets."

Test subjects were delighted, when they opened the silver bullets, that the beer inside produced a rich foamy head. Miller Lite had almost no foam at all. Beer consumers, the Coors people learned, drink with their eyes as well as their mouths. But taste was important, too. The extra complex carbohydrates in the test brew lent it a subtle undertaste. Jeff called the flavor "grapefruit-banana." Miller Lite lacked any such undertaste. Even in blindfolded taste tests, the public preferred the unlabeled Coors light beer nine to one over Miller Lite.

By now, Coors's situation was desperate. Despite expanding into three new states, Coors was selling less beer than a year earlier. Sales in 1977 were down 5 percent and, owing to the complications of shipping to the new territory, earnings were down almost 12 percent. The last quarter of 1977 had been particularly bad, with earnings half what they'd been a year earlier.

The Coorses' financial picture was so grim that when they needed to raise $5 million to pay an inheritance tax bill, the only buyers of Coors shares they could find were each other. When Aunt Gertrude died, the family held its collective nose and borrowed from the National Bank of Denver to pay the taxes on time. But when they put 400,000 new brewery shares on the market to pay off the National Bank debt, the stock went begging. Nobody wanted shares in a failing brewery beset by labor troubles. The calamitous offer pushed the stock price down still further. Another family trust finally bought the shares—at an inflated price. It was a thoroughgoing disaster.

The planets were lining up to force a change at Coors. The AFL-CIO boycott surely was contributing to the market-share drop, especially in California. Anheuser-Busch, having recovered all the market share it lost during its hundred-day Teamsters strike and smelling the blood drawn by the AFL-CIO, was coming after Coors in California with discounts, price promotions, and a bottomless-pockets advertising blitz. August Busch III didn't want to return Bill's favor, after all. Miller, which had sold twice as much beer as Coors in 1977 and was already the country's number-two brewer, attributed almost all of its growth to Miller Lite. By now, light beers constituted some 8 percent of the market, and Miller Lite had most of it. While the elder Coorses—now sixty-one and sixty-two years old—were not capable of responding to the AFL-CIO's bruising boycott or learning from Busch's self-interested settling with the Teamsters, Peter thought they were perhaps ready to consider Jeff's light brew. When he sprung the news on Bill and Joe that they'd been brewing a light beer, neither of the elders was surprised. They'd heard rumors. They accepted the brewing rebellion gracefully—even declared the beer pretty good—but they still did not give the go-ahead.

Shelton let slip to a reporter that Coors was thinking of entering the light market, and the reaction was like a sonic boom. Distributors, retailers—even individual customers—flooded the company switchboard asking, "When do we get it?"

Finally, the elders folded.

Bill put up a brief fight about the brewing process Jeff had selected; he'd have done it a different way entirely. But Jeff had brewed a winner without his gifted uncle, and it visibly stung Bill. He spent his theatrical ire over laboratory methods, insisted on a few minor changes, and then he declared the beer good—good enough to wear the Coors label.

The shirtsleeved engineers in packaging, however, set their heels against it. A second product would require all kinds of expensive changes on the can and bottle lines. They said they couldn't do it, and Bill couldn't help siding with his kind against the marketers. Their objections delayed the release for more agonizing months.

When the engineers finally gave in, Peter convinced his uncles the new beer was going to need a big advertising push. He got an ad budget of $33 million for the coming year. It was paltry compared with those of Miller or Anheuser-Busch but it was a lot better than $12 million. In February 1978—three full years after Miller Lite exploded onto the beer market—the Colorado brewers announced that Coors Light would be in stores before the end of summer.

David Sickler was cruising the dilapidated neighborhoods of East L.A. in the twilight, radio on, idly crisscrossing block after block. He noticed lots of Coors neon in bodega and barroom windows and lots of Mexicans drinking beer on their stoops, enjoying the first cool breath of evening. More often than not, the beer they were drinking was Coors.

"Seven-twenty KABC news time," the radio announcer said as Billy Joel faded through the last notes of "I Love You Just the Way You Are." "Hey, good news for you beer drinkers!" the announcer continued. "The Adolph Coors Company says it's finally getting into the light-beer game and will have a Coors Light on the market by summertime. Seventy-two degrees and cloudy. More great music after this."

Damn, Sickler thought. He'd known Peter would eventually convince his father and uncle to make a light beer. He figured it would taste good and sell well. That's why he'd been racing to inflict as much damage on the company as he could before Coors Light was born. Another year and Coors would have limped to the negotiating table. Now it might never happen.

Sickler drove back downtown through the high-rise maze and let himself into the AFL-CIO building. George Meany had come through with a budget of $32,000 dollars to run the Coors boycott. That wasn't an annual budget, but rather all the money the labor federation planned to spend, regardless of the boycott's length. Sickler, though, considered his budget almost unlimited. As long as he was running a federation-sanctioned boycott, he decided to claim all the AFL-CIO's resources as his own. He called locals all over the country asking them to contribute time, work, beds, and money. He felt comfortable walking into any local's office to use the phone and photocopier, felt justified in claiming the time of any AFL-CIO staff member. Organizing a road show of strikers who would talk to any group that gave them a forum, Sickler lodged the strikers at the homes of local members, used the cars of local members to ferry them around, and cadged discount meals for his group at union restaurants.

Sickler was usually effusive about the effectiveness of the boycott, but today, hearing about Coors Light, was a low point. He walked listlessly through the empty building and sat at his gray steel desk.

Bill and Joe Coors might be reactionary, he reflected, but they were educable. Those two brontosaurs were adapting—however slowly and painfully—to many new realities. Bringing in Art Stone had been a start, and now, Coors Light. As Sickler flipped through the stack of mail heaped on his desk, his mind drifted to the problem that vexed him night and day. How could he spread the Coors boycott beyond the thinning ranks of labor? Sickler believed that all was fair in a fight against a rich and ruthless corporation and until recently his scorched-earth PR tactics had been routing the Coors brothers. But the company was getting smarter, no doubt about it. Just months ago, Sickler had been able to say anything, knowing Coors would say "no comment." But Peter had talked his father and uncle into setting up a six-person public relations department. They'd hired a pro from conservative Pepperdine College in Malibu to be vice president for public affairs—a title neither Mr. Coors nor the first Adolph could have stomached. The company was meeting Sickler now on any battleground he chose.

Sickler had gotten bills introduced in the Oregon and California state assemblies, for example, proposing a ban on the sale of unpasteurized beer as unhealthy. But in a moment of uncharacteristic political savvy, the brewery had sent a team of lobbyists—led by Joe's University of Colorado friend, Cliff Rock—and killed the bills.

Sickler had begun to tell people in California that Coors had donated $2 million to the National Rifle Association, which, in the context of Joe's politics, was readily believed by both antihunting activists and the millions supporting stricter gun control. As Sickler had hoped, Coors answered the charges by saying it didn't support the NRA—an assertion Sickler splashed across a flyer he sent to NRA members. Organizations on both sides of the gun question—consumers in urban California and their counterparts in the gun-toting frontier states that made up much of Coors territory—announced boycotts.

But the brewery parried that thrust, too. Max Goodwin—the company's decorous and orderly chief financial officer—had come up with a solution. Goodwin was a collector of *schutzen* rifles, an arcane type of turn-of-the-century target gun. These were elaborate, single-shot guns, useless for hunting or combat. Goodwin convinced the board to spend $20,000 on fancy display cases and truck his firearms to more than fifty gun shows in a single year as the "Coors Gun Collection." It was a perfect message; they were guns, all right, but relatively inoffensive both to antihunters and to those wanting to lower the gun-related murder rate. The Coors gun hoopla evaporated.

Pawing through the mail, Sickler came to *Beer Marketers Insights* and flipped to the California statistics. Good. Coors market share was still dropping, though Sickler had no idea whether the boycott or the combined force of Anheuser-Busch and Miller was responsible.

Next, Sickler opened an envelope from AFL-CIO headquarters and read some bad news. A small item clipped from the *Washington Star* said the American G.I. Forum, the national Hispanic-veterans group, was reversing an earlier position and accepting a donation from Coors. "Mr. Coors is now committed to helping Chicanos improve their status of life," said the organization's president Manuel Fierro.

"Scumbag," Sickler muttered. Fierro had helped lead the fight against Joe Coors's Senate confirmation to the board of the Corporation for Public Broadcasting. Now he'd been bought off with a couple of big checks.

Coors was clearly getting smart about Hispanics. When it expanded into eastern Texas, the brewery not only gave a distributorship to ex-astronaut Alan Shepard (and turned down Spiro Agnew), it also awarded five distributorships to people with Spanish surnames and made a big deal out of it.

Coors had also hired one of its most vocal Hispanic critics, Joe Benites, away from his job as president of LULAC—the League of United Latin American Citizens. As a public relations officer, Benites got Coors to start spreading scholarship money among Hispanics and then wangled a spot for the company on LULAC's corporate advisory board. Now Benites was here in Los Angeles organizing a campaign to unseat Hispanic councilman Richard Alatorre because Alatorre—at Sickler's urging—had filmed a boycott-Coors commercial in Spanish.

Coors's Hispanic PR drove Sickler crazy. He'd just been to Golden and Hispanics were as sorely underrepresented at the brewery as ever—especially in management. The white Rocky Mountain monoculture that prevailed at Coors remained oppressive. "If you want to keep your job, don't speak Spanish here," Hispanic Coors employees told Hispanic newcomers. "Lose your Mexican accent, and don't spend too much time in the sun."

Why didn't Manuel Fierro understand this? Sickler asked himself. Why didn't Joe Benites? Were they so narrowly focused that they couldn't see beyond the coffers of their own organizations? If they were willing to ignore Hispanic workers at Coors, how was he going to recruit Hispanic consumers to the boycott?

There was no sense of common cause with workers today, Sickler realized as he threw the rest of the mail on his desk and stretched in his chair. And it was no wonder. Labor unions, with their odious "grandfather clauses," had been openly racist for years. And homophobic. Another image from the trip to Golden flashed before Sickler. The strikers had held a fund-raising dance, and two gay activists who'd flown in from San Francisco had danced together. A group of strikers had surrounded Sickler. "What the hell is this?" they'd demanded, pointing at the two men hugging.

"They're here to help," Sickler had whispered, drawing the men outside so the San Franciscans wouldn't hear. "We've got a lot of support in the Bay Area."

"Screw that," the strikers had told him. "We don't need faggots. . . ."

"Yes, we *do*," Sickler had snapped. "You want a boycott in California, you *need* those guys. Now shut the fuck up and see to it nobody bothers them."

Nobody had taken a swing at the emissaries from San Francisco. But, Sickler reflected as he rose to walk to the water cooler, it was going to be hard to create that missing sense of common cause. Not only between labor and gays, or labor and minorities: The civil rights movement had long been criticized for relegating women to supporting roles. Blacks and Hispanics, suffering on the same side of the street, barely acknowledged each other. Environmentalists seemed to feel more allegiance to trees and birds than to people. "Solidarity forever," he muttered ruefully as he crumpled his cup.

Back at his desk, Sickler's eye fell on a photograph he'd tacked to the wall. It was a full-size black-and-white glossy news shot of the picket line. UNFAIR, a few of the signs said. And: WHEN WILL COORS SEE THE LIGHT? But something else caught Sickler's eye. A lot of the signs mentioned Joe Coors personally. Not Bill. Joe. WILL ROGERS NEVER MET JOE COORS, read one. JOE FOR FÜHRER, read another. Sickler found that odd. Bill had always run the brewery. Bill was the one the workers always saw.

Sickler stood looking at the photo a long time, thinking.

12

Texas Stranger

As marketing became increasingly important in the beer business, the ghost of Ad Coors began hovering around the brewery. As the oldest son, Ad had been groomed to run the whole company in a way that the engineering-focused Bill had not. Allergic to beer and untrained as a brewer, Ad was not obsessed, as Bill was, with product over sales. He'd always argued that "appealing to the market is every bit as important" as brewing excellent beer, so perhaps he'd have been better suited to taking on the likes of John Murphy and August Busch III.

The stress of trying to fill shoes he wasn't born to was eating Bill alive. As he'd tell anyone who'd listen, only his twenty minutes a day of transcendental meditation kept him from folding up altogether. The craziness of putting every beer drinker on the psychiatrist's couch and figuring out what special beer he wants was like trying to grab smoke—nothing at all like the tangible mechanical problems that used to occupy Bill's time.

Though the boycott was spreading and Anheuser-Busch and Miller were storming the barricades, the Coors brewery was a long way from going under. The family rule against borrowing meant its mountain of cash—some $70 million in 1978—was unencumbered. Coors could survive a lot of mistakes on a cushion that big. But there was no denying that on Bill's watch the brewery was suffering its first reverses since Prohibition.

Bill had no idea how to stop the rot. Peter claimed to have ideas. But

Peter was only thirty-two years old, and every time he opened his mouth his arguments threatened to steer the brewery further from the traditions that had made it great. Peter thought more about money than he did about beer. In fact, it sometimes seemed that Peter didn't care as much about making a great beer as about fancy tricks to sell it. Peter seemed to have no faith in the grand old engineers of the brewery who'd worked side by side with Dad. He wanted only to hire more fast-talking Visigoths from the East. That wasn't the way Adolph the founder or his quality-conscious son had seen the world. It wasn't the way Bill was reared. It didn't seem entirely honest.

Frightened and depressed, Bill did what he usually did when his back was against the wall. He looked for a battle to fight, on a field where he had confidence. He had already pushed the union into a strike it was sure to lose; so he looked beyond Golden.

Bill decided to join his brother on the political barricades in defense of the free enterprise system. He launched a spirited fund-raising campaign for a conservative lobby called the U.S. Industrial Council. "Today we face more anti-business legislation with more bureaucratic rules than ever before," Bill wrote on Coors letterhead to hundreds of wealthy business owners.

> The number of bureaucrats and special interest groups trying to ram anti-business legislation through Congress is staggering. They include liberals, unions, so-called consumer protection advocates, and economic policy pressure groups who oppose tax relief for businesses and incentives for personal investments. If anti-business legislation is allowed to proliferate, then one day you and I will be handing over to the federal government the keys to our businesses.

Bill's entry into the political arena was narrowly tailored. In defense of business unfettered by government regulation or taxation, Bill stood shoulder to shoulder with his brother. But when it came to the rest of Joe's conservative agenda, Bill pulled back.

He didn't live with a born-again Christian the way Joe did with Holly, so he wasn't as offended as Joe by perceived affronts to Judeo-Christian tradition. He did not share Joe and Holly's distaste for homosexuals. Bill didn't hang out with gays, but he lived his own kind of alternative lifestyle—chanting a mantra for twenty minutes every morning, pursuing

"New Age" health remedies—and that lent him a personal tolerance Joe couldn't muster. Bill didn't have much interest in passing judgment on another person's private life. He didn't share Joe's either-or personality. He had strong opinions, but unless the subject was brewing and the opponent a younger Coors, a debate could sometimes move him to reconsider. This was the "ambivalence" that Joe's assistant Cliff Rock had detected.

Bill received a letter in 1978 from a probusiness Republican named Kevin Johnson, who worked for the San Francisco Chamber of Commerce. Johnson had previously been fired from his job as city administrator of Orlando, Florida, because he was homosexual. As a conservative, Johnson was furious that organized labor was trying to recruit gays into its fight with the Adolph Coors Company. Gays had real enemies, he wrote to Bill, such as the so-called Briggs Amendment, an initiative on the coming California ballot that would bar gays from teaching in public schools. Bill sent a handwritten letter back, along with a $1,000 check to help fight the amendment. "Love," Bill wrote to Johnson, "is unconditional."

After corresponding with Johnson, Bill ordered his personnel department to remove all questions about sexual orientation from the preemployment lie detector test. (The one asking for "any information about subversive, revolutionary, or Communistic activity" remained.) Bill also added the words "sexual orientation" to the brewery's antidiscrimination clause, making Coors the first major U.S. brewer specifically to bar discrimination against gays.

It was out of character for Bill to grant interviews but after corresponding with Johnson, he gave one to *The Advocate,* the national gay magazine. In the interview, Bill convincingly refuted rumors that Coors was donating a penny for every can of beer sold to Anita Bryant's antigay crusade.

It worked. *The Advocate*'s publisher examined Coors's antidiscrimination policy and editorialized that gays should drop their boycott of Coors products.

Bill also split openly with Joe on the Equal Rights Amendment. To Joe, ERA was a slap at Judeo-Christian tradition and a deplorable example of interest groups mewling for "rights." To Bill, ERA made sense. While Joe's wife Holly held conservative Christian values about a man ruling the household, Bill's second wife, Phyllis, was much younger and enjoyed engaging Bill in argument about the changing role of women.

While Joe had five sons, four of whom had devoted their lives to Christ, Bill had three daughters, none of them born-again Christians. (His son, Scott, was only eleven years old.)

In early 1978, Bill mailed the following letter to the Mexican American Legal Defense and Education Fund:

> My interest in equal rights for all people has intensified over the past months as time runs out for getting the E.R.A. passed in three additional states, if the extension is not finally adopted.
>
> I have always supported women in their drive to achieve equal employment, equal pay, and equal responsibility. In this struggle for equal rights, I am sensitive to the special problems sometimes facing chicanas. . . .
>
> I am, therefore, enclosing a check for $1,000 as a personal contribution to MALDEF's chicana rights project for research and education projects for chicanas.

Bill wanted the check kept as quiet as all other Coors philanthropy. Besides, this wasn't a brewery contribution. It was personal. Bill was mindful that word of mouth about the check might help distinguish him from other Coorses and perhaps help the brewery. But he was also impulsively breaking his own political trail.

After three months of arguing, the MALDEF board returned Bill's check along with a curt letter of refusal. But Bill wouldn't let it go. He immediately wrote back:

> In reply to your letter of March 7, now that the American G.I. Forum and presumably the other major Mexican American organizations have called off the boycott, is it now appropriate that a contribution from me to MALDEF be accepted? If so, could you please advise me.

Thus began a six-year effort by Bill Coors to give MALDEF a thousand dollars, an effort that arose from Bill's desire to distinguish himself politically from his brother and which would culminate in one of Coors's boldest—and most desperate—efforts to rid itself forever of boycotts.

"Our business plan, in one word," Bill Coors told *Forbes* magazine in October 1978, "is survival."

Two months after introducing Coors Light, the company was in worse shape than ever. Those intrepid investors who'd held on to Coors stock since its first public offering in 1975 had lost half their money.

Coors Light was proving a disappointment, and the Coors board, product-oriented as ever, was groping in the dark, asking, if it tastes so great, why doesn't it sell?

Peter thought he knew. The Coors Light can was the same creamy yellow as the regular Coors can. Peering through the coolbox door, it was hard to tell them apart. Only if you looked closely could you see the word "Light" scrawled across one in a thin script.

Peter was also disappointed with his ad budget, which though expanded, didn't have enough firepower to launch a product as important as Coors Light.

They think they've given in by allowing us to make it, Peter grumbled to his advertising staff. But if they won't let us *sell* the can, the beer inside might as well be Kool-Aid.

Anheuser-Busch, on the other hand, was roaring. It sold almost a third more beer in 1977 than the year before and made more money on every barrel. Its 1977 profits hit a record, rising more than 65 percent above the previous year. Anheuser-Busch even stole Paul Newman, Coors's longtime high-profile fan.

"All the good things about Coors are simply outweighed by the company's violations of people's privacy and rights," Newman had told *Time* magazine when the strike began. August Busch III had pounced on the opportunity. Newman's great passion was auto racing, and Busch offered to sponsor Newman's team to the tune of a million dollars a year, provided Newman's car wore a bumper-to-bumper Budweiser logo.

Over at Miller, John Murphy was boosting his own marketing budget to astronomical levels. Miller now was the number-two beer in the country, earning almost three times as much as Coors. A reporter, noting that Miller Lite was aimed straight at the Coors market, quoted Murphy as saying, "We're going to teach those damned engineers up in Colorado how to sell some beer!"

Murphy later denied saying it—but he denied it with a laugh.

A pall fell over Bill. Everybody noticed he was distracted and bored in board meetings. He said less, and deferred more to Joe. Bill was sixty-three and had the vigor and health of a man twenty years younger. But it was hard to avoid the conclusion that the late 1970s felt like the beginning of the end of his career at Coors. The tremendous challenges the company faced were not ones that engineering could solve. Except for modifying the brewery to accommodate more products and more different packages, the future belonged not to engineers, but to the Visigoths dancing on the grave of brewing integrity. Bill would never admit as much to Peter, but he did—sort of—to reporters. "Making the best beer we can make is no longer enough," Bill said gloomily. "If we had our druthers, we'd choose the old mode."

Because Coors was sold in only sixteen states, it spent, on average, 20 percent more per barrel on advertising to reach the same number of people as the national brands did. The brewery paid more to reach fewer people because it couldn't buy national media. Bill had once told *Newsweek* that Coors "had a built-in safety valve" because people back east were clamoring for its beer. If the company needed to sell more beer, Bill had boasted, "all we have to do is expand our market." But as Peter sat staring at a map of the United States, expansion didn't look so easy. A-B and Miller were pushing hard in the West, in part, because the eastern markets were saturated with beer brands. Sure there was the "Coors mystique," but that might disappear when people in Virginia and Pennsylvania could buy it in their supermarkets. Coors beer was good, Peter figured. But it might not be *that* good. Even if the mystique remained, shipping to New York from Colorado would bite severely into profit margins, and Peter knew how Uncle Bill felt about building a second brewery.

Peter also worried about the boycott. Isolating its effect on sales when A-B and Miller were doing blitz marketing was difficult. But Peter knew the boycott hurt more than the company was willing to admit. Ten percent of sales was not an unrealistic assessment of the hit. The boycott was worst in California, but it was doing damage in other western states as well, even those without strong union membership.

Among the untapped territories east of the Mississippi River were Illinois, Michigan, New York, and New Jersey. These were huge markets and heavily unionized. Selling Coors there was going to be murder. But no one could talk Dad and Uncle Bill into making peace with the unions. Now they were trying to push the union into a decertification—to get rid of the union once and for all—and they'd probably win it. That would make Coors the only major brewer in the country without a union bug on its label.

Battles for Detroit and Pittsburgh were coming up.

"A corporation's public image is the most important asset a company has," Peter told the Denver Kiwanis Club. That was as close as he allowed himself to come to calling the company's militant antiunion stance a mistake. He'd argued about Press Tab and the ad budget and he and Jeff had pulled an end run to create Coors Light. But Dad and Uncle Bill were lunatic on the subject of the boycott. "A monument to dishonesty and immorality," Uncle Bill was fond of calling it. Peter's own father, strangely, sounded less strident. "We're not a bunch of professional managers who'll give the unions anything they want and then retire in five years," Joe told *The Wall Street Journal*. "We're owner-management. There's more at stake."

It was a solid, sober point to make. Any businessman could appreciate the sentiment and it left open a door to compromise with the union. But in the same article, Uncle Bill blurted, "I see no resolution to our conflict with the unions. We're convinced we can sell beer without them."

Such a comment, Peter knew, only challenged the AFL-CIO to prove Uncle Bill wrong.

In 1978, it was not at all certain that the Adolph Coors Company would live to see the end of Jimmy Carter's presidency. Coors was about to be ground to dust between Anheuser-Busch and Miller, and was not even trying to fight its way out. The only question seemed to be whether Coors would disappear entirely or carry on as a subsidiary brand of A-B or Miller.

And then, as in a cheap western, a lone stranger rode in from Texas to save the day.

When John Nichols was a hell-raising senior at Amarillo High School in Texas and trying to decide where to go to college, his mother took out a map of the United States and drew a thousand-mile circle around Amarillo. "You can go to college," she said, "anywhere outside that circle."

Nichols chose the University of the South in Sewanee, Tennessee, and went on to earn an M.B.A. at Columbia University. It was the early 1960s, the heyday of brand marketing, and Nichols, now directing his fearsome energy toward a career, was in a hurry. He wanted to be at the top of the marketing profession as fast as possible. Burning with impatience and physically compact, Nichols gave the impression of having too much personality squeezed into too small a package. Some short men avoid standing too close to taller ones. But not Nichols: Shoulders squared, fists balled, he'd get in close—right under the other man's chin—and squint up aggressively like Popeye with a West Texas accent. Lucky for him, he had the brains to back up such a personality, and he rose like a rocket through one of the nation's premier ad agencies, Leo Burnett and Company of Chicago, creator of the Marlboro Man. He learned brand marketing at the feet of the elderly Leo Burnett himself, in the last years before Burnett's retirement.

Nichols quickly claimed a number of stunning successes. Burnett assigned him early in his career to Procter & Gamble's Lava soap, a soap for "extra dirty" hands which was mysteriously dwindling in market share. Nichols deployed researchers lavishly, the way an infantry captain does skirmishers. Lava's slump, it turned out, owed to a shrinking number of farmers and blue-collar workers nationwide. Nichols repositioned the soap as perfect for getting kids' hands clean. He targeted the advertising at mothers instead of grease monkeys, and the product revived.

Nichols won a similar redesign victory for Pillsbury's canned cake frosting. The competition, Betty Crocker, had about 80 percent of the market, though the two products were all but indistinguishable. Betty Crocker was selling theirs as an emergency staple, to be used when there wasn't time to make frosting from scratch. Nichols's research, though, showed consumers didn't consider canned frosting a substitute anymore. They liked it better than their own because it was consistently smooth. Nichols and his people positioned Pillsbury Supreme as "so spreadable you can spread it with a paper knife," and it was soon sharing the market about evenly with Betty Crocker.

By the time he was thirty-five, Nichols was the youngest management director Burnett had ever had. He was a slash-and-burn boss, brutal on incompetence, quick to fire, yet generous, too, with merited praise and reward. Nichols's colleagues presented him with a wall plaque that read NOTHING IN MODERATION.

But then Burnett was taken over by a man who believed in "zero client unhappiness"—which amounted to never telling clients what they don't want to hear. Disillusioned and too impatient to wait out such a regime, Nichols quit. To him, no other ad agency matched the standards of the old Leo Burnett, so he got out of the business. He went back to Texas to open a chain of barbecue restaurants.

When it became clear to Nichols that he'd never raise the necessary capital to become a barbecue king, he began looking around for something else to do. On October 18, 1978, he typed a four-page letter to a man he'd never met: Bill Coors.

"We are in a unique position to help one another," he began. "I am eminently qualified to help you reposition Coors beer and take market share from your major competitors. You are eminently qualified to make me an independent businessman. . . ."

The deal Nichols offered was this: He would come to Coors and set up a proper marketing department, staffed by professionals he knew from his days at Burnett. He would write a long-range strategy for Coors, help the company define market segments and create products. He'd stay two to three years and when he left, Coors would be a competitive marketer.

In return, Nichols wrote, Coors would give him a beer distributorship in Texas.

That Bill Coors did not immediately tear up Nichols's letter is testimony to the brewery's desperate straits. Nichols's letter represented everything Bill detested; it was brash, immodest, impatient, and abrim with what Bill considered marketing bullshit. That Pillsbury could take market share from Betty Crocker, as Nichols described, by saying "you can spread it with a paper knife" struck Bill as more depressing than inspiring. Why bother making a good product, Bill felt, if a silly slogan can undo you?

Moreover, Nichols's letter demonstrated an appalling lack of loyalty. His long list of achievements with Lava, Pillsbury, Secret deodorant, and Tums weren't battle ribbons; they were hickeys on a whore. The man would "segment" and "market" cyanide if there was a buck in it.

Nothing in the letter showed any particular affection for Coors. If Augie Busch made him an offer he'd probably have gone there as willingly.

Nichols's request for a distributorship was particularly repellent to Bill. Bill had a rule: No former Coors executives could get distributorships for the asking. They had to earn them from scratch like anybody else. Like his brother Joe, Bill was powerfully ambivalent about his distributors. He considered the distributor's position a sacred trust, to be handed only to those thoroughly vetted and deemed most worthy. On the other hand, Bill barely tolerated the distributors, and despised these "most worthy" businessmen. Many of them, traditionally, were far richer than Bill and Joe themselves. Yet they complained constantly—about Press Tab, about advertising, about the boycott, and about the high costs they incurred to keep the product fresh. They also represented the one link in the farm-to-brewery-to-consumer chain that Coors didn't directly control. That in itself was an irritant to Bill, as it had been to his father and grandfather. If not for antiquated laws preventing breweries from selling directly to retailers, Bill would happily have cut out the middlemen.

That John Nichols aspired to be a Coors distributor made him suspect. That he wanted to snatch the position through a back-door deal made him sleazy. Nichols was precisely the type of Visigoth that had ruined the brewing industry. At any other time, Bill would have tossed the letter in the trash and washed his hands afterward.

But the figures on the first half of 1978 were in, and they were the worst ever. Sales were down 12 percent and earnings almost 50. Sometime between January and July, Anheuser-Busch had passed Coors as the biggest seller in California. Wall Street was openly discussing Coors as a takeover target.

This was Bill's trial. As he set Nichols's letter on his desk beside the first- and second-quarter financial reports, the portraits of his father and grandfather looked down on him. Adolph and Adolph Jr. had faced down Prohibition. They'd kept the brewery alive by making the odious malted milk and ersatz near-beer.

Adolph had been sixty-eight when Prohibition took away his livelihood. Bill was now sixty-three.

Bill didn't want Nichols in his brewery. He didn't like him, and he detested what he represented. But Adolph and Adolph Jr. hadn't wanted to make malted milk or that foul-tasting Mannah. They'd done it because they'd had to. They'd done it because if they hadn't, the Adolph Coors Company would have joined eight hundred other breweries killed by Prohibition.

Bill could not place his father's and grandfather's brewery at risk. He picked up Nichols's letter. If saving the brewery meant inviting this Visigoth inside the gates, he would do it. He didn't like it, but he would have to adapt.

13

The Paw Print

Bill wanted the foul deed done as quickly and painlessly as possible. Peter should hire Nichols, he said, thrusting the letter into his nephew's hands, and not make a big search for "the best person." They were all pretty much the same. This guy wanted to work for Coors. They should hire him and get it over with.

Nichols waded into the wreckage of the Adolph Coors Company in late 1978 and took stock. Coors Light was late, and being handled badly. Regular Coors was moribund. The family still had no plans for a super-premium beer to compete with Michelob, Löwenbräu, and the imports; no plans for a "popularly priced"—inexpensive—beer; no clear idea about expanding into new territory; no apparent commitment to serve the market at all.

Peter at first wanted to make Nichols's marketing department answerable to sales. The sales director, an amiable Portuguese American named Fred Vierra, had joined the company as an administrator in the can plant and was in charge of sales—in an area where he had neither training nor experience—only because Joe Coors liked him personally. Nichols didn't object to Vierra—he seemed smart and easy to work with. But making marketing subordinate to sales would put a layer of management between Nichols and Peter. Nichols refused, and Peter immediately backed off the idea. But Nichols noted that the family's desire to diminish his authority reflected their fundamental hostility toward all he represented. He wouldn't fully understand how deep that resentment ran for another three years, when he reached the point of preparing a lawsuit against Coors to protect himself from their wrath.

Nichols's predecessors, Art Stone and Lee Shelton, had made a couple of entertaining commercials, but Nichols could not see where they were supposed to take the product; there was no coordination among radio, print, and outdoor advertising; no overarching concept of the product's function in the marketplace. Nichols—whose only standard was sales and increased market share—had learned from experience that a unified strategy was far more important than the "execution" of any particular ad.

Nichols scrutinized the marketing department and was tempted to march through it with a chain saw. But he told holdovers from Lee Shelton's era that he'd make no changes for several months. "You're probably doing some things right," he told them. For the moment, he had bigger tasks. He hung the NOTHING IN MODERATION sign on his office wall and sallied forth to do battle with the board.

"You're going to have to spend money," Nichols said during his first meeting. Bill, Joe, Peter and Jeff, Max Goodwin, sweet old Lowell Sund, and big blustery Bob Mornin all looked at Nichols as though he'd landed from Jupiter.

"Lots and lots of money," Nichols boomed. "If you're not willing to do this, there's no point in going forward."

"How much money?" Max Goodwin finally asked.

"I'd say about forty million dollars," Nichols said. "The first year."

A gasp.

"Forty million dollars?" Bob Mornin asked. "Are you kidding? What do we get for forty million dollars?"

"You get the beginnings of a serious marketing strategy."

"I mean, how quickly will we see payback?"

"You could earn it back the first year," Nichols said. "But I don't know. Marketing is not a barley auger. You can't factor its value precisely."

"Now look," Mornin said, huffing like a locomotive. "When I put in a new can line, I can tell you *exactly* what the payback time is going to be."

Nichols opened his mouth to explain, but Bill Coors spoke first.

"God damn it, Bob," he said. He gestured at Nichols without looking at him, the way he would a piece of machinery. "He's the expert. If he says we have to spend forty million dollars, we'll spend it."

Nominally, Nichols reported to Peter, but only in the way a gruff old twenty-year sergeant "reports" to a brand-new second lieutenant. After that first board meeting, it was clear to Nichols that the poor boy had no autonomy. He could hardly take a leak without clearing it first with his father and uncle. Peter lacked the sacred credentials of an advanced engineering degree and was tolerated only as the family's emissary to the dark side of the brewing business, the mysterious and contemptible worlds of marketing and distributing. For all his charm, there was a sadness around Peter's eyes, Nichols thought, a visible pain at bearing so much responsibility while enjoying so little power and respect. Peter knew not a damned thing about marketing. He had been locked up in Golden since taking his business degree. The only good thing Nichols could say about Peter was that he was willing—yea, desperate—to learn. And that, Nichols supposed, was all he could ask.

Nichols led Peter through the steps of hiring the brewery's first grown-up ad agency—Ted Bates and Company of New York—and it was like taking a kid to Disneyland. Flying around the country for power lunches with the best minds in marketing was heady stuff for the thirty-two-year-old novice. Nichols couldn't help chuckling over the way Peter came alive when on the road. He started to like this bright, vulnerable protégé.

But when they returned to Golden after their marketing tours, a gloom fell over Peter. Whenever Bill and Joe were feeling angry at the sleight of hand required to sell beer, they took it out of Peter's hide. Nichols could tell when Peter had been subjected to another shouting match. He'd be dragging his lanky frame along the gray-tile walls looking utterly whipped.

"It's tough on you, ain't it," Nichols said one evening when they were alone in the office.

"At times it is, yes," Peter said.

"Let me ask you something, Pete," Nichols said. "If you had your druthers—if you could do anything—what would it be?"

The stress evaporated from Peter's face. "A ranch," he said, staring into middle distance. "A nice little ranch on the front range. Nothing too big. And, I don't know. I'd hunt. And fish."

Nichols felt a rush of pity for this tortured kid. Worth tens of millions of dollars, and all he wants to do is enjoy it a little. "Peter," he said, "why don't you do it? Why do you need this aggravation? Buy your ranch. Retire."

Peter looked at Nichols as though he were crazy. "I can't," he said. "I don't have the money."

Nichols laughed.

"I'm serious," Peter said. "I don't have a dime. Everything is in trusts and whatnot. If I don't work at the brewery, I'm cut off."

Christ, Nichols thought. Bondage. "Well?" he finally asked. "Why not? Leave the money. Get a job where you don't have to fight with your father every day."

Peter laughed sadly. "Where am I going to go? I don't have experience. I don't have skills. I'm not even sure I have the smarts to make it outside."

The implications of this appalling admission—that, if he was unfit to work outside the company he was unfit to work within it—were left hanging.

Nichols didn't have much time to brood over the young man's poor self-image, though. He'd begun calling colleagues at Burnett and other agencies, recruiting an entire marketing department at once in the same way he'd assemble an all-star football team. This was their chance to build a marketing department from scratch, he told them. They had a decent budget and a blank sheet of paper. He couldn't pay them much, but it would be fun.

Nichols's reputation induced almost everybody he invited to Colorado to leave the big time and join him. Nichols and his wife, Mary Ann, coached the newcomers through the lie detector test, carved out office space for them, helped them find housing, and quietly advised them to leave their Hermès ties in the closet. Nichols's young marketers swarmed the brewery in their Armani suits—young, cocky, ribbing each other, sparkling with ideas. In the space of three months, Coors had its first real marketing staff. At the eleventh hour, the cavalry had arrived. The slick new marketers had only one question for Nichols: Did they really have to attend Marilyn Coors's Bible classes?

To keep himself focused on the company's life-threatening problems, Nichols doodled a "map" of the beer market. It looked like a malformed paw print, with a big heel blob at the bottom, a smaller ball blob above it, and four toe blobs arrayed across the top. Michelob dominated the big toe, the superpremiums that made up 12 percent of the beer market, and next to Michelob, Nichols wrote, for lack of a better name, "Coors Superpremium." Coors had to have a superpremium, and fast. Without a superpremium, the distributors were locked in a gunfight with a half-empty Peacemaker.

Across the line of other toe blobs—dark, nonalcohol, and "popularly priced"—Nichols penned in frustration, "Coors? Coors? Coors?" Perhaps these weren't as urgent as the superpremium market, but the company needed to think about branching out.

Nichols concentrated now on the heel and the ball of the footprint, where Coors did have beers. The heel blob, the biggest, was the market for regular, so-called premium beers. In its center, Nichols scrawled "Budweiser."

The ball blob represented the light-beer market. In its center, Nichols penned in "Miller Lite."

Nichols scribbled "Coors"—regular Coors—near the top of the premium beer blob, close to the light beer, because Coors had always been lighter-flavored than its competitors. At the bottom edge of the light-beer blob, toward the regular beer blob, Nichols wrote "Coors Light," which had more calories than the other light beers.

The problem was obvious: The two Coors beers were right next to each other. Coors Light and regular Coors, "America's Fine Light Beer," were indistinguishable in the public's eye. Coors was trying to fight a multifront war with only two cannons, wheel to wheel and pointed in the same direction. Nichols drew arrows from each beer, directing each into the center of its respective market. They had to push their images apart, he told his young marketers.

Nichols looked at the research Peter had requisitioned when producing Coors Light. He understood that people didn't enjoy drinking Miller Lite—he didn't, either. Coors Light couldn't claim to be less fattening than Miller Lite but it had something the other beer didn't: the unimpeachable taste of Coors. *"Taste taste taste,"* he scribbled. Taste was still Coors's strongest selling point: For this, Nichols admired Coors family tradition.

And thank God the family was changing the design and color of the regular Coors and Coors Light cans. Even before Nichols arrived, they'd asked the art department to produce about thirty new designs for Coors Light. The one they picked—a plain silver can with the logo in strong red—was an eye-popper, strikingly different from anything else on the beer shelves. Bravo, Nichols told the art department.

But however much Nichols complimented the Coors staff on the things they did right, the old-timers at Coors treated him like a disease they didn't want to catch. He and his team of irreverent, fast-talking marketers were like a virus inside the brewery, an alien presence that everybody feared would transform Coors from a quality-driven, genteel family business into a heedless corporate monster. Conflict between the two cultures was constant. Coors's no-return bottle at the time was a squat, ugly cylinder with no neck. A beer bottle's neck, Nichols knew, is one of its most important features—a handhold, distinctly phallic, that communicates what is inside the bottle. A tall, thin neck implies lightness, elegance, femininity. A short, thick neck bespeaks dark, weighty strength. The neckless bottle was all wrong for Coors.

The marketing and engineering departments at Coors were meeting one afternoon to consider bottle designs that had been lathed out of solid amber for the marketers to compare. As the dandies from marketing passed the prototypes around the table, a bottle-line engineer exploded in anger.

"We don't need a new bottle," he said. "The one we have goes through the line easily. And without a neck, we can get an extra layer on the pallet."

"Well, that's just great," the marketer holding the prototype sneered. "Nobody wants to drink out of the thing. So what does it matter how many you can get on the pallet?"

The exchange reverberated through the brewery, confirming each camp's worst expectation of the other.

It was time for one of Bill's quarterly speeches to the Coors workers, and Nichols invited his team to listen. It was kind of required, he told them sheepishly. They walked together from the marketing department, a gang of wise-guy city kids in creamy Perry Ellis fashions shouldering past the regiments of engineers with pocket savers. The marketers took their seats in the second row of the sixth-floor auditorium, directly behind Peter. Bill took the stage.

"I've been advised to be careful in my remarks," he said, "because my words have been frequently misconstrued by the press and caused the company some bad publicity."

Good, Nichols thought. That's all we'd need.

"But," Bill continued, "I feel I really must say a few words about Jane Fonda."

Oh, my God! Nichols gripped the back of the seat in front of him.

"That woman," Bill said, "betrayed the nation. She deliberately traveled to the enemy camp to give them aid and comfort in time of war." He stepped around the podium. "As far as I'm concerned, she is a traitor!" Nichols put his face in his hands. She went to Hanoi six years ago, for Christ's sake. The war has been over for three.

Nichols glanced at his marketing crew as Bill segued from Jane Fonda to international communism. The young men were staring at Bill, aghast. "I've known for some time a communist cell is operating right here at this brewery," Bill said. Someone in the audience snorted, and Bill became furious, glaring into the lights, tendons taut in his throat. "There *are* communists in this brewery," he spat, jabbing a finger. "And if you don't believe that then you don't know communism!"

Nichols heard a throat clearing to his left and glanced over. His entire staff was leaning forward, glaring at him as though to say, "We left good jobs for *this?*"

Bill finally wrapped up the meeting and Peter flew out of his chair like a stone from a catapult. He ducked his head and raced through the crowd, Nichols hard on his heels. Peter sped into his office, but Nichols stayed with him, flying past Peter's alarmed secretary.

"Close the door," Peter whispered to Nichols. A look of pure grief contorted his face. "Is my uncle a nut?" he asked.

"You tell me," Nichols said angrily.

"He wasn't drunk," Peter said. "I don't think."

"Well, this shit's got to stop," Nichols said. "We can't have it. It's bad for morale."

"I agree," Peter said, slumping into his seat. "I don't understand it. He gets on these tangents."

"Well, he has to cut it out," Nichols said, pacing. "And another thing: I don't like Marilyn asking my people to go to her Bible classes. It isn't appropriate."

"She's just inviting—"

"Peter, she's the wife of the damned vice president of sales and marketing. Of Peter Coors. And they're Coors marketing. You can't expect them to shrug it off. It isn't right."

"Well, they should know there's no pressure," Peter said. "But I'll tell her."

"Good. And something else."

"What?"

"Press Tab Two," Nichols said. "It's got to go. And I mean now."

A look of horror crossed Peter's face. "Oh, no," he said. "I'm not walking into that one. I voted against it once and got my head handed to me."

"Peter, it's killing us. Which one is behind it?"

"Both, really," Peter said. "But probably my dad more than Uncle Bill."

"Why?"

Peter puffed himself up in his chair like a tin-pot potentate. "'A dollar a thousand we save,'" he said, mocking Joe's deep voice. He looked up at Nichols with a shrug. "They say it's the better top. It *is* the better top. It doesn't cause litter."

"Nobody can open the goddamned can, Peter. Bartenders won't serve it. You've got distributors ready to wring our necks."

"Jeez, don't talk about distributors," Peter said. "That's the *last* thing Dad and Uncle Bill want to hear."

"Peter, talk to them. Put a stake through the heart of that god-awful Press Tab."

Peter gazed up at Nichols like a terrified soldier refusing to budge from a foxhole. After a long moment, Nichols walked out.

Nichols and his team dealt with Coors family quirkiness by ignoring it as much as possible. The marketers worked like crazy. Within three months, they'd put together a campaign for Coors Light. In the commercials, a hardworking man finishes his shift and asks for a beer. "Coors *Light*?" he asks. "I work hard all day and you give me a *light* beer?" But after tasting it, his face blooms in a wide smile. "I am surprised," he says. The ads started running as soon as the new silver cans hit the stores. The slogan: "The Surprising Taste of Coors Light." Like an underexercised horse spurred to a trot, Coors Light began to move.

But as Coors Light lunged forward, Press Tab Two yanked back on the reins. At every marketing meeting, Nichols and Vierra hammered on Peter to take their case to Joe and Bill. Alcoa had just developed— and 7Up was test-marketing—a pivoting stay-on tab that would eventually become the industry standard. Here was a nonlittering alternative to Press Tab Two. But no matter how hard the marketing people pounded Peter, he wouldn't fight Bill and Joe about Press Tab Two. Like the union, Peter considered this an issue beyond argument and wasn't willing to suffer for a doomed cause.

Nichols suspected Bill was belittling Alcoa's invention because once upon a time that same company had told him an aluminum can was impossible. Finally, Nichols took the task upon himself.

"Bill. Joe," he said in his gruff West Texas tone when they were gathered with the board one afternoon. "I'm here to tell you the Press Tab has got to go."

A tense silence fell. Everybody on the board knew Press Tab Two was a stinker, but like Peter nobody was willing to go to the wall over it with Bill and Joe. Mornin, Sund, Goodwin, Peter, Jeff, and the others froze in their seats.

Bill looked over at Joe but said nothing. It often seemed to Nichols that for all his prominence within the brewery, Bill ultimately deferred to his younger brother. Maybe it was because Joe's sons were in line to inherit the place. Or maybe it was because Bill knew Joe was more stubborn and there was no point in fighting him.

Joe's face grew dark red. "No way," he snapped.

"Joe, you get an E for effort, but this dog just won't hunt no more. Coors Light has a chance of success. Don't hold it back with the Press Tab."

"Press Tab Two is superior to the ring-pull. The problem," Joe said, leaning forward in his chair accusingly, "is the advertising."

The board members silently swiveled their eyes to Nichols like spectators at Wimbledon.

"The what?" Nichols asked.

"The advertising!" Joe snapped. "You haven't advertised how to use Press Tab Two properly."

"Wait a minute," Nichols said. "You want me to divert advertising resources to instructing people how to *open the can?*"

"There's nothing to it," Joe said peevishly. "Look." He produced a golf ball and a can of Coors. He rolled the golf ball over the top of the can and the tab opened with a hiss. "There," he said.

"Now let me see if I've got this straight," Nichols said, holding up a palm. "You want me to take money we *could* be using to build market share, and use it instead to tell people they'd better carry a golf ball if they want to drink Coors?"

Joe scowled at him like an Easter Island statue, his long head tipped back and mouth set in a hard frown.

"Joe," Fred Vierra said, "let's subject it to scientific testing. Let us run a survey and quantify consumer reaction to the Press Tab. If the results come back negative, will you let it go?"

"I'll agree to the survey," Joe said.

"I will, too," Bill said. Everybody else at the table let out a long breath.

Nichols took advantage of the pause to bring up his other desperate cause: the need for a superpremium beer in the product line.

"Aw . . ." Jeff said.

"What?" Nichols asked. Jeff was directly in charge of brewing. His support would be crucial.

"We just got finished making a light beer. Now you want us to make *another beer?*"

"We need something in the Heineken/Michelob market. We need it immediately."

"I suppose it doesn't matter *what*, just *something*," Jeff said, flapping a hand dismissively. "Something you can 'segment,' 'position,' whatever. Just something in a bottle."

"Jeff," said Peter, "get off it. Coors Light is succeeding because it's good. The campaign is helping it. But product . . . We're asking you to make a good beer."

"Oh, so quality is still important," Jeff fired back. "That's nice to hear. I thought it was all image. And I suppose you'll want a fancy new bottle for this 'superpremium' as you call it, which means retooling the bottle line. They're going to love *that* downstairs."

"Boys," Bill said.

"Coors regular and Coors Light are the best beers we can make," Jeff said.

"Stop saying 'Coors regular,' for God's sake," Nichols said. "It sounds like gasoline. Call them Coors Light and Coors Premium. Or, if you like, use the trademark from the damned can: Call the premium Coors Banquet."

"I don't see what difference it makes here in the boardroom," Jeff said.

"It makes all the difference," Nichols said. "It's an attitude that filters from us to the brewery to the distributors to the retailers. Nobody should *ever* call it Coors regular. I told the same thing to Kentucky Fried Chicken. They were calling it 'regular' and 'extra crispy.' I got them to say 'original recipe.' Regular makes people think mediocre."

And that was pretty much how conversations about the superpremium went. They heated up and flew off on tangents, with Nichols getting nowhere.

It was time to lighten up and clear the air with a little good news. Nichols brought along to the next board meeting a tape of a commercial for Banquet that his people had just finished shooting.

"Now I don't want you to focus too much on the *commercial* as much as on the *strategy* here," Nichols said as he dimmed the lights. "Remember: We're going for a new *positioning* of Coors premium."

The spot opened like the ads Coors had been running for thirty years—burbling brooks, Rocky Mountain vistas. "It ain't no flatland beer," said the announcer. "It ain't no city beer. It ain't no downstream beer." Cowboys rode through the frame, driving a herd of sheep across a spectacular Rocky Mountain tableau—as macho an image as Marlboro Country. "Come," the announcer concluded as a hand pulled a glistening six-pack out of an icy stream, "taste the high country."

Nichols held his breath.

"Heinie Foss," Bill said, referring to one of his friends, "wishes we'd just go back to the mountain-stream ads."

"I like the slogan," Joe said.

"That one cowboy," Jeff said, "he's a little rough-looking isn't he?"

"Let's not focus on the *ad* as much as what we're trying to do with the *product*," Nichols said.

"We're repositioning it," Peter piped up. "We're trying to strengthen its macho image, to compete better with Budweiser and differentiate Coors regular—ah, Banquet—from Light."

"Get rid of the sheep," Bill said. "Real cowboys don't bother with sheep. Cattle's the thing."

"Nobody really herds livestock on horses anymore, do they?" Jeff asked.

"Gentlemen," Nichols said, "the *strategy*. . . ."

It was hopeless. The meeting dissolved into a rambling commentary on the commercial. Nobody wanted to talk about strategy, Nichols realized. Nobody even had the vocabulary. So Nichols excused himself. As he left, he noticed with grief that Peter was arguing with Jeff about the sheep.

Max Goodwin slipped out the door behind Nichols. "John," he whispered conspiratorially, "I've got to make a presentation to Bill and Joe about whether to buy the company a Lear jet."

"A Lear jet?" Nichols asked, appalled. "We're bleeding from every orifice and they're thinking of buying a *Lear jet?*"

"Their friend Cal Fulenwider put the bug in their ear," Goodwin said. "'Charlie Gates, too. He has a plane of his own and he told them, 'You're bigger than I am.' So that's got them all fired up."

"Who's Charlie Gates?" Nichols asked.

"Gates Rubber. They make fan belts here in Denver."

"Shit."

"I've done the figuring," Goodwin said, "and it doesn't make sense at all."

"Of course it doesn't."

"Will you help me put together a presentation? I mean a really professional one, the kind your people do."

Nichols lit up. For the first time, someone on the board besides Peter was acknowledging that Nichols might have something to teach the mighty Adolph Coors Company Nichols found himself pumping Goodwin's hand like a fool in bliss.

The next day, he assigned a couple of people to prepare slick charts and graphs and to help Goodwin rehearse the presentation.

When the time came, the financial officer stood at the boardroom easel and with brutal precision struck down every conceivable reason for buying a Lear jet. The jet would not pay for itself because Coors executives didn't fly often enough. Maintenance, insurance, airport fees, fuel, and the pilot's salary would burden the company's already stressed bottom line.

Goodwin spoke for nearly half an hour, flipping through colorful charts of rock-hard data. He thanked the board for its time, and sat down.

Nichols nodded approvingly. The man had studied hard, practiced well, and delivered a devastating presentation.

"Well . . ." Joe was the first to speak. "I want one." He looked at Bill

"Me, too," Bill said. "Max, buy one."

Nichols groaned. But he hadn't yet heard the worst.

They charged the jet to his marketing budget.

14

Ideological Kooks

Dorothy Silverthorn's phone rang at two-forty in the morning. She scooped it up before it could wake Jim. "Hey," a sultry woman's voice said. "Your husband's down at the Aloha Striptease Club, drunk on his ass."

"My husband," Dorothy said sleepily, "is right here next to me." She hung up.

A few minutes later, the phone rang again. "You know when Jim says he's going to union meetings at night?" the woman's voice said. "He comes to meet me. . . ." Dorothy hung up, lifted the receiver off the cradle, rolled against Jim's broad back, and fell asleep.

It had been this way for weeks as 1978 drew to a close. Daytime calls from company managers offering "one last chance" to come back to work. Earnest-sounding calls from scabs urging Jim to vote to kick out the union. Then these smarmy calls in the wee hours. One way or the other, Dorothy was glad it would soon be over.

The strike now existed in name only. Almost three quarters of the workers had crossed the picket lines to work. The diehards pushed mimeographed flyers under the doors of those who'd gone back to work:

After God had finished the rattlesnake, the toad and the vampire, he had some awful substance left with which he made the scab. Judas was a traitor to his God. Benedict Arnold was a traitor to his country. You are

a traitor to yourself, your family, and to your class. I won't wish you
Luck, but you'll need it.

The hot prose didn't convince anybody to give up a paycheck and
rejoin the picket line, but David Sickler was glad to see that a core
remained who felt strongly enough to write such a stinging letter.

Still, the union had never been weaker.

Coors couldn't legally petition for an election to decertify Local 366
until a year had passed since the strike. What's more, the company still
hadn't settled the issue of the demoted leadmen. Until all the charges of
unfair labor practice were settled, the Labor Department said Coors
couldn't try to get rid of Local 366.

Once the one-year mark passed on April 5, Coors surrendered in the
leadmen case. The brewery reinstated the leadman position, offered the
demoted leadmen their jobs back at full salary and an aggregate quarter-
million dollars in back pay. Local 366 accepted. Back in April, the union
appeared to have won one.

But by now, in December, Silverthorn had come to understand that
Coors had bought the bargain of a lifetime. The company's original replacement of the union leadmen with nonunion women and minorities
was a triple whammy. It pit the union against the company's other aggrieved critics. It painted a positive affirmative-action image on the company. And it had helped push the union into the disastrous strike.

And now, by rolling over completely to all the union demands, the
company cleared the way for a vote to get rid of Local 366. All for a
quarter-million dollars.

With the decertification vote approaching, company literature was
slipped under the door several times a week. Coors managers walked
around with black buttons saying, VOTE NO: ASK ME WHY. To assure a
vote against the union, the company had offered a surprise, last-minute
10 percent wage increase.

A few hours after the last smutty phone call, Silverthorn stood at the
gate with DeBey in the whipping December wind watching brewery
workers pass. Later today they would begin casting votes on whether to
keep Local 366 of the AFL-CIO, or to become a nonunion shop. But
every militant had long since been replaced. The only people filing past
to vote on the union's fate were strikebreakers and scabs.

"Fucked up," DeBey said.

"Got that right." Silverthorn nodded, hunched in his jacket.

"Whole system. Totally rigged."

"Totally."

"Drive our guys out, *then* vote."

"Yup."

"Get thumped."

As it turned out, the union did better than expected. Even with company pressure, the last-minute wage increase, and the union barred from campaigning on brewery grounds, Local 366 got a third of the votes.

"This is the Coors employees' declaration of independence," Bill Coors jubilantly told reporters. "For the first time in forty-four years we will be able to deal directly with our employees."

It also meant that for the first time since 1933, Coors beer would leave the loading dock without a union bug on its label. Coors was now America's only nonunion mass-produced beer.

A couple of months later, an AFL-CIO official showed up at the union hall on Independence Street to bury the local. He took the charter off the wall, loaded files into the trunk of his car, pocketed the keys, and drove off. Local 366 was gone. The building would soon be sold to the Steelworkers. The AFL-CIO-funded boycotters moved their headquarters to an old trailer on East Street, but would soon be run out of there, too. The Adolph Coors Company simply bought the entire street from the City of Golden and evicted them.

By this time, David Sickler was running the AFL-CIO's biggest organizing committee, in Los Angeles. Plus he was still running the Coors boycott. When Local 366 folded, the AFL-CIO gave him no specific orders. But the federation still had Coors on its boycott list, so Sickler felt free to continue using AFL-CIO personnel and resources to promote it. The job was no less important to Sickler now that Local 366 was gone; it was just different. Until now, his goal had been to bring management to the table. Now, his goal was to destroy the Adolph Coors Company.

Revenge was only part of it. Sickler wanted corporate America put on notice that if it treated workers the way Coors did, organized labor would draw blood. It had been a long time since organized labor had shown itself capable of throwing a punch. Union membership, declining since the early 1960s, was in free fall. The movement had to show working people that labor was still an ally worth having, Sickler believed, that it was strong and smart enough to command the boss's respect. Taking down Coors would change the battlescape for sure.

Sickler's Mexican-American friends told him about Bill Coors's letters and check to MALDEF, and it made Sickler smile. It was clever of Bill Coors to pretend to stand for the Equal Rights Amendment and at the same time give brewery money to the anti-ERA Heritage Foundation; and very slick to pronounce himself in support of gay rights while donating money to the Committee for the Survival of a Free Congress, which campaigned for hard-core Christian conservatives.

Sickler ruffled in his file drawer for Bill's pro-gay rights interview in *The Advocate*. Okay, Sickler muttered. Let's play ball. He cut out the interview and editorial, then flipped through the magazine, clipping graphic personal ads ("GWM, 70, seeks young boys for rimming & fisting") and notices for nipple clips, whips, and black leather masks. He arranged the ads around Bill's lavish praise of gay rights and made dozens of photocopies. Chuckling, Sickler spent the rest of the afternoon stuffing the flyers into envelopes and addressing them to the John Birch Society, the Reverend Jerry Falwell, Anita Bryant, and other Christian-right activists.

Falwell took the bait. "The fact that Coors would lend support to the homosexual community and solicit their economic participation," he told a conservative newsletter, "degrades them in my opinion to the lowest echelon of their industry." Suddenly, the Coors brothers had enemies where they once had allies. Though conservative anger against Coors never amounted to a serious boycott, it did harden the Coorses' bunker mentality, their sense that the world was ganging up on them.

Larry Gold, the AFL-CIO's chief counsel, worried that Coors would sue. He kept telling Sickler to let the boycott die. "You're going to cause trouble," Gold said often, to which Sickler would respond, "I hope so. It's about time the AFL-CIO stirred up some trouble." Sickler kept glancing at the photos of the Coors picket lines hung above his desk. Something about this boycott felt different to Sickler than others that had fizzled. Those anti-Joe Coors signs outside the plant told him that Joe's stridently right-wing politics had touched a nerve with the Coors workers. That the anger fueling the strike had run deeper than such specifics as the leadmen, the spot urine tests, or seniority. Even the lie detector, Sickler knew, hadn't been enough to inspire fourteen hundred workers to give up their paychecks.

In one sense, Sickler knew, Jim Silverthorn was right; dignity issues don't mean shit. At least not individually. But enough of them together, in the context of Joe Coors's well-publicized conservatism, did add up to something. Joe Coors stood in direct opposition to ordinary people's interests. He hated unions because they challenge the authority of business owners, but that meant he abhorred the thought of working people having some say over how they did their jobs. He opposed taxes to pay for poor-people's programs because they redistributed wealth, but that meant he didn't want to give those down on their luck a helping hand. He reviled public education as a government power grab, but public education was the only way most people's kids were going to get ahead. He rejected the civil rights, gay rights, and women's movements as assaults on "tradition," but those traditions reserved privilege for straight white men and put high hurdles between everybody else and the American dream.

A shock of embarrassment jolted Sickler. All that time, those fourteen hundred doomed bastards striking Coors had understood what the Coors boycott was about. They probably couldn't have articulated it, but they'd known. It was about Joe Coors. It was about class.

We were the ones who had tunnel vision, Sickler thought, as he pawed through his desk looking for the flyer the Local 366 activists' had put under scabs' doors. "A traitor to your class," it said, just as Sickler remembered. We so-called union leaders failed to see the potential for a national movement supporting the Coors workers, Sickler thought. Maybe those fourteen hundred broken unionists could win something yet. Something bigger than themselves. Something bigger than Coors.

Sickler got up from his chair and began pacing. Joe Coors wants to be the country's leading conservative. Okay, we'll make him the country's leading conservative. We'll shop Joe Coors and his politics to gays, blacks, Hispanics, women, the poor . . . to ordinary working Americans. We'll make the Coors boycott a national referendum on the conservative agenda.

Sickler opened the Coors annual report to Joe's stiff, bespectacled portrait. This was the face of the enemy, he mused. Well, Sickler thought, he was about to meet his match.

Sickler knew he had to be careful. He couldn't just issue an ideological appeal for everybody to boycott Coors because of Joe's politics. Americans didn't like to think of themselves as ideological. He had to be subtle about it, he thought as he sat down and reached for a legal pad. Sickler wrote "blacks" on his pad and wrote "EEOC complaint" underneath. Under "women" he wrote "no rest rooms" and "underrepresented." Under "gays" he wrote "lie detector," and so on. The boycott could certainly be sold to trade unionists around the country on the basis of what *Business Week* recently called Coors's "ideological anti-unionism." But spun correctly, the boycott could also be sold to blacks. Spun another way, to Hispanics. Spun yet again, to women, to gays, to environmentalists. And underlying each appeal, like a bass riff, would be a constant reminder of the Heritage Foundation and Joe's racist, sexist, elitist politics. Without knowing it, David Sickler was beginning to do what John Nichols was doing at Coors. He was segmenting the market. Not for beer, but for a beer boycott.

Bill had been saying for years that the lives of Coors workers would improve without a union. Now that they'd voted the union out, it was time to deliver.

The company boosted wages yet again, created a formal grievance procedure, and required meetings between workers and management to raise personnel concerns and generate ideas for improving operations. Bill even insisted on buying a disused Safeway supermarket adjoining the brewery and turning it into a lavish health club for the free use of employees. In typical guru-speak, he called it a Wellness Center. Use it, he urged, on company time.

Most significant to John Nichols, though, was that the company was answering the boycott's legitimate accusations by sincerely recruiting and promoting women and minorities. The Adolph Coors Company was undeniably a culture of white men, but this was more a question of ignorance and isolation than active bigotry, Nichols felt. Now that nobody was forcing them to do so, Coors was starting to do the right thing and diversify.

Nichols sensed that Peter, Joe, and Bill were relieved to be cleaning up the brewery's act. Mostly, they wanted the boycott to go away. But Nichols also felt the Coorses were fundamentally decent. They'd been foolish about labor relations, yes. Bullheaded about marketing, certainly. But to a fault, Nichols found them honest and good-hearted. None of them was racist, he told Mary Ann. The AFL-CIO charges hurt their feelings as well as their pocketbooks. As long as they didn't appear to be "knuckling under to the union," they seemed to be genuinely relieved to make theirs a friendlier company. The improvements were slow, but Nichols was noticing an increase in the number of black, brown, and female faces in the brewery. Maybe, he told Mary Ann, this company can survive.

Then again, maybe not. Peter Coors walked into Nichols's office one afternoon ashen-faced.

"What's wrong?" Nichols asked.

Peter blushed and ducked his head, signaling to Nichols that he was about to deliver an order from his father and uncle that Nichols was going to hate.

"What now?" Nichols asked.

"We have to make a commercial with Eva Gabor," Peter mumbled.

"With *whom*?"

"Eva Gabor," Pete said, coloring deeply.

Nichols closed his eyes. He and his crew had been working themselves ragged to reposition Coors and Coors Light, to develop a strategy the company could build upon for years—the way Pillsbury did with the Pillsbury Doughboy and Marlboro did with cowboys. It took luck, smarts, and discipline to bring such a campaign to fruition. Every radio ad, TV commercial, and in-store display had to fortify the campaign's themes, the grand vision of the market niche. For Coors Light, the theme was surprising good taste. For Coors Banquet, taste the high country. Nichols shot print and outdoor ads at the same time commercials were being filmed, so that they contained the same people, wearing the same clothes, in the same settings. He resisted fighting with the Coorses about execution. Bill had been adamant, for example, against sheep in a Coors ad. Texans don't like sheep, he told his Texan marketing chief. But Nichols hadn't taken the bait. His primary goal was to teach the family that strategy is more important than such details. He'd reshot the commercial using cattle instead of sheep. And he'd charged ahead, with Bill's blessing, sponsoring the Professional Rodeo Association, a sport that had been overlooked by Budweiser and that reinforced the "high country" image. The Coors and Coors Light campaigns were young, but Nichols was sure they had the potential to carry their products for years, slowly building share. All the Coorses needed was single-minded focus.

Eva Gabor?

The prospect of shooting a commercial with the aging Hungarian star of *Green Acres* was bad enough. What the request said about the family's misunderstanding of strategy devastated Nichols. He sat back in his chair and laughed sadly. "I'm listening," he said.

"She's a friend of my mother," Peter said.

"Oh, Peter. . . ."

"And her husband is a big contributor to the Republican party. We have to use her." Peter pulled up a chair at Nichols's desk. "But listen. Maybe it isn't so bad. We'll use her for Light. Women drink light beer."

"Women drink two percent of it," Nichols barked. "You know women aren't beer drinkers, Pete. Christ. She's a friend of your mama. Like this is some dime-store operation."

"I tried," Peter said, gazing sadly at Nichols's desktop. "I really did. But they're not budging on this one."

Nichols started up out of his chair, to go talk sense into Bill and Joe. But then he flopped back into his seat. To hell with it, he figured. I'll make the commercial.

"But you tell your father and uncle that this spot gets run through the focus groups like any other. If it bombs, we don't run it, got that?"

Maxxed out in time and energy, Nichols had to divert $40,000 and a sizable crew to shoot and field-test a Coors Light commercial starring Eva Gabor. Slathered in makeup, her platinum hair shellacked into place, she looked like something from a wax museum. Her over-the-hill Gypsy-seductress act was plain embarrassing. "Who is this hooker?" the men in the focus groups yelled. "What's she doing selling beer?"

Nichols loaded Peter with the brutally negative results. "Here's all the ammunition you need. The spot can't run, ever."

Peter got the job done. But for days afterward, he seemed subdued. Nichols wondered how much more of this the boy could take. Peter's dark hair was showing strands of white. Nichols mentioned it to Mary Ann.

"Marilyn looks the same way," Mary Ann said. "We were talking at school this morning, and this look came over her face. I asked her what was wrong, and she got all choked up. She told me, 'This isn't what I bargained for.' That's what she said. She said she and Peter had planned on having a little ranch."

Nichols shuddered to imagine a lifetime of fighting Bill and Joe Coors. Nichols had only been around a year and a half and his ears already rang from banging his head against the wall. The distributors loved Nichols's work; at the latest national meeting Nichols had un-veiled a new "Taste the High Country" spot and the distributors had leapt to their feet and cheered. And market share was creeping up. But it seemed to Nichols that every time he took a step forward, the family jerked him back.

Nichols was desperate to place a Coors product in the fast-growing superpremium market and was pushing three strategies at once. Jeff had cooked up the first one, a homegrown product, to rival Michelob. It would have a richer flavor than the other Coors beers, and 4 percent alcohol instead of 3.6.

A good product, Nichols thought when he tasted it. We have a chance with it. But the family insisted on naming it "Herman Joseph's 1868," to honor the two middle names of the company founder and the year he emigrated to America. Nichols thought "Herman Joseph" sounded too much like "Henry Weinhard," a currently popular competitor, but he couldn't get the Coorses to see any such similarity. When Nichols tried to get them to design an attractive, square-shouldered bottle for it, they sided with their bottle-line engineers, who didn't want to be bothered handling a new package. The fine new beer was packed in the ordinary squat Coors bottle with a dull black label, giving the product, in Nichols's view, all the appeal of a mortar shell. As Nichols predicted, Herman Joseph's 1868 flopped. About the only place he ever saw it was in the miniature refrigerator aboard the Coors Lear jet.

Never mind. A marketer has to be able to step over failed products like a battlefield officer charging over his own dead. Nichols redoubled his efforts for superpremium strategies two and three, which involved becoming the U.S. distributor for an import. The biggest per-capita beer drinkers in the world, Nichols knew, weren't the Germans but the Belgians. Nichols had been putting out feelers to Stella Artois of Belgium, the biggest seller in Europe.

Nichols was simultaneously investigating an approach that had come in over the transom from the Pelforth brewery in France. Pelforth had a contract to brew a pseudoimport called George Killian's Irish Red Ale, and was looking for an American brewery to do likewise in the United States. Nichols found Killian's interesting. The giant Irish brewer Guinness had long since bought up all its competitors' breweries in Ireland. But George Killian Lett of Dublin, heir to a small brewery, had refused to sell out. Lett, a puckish, bearded fellow of about fifty, didn't make any ale, but lived in the old family brewery and against terrific pressure from Guinness had held on to his family's recipe and trademark. He'd contracted both out to Pelforth, which was doing pretty well selling

French-brewed "Irish" ale in France. Nichols liked the idea of a pseudoimport. It mimicked Löwenbräu's successful strategy of domestically
brewing an "import," which let Miller collect import prices without incur-
ring grievous overseas shipping costs.

Bill resisted. Making beer to somebody else's formula was anathema.
The bottle-line engineers hated the idea, too, since Nichols had made it
clear that the robust George Killian's would require a distinct bottle
design. The standard Coors bottle, with its sloping shoulders, would be
entirely wrong.

Nichols pleaded and cajoled. He told Bill and the bottlers that he
understood their concerns, that there were legitimate engineering challenges, but that Coors had always proven itself up to such tasks. When
coaxing failed, Nichols pounded the table like a wrangler at a Saturday
night brawl. Right now! Coors needed a superpremium in the marketplace! Killian's was the best and quickest shot, and it had to be bottled
right, God damn it!

Nichols won.

But the day that Bill gave in, his eyes took on that distant, resigned look.

One day soon after, Nichols was on his way out to lunch when he
passed a dashingly handsome, smartly dressed young man standing in the
reception area. Two hours later, when Nichols returned, the man was
still there, looking peeved. Nichols walked over and introduced himself.
The man turned out to be Viscount Philippe de Spoelberch, scion of the
family that owned Stella Artois. The family had some $250 million to
invest overseas, he said, and had been thinking of a partnership with
Coors. This was exactly what Nichols had been praying for when he put
out his feelers to Stella Artois. De Spoelberch had made an eleven o'clock
appointment with Jeffrey Coors, he told Nichols. Jeff had apparently
forgotten.

Nichols was mortified. The de Spoelberchs were billionaires—they
could buy the Coorses with petty cash. A partnership with Stella Artois
could be a lifesaver.

"This Jeffrey Coors is a strange fellow," de Spoelberch said, graciously
making light of the gaffe. "I think he likes hops more than women."

The talks with Stella Artois went nowhere.

To Lyn Nofziger, Ronald Reagan's so-called friends came in two flavors:
natural and artificial.

The artificial ones were the rich California Republicans who had heard Reagan's pro-Goldwater speech in 1964 and had sought him out to unseat Democratic Governor Pat Brown. That was when Nofziger had come on board as press secretary. He'd watched this pin-striped group of wealthy industrialists use Governor Reagan to protect their narrow business interests. Ford dealer Holmes Tuttle, industrialist Justin Dart, oil man Henry Salvatore: To Nofziger, these were the fat cats. They had no particular ideology, just a rich man's desire to maintain the status quo and forestall regulation.

Nofziger put up with the fat cats because they pumped rivers of their own money into Reagan's campaigns and raised more from their wealthy friends. But Nofziger prided himself on being an "ideological kook," a taproot Republican who reached down to the pure aquifers of Buckley/Goldwater conservatism. The fat cats were for him an expedient in the bare-knuckle political game.

Then there were Reagan's other friends, the natural ones, the ideological soul mates. Chief among them was the brewer from Colorado named Joseph Coors. Nofziger first met Coors in 1968, when Reagan was ripping up the Board of Regents of the University of California and making forays outside the state to gauge his political future. Nofziger went with Reagan for the speech at the University of Colorado where he met Joe and was impressed by the depth of his beliefs. They'd met again in Nixon's White House, where Nofziger blew dust from the American Enterprise Institute report and encouraged Joe to found a plainly conservative think tank.

They made a funny pair—tall, soft-spoken Joe and the attack dog Nofziger, short, portly, and gravel-voiced with a Vandyke beard. Nofziger recognized that Joe was as much of a kook as he was.

Joe had no sense of humor, Nofziger knew—he would never call himself a "kook." You couldn't hang out and have a laugh with the guy. And he was one of the most politically unsophisticated men Nofziger had ever met. He had no strategic savvy or startling vision, only a mawkish way of saying the obvious. But Reagan was going to need men like Joe Coors, Nofziger knew. The more powerful Reagan got, the more the fat cats and hangers-on would dilute his positions. Men like Joe would keep him honest.

Joe Coors also happened to have a pantful of money.

Nofziger saw to it that when Joe wrote Reagan, Reagan wrote back. When Joe called, Reagan took the call. After a while, it became clear to

Nofziger that he didn't have to bother; Reagan genuinely liked Joe Coors. They were of a piece—simple men of uncomplicated vision, conservative in their gut, rooted in the West and instinctively mistrustful of the East. On several occasions during the 1970s, Reagan found reason to visit Joe and Holly, often alone. Reagan would be leaning against the kitchen counter while Holly cooked and Joe set the table. Holly was a peach. Charming and talkative, she possessed the public personality her husband lacked. She threw grand parties, organized Republican women into myriad volunteer organizations, and was an ever-optimistic cheerleader for the cause. Reagan loved her like a sister. When the operatives and fat cats and party hacks swirled too thickly around him, Reagan found shelter in Holly's kitchen. Joe and Holly were his touchstones, and they adored him.

And Joe was Johnny-on-the-spot with the checkbook.

After Reagan took the White House in 1980, Joe made clear in press interviews that he wanted to be in the Cabinet. "If the governor wants me, he knows my phone number," Joe said. Nofziger read this with a chuckle. That a rube like Joe Coors would think himself Cabinet material was a hoot. But Nofziger kept the Coloradan close, asking Joe and a handful of other patrons to meet regularly and make staffing recommendations. They called themselves the "transition advisory group." Everybody else called them the "kitchen cabinet."

Reagan's lawyer and soon-to-be attorney general William French Smith called the group a "pretty good cross-section" of Reagan's world. *The Washington Post* called it a "spectrum" that ranged "from millionaire to multimillionaire; from middle-aged to elderly, and all white male."

Nofziger raised the homogeneity problem in a kitchen cabinet meeting. "We're all white men," he said, "and with the exception of Nofziger, all of us have names that are easy to pronounce. It could create a negative impression of the new administration." Joe and the others stared at him. Nofziger was sure none had the slightest idea what he was talking about.

The chief counsel for Beatrice Foods called John Nichols one afternoon to offer a stunning opportunity. Beatrice had been one of the first U.S. corporations to take advantage of opening Chinese markets. Now the Beatrice lawyer, a longtime friend of Nichols, was inviting Coors to represent the American brewing industry on the next China-bound trade mission. Hell, yes, Coors is interested, Nichols told him. That's a billion potential Coors drinkers. He practically ran to Bill and Joe's office with the news.

Joe was on the phone. Bill put his finger to his lips and waved Nichols in.

"White House," Bill whispered, grinning. "I think he's being told he's not going to be secretary of commerce. Look at him. Mad as hell."

Joe frowned darkly into the phone, plugging his other ear.

In an excited whisper, Nichols told Bill about the call from Beatrice.

"Red China?" Bill asked.

Nichols hadn't heard it called that in years.

"No way," Bill laughed. "Joe would never go for it."

"We're talking a billion people, Bill. It's a Republican initiative. They're opening up over there."

"Naw," Bill said. "They're communists. They're not going to do business. I wouldn't trust 'em."

"Bill . . ." Nichols said.

"Know what, John? Marco Polo brought brewing *from* China. They've been brewing over there longer than we have. Why would they want to learn from us?"

Nichols wanted to shake the man. They don't want to talk about brewing, you idiot! They want to talk about marketing, distribution, branding! All the things our country knows! All the things they're trying harder than you to learn!

But what the hell, Nichols thought, as Joe grumbled into the phone beside them. These guys don't get it and probably never will. There go a billion customers. Have at it, Miller. All yours, Anheuser-Busch.

Suddenly, Joe raised his voice and Nichols turned.

"All right then, I'm serious about Interior," Joe said. "It's got to be Watt. . . . Yes, James Watt."

Joe's fourteen years of campaign contributions, radio ads, introductions to wealthy Coloradans, and genuine friendship hadn't exactly bought him the right to appoint Reagan's interior secretary. But he had earned the privilege of being heard. Interior secretaries traditionally come from the big empty western states, where the department controls vast sweeps of territory. This was the natural Cabinet appointment on which to consult Joe.

It happened that Joe's protégé was a perfect fit for the Reagan Cabinet. In the previous three years of running Joe's Mountain States Legal Foundation, James Gaius Watt had lit up the conservative firmament with high-profile cases. Watt and his ten attorneys had argued against wilderness protection, against utility rate breaks for the poor, against the restriction of grazing on public lands, against punishments for polluters, against even Bill Coors's cherished Equal Rights Amendment.

Reagan had battled all his political life against the Environmental Protection Agency, the Bureau of Land Management, the Department of Education, and other federal authorities. He was now selecting Cabinet officers in part for their hostility to the agencies they would lead. Watt's key qualification to lead the Interior Department was precisely that he had spent much of his career resisting it.

Joe also directed Reagan's transition team to a band of extremely conservative Colorado legislators known in Denver as "the house crazies." Ann Gorsuch, for example, had resisted toxic waste regulations and tried to reopen a toxic dump closed for safety reasons. She'd also once hired James Watt to block the EPA from enforcing air pollution laws in smog-choked Denver. Reagan took Joe's advice and appointed Gorsuch chief of the EPA In turn, Gorsuch chose former Coors attorney Thorton Field, Colorado's chief lobbyist against toxic waste regulation, to enforce toxic waste law. Gorsuch's husband, Robert Burford, became director of the Bureau of Land Management.

Reagan accepted one more recommendation from Joe, making Colorado state representative Tom Tancredo, who had opposed bilingual education and immunizing schoolchildren, western director for the Education Department. "Too much government in the realm of social services takes away the individual's responsibility," Tancredo argued.

Even the harshest critics of the "house crazies" never suggested the legislators acted out of personal interest. Simply, they were "less concerned about public health than the burden on industry," as one Colorado health official told *The Washington Post*. "I don't think they were in anyone's pocket," the official continued. "They obviously had very deep personal convictions about the problems of over-regulation [and] . . . this led them to do exactly what industry wanted."

Such was the case throughout the new administration. Ronald Reagan was assembling the most ideologically committed administration in recent memory, staffed with people uniquely equipped to run the tiniest policy detail through a clearly articulated philosophical matrix. Reducing the size and power of the federal government, in all areas but defense and the maintenance of public order, was paramount, followed quickly by anticommunism. They swore to use their huge electoral mandate to transform American government "radically." The purity of their beliefs and their unanimity promised to make Reagan's the most dynamic presidency—albeit in precisely the opposite direction—since Lyndon Johnson's.

Reagan's debt to Joe went beyond campaign contributions and staffing suggestions. Upon winning the election in November 1980, Reagan was presented with a cube-shaped volume titled *Mandate for Leadership: Policy Management in a Conservative Administration.* More than three hundred people had worked on it for the better part of a year. Its eleven hundred pages scrutinized every department and agency, critiquing its mandate and history and making dollar-specific recommendations. Much of what became known as the Reagan agenda—the severe pruning of social services and the vast expansion of the military—was outlined in *Mandate for Leadership.* It had been produced by the Heritage Foundation, of which Joe Coors was founder and still a director.

What made *Mandate for Leadership* different from, say, a Brookings Institution policy paper was its touting of ideology over pragmatism. "The self-appointed guardians of political fashion . . . advise the new president to 'avoid ideology,' "wrote Heritage president Edwin Feulner, Jr., in the book's foreword. "But a successful statesman is first of all a strategist with vision: pragmatism is a wise mentor but a dangerous master."

The Reagan transition team proudly pointed to *Mandate for Leadership* as its operating manual. It was Joe's dream come true. The tome explicitly trumpeted the conservative ideology that Joe had nurtured during the previous quarter century. Now the President, by crediting Heritage with crafting his agenda, showered prestige on Joe's institute. The synergy that Joe Coors and Paul Weyrich had worked since 1973 to create—in which conservative theory, research, and political power would feed off each other—was now real. Seven years after its founding, Heritage was Washington's most powerful and influential think tank.

Only thirty years had passed since Lionel Trilling had declared liberalism the "the sole intellectual tradition" in America. "Now," Feulner wrote, "the clichés of liberalism are stale: they have lost their power to motivate or to inspire; they have also lost their power to govern." The conservative revolution had swarmed out of the hills and taken the capital—with Joseph Coors as chief quartermaster.

15

We Can Get
to All of You

David Sickler was nominally in charge of the Coors boycott, but the real inspirers of the movement, Sickler knew, were Joseph Coors and Ronald Reagan.

It wasn't only the substance of the new presidency that offended those who hadn't voted for Reagan—the huge tax cuts, the bellicose rhetoric about the Soviet Union, the military buildup, and so forth—but also the style.

"In the first few days of the Reagan Administration," wrote *The New York Times*, "business came to town—ferried to the inauguration, in part, by an air force of some four hundred corporate jets. They traveled by limousine, threw lavish parties, and generally made their presence felt in numbers that Washington had not seen in recent years."

Sickler sensed that a great many people felt left out of this limousine-and-corporate-jet soirée and the socially conservative groundswell that went with it. But Sickler sometimes had to remind himself that most Americans disliked thinking politically. It was hard to get them to vote, let alone stuff envelopes, walk precincts, man phone trees, or do any of the other mundane but essential work that went into building a political movement. Politics and religion were the two topics polite people avoided discussing. Direct appeals to "get involved" in the boycott, Sickler understood, were never going to work.

But one thing Americans loved to do, Sickler knew, was shop. If Sickler could make people believe they were "doing something" against Reaganism by the way they spent their money, the sky would be the limit. In other words, he had to convince people they could say "Up yours" to Ronald Reagan and all he represented, simply by buying any beer other than Coors.

That was the strategy. Tactically, Sickler attacked Coors not only one interest group at a time, but one neighborhood at a time. He organized informational pickets in front of liquor stores. A store owner who got tired of the pickets could get rid of them by refusing to handle Coors. Sickler was careful to picket all the stores in a neighborhood simultaneously, so that they could all drop Coors at once without fear of competition. Once every shop, bar, and restaurant in a neighborhood was free of Coors, the boycott battalion moved on.

Sickler traveled California, sleeping in union members' homes, talking up the boycott to locals, civic groups, and PTAs—to anybody who would hand him a microphone. A couple of weeks after speaking to a supermarket checkers' local in Los Angeles, he got a call from the local's business agent.

"God damn it, Sickler," he said. "You just got one of my best girls fired."

"What do you mean?"

"After hearing your speech, she started hassling *customers* for buying Coors beer. The manager finally fired her because she wouldn't ring up the beer for a guy."

"I'll be right down," Sickler said.

He picked up the business agent and together they went to the supermarket. After a few minutes in the manager's office, Sickler and the business agent convinced him that the young woman wouldn't rag customers over their beer choices again and that it wasn't worth going through a firing grievance. As he was leaving the store, Sickler took the young woman aside.

"Listen," he said. "I really appreciate your enthusiasm for the boycott. But don't get yourself fired. You shouldn't harass a customer for buying Coors."

"Pissed me off," the woman said. "He was the only guy all week who wouldn't switch brands."

When Sickler was in San Francisco organizing boycott events, he heard KQED, the local public radio station, announce "Coors Day" to honor the brewery for a generous contribution. Sickler called Howard Wallace, the activist who'd helped break the Teamsters' antigay policy, and now the northern California coordinator for the Coors boycott. Hours after KQED's announcement, an angry crowd appeared outside the studio. "Coors Day" was abruptly canceled.

Coors fought back. The company's lawyers filed a $145,000 lawsuit against Wallace, accusing him of conspiring to restrain trade and reduce competition. Wallace, who now worked as a theater janitor, learned from an article in the *San Francisco Chronicle* that he stood accused of violating the Sherman Anti-Trust Act against the Adolph Coors Company.

Coors demanded, as part of the discovery process, a list of Wallace's associates. The judge, though, suggested Coors might have "ulterior motives" for the request, and the lawsuit was eventually dismissed as "far-fetched." All Coors got out of it was renewed ill will in the gay community.

Sickler watched for signs that the boycott was pinching. An article in *The Wall Street Journal* described an internal conflict at the brewery in which Peter wanted to concentrate ad dollars on selling beer, while his uncle Bill—who took the boycott attacks personally—wanted to divert ad dollars to a more generalized campaign polishing the company's public image.

Another indication of the boycott's success was Coors's well-publicized switch from composite pads in their Enzinger beer filters to pure cotton. Somebody had started a rumor that Coors beer was contaminated by the asbestos pads through which it was filtered. In fact, Sickler knew, just about everything contains asbestos fibers. *Brewer's Digest* had published a study that found soft drinks contained almost three hundred fibers of asbestos per liter, most American beer contained between six hundred and twelve hundred, and Chicago drinking water contained more than thirty-eight hundred. Coors, by comparison, contained fewer than two hundred per liter, probably because the asbestos in the Enzinger filters combed them out. The switch to cotton showed Coors was desperate to answer every boycott charge, no matter how wild.

Sickler also kept an eye on Coors distributors. Several had started to handle soft drinks and candy as well as beer, which Sickler took as a sign the boycott was working. A group of distributors griped to *The Wall Street Journal* about Coors, describing such embarrassing blunders as Press Tab Two, deriding the lag in starting a marketing department, scorning a sales force that obsessed over beer temperature but gave no support for displays and advertising. "They're more interested in policing your inventory than helping you move it," one distributor said. But most of all, the distributors were furious at the family for picking a no-win fight with organized labor. "As much as I might sympathize with Coors's dispute with the unions, I think the only solution to the boycott is to make peace with [them], something we've suggested all along," one Iowa distributor told the *Journal*. "The brewery will never get anywhere trying to back the unions into a corner, and meanwhile we'll just keep suffering."

Nichols was sensitive to the plight of the distributors. He'd been at Coors two years and was about to become a distributor himself.

A slot in Texas wasn't going to open soon, but the company was planning a move into Tennessee and Nichols asked for a distributorship that would cover the middle third of the state. He'd gone to the University of the South at Sewanee and occasionally lectured there, he told the board. He knew businessmen and politicians all over Tennessee and owned a house near Nashville. He was a natural fit.

The board, bound by contract to give him a distributorship at the end of two years, agreed.

As Nichols was wrapping up in Golden, he suggested to Bill and Joe that they encourage distributors to organize themselves into a committee for transmitting their concerns to the brewery. It would be better than having them bellyache in public, he said. Bill liked the idea, but, in what Nichols considered typical boss-man fashion, didn't trust the distributors to elect their own committee. Bill handpicked it himself.

Nichols, in his crossover role as brewery executive and future distributor, was one of Bill's choices. The committee quickly submitted six resolutions that had a decidedly pro-Peter, anti-Bill cast. One resolution questioned the utility of "corporate image advertising"—which Bill was pushing—over Peter's preferred sales-oriented ads; another expressed "full confidence in Peter"—pointedly leaving out the other Coorses. The most explosive begged the company to make peace with the unions. "We feel that we must accept the premise that unions are a 'fact of life' and learn, together, how to deal with them effectively."

"Dad and Uncle Bill want your hide," Peter told Nichols. "They think you're behind the union resolution."

Nichols wrote Bill and Joe a formal letter denying that he'd led the distributors into the union resolution. But he couldn't help adding, "It would seem that financial survival of the Brewery and the distributor organization requires finding an accommodation with the unions that does not sacrifice your principles." Peter told him later the letter only made the elders angrier.

Bill believed the labor movement was lying and cheating to destroy the Adolph Coors Company. As a patriotic American businessman, he felt he had to resist. "Does anybody here know what Augie Busch's political beliefs are?" Bill asked the crowd at his annual Christmas address. When nobody answered, he said, "I thought not. I guess selling beer is more important to him than being a good citizen." Bill said he didn't mind suffering financial losses over the family's politics. "This is the kind of war we want to get into, not shy away from," he told *The Wall Street Journal.*

A kind of mild madness descended on the brewery as Nichols prepared to leave. A directive issued from Bill's office: Use of the Wellness Center is now mandatory for all employees, along with participation in team sports. You have to be fit, he told *The Wall Street Journal,* "to survive."

Peter called sales vice president Fred Vierra into his office. Sales were starting to rise and Vierra thought he was about to be praised. Instead, Peter fired him.

"What?"

"I'm not happy with you," Peter said vaguely.

"Why not?" Vierra asked.

"I just think it's time for you to go," Peter said, failing to make eye contact.

Vierra went to Nichols, who thought he knew what was up.

"Peter wants to run this company, and while you and I are here, telling him what to do, he doesn't feel like he's in charge," he said. "I'm getting out of his way. He's got to get rid of you, too."

Bill and Joe Coors, who liked Vierra, were likewise shocked. Bill asked Vierra to take over a new food-products subsidiary, but Vierra declined. Joe invited Vierra to his house and asked him to stay in his job. "I'll order Peter not to fire you," Joe suggested. Vierra shook his head. He was too angry. "I'd just be rooting for Peter to fail," he said.

Peter replaced Vierra with one of the Coors old-timers from distribution.

"Let me help you hire *my* replacement," Nichols begged, as Peter watched him empty his desk into boxes. "I know all the best people in marketing. You're going to want the best."

"I don't know," Peter said evasively.

"You don't *know?*" Nichols said. "What do you mean?"

"Dad and Uncle Bill have their own ideas," Peter said.

"Make sure they do it right this time." Nichols took down the NOTH-ING IN MODERATION sign.

"They're looking all over the beer industry," Peter said.

Nichols turned to look at him. "Well, that's stupid," he said. "Everybody worth a shit in the beer industry is already working for Anheuser-Busch and Miller. They have to look outside the beer business."

"They want a beer guy," Peter said.

"What for?" Nichols cried. "Brand marketing is brand marketing."

"It's because you say things like that . . . that's why they don't want your advice," Peter said.

Jerry Steinman, editor of *Beer Marketer's Insights*, wrote a sympathetic story about the Coors distributors' fight with the brewery. Bill fired a letter off to Steinman. "You have dealt us a low blow," he wrote his old friend. "Just how many of these blows we can continue to absorb and still come up for air is debatable, but there is a limit." He ended with his public-spirited argument against settling the boycott: "Winning our fight is just as important to our industry and to the long-range survival of our country's free market system as it is to ourselves."

A clerk at the March of Dimes chose this moment to make an error of protocol that sent Bill into paroxysms of wounded fury. Thomas Donahue, secretary-treasurer of the AFL-CIO, was to chair a fund-raising dinner for the March of Dimes. Bill Coors was among the philanthropists who received an invitation bearing Donahue's signature.

"Dear 'Brother & Sir,'" Bill wrote Donahue after receiving the letter:

I was touched by the attached invitation. How delicate of you, my self-appointed executioner, to invite me to dinner. Do manners and decency still exist in the AFL-CIO? You had led us to believe that they did not.

No, Tom, I won't be attending. My stomach is not strong enough to consort with persons like [AFL-CIO President] Lane [Kirkland] and yourself who condone and encourage the AFL-CIO in its efforts to destroy my Company. How proud you must be of your tools of destruction—the lies you tell about my Company and its people, the disparagement of its products. You must swell with pride at the dishonor these tools bring you. . . .

If and when the dust ever settles on this conflict, I give you my personal guarantee that the AFL-CIO will have spilled one hundred times more blood than we. If you would ever bother to do your homework, you would learn that you can only get to a part of us, and we can get to all of you. Come out some day and meet the 10,000 people of Coors who have dedicated themselves to that task.

Disgustedly yours,
William K. Coors

Donahue wrote back, apologizing for the clerical mistake, but adding, "I am concerned about the paranoia which your letter demonstrates. I always thought you were the practical one in the family, but to read your statements swearing vengeance against the AFL-CIO over a fight you started, seems to me more ideological than practical."

Copies of the exchange made the rounds of boycott activists and eventually filtered through the ranks at Coors. Nichols privately agreed with Donahue on one point: Bill was too emotional about the boycott. It hurt sales, sure. But not as much as Anheuser-Busch and Miller. They were the real threats. Fighting on a political as well as a marketing front—especially when the political front was unhinging the company chairman—was exhausting. Even if the AFL-CIO was smearing and insulting the company, Bill needed to get his mind off it. His outbursts only inspired the brewery's competitors.

It occurred to Nichols that Anheuser-Busch and Miller must be enjoying Coors's punishing bouts with labor. As he prepared to open his distributorship, Nichols hired a private investigator, a retired FBI agent named Jack Barron, to see if A-B was slipping the boycotters under-the-table assistance.

On stationery bearing a silhouette of Sherlock Holmes, Barron wrote that there was "strong probable cause" that Anheuser-Busch was funneling money through the Teamsters into the boycott campaign. A-B and the Teamsters had made an unholy alliance years earlier, he said, to strengthen both Budweiser and the Teamsters in Alaska. Barron's primary piece of evidence that something similar was going on in the AFL-CIO Coors boycott was that the Teamsters were participating. George Meany had expelled the Teamsters from the AFL-CIO in 1957 in disgust over Jimmy Hoffa's corruption, and the two labor organizations had been competitors ever since. To Barron, only Anheuser-Busch collusion explained the Teamster's participation.

Barron, though, was missing precisely what Sickler had identified as the difference between the Coors boycott and others: ideology. The AFL-CIO and the Teamsters raided each others' membership and competed tactically, but against a foe as ideologically antilabor as Coors, they easily stood shoulder-to-shoulder. Both labor organizations had much to gain by whipping Coors into submission; Teamsters delivered most of the beer in the country, and the AFL-CIO wanted to reorganize the brewery. Beyond that, even the most jaded and cynical Teamster or AFL-CIO boss was at heart a union man. And Joe Coors had established himself as unions' number-one enemy. It was 1981, after all. Ronald Reagan had that April annihilated the Professional Air Traffic Controllers Organization (PATCO), signaling the administration's fundamental hostility to unions and ushering in labor's darkest period ever. Trade unionists everywhere were eager to hit back any way they could. With David Sickler out there heaping the sins of the right wing onto the back of the Adolph Coors Company, supporting the boycott was pleasant work.

On top of the growing boycott, the distributors' revolt, and Jerry Steinman's "low blow," Bill received appalling news.

The brewing water was contaminated.

Springs Fourteen and Nineteen, the wells closest to the can plant, contained cancer-causing solvents that were used to clean cans. The culprit was probably a cracked sewer line that appeared to have been leaking for several years. Springs Eighty and Eighty-one were also tainted by solvents, though the source of this contamination wasn't clear. All four springs were used to make beer.

It was Bill's worst nightmare. His grandfather had built the brewery in Golden to take advantage of Clear Creek. For decades the company had boasted that its beer was "Brewed with Rocky Mountain Spring Water." The purity of the water differentiated Coors from the "downstream" beers its ads derided.

For Bill, the news was painful on another level. Bill loved the Rocky Mountains. He took pride in their pristine beauty and believed in conservation. He had developed the aluminum can, defended the disastrous Press Tabs, and invented can recycling in large part to thwart litter. He'd redesigned the malthouse to recycle water. He'd built a state-of-the-art waste treatment plant that he shared, free of charge, with the nearby Colorado School of Mines. And he'd devised a way to pipe the steam generated by the brewery to heat classrooms and dormitories at the School of Mines. He even drove a little blue experimental electric car. Every day he pulled into his customized parking space, plugged in, and went to work, where, if he had a minute, he'd bend your ear about the world's ecosystems and the fragility of the environment. Now, he had to face his own brewery's pollution.

Federal law required Coors to report the contamination at once. Both Bill and Joe knew that meant an army of inspectors would swarm the brewery grounds. Coors would be dragged before state and federal health officials and forced to pay a huge fine. They might have to shut down until the problem could be fixed. The massive publicity, on top of the A-B/Miller onslaught and the boycott, could finish off the company.

It was out of the question.

As Coors executives admitted almost a decade later, the company decided to keep the contaminations secret. Its water engineers believed the solvents—TCA, PCE, TCE, 1,1-dichloroethylene, and 1,2-dichloroethene—were so volatile that they would evaporate harmlessly as the engineers pumped out the polluted wells. The engineers quietly began pumping the tainted waters of Springs Eighty and Eighty-one into a stream called Kinney Run. They pumped out the fouled waters of Spring Nineteen, too. By the time the affair came to light, they could not remember where those waters had gone.

The destination of Spring Fourteen's dirty water, though, was unforgettable. Clear Creek had been the heart of the Adolph Coors Company since the founder first built his brewery on its banks. Bill's grandfather had given the sparkling creek its sacred purpose. Bill's father had used it to bathe the busy brewery's fevered brow, passing it through the plant's cooling towers, returning it warmer but clean to its bed. Now Bill's legacy would be that he'd poisoned it by dark of night, repudiating both his environmentalist principles and his reputation for honesty, and making a mockery of the river's name.

John Nichols borrowed a million dollars to open his Nashville distributorship and lost it all within a year. Adding up the calamities, Nichols could draw no other conclusion than that Coors had deliberately destroyed him.

The trouble started with Nichols's first order of beer. He could only unload two cars a day, so he asked for eight carloads of beer to be delivered over the course of the first week. For reasons never explained, all eight carloads arrived at once. Because six of them sat too long in the searing Tennessee sunshine, Coors made him destroy all the beer they held at his own expense. Before the end of his first week, the debacle had cost Nichols six hundred thousand dollars.

Then Nichols learned that he was being charged 20 percent more for his beer than any other distributor. It was cheaper for him to buy inventory from the Coors distributor in Jacksonville, Florida, than to buy it directly from the brewery, and he did so a few times when Jacksonville had a surplus. He wrote the brewery letter after unanswered letter asking why his price was higher. "I do not wish to believe that anybody maliciously set out to impede our success," he wrote Peter. Peter never responded.

Shipments were late. Permission to engage in competitive discounting was denied. In all its dealings with Nichols, the brewery was so antagonistic that Nichols had to ask it "to do some real soul-searching about its attitude" toward him. "We are not the enemy!" Nichols wrote plaintively.

Nichols made his share of mistakes, too, but they were minor, he felt, compared with the actions of the brewery. He finally filed for bankruptcy protection and lined up a buyer. But Coors went around him and told the buyer that Nichols's price was too high. The deal vaporized.

Nichols decided to sue. "The brewery maliciously set out to prevent [our] financial success," he wrote in a draft press release. "And it has done a good job of it to date."

In the end, though, Nichols's lawyer advised him not to file the suit. Coors would drag the fight out indefinitely, he said. "Even if you win, I'll have all your money," the lawyer told Nichols. "Walk away."

Nichols tried to take his lawyer's advice and put the experience behind him, but the brewery interfered with that, too. A friend at the Ted Bates ad agency eagerly snapped Nichols up, but a few days later had to call and rescind the offer. Bates now had the Coors Light account, and the brewery had threatened to switch to another agency if Bates hired Nichols. When Nichols began calling friends at other agencies, he found Coors had apparently gotten to them, too. Nichols was told that Coors had said no agency that hired him would ever get Coors's business. Nichols recognized the irony. It was he who had turned Coors into a corporation that spent almost $50 million a year on advertising. Nobody was willing to risk losing a piece of that.

Nichols was out of work for six months, with a child in college. Finally, a tiny agency in Warren, Michigan, hired him at a fraction of his former salary. For Nichols, it was like exile. Many months later, Coors dropped Ted Bates as its agency and the agency hired Nichols—as president.

Long after the collapse of his distributorship, Nichols flew to Golden for a meeting with Coors's lawyer to tie up loose ends. Nichols walked out of the lawyer's office at the end of the meeting, and there in the hallway stood Peter Coors.

Peter fidgeted awkwardly for a long silent moment, biting his lip.

"Hello, Peter," Nichols said frostily.

"Hi, John," Peter said to his old mentor. They stood looking at each other for a long moment.

I saved your ass, Nichols thought. I gave you a marketing strategy you can ride for a decade. I made you a hero in your company. "I've got to know something Peter," Nichols finally said, stepping in close and peering up. "After all I did for you, why did you do this to me?"

Peter turned red and looked at the floor. He leaned down close to Nichols's ear and whispered, "It's my dad. You taught me to argue with him."

Then he turned on his heel and walked out into the sunshine. Nichols never saw him again.

Allan Maraynes opened the envelope from the AFL-CIO and withdrew the bright orange flyer. "BOYCOTT COORS!" it read. Coors forces employees to take lie detector tests. Coors strip-searches employees. Coors discriminates against women, blacks, Hispanics, and gays. The flyer made the Adolph Coors Company sound like a miniature fascist police state.

Perfect, in other words.

Maraynes was a producer at CBS's *60 Minutes* and handled most of the show's stories about businesses. A slim, elegant man with fashionably long hair and a neatly trimmed beard, Maraynes had produced the devastating piece that revealed the tendency of the Ford Pinto to explode when hit from the rear. He also exposed fraudulent drug companies and toxic polluters. The Coors story seemed to be the kind he liked. Maraynes called the name on the bottom of the flyer: David Sickler.

Sickler was ecstatic that the highest-profile news show in the country—one with a reputation for tough corporate reporting—was finally on the Coors story.

Maraynes asked for evidence to back up the charges on the flyer, and Sickler sent him a stack of notarized affidavits from replaced strikers attesting to sex-related questions on the polygraph, discrimination, and unwarranted searches. Maraynes flipped through them and realized that all these cases were years old.

"Well, we haven't had our people inside the plant in five years," Sickler told him. "That's the whole point."

"I need to know about *current* abuses against employees," Maraynes said. "*That's* the story."

At this point, Sickler made a crucial mistake. He failed to notice the direction Maraynes's expectations were heading. Maraynes was used to breaking stories about corporations that committed specific illegal acts— hushing up dangerous defects, willfully polluting, pushing unsafe products. The Coors boycott story, Sickler could have explained, lived on a different plane entirely. It didn't just exist in the here-and-now. It was about the Coors family's support for organizations that hurt women, gays, minorities, and working people and the family's self-identification as right-wing antiunionists. It was about organizing the Left under a single banner and about politics and corporate ideology. Mainstream journalists are not usually tuned to the frequency of class struggle. But had Sickler been clear about the boycott's nature from the start, he might have killed the story—and averted a gathering catastrophe.

Instead, he fed Maraynes's dangerous expectations. He promised to find recent cases of employee abuse.

In the meantime, Coors's public-relations chief asked Maraynes to fly to Golden, without a camera crew, to let Coors plead its case in private. Maraynes rarely allowed story subjects to "preinterview" off the record. It gave them, he felt, an unfair advantage.

This time, though, he accepted the invitation. He believed he was immune to corporate PR.

A Coors public relations team met Maraynes at the airport and walked him through the brewery. They, not Sickler, first explained to Maraynes the ideological nature of the boycott. The AFL-CIO didn't like the Coors family because of its politics, the Coors people told him. That was what this was all about. They showed him their improved affirmative-action record. They showed him state data indicating that Coors was one of the highest-paying companies in Colorado. They showed him the Wellness Center. They made no apologies for the lie detector test because, they said, it helped ensure the family's security. Besides, they said, many other corporations used the polygraph, too. As for searching employees for drugs, they pointed out it was only prudent when employees handled potentially dangerous machinery. Maraynes found the Coors people relaxed and confident; they seemed to have nothing to hide.

He could have the run of the brewery, they told him. Talk to anybody, film anything.

The Coorses weren't quite as relaxed as they wanted Maraynes to believe. At the urging of the public relations chief they'd hired from Pepperdine College, Bill and Joe had agreed to hire a Texas PR firm whose specialty was preparing company executives for media interviews. Old Mr. Coors would have been apoplectic at the thought of spending money on such a thing. But the specialists earned their keep. "What are the questions Mike Wallace could ask that you'd least like to answer?" they asked Bill and Joe. Then they set up a camera and playacted the interview, hammering Bill and Joe mercilessly with aggressive questions and fine-tuning their responses. They carefully selected the clothes Bill and Joe would wear (open-neck shirts with sweaters), and even switched Joe's photosensitive glasses for ordinary lenses so they wouldn't darken under the television lights and make him look like a thug. For Bill and Joe, the expenditure of time and money on something as ephemeral as media prep was culturally shocking. It was also some of the smartest money they ever spent.

Maraynes stayed in Golden a couple of days. He walked the brewery unescorted, making himself as conspicuous as possible. He went from bar to bar at night, introduced himself, handed out business cards, and said he was interested in hearing horror stories about Coors. Nobody came forward in the bars. Nobody called him at his motel.

He figured that nobody wanted to talk to him right there in Golden. They'd call when he got back to New York.

Nobody called.

As for David Sickler, he kept promising juicy recent cases, but never delivered. His cases were old. "Our people haven't been in the plant in five years," he repeated.

If things were worse five years ago when there was a union, Maraynes thought, maybe the problem was the union.

Maraynes recalled the first story he'd produced at *60 Minutes,* a profile of Boston University president John Silber. Silber was constantly under fire at the time from students and faculty for being, in their words, a "fascist dictator" on campus—abusive to students, capricious in disciplining faculty, a genuine monster. But Maraynes had come to see Silber as a decent man who simply held conservative political views that were unpopular on campus. The story Maraynes ultimately produced was one of a man pilloried on phony charges as punishment for his politics.

The Coors story was starting to feel to Maraynes like the Silber story.

At Sickler's urging, Maraynes flew to San Francisco. Howard Wallace—the gay activist and theater janitor sued by Coors for violating the Sherman Anti-Trust Act—had organized a group interview with a Catholic priest, a black activist, a Jewish woman who worked for the United Farm Workers, a woman who worked for the National Gay and Lesbian Task Force, and a Mexican-American community leader. They sat in a circle, Mike Wallace asking questions, and ran through the litany of charges against the Coorses: the lie detector, the history of discrimination, and most of all the family's support for Ronald Reagan and the conservative agenda. The interview lasted two and a half hours, and with every word Maraynes became more convinced that the Coorses' story was the equivalent of Silber's. The Coors family was being punished for its political beliefs. The thought of the AFL-CIO scoring political points by smearing a good company offended Maraynes. This wasn't another corporation-as-scoundrel story, he figured. The real story was the opposite. The AFL-CIO was the villain and Coors the victim.

He didn't let Howard Wallace know he was thinking this way, though. "That was terrific," Maraynes told him when the group interview was over. "I don't know how you did it."

Sickler was interviewed personally by Mike Wallace. Speaking in a San Francisco union office, he ran through all the same charges as the San Francisco activists had. But like Maraynes, Wallace wanted specifics.

"Give me an example," he pressed, "over the last five years of illegal search and seizure."

"In the last five years?" Sickler asked.

"Yeah."

"I have no example." Trying to gather his thoughts under the glaring TV lights, Sickler started to point out that the union had struck five years ago and been kicked out, but that the boycott had since pressured Coors into cleaning up its act.

Wallace bored in with questions about the lie detector. "All kinds of companies [use the polygraph]," he said. "And you're not boycotting them."

"No, we don't," Sickler said. "And many of those companies have union contracts."

"That's really the nub of the issue," Wallace said. "They got rid of the union."

"That's right."

The lights were hot and they took a break. When Mike Wallace was out of earshot, one of the cameramen muttered to Sickler, "I've got to hand it to you. Not many people can stand up to Wallace when he's in one of his 'gotcha' moods. You're doing well."

Wallace's interview with Bill and Joe took place in the elegant living room of the old mansion, a stark contrast to the peg-board-and-fluorescent-light backdrop of Sickler's interview. Bill and Joe were smooth and relaxed. They freely admitted they wouldn't have invited *60 Minutes* to Golden if the boycott hadn't been hurting them. They denied abusing workers, unapologetically defended the use of the lie detector, and reiterated their invitation to *60 Minutes* to talk to anyone at Coors. The way Wallace framed the questions, the issue remained Coors's current business practices, not the family's politics.

The Texas public-relations consultants arranged an informal "brown bag" meeting for the *60 Minutes* crew to meet a group of Coors employees, with Bill and Joe in attendance. Sickler heard about it and called Maraynes. "It's a setup," he said. "They're going to handpick them. And anyway, nobody would criticize the company with Bill and Joe there."

"We know. Don't worry," Maraynes said. "We're going to film it, but I'm not going to use it."

In the final editing, though, the "brown bag" meeting became the centerpiece of the story. Employee after employee took the microphone to praise Bill and Joe for their integrity and the brewery for its high wages and generous benefits. A Hispanic foreman and a woman construction supervisor told of advancing more rapidly at Coors than they would have elsewhere. The camera kept flitting back to Bill and Joe, who beamed proudly.

None of the interviews with the strikers was aired. Neither was the group interview with the activists in San Francisco.

Sickler watched the segment in a motel room while visiting Denver, and if he hadn't been on the first floor he'd have jumped out the window. First of all, he'd fallen into the same trap that Joe Coors's media coaches had foreseen: Sickler's photosensitive eyeglasses had darkened under the bright TV lights, and nobody on the crew had bothered to tell him. He came off looking like a gangster. The camera kept an extremely tight close-up, too, which made him appear all the more threatening. The steel-desk-and-peg-board backdrop of the union office looked nasty beside the living room of the Coors mansion. None of Sickler's broad charges against the company made the show; most of his air time went to admitting he had no examples of recent abuses. So when Sickler agreed that Coors was singled out for boycott because it got rid of the union, he sounded like a stereotypical union boss focused on nothing broader than wresting power for himself. In ten minutes of television, *60 Minutes* had reduced the Coors boycotters to petulant spoilsports. Anybody watching the show would have thought the campaign against Coors was no different from, say, the failed J. P. Stevens boycott: a big union versus a big company. Nothing more.

16

Hi Ho, Critical Mass!

Inside Coors: jubilation. Vindicated! Even the liberal media agree with us! *60 Minutes* was the top-rated show on television; more than a quarter of all TV-watching households tuned in each week. The Coors segment surely would put a stake through the heart of the boycott.

Things were looking up. California market share was rebounding slightly on the strength of the "Surprising Taste of Coors Light" ads. Press Tab Two was gone, replaced, finally, by the Alcoa tab. The moves into Arkansas and Louisiana—the first big plunge eastward—were going well. After so many frightening years, this taste of good news was heady enough to nudge Bill an inch. He was still against building a second brewery or even buying land against the eventuality. But he was willing enough to option a vast swath of land in Virginia. It was no ordinary land; it bordered Shenandoah National Park, at the feet of the four-thousand-foot peaks of the Blue Ridge. In its proximity to its region's water's source, the site was about as close a replica of Golden as could be found on the East Coast.

When it became clear that Bill Coors really wasn't going to build a second brewery anytime soon, the excitement of optioning the Virginia land quickly faded. Everybody at the brewery noticed that Bill was with-drawing. The *60 Minutes* coup seemed to cheer him only momentarily.

His mind wandered in meetings. He appeared silent and morose. He was seen less and less walking around the plant. His long-standing open-door policy—by which any brewery worker could come talk to him—was quietly rescinded. Now workers with ideas or complaints had to go up through layers of middle management before they might hope to reach Bill. For the first time, Bill didn't deliver his annual Christmas address to the brewery workers; Peter did. And Bill stopped playing piano at the retirement parties of brewery workers.

Bill's first wife, Geraldine, had just died and although they were long divorced and both remarried, people thought that perhaps her death was the cause of his depression. His speech to the shareholders that year had none of the homespun wit for which he was beloved. He stood at the podium, rumbling in a monotone, about the brewery's plan to get rid of the public-image-building "We Are Coors" campaign that he'd pushed, in favor of the hard-sell strategy preferred by his nephew. Bill even mentioned offers to buy the brewery. "It pains me to say it," he said, "but brand loyalty rather than quality often dictates people's buying habits."

Fred Vierra, fired by Peter Coors for reasons he never understood, was in Washington, D.C., when one of his old Coors distributors called him. "Fred, things are worse than ever," the man said. "At least when you were there you'd listen to us. This new guy has turned the sales department back into a goon squad."

How odd, Vierra thought. Peter was always the distributors' champion and Bill was their nemesis. Maybe Nichols was right. Maybe in his eagerness to prove that he ran the show, Pete had chosen incompetent managers. And it had worked against him, because now the distributors wanted Vierra to go around him to his uncle.

"I'm sorry to hear it," Vierra told the distributor, "but there's nothing—"

"You can get to Bill," the distributor said. "Please, Fred. We're dying out here."

Fred agreed to try, and as the words left his lips he was sorry. But having committed himself, he dialed Bill's home number. Phyllis answered.

"I just did something really stupid," he said, and told her what the distributor had asked of him.

"Come up for dinner the next time you're in town," Phyllis said warmly.

That turned out to be soon, and he went not for dinner but for tennis on Bill's backyard court. They played a set and then reclined in the shade with glasses of beer.

"I need to share with you some problems the distributors have told me about," Vierra said.

"Wait a minute," Bill said, holding up a hand. "Let me tell you." And he listed, with startling accuracy, all of the distributors' gripes.

"Why don't you do something about them?" Vierra asked.

"Pete is running the brewery now," Bill said. He took a long, thoughtful sip of his beer and set down the glass.

"Pete has failed," Bill said softly, looking into Vierra's eyes with that plain-Jane honesty of his. Even coming from Bill, who always played his cards faceup, such a bald indictment of a nephew shocked Vierra.

"But I don't blame him," Bill continued. "You know he's tried to resign several times."

Vierra wasn't surprised. Pete had never seemed happy in his job. "What's stopping him?" Vierra asked.

"His father," Bill said matter-of-factly. "Joe has very clear ideas of what he wants from Peter, and he's not going to let Peter walk away."

"Damn . . ." Vierra said.

"It's how we were raised," Bill said. He picked up his glass again and studied it. "We all faced it," he said, peering through his beer. "There are more kinds of child abuse than the ones you usually hear about."

Joe interrupted a San Diego banquet with some six hundred Coors distributors and salespeople to gather them in front of a large-screen TV. It was President Ronald Reagan's first State of the Union Address and Joe insisted everybody watch it. The triumph of Reaganism was, for the brewer from Golden, Utopia. He didn't want to miss a minute of it.

Joe was deluging the White House with letters recommending people for jobs. He didn't always get what he wanted. Anti-ERA activist and Eagle Forum founder Phyllis Schlafly, whom he recommended for "any important spot," was left out. Elizabeth Dole, whose appointment Joe fought bitterly on the grounds she had once been a Democrat, nevertheless became White House public liaison chief. But Joe was learning the relentless ways of Washington, and if he couldn't keep Dole out he could at least put one of his own on her staff. He reminded the White House that he was contributing $10,000 to Nancy Reagan's White House restoration and in the same letter requested that New Right activist Morton Blackwell be given a job on Dole's staff. The request was granted within a week.

Joe's wife, Holly, set up an organization called Citizens for a New Beginning, to promote the Reagan agenda. "There seems to me to be a very urgent need to let the many dissident groups know that President Reagan has a sincere concern for the Poor [sic], before they become enflamed during the hot summer months," Holly wrote Elizabeth Dole on her cursive-print typewriter. "While the Republicans are often blamed for being uncaring and heartless toward the Poor, I believe that perception can be changed to one of concern." When she got no answer from the White House, Holly organized a Foundation for the Poor to "address the problems of 'the Poor' through the active participation of the concerned evangelical church leaders in America in cooperation with the Free Market Economy."

Joe and President Reagan corresponded frequently and with great warmth. Joe never called Reagan "Mr. President," but rather, "Ron." Joe's handwriting was awkward, so he almost always dictated his notes. Reagan frequently handwrote his notes to Joe, and then had them typed up on White House stationery before sending them. Reagan appointed Joe, along with the actor Charlton Heston, to his Task Force on the Arts and Humanities. He installed Joe on the Presidential Commission on Broadcasting to Cuba. He made him civilian aide for Colorado to the secretary of the army.

Joe was particularly voluble on matters of defense. He warned Reagan to get "tough" on those advocating a nuclear freeze, praised the sale of AWACS radar planes to Saudi Arabia, and encouraged use of the term "neutron weapon" over "neutron bomb" to "take away some of the severe criticism that this device has incurred." And the one area where Joe enjoyed direct policy input was strategic missile defense.

The notion of shooting down Soviet warheads was first broached in 1962 by physicist Edward Teller, the scientific and political force behind the hydrogen bomb. Right after Reagan was elected governor in 1966, Teller invited Reagan to the Lawrence Livermore Laboratory at the University of California at Berkeley, where the X-ray laser, centerpiece of the future "Star Wars" vision, was being developed. Teller found Reagan keenly interested in missile defense and quick to grasp the technical concepts. At that time, Reagan was developing a deep belief in the biblical prophecy of Armageddon, repeatedly saying in private that the final battle between Good and Evil was at hand. "For the first time ever," Governor Reagan told a governor's-mansion guest in 1971, "everything is in place for the battle of Armageddon and the second coming of Christ." Certain that Armageddon would be a nuclear war between the United States and the Soviet Union, Reagan dreamed of defending American soil from enemy missiles. Teller made it his business to stay close to Governor Reagan as an informal science adviser on everything from nuclear power to earthquake-proof architecture.

Joe Coors had likewise known Edward Teller for years; their paths had crossed frequently in anticommunist circles. Knowing Joe was close to Reagan, and sensing that Reagan had a big political future, Teller invited Joe to Livermore during Reagan's term as governor and bemoaned the tragic vulnerability of the United States to enemy attack. Joe needed no lectures on the Soviet menace. Simultaneously shooting down hundreds of warheads flying every which way at Mach 4 would be difficult, Joe understood. But it was at heart just another engineering problem, and Teller's whole operation smacked of top-notch engineering. Joe was sold.

Reagan and Joe Coors also each made his own pilgrimage to the North American Aerospace Defense Command (NORAD), the high-tech redoubt in the Colorado Rockies from which nuclear war would be fought. Reagan and Joe separately experienced similar reactions when technicians simulated on the "big board" an incoming missile attack. "It's nice to know," Joe said later. "But it also told me that it was too late to do anything when the warheads are over Canada heading for our cities." Reagan told a reporter about the "irony" that "with this great technology of ours . . . we cannot stop any of the weapons." Reagan spoke several times on the radio during his governorship about the need for missile defense, and by the time he became President he was well primed on the issue.

As soon as Reagan was inaugurated as president, Teller made his move. He persuaded Reagan to appoint one of his young protégés national science adviser. Then he recruited a small group of oilmen, industrialists, and others who he knew had the President's ear. Some had been on the "kitchen cabinet," some hadn't. The group was led by kitchen-cabinet member Karl Bendetsen, who as an army colonel during World War II had directed the internment of 100,000 Japanese Americans. Joe Coors was among those recruited to Teller's group, which called itself High Frontier.

High Frontier first gathered in September 1981 and enjoyed such clout that they met in the White House with presidential assistant Ed Meese just nine days later. Teller told Meese during the meeting that the United States could achieve "assured survival," thus setting up an expectation that would drive missile defense for years. Bendetsen followed the meeting a month later with a long letter to Meese in which he made sweeping promises about the feasibility of the X-ray laser and even promised it within four years—all without the knowledge of the scientists working on the project at Livermore.

Four months after meeting with Meese, High Frontier was scheduled to meet for fifteen minutes with President Reagan. Reagan was so intrigued, however, that he let the meeting run more than an hour. The group verbally delivered to Reagan the information Bendetsen had written to Meese, and added a few refinements. The 1972 Anti-Ballistic Missile Treaty was no impediment to Star Wars, they said, because the treaty allowed either party to withdraw on six months' notice if it believed its "supreme interests" were endangered. Such was the case now, High Frontier told the President, because the Soviets were on the verge of deploying "powerful directed-energy weapons in space," an assertion they never supported and which turned out to be untrue.

Reagan wrote Bendetsen a note thanking him. "You can be sure that we will be moving ahead rapidly with the next phase of this effort."

When Peter set out to replace John Nichols, his father and uncle were adamant. We want a beer man this time, they told him. We want someone who understands the culture of brewing. Peter tried to explain, as Nichols told him, that any beer marketer worth hiring was probably already at Anheuser-Busch or Miller. Bill and Joe didn't listen. A beer man, they insisted.

Peter found one at the dying Joseph Schlitz Brewing Company who would satisfy his elders' criteria as well as his own. Bob Rechholtz was a nomad of the marketing trade. He'd served at Procter & Gamble—the undisputed heavyweight in brand marketing—and at Liggett and Myers tobacco before joining a sinking Schlitz as vice president of sales and marketing. The "Drink Schlitz or I'll Kill You" ads had just pushed the company over the brink. When the Uihleins wouldn't follow Rechholtz's advice—return to the original Schlitz recipe and start over—he'd started looking for work again. To Nichols's staff still toiling at Coors, hiring a marketer from Schlitz was like poking around in the wreckage of a crashed airplane to hire a pilot. But Bill and Joe wanted a beer man, Rechholtz was available, and his experience was broad.

"I don't believe in marketing," Bill Coors told Rechholtz over lunch at Rolling Hills Country Club. "A company that makes an excellent product shouldn't have to jump through hoops to get people to buy it."

Peter started to say something, but Bill held up his palm. "There are a lot of people in this company who feel the way I do. Production people. Engineering. We weren't raised to do marketing."

"I understand," Rechholtz said.

"I doubt you do," Bill said. "Quality and integrity have always been important to this family. At times this new way of doing business seems to fly in the face of those values." Bill took a sip of his Coors Banquet. "That said, I know we need to do business the modern way. We've taken some painful steps in that direction, and we're committed to continuing. But you have to do your part. You'd have two jobs, really. You not only have to make the company the smartest in the business, you also have to *get the company to accept you.*"

Bill was just coming off his experience with Nichols, who had made no visible effort to integrate himself into Coors. Nichols had raised his voice in board meetings and snubbed the Christmas party. His people had been rude to the brewing and bottle-line engineers. And they treated like an idiot anybody who might suggest that $50 million was a lot of money for something you couldn't put your hand on. Intoxicated by the logic of his profession, Nichols had assumed Coors would adapt itself to him if the bottom line improved. He'd misjudged.

As Peter walked Rechholtz through the marketing department, the staff—Nichols's slick outsiders—were struck by how physically alike the two men were. Both were tall, thin, and handsome, with straight brown hair going gray. They shared a tense reserve, a stiff, faintly forbidding air. Nichols's young Visigoths felt the old Coors culture, the dreaded Prussian frostiness, reassert itself as surely as winter follows fall. They knew their days were numbered.

Bob Rechholtz did what Nichols had not; he fired several people right away to make room for his own hires and declared everything that preceded him inadequate. He scrapped the "Surprising Taste" ads that had launched Coors Light upward as well as the "Taste the High Country" ads that had stopped the slide of Banquet.

"Taste the High Country" was meaningless, he said, and the "Surprising Taste" campaign only drew attention to the fact that light beer didn't taste very good. Rechholtz hung his new campaigns around the slogan "Made for the Way You Like to Drink Beer."

The Nichols-era marketers who were being pushed out the door couldn't understand Rechholtz. He abandoned Nichols's practice of keeping commercial actors in costume to shoot the still ads and in-store displays, so that all the ads would look like one another. Under Rechholtz, television sent one message, print another, radio another, and in-store display yet another. His swift, sweeping judgments struck Nichols's people as more erratic than bold.

Rechholtz knew he was coming on strong. He believed he needed to do so, to prepare the company for a radical plan. Bob Rechholtz intended to transform the Adolph Coors Company from a regional brewer to a national one—sold in all fifty states. If anything was clear in the modern beer business, it was that regional brewers were doomed. Only the nationals would survive. Rechholtz described his plan to the board in terms of "critical mass."

"Critical mass," he said, "is best defined as that share of the market which provides enough marginal contribution to competitively market your brands."

"Say what?" Peter's big brother Jeff asked irritably.

"Coors has to grow big enough to meet the big boys on the playing field," Rechholtz interpreted. "Right now we're at about an eight share. I'd define critical mass as fifteen to twenty."

Coors couldn't do that if it sold only in the West and South. The time had come, Rechholtz said, either to grow or die—to meet Anheuser-Busch and Miller on the national battlefield or prepare to go the way of Schaefer, Rheingold, Lone Star, and any number of other dead regional brewers.

"We're in twenty states now," he told the board, "which are home to only thirty-five percent of the population. People are drinking Coors beer back east anyway. They want it. We should give it to them." He explained once again the cost-effectiveness of national advertising.

"How are you going to finance it?" Joe asked. "This company doesn't borrow money."

"You'll have to forgo profit," Rechholtz answered quickly, and a wave of fidgeting went around the table. "I'm not saying 'no profit.' I'm saying 'less profit'—in the near term. It will pay off."

Jeff was furious. "We did fine when we were making one beer and selling it in eleven states," he snapped. "Since we've started bringing in these guys"—a wave at Rechholtz—"we've fouled up our lines with more and more products, we've sold them in more and more states, and we're not making any more money."

"The world has changed," Peter said.

"The world changed a lot on our grandfather and great-grandfather," Jeff said, gesturing at the portraits. "They didn't give up their principles. They held tighter and tighter to what they believed, and it saw them through."

"Either we go national," Rechholtz said, "or we end up a subsidiary of someone else's brewery."

"There were twelve hundred breweries in the United States when I was born," Bill said, "and seven hundred fifty when Prohibition ended. Now we're down to fewer than thirty." He looked into space for a moment. "I'll be damned," he said. "Consolidation has killed off more breweries than Prohibition. That's a hell of a thing, isn't it?" He stared meditatively at the tabletop.

"If you don't want to borrow, I respect that," Rechholtz said. "But it means a short-term reduction in ROI. You know I've personally bought a large block of Coors stock. I have faith in Coors. My fortune is hitched to yours."

Rechholtz preached critical mass every time he met with the board. The conversation about national expansion went on for months, and there never came a day where everybody enthusiastically signed onto Rechholtz's bold plan. Instead, active resistance slowly melted. The men around the board table—Joe, Bill, Lowell Sund, Max Goodwin, Al Babb, Bob Mornin—had all come of age when "the old gent," Adolph Jr., ran the company like a friendly mom-and-pop operation. The characteristics that differentiated Coors from Anheuser-Busch—that made them all so proud to be part of Coors—were small-scale attention to quality, identification with the West, and disdain for the hollow showmanship of advertising. All that was slipping away. The Adolph Coors Company was on its way to becoming Anheuser-Busch—if it was lucky. If it wasn't, it was on its way to disappearing.

In their ambivalence about what the company had to do to survive, the board made its support more tacit than explicit. For Bob Rechholtz, the Coors board wasn't a cheering section and it wasn't a supportive platform from which he could spring into the future. It was an anchor: movable, but only with great effort. He was more or less on his own.

"The most you need to advertise," Joe told Rechholtz at one meeting, "is five million dollars."

Rechholtz suppressed an urge to guffaw. He had in mind a figure twenty times that.

"Put the product on the shelf and let people know it's there," Joe went on. "That's all you have to do."

Rechholtz took a deep breath. He knew that direct confrontation had ruined Nichols. There were better ways to deal with Germanic authoritarians. Patience, he told himself, and figures. Joe is an engineer. Take him through the numbers in an orderly way.

"Total beer-industry spending on advertising is about five hundred million," Rechholtz said patiently. "We have an eight share. So we have to spend at least eight percent of five hundred million, right?"

Joe scowled. He could see where this was going.

"That's at least forty million dollars," Rechholtz went on. "But then, we can't make the national media buys, and we don't reach two hundred and fifty million Americans with every spot; we reach only ninety million. So to have the same viewer impact—as many pairs of eyes seeing our spots the same number of times—we have to spend more than twice as much. But say double. Say eighty million dollars.

"But even that won't do," Rechholtz pressed. "Because we don't want to be at eight share. We want to be at fifteen to twenty share."

"But," Joe bored in, "you can't *guarantee* results for that money, can you?"

"No," Rechholtz said crisply. "You're right. There is an element of the theoretical."

"You guys," Joe said disgustedly. "You're going to bankrupt the company."

Rechholtz was skilled at managing the board, though. They were used to spending about 1 percent of sales on advertising. Rechholtz got them to commit a breathtaking 10 percent of sales—$90 million. That was almost twice the previous year's ad budget—and twice what Coors was earning in profit. The old men on the board—Bill and Joe included—were in a state of shock. "There is a blood-letting going on in our industry," Bill told the *Denver Post*. "We are not giving in or going under."

Among the people Rechholtz brought from Schlitz was a young market researcher named Bob Schieffer. Schieffer had joined Schlitz in 1973, shortly before Bob Uihlein cheapened the product, setting off the calamitous chain reaction that crippled the company. To introduce the new man to the board, Rechholtz asked Schieffer to prepare a presentation on the beer market. Schieffer had prepared such reports annually at Schlitz and found them a cinch. Beer was heavily taxed, so it was easy to track sales geographically—and the maps made pleasant viewing.

Peter was entranced at Schieffer's charts—like a newly discovered Stone Age tribesman bewitched by a pocket mirror. "Gosh," he kept saying, as Schieffer flipped through simple data. "Gosh."

Was it possible, Schieffer wondered, that Nichols had never done this?

Schieffer had been given only thirty minutes in front of the board, so he moved rapidly. "A quarter of all beer is drunk by eighteen- to twenty-four-year-olds," he said, scribbling on a whiteboard. "After twenty-four, beer consumption drops off sharply, especially if the consumer gets married. What this means is that every six years, a quarter of all beer drinkers are new to the category."

A buzz rose from the table.

That was the most elemental of beer-market facts, Schieffer puzzled, and yet they seemed to be hearing it for the first time. He was awed, but he had to conclude that Nichols, a marketing giant, had never done this.

Encouraged, Schieffer plunged ahead. He thumbnailed America's beer-drinking demographics, including the statistics showing that women were drinking more beer.

Fifteen minutes into his talk, Schieffer looked up from the whiteboard and saw he'd lost his audience. Joe was asleep in his chair. Bill was awake but studying his thumbnail. Jeff was looking at the ceiling with a sour look on his face. The rest sat like andirons, except Peter, who was nodding at Schieffer's points and taking notes, as though by the force of his interest alone he could make Schieffer succeed.

It became clear to Schieffer that Nichols probably had done all this, but that everybody on the board had forgotten. They turned off. They developed narcolepsy. All but Peter, who had to pretend that this marketing stuff was new in hopes they'd catch his enthusiasm.

Deflated, Schieffer moved on. "As we move east," he said, "we should upcharge to between Michelob's price and the imports."

Bill came alive. "Charge more than in California?" he asked.

"The data indicate yes," Schieffer said. "In the states we're about to enter, Coors is considered special. It could—and should—carry a higher price than in California."

"That," Bill said, "would be unethical."

"Excuse me?" Schieffer asked. In all the market-analysis briefings he'd given, nobody had ever raised pricing as an ethical dilemma.

"It would be wrong to charge customers in one state more than in another," Bill said. "How could we possibly justify that?"

"In states like Indiana, they *expect* to pay more," Schieffer said, "because they consider Coors exotic, and better than average. They're not used to it the way they are in California. You might even do yourself harm if you *don't* charge more back east. At too low a price, people are likely to think there's something wrong with it, that it's old or stale."

"First of all," Bill said, "pick another example. We won't be selling beer in Indiana."

"Why not?"

"Indiana law prohibits selling beer from a refrigerated case," Bill snorted with a glance around the table. "Can you imagine? You can't buy a properly cared-for bottle of beer in Indiana. That's government for you."

"Illinois then," Schieffer said. "We'll sell more beer, and earn more on it, if we upcharge."

"I won't do that. My father wouldn't have stood for it." Subject closed.

While the board arm-wrestled, a small team of Coors brewers and marketers was working on a nonbeer product with huge potential: spring water. Perrier had exploded onto the scene in 1977 and the bottled-water craze was still swelling. The market was a natural for Coors, given its century-old reputation for excellent water. But when Coors taste-tested its brewing water against Perrier, Evian, and others, it rated surprisingly low. Good as Coors beer was, the plain water from its wells was humdrum. Putting Coors water on the market might not only fail, but might also damage irretrievably the reputation of the beer. The discovery led the team to an idea that would prove huge—for everybody but Coors: flavored spring water.

Perrier hadn't yet introduced citrus-flavored waters, nor had anyone. To capitalize on a pure-water image without letting anybody taste its unadulterated water, Coors invented no-calorie fruit essences. Coors water taste-tested well when flavored with these, and focus groups seemed attracted by the Coors logo on a bottle of drinking water.

Bill was unenthusiastic. He worried the brewery might run out of water. He also knew water used for brewing was not required to be inspected, the theory being that the alcohol in beer purifies it, but water sold plain would invite federal snoops. An unappealing thought in the best of times, federal inspections while Coors was secretly flushing contaminated wells would be unthinkable. Bill killed the water project. A few months later, Perrier released its fruit-flavored waters, competitors followed suit, and Coors missed a booming market its own engineers had pioneered.

Working with the brewers downstairs, Rechholtz's people envisioned a richer, more full-bodied addition to the product line aimed straight at those who considered Coors too watery. The brewers came up with a formula they called "Bud Killer," and in taste testing it consistently beat the King of Beers. After about six months of brewing and field testing, the team felt ready to approach Bill.

The old workers' bar in the basement had been converted by Bill Moomey to a "hospitality lounge" for brewery tourists. But upstairs on the sixth floor of the brewery was a tiny windowless executive "bar" with shallow maple-veneer paneling and light-up beer taps—like a bar in a county airport. Every Thursday after work, Bill, Joe, Peter, and Jeff would hold court there. To be invited to a Thursday beer was an honor and an opportunity; Bill summoned the marketing team working on Bud Killer.

The marketers led off with a blizzard of dry field-testing data. The beer they officially dubbed Coors Extra Gold scored so much with this group and so much with that, did better in this region, worse in that. Bill, sipping a George Killian's Irish Red Ale, drummed his fingers on the bar. Where beer was concerned, he had the finest eye, nose, and palate in the country. Why should he listen to a random bunch of lugs?

Noting Bill's impatience, the marketers hurried along, concluding that the current formula—which could be produced at reasonable cost—had a fighting chance against Budweiser.

"Fine, fine," Bill said. "Thank you. Let me see the beer."

He opened one of the unlabeled bottles. He put his nose to the top, took down a clean glass, and poured it expertly, generating an inch of foam. He held the glass to the light. Sniffed again. Finally, while the Extra Gold team held its breath, he took a sip. He thought about the sip. Then he took a long draft, and sat thinking about it. He took another sip.

"It's good," he said.

The Extra Gold team exhaled.

"But . . ." Bill said. He walked behind the bar and pulled from the refrigerator a cream-and-blue can of Coors Banquet. He poured a glass three quarters full. Then he picked up his glass of Killian's and poured a dollop into the glass of Banquet. He swirled the mixture, sniffed, and took a swallow.

"This is better," he said, putting the glass on the bar. "Let's go with this."

In horror, the team leader reached for the glass, sniffed, and took a sip. He paused, then handed the glass to the man beside him. One by one, the Extra Gold team tasted Bill's impromptu mixture. The truth was too awful.

Bill was right.

Gary Naifeh was another Schlitz marketer Rechholtz brought to Coors. Short and dark with a black mustache, Naifeh had spent four years in field sales and four in marketing. He knew both tactics and strategy. More than that, the thirty-three-year-old Texan had the personality Rechholtz wanted: He was a high-strung, single-minded pit bull of a marketer. A Nichols type, but one Rechholtz could buffer. "This is a very unaggressive company, and there's a chance it could disappear," Rechholtz told Naifeh when he brought him aboard. "The problem is the family; they are very conservative, in all senses of the word."

Rechholtz handed Naifeh the company's number-one assignment: Coors Light. After an initial surge, sales of the light beer were flattening out. "Light is life-and-death to the brewery," Rechholtz told Naifeh. "You've got to find something to jump-start it."

Naifeh agreed with Nichols's assessment that customers couldn't tell the difference between Light and regular Coors. Light needed a special handle, a call, or—as Naifeh put it—"a story people will listen to."

Everybody who worked at Coors at the time—right up to Bill himself—takes credit for what happened next. The nickname the test marketers had given their unmarked cans of Coors Light had caught on inside the company when the silver-and-red can was developed. Company people now used the name with distributors, who used it with retailers, who must have used it with customers.

Or maybe it was just coincidence. Maybe it simply made sense to call a sleek, shiny metal cylinder a "silver bullet."

Either way, the name caught on independent of the brewery. Distributors in Texas began reporting that college students were using the phrase. Bill's daughter called from college in Missouri to say the way they ordered Coors Light there was to yell, "Hi ho!" to the bartender, in imitation of the Long Ranger, who loaded his six-shooter with silver bullets.

Naifeh was going through files one afternoon and came across a newspaper ad that a Nebraska distributor had run. It showed a cowboy's gunbelt, and in every bullet loop there was a can of Coors Light. Also in the file were letters from Coors's lawyers frantically ordering the distributor to stop using the phrase "silver bullet": Coors might get sued by the studio that owned the rights to the old Lone Ranger TV show.

Nonsense, Naifeh thought. It took him one phone call to learn that the phrase "silver bullet" hadn't been registered as a trademark. Naifeh registered it, and ordered the "silver bullet" built into all Coors Light advertising.

Overnight, he had a whole new product.

17

The Founding
Fathers Died Broke

It was one of those infernal New York August days when the sky shimmers sickly silver-brown. Azhure Bhorne, a New York University student, was walking west on East Twenty-third Street, along the edge of the swank Gramercy Park district, when she noticed a crowd forming in the street up ahead. Bhorne thought a movie star must be passing.

Fire engines roared up from behind her. She searched the buildings ahead for smoke and saw instead the strangest sight—a woman, naked, on a balcony high above the street, shouting. Bhorne glanced around for lights and cameras; there was always a movie or TV show being shot somewhere in Manhattan. But she saw no movie gear. She looked up again, and to her horror the naked woman swung her arms like a diver and leapt from the balcony. Transfixed, Bhorne followed her down, not believing the woman would really hit the pavement.

Back in Golden, Fred Vierra and his wife, Roxanne, drove up Bill and Phyllis Coors's long driveway and parked at the spectacular Table Mountain house. The pain of being fired by Peter remained, but Vierra cherished his friendship with Bill and Phyllis. They were two of the smartest and warmest people he knew, and an evening at their house was always fun. As the Vierras walked toward the door, they could hear dinner guests talking above them on the massive deck overlooking Golden Valley.

Phyllis seemed subdued as she handed them drinks.

"Hello, Bill," Vierra said, extending his hand as he stepped onto the deck. Bill shook, looking away. A nerve quivered in his cheek.

"Anything wrong?" Vierra asked.

"No," Bill said quickly. Then he leaned close to Vierra and said quietly, "Yes. We just got terrible news about my daughter Missy. She's taken her own life."

Vierra stepped back, his hand over his mouth. "Oh, my God!" he said. He had heard from Coors old-timers about Missy's troubled childhood. How creepy, Vierra thought when he heard the details, that she chose to kill herself the same way as her great-grandfather. Vierra put his hand on his friend's shoulder. "Oh, Bill, I am so sorry." He looked around at the other guests laughing and talking. "For heaven's sake, why don't you send us home?"

"No," Bill said, squaring his shoulders. "I'm better off with you here. Where's Roxanne? I haven't said hello."

Taste? Gary Naifeh thought, as he looked over John Nichols's old memos, centering the Coors Light campaign on *"taste taste taste."* Who cared about taste? People drank beer for the image. And they drank it for the buzz. He took out the word "taste" and aimed new ads at active young adults who played hard and drank hard. The Silver Bullet became "The Beer That Won't Slow You Down."

Naifeh's next step was to attach Coors Light to a holiday. Beer promotions and sale-pricing for long weekends such as Memorial Day, the Fourth of July, and Labor Day boosted sales astronomically. But all of the big three summer holidays were devoted to Coors Banquet, and its crew wasn't willing to share any with Coors Light.

New Year's Eve was a drinking holiday, but not for beer. Naifeh considered Christmas, Thanksgiving, Easter, even Columbus Day. He settled on the as yet undiscovered and seemingly perfect beer holiday: Halloween.

"It's a *children's* holiday," other Coors marketers argued. "We'll get killed for marketing to kids."

"Bullshit," Naifeh said, rocking from toe to toe like a racehorse at the gate. "I've been to more Halloween parties as an adult than I ever went to as a kid. If people think of Halloween as a children's holiday, it's because we haven't redefined it for them."

Halloween was barely six months away. There was no time for market research or focus groups. Naifeh wasn't a product of Columbia or Wharton; he'd gotten his M.B.A. at Texas Christian University and his real education on the loading docks of the hundreds of distributors he'd called on during his career at Schlitz. It was the guys on the docks he wanted to titillate, not only so they'd work their butts off to get Coors positioned right in the stores, but also because if deliverymen liked his ads, so would steelworkers, mechanics, and all the other regular Joes who constitute the backbone of the beer market. Rather than subject Halloween to focus-group testing, Naifeh went with his gut. He grabbed an idea from the ether: Beer Wolf, whom you need a silver bullet to kill. He whipped up a commercial showing a man in a hairy suit whistling at women—easily the most lowbrow ad Coors had ever produced.

It was just the kind of rough-and-tumble work Rechholtz expected from Naifeh. Rechholtz brought him to a board meeting to describe the Halloween campaign.

Naifeh looked around the room and wondered what he'd been thinking. There sat prissy-Christian Jeff, stone-grim Bill and Joe, and all the antediluvian squareballs that constituted the rest of the board. No way he could sell them the campaign. More likely, he thought, they'd fire him on the spot.

But he explained his thinking on Halloween. "It's a major party holiday with a strong theme," he said. "What I'm about to show you is daring."

"You shot a commercial without clearing the storyboard?" Jeff asked.

Naifeh felt his mouth go dry. But he lowered the lights and played the ad. Board members watched the hairy man whistling at women. Naifeh watched the board. The spot ended and the lights came on. Jeff's face was bright red. Joe frowned into middle distance. Bill stared at the television screen with a scowl that might have melted it. The other old men looked like they'd been gut-shot. On the wall, Adolph the founder and his straightlaced son didn't look pleased, either.

Good God, Naifeh thought. I'm dead.

Suddenly, Bill slapped the tabletop with his palm, threw his head back, and laughed like a madman. "That's the funniest goddamned thing I've ever seen," he said. Everybody else started laughing, too. All but Joe, who sat as still as a craggy chain-saw sculpture.

"I find it offensive," he said.

"Oh, come on, Joe," Bill said, wiping his eyes with a handkerchief. "You should watch more television. This is what's going on in our culture."

Joe grunted and gave a backhand wave.

Beer Wolf became the Coors Light Halloween mascot. Distributors snapped up $600 Beer Wolf suits to dance in parades and at football halftimes. People laughed at the Beer Wolf gimmick. And they bought the Beer Wolf beer.

But having to resort to such sophomoric imagery took its toll on the old-timers who had worked alongside old Mr. Coors. Not long after Beer Wolf appeared, Lowell Sund told Bill he wanted to retire after thirty-seven years at Coors. "It isn't fun anymore," he told his old friend. The younger generation was taking over. Bill and Joe had just agreed to create a four-man "office of the president" to include Peter and Jeff as ostensible equals. Rechholtz had been named to the board of directors—a marketer, to sit alongside the likes of Max Goodwin and Bob Mornin—and he had told *Business Week* that marketing "is what this industry is all about."

"He's right," Sund told Bill gently. "The company is going in a new direction, and I don't feel like going there with it."

"I know what you're saying, Lowell, but damn, we need you here," Bill said. "We need the old-timers to remind us who we are."

"I've done my bit," Sund said.

Bill said he understood, but asked Sund to do him a favor.

"Would you stop in and see Pete from time to time?" he asked. "Kind of keep him under your wing? Pete's going to need all the help he can get."

Sund said he would, and soon after, he left Coors for good.

The marketing department was moving at warp speed. Relying on his research that showed most beer is drunk by eighteen- to twenty-four-year-old men, Rechholtz and his people centered ads on bombshell women. "We never even used to put people in our ads," said longtime plant manager Al Babb. "Now *this*."

One spot produced by Rechholtz's people showed a couple of guys sitting at a bar watching women walk through the door. "That one's a Michelob," they said as a plain-faced woman walked in. "That one's a Heineken," they said as a prettier woman walked in. Then a Bo Derek look-alike entered. "And that one's a Coors."

"This is just terrible," Max Goodwin told Bill. "Your father wouldn't have stood for it."

For some reason, the comment made Bill explode. "God damn it!" he shouted. "These people are the experts! We have to give them a chance!"

Goodwin retreated, stung. He didn't blame Bill. He could see that tradition-smashing was taking its toll in stress. But that was the problem. Goodwin wondered whether the exertion of change wasn't warping Bill's judgment. It seemed to Goodwin that because the old Bill felt marketing and advertising were sleazy by definition, the new Bill had decided the raunchier the better.

David Sickler had figured, after the *60 Minutes* segment, that he'd be tarred and feathered by the labor movement and the boycott would collapse. He had, after all, come off as a buffoon and a bully, and the whole purpose of the boycott had been left out. Nobody watching it, he'd thought, would have a reason to continue boycotting.

But he was wrong. Instead of giving people a reason to stop boycotting, the segment seemed only to have reminded people that the boycott was still going on. The segment may indeed have turned off those people who wouldn't have boycotted anyway. But those inclined to boycott interpreted the segment as a re-call to arms. Sickler found his phone ringing constantly from union locals, women's groups, black and Hispanic organizations, environmentalists, and gays wanting to offer their services. The boycott grew bigger and more energized than ever.

This did not go unnoticed at Coors. Boycotters were back in the news, staging demonstrations and press conferences to denounce the company afresh. The boost in sales that Coors expected after the *60 Minutes* segment never materialized. Sales remained sluggish, and though it was impossible to comb apart the effects of the boycott and the effects of the combined Budweiser-Miller attack, it was depressingly clear to everybody at Coors that the boycott was just as much of a drag on the company as ever.

Bob Rechholtz, Bill, and Peter were walking through the brewery one morning when the marketing chief took courage to speak plainly about it. "Much as I may agree with Joe politically," Rechholtz began, "the attention he draws is hurting us."

Pete stopped walking and held up both palms. "Nope," he said, with a choked laugh. He shuddered and walked away, unwilling to discuss it with Rechholtz and Uncle Bill, let alone be drawn into confronting his dad over it.

"Well?" Rechholtz asked Bill as Pete disappeared around a corner. "What do *you* say?"

"I don't disagree with you," Bill said mildly.

"But is it something we can fix?"

"I don't see how."

"We could talk to Joe," Rechholtz said. "Ask him to take a lower profile."

"There's no way," Bill said.

"No way to talk to him?"

"No way to talk to him, and no way he'd agree," Bill said. "This is his moment. He's waited twenty years to see Ronald Reagan president."

"He's hurting the brewery," Rechholtz said. "He keeps the boycott going."

"That can't be helped," Bill said. "Did you know the founding fathers all died broke? It's a fact. They suffered terrible business reverses for their politics. I would never ask Joe to soft-pedal. It wouldn't be right."

Rechholtz dropped the subject, for the moment. But the boycotts were a major nuisance. Rechholtz had high hopes for the African-American market. Blacks were trendsetters in music and style and he wanted to capitalize on that. They hardly drank Coors because, as the backbone of the malt liquor market, they figured it too watery. But their indifference spelled opportunity. The market was untapped. Because blacks weren't big Coors drinkers, they weren't big boycotters. Rechholtz thought Coors's new relationship to minorities would help. Having once been accused of discrimination, the company now was being held up as a model of affirmative action. The EEOC had recently put Coors on its list of exemplary companies. Bill had just hosted a reception for the Congressional Black Caucus in Washington.

Rechholtz assigned Naifeh to explore inroads to the black community. Full of optimism, the little Texan began working with Uniworld Group, a black-owned ad agency, on a whole new campaign.

The fresh approach to the black community inspired a jolt of optimism among the marketers. It was a new, bold initiative, and it made Rechholtz and his crew feel like they were finally acting, instead of constantly reacting. Faint suggestions of hope trickled in. Although August Busch III had gotten over his fear of diluting the Budweiser trademark with a light beer and was pushing Bud Light, Coors Light was meeting the

challenge and keeping up. Slowly but surely, George Killian's was growing, too. Even with the boycott, 1983 was the best year Coors had had
in ages; sales topped a billion dollars for the first time and yielded a
respectable 8 percent return. At the Christmas party in 1983, Gary Naifeh
was reaching for yet another glass of the delicious "Winterfest" beer Bill
brewed specially for the party when he felt an arm snake around his
shoulders. He looked to his right, and then up. Joe Coors was towering
over him, beaming down with a wide smile. "I just want you to know,"
he said, "that we're glad you're here." It was the first time in Naifeh's
eighteen months at the company that Joe had spoken directly to him.

On February 23, 1984, Bill arrived at the Quality Inn of downtown
Denver to address a meeting of minority business owners. Inviting the
68-year-old brewer had been a gutsy move; ethnic boycotters might easily
have accused the businessmen of selling out. But these were fundamentally conservative people and they welcomed a chance to demonstrate that
neither blacks nor Hispanics think in lockstep.

Bill greeted friends among the crowd of well-dressed, well-to-do
blacks and Mexican Americans. As he mounted the stage, he found himself overwhelmed at the opportunities America offered. He'd noticed he
was more emotional since Missy's death, but even so, who could fail to
be touched by this banquet hall full of prosperous minority entrepreneurs?
Five generations ago, some of these people were slaves. Slaves! Not even
considered people. As for the rest, many of their parents—maybe even
these same people—had swum the Rio Grande with nothing but dreams
of a better life. They were a lot like Bill's own grandfather. And now
look—a banquet hall filled with prosperous minority entrepreneurs, who
paid taxes, provided jobs, and generated wealth.

Bill had seen a bit of the third world. As a member of the board of
Outward Bound in 1974, he had climbed Tanzania's Mount Kilimanjaro
at age fifty-eight. He'd stayed on in Africa to tour and been appalled at
what he'd seen of squalor, oppression, and thwarted lives. Some of these
same people might have ended up scratching the earth for their wretched
living, he thought as he stood at the podium. What a difference freedom,
opportunity, and education made.

Bill began talking, extemporaneously as always, on his favorite topic:
the American free enterprise system.

"We have to understand how great it is," he said, "and how fragile."
Bill tried to draw a parallel between his family's story and that of those
sitting before him. America was a land of immigrants, he said; "we are

all ethnics. . . . Whether you stowed away on a boat across the ocean or waded across the Rio Grande River makes no damn difference."

Black Americans, he said, were beneficiaries of a historical irony; the slave traders of old actually did them a favor. "The best thing they did for you was to drag your ancestors over here in chains."

A ripple went through the crowd, and Bill sensed he'd used too strong an image. All he'd wanted to suggest was how much better life is in America than in Africa. He tried to explain, saying if the blacks in the audience could visit Africa, they'd never get over the contrast with this land of opportunity.

The room was oddly silent, and Bill grew nervous. He wasn't used to blacks. He hadn't grown up around any, and few went to Exeter or Cornell in the 1930s. Awareness of the black minority had been thrust upon him in the fifties and sixties, when they were challenging traditions and urging the federal government toward what Bill considered ever-more intrusive policies. Bill's personal decency—he felt he bore black individuals no ill will—conflicted with his conservative dislike of the African-American political agenda. Because he spent so little time around black people, he'd never had the opportunity to sort out these contradictory feelings. He found himself trying to do so now, aloud, before a roomful of blacks.

Bill shifted to education. That's what was missing over in Africa. "In Rhodesia, the economy was booming under white management," he said. "Now, in Zimbabwe, under black management, it is a disaster."

That struck the wrong note, too, making his argument sound racial. Bill tried again, focusing once again on education.

"It's not that the dedication among the blacks is less," he said quickly. "In fact, it's greater. They lack the intellectual capacity to succeed, and it's taking them down the tubes."

The business owners in the room seemed to hear Bill as he wanted to be heard—defending free enterprise, education, and opportunity. Bill received a warm hand of applause and thought the talk had gone well.

Gary Naifeh was feeling good on the morning of February 24. He'd just returned from a session with Uniworld Group in New York, crafting a strong, sexy campaign directed at blacks. Coors had a shot in that community, he thought. A good shot.

He sat down to coffee and a newspaper, while his wife Cathy went upstairs to get dressed. Cathy was in the bedroom when she heard Gary scream.

"I can't believe it! Shit! I can't believe it! God *damn* it." He was stomping around the living room; Cathy thought he'd gone mad.

"What is it?" she cried, rushing down the stairs.

"Look!" he shouted, thrusting the newspaper at her. Across the top of the front page of the *Rocky Mountain News* business section was an inch-high headline: COORS CALLS BLACKS "INTELLECTUAL" INFERIORS. A three-column shot of Bill Coors accompanied the article.

"Finished," Naifeh muttered, as he sank into the couch. "Everything I've been working on. . . ."

Across town, Bob Rechholtz was enjoying a quiet breakfast with his wife. Months like these seemed to justify his choice of profession. Miraculously, Rechholtz was delivering Coors growing market share and solid ROI at the same time. Coors Light, riding the Silver Bullet, was on its way to becoming the number-two beer in Coors's territory. And profits were higher than the company had ever seen. Rechholtz was a restrained man but he relished the tingle of success. Then he opened the business section. "Honey," he said, "I don't think we can continue to hold our Coors stock."

Bill was livid. "I never used the word 'inferiors,' " he sputtered. Joe, Peter, Jeff, and Bob Rechholtz had gathered in his office for the postmortem.

"It's typical of the liberal press," Joe said.

"Are the quotes accurate?" Peter asked Bill.

"I didn't say it," Bill said, "because I don't believe it."

"Uncle Bill," Peter pressed. "What about the quotes? Are they accurate?"

Bill ran his eyes over the page. "I don't know," he said grumpily. "I suppose so. But they're taken entirely out of context."

"That's what they do," Joe said. "They get your words right but twist their meaning, so they stay just this side of libel."

Peter turned to Rechholtz. "In future," he said, "when Uncle Bill is going to speak publicly, have someone from the company accompany him with a tape recorder."

"Good idea," Rechholtz said. They spoke as though Bill wasn't in the room.

"They applauded!" Bill said. "They even defended me afterward. Listen to this." He picked up the paper. "'Actions speak louder than words,' one of them says."

"Uncle Bill . . ." Peter began.

"No, listen!" Bill said, his voice rising. "'Denver's black community has received generous support from Bill Coors and the Adolph Coors Company.' Their words!"

"It doesn't matter what the people in the room thought," Peter said. He turned to Rechholtz. "We have to make a statement." Already, the National Association for the Advancement of Colored People, the National Urban League, and a raft of black city and state legislators were calling for Bill's head on a pike. The NAACP called Bill's speech "abominable."

"I think Coors has invited some kind of economic boycott," city council member Hiawatha Davis told the *News,* apparently unaware one had been in effect for six years. "Coors has invited the outrage and hostility of a whole people by what I think is an absolute supremacist view." Distributors were calling the brewery in despair; retailers were demanding Coors "get its racist beer off our shelves."

Bill held an excruciating press conference to explain his words. He admitted the accuracy of the quotes in the *News* article and said they'd been "an unfortunate choice of words." The failure of Zimbabwe, he said, was not racial, but educational. "The lack of success is due to a lack of a trained mind," he said. It didn't help.

A fathomless gloom settled over the brewery. Charges of discrimination had always been painful for the Coorses, not least because, in the old days, they were true. Until pressed by activists, Coors had pretty much ignored women and minorities. But the company had come a long way since then. The president of the Colorado women's political caucus had, shortly before Bill's gaffe, called Coors "one of the most progressive employers in the state of Colorado." Now, though, the *Rocky Mountain News* blared: OUTRAGED BLACKS SAY COORS INSULTED ENTIRE RACE.

Bill filed a $150 million lawsuit against the *News,* which only made the boycotters angrier.

Coors's public relations department shouted long and hard about the company's improved record of hiring and promoting minorities. But it didn't do any good. The boycotters interpreted the changes in Coors's corporate behavior as proof they were winning, and inspired them to redouble their efforts.

But even more confusing and frightening to the people at Coors, the boycotters occasionally let drop that their campaign wasn't really about Coors's treatment of its workers at all. "The Coors company may have cleaned up their act, but I think we will carry the banner of the Coors boycott simply on the level of Reagan being our enemy, and Reagan's friends are also our enemy," a Washington, D.C., labor leader said. In other words, the Coorses were being punished not for what they did, but for who they were. The boycott was ideological. The other side was as committed to its cause as Joe was to his—and everybody knew how committed that was. Coors was in for a long fight; the boycotters were true believers.

The boycott was like one of those cancers that is "almost always" curable. Nobody at the brewery really thought it was going to kill the Adolph Coors Company, especially during those times when the boycott was in remission. But there was always the cold fear in the back of everyone's mind that maybe the boycott would spread suddenly. Or maybe it would slowly and progressively whittle down the company's health past the point of recovery. To have the boycott thrust into the news after Bill's speech was like an unexpected metastasis. Suddenly, the boycott appeared potentially fatal. It was time for radical surgery.

part
Three

18

Fix It

Bob Rechholtz sat down, and with his customary confidence wrote what he called a "white paper" to Peter Coors. The brewery is in mortal peril, he wrote. Unless the family abandoned—right now—elements of the selfsame culture that made it great, it would lose its brewery. Rechholtz then listed the company's "barriers to success," working from the symptomatic inward.

The market holes were obvious: Coors still fielded no "popularly priced," or inexpensive, beer; no dark beer; and no malt liquor. Rechholtz also asked the company to get over its aversion to the hot new wine cooler market.

The marketing department needed more money and more power, he wrote. Production and packaging people should not be allowed to veto products, for example, simply because they didn't want to handle them.

The core of the problem, though, was the family's bone-deep resistance to the very idea of marketing. The Adolph Coors Company distinguished itself by making an excellent product, Rechholtz wrote, but it had taken product orientation too far. Like it or not, the world had changed; marketing was now at least half the game. This challenge should be embraced, not resisted. Crafting a great image took just as much genius and sensitivity as crafting a great beer. No amount of marketing would sell a lousy product. Coors's product was the best there was; it deserved marketing support of the same quality.

Rechholtz next repeated his concern about Joe's politics. Joe was back in the news. Ed Meese was moving from presidential counselor to attorney general; Joe wanted Meese's old job and was both explicit and public about it. Not that there was any chance he'd get it. Mike Deaver, Reagan's director of communications, thought it "hilarious" that Joe—whom Deaver privately called "Daddy Warbucks of the Republican party"—thought himself fit to be presidential counselor. Still, Rechholtz didn't like seeing Joe in the limelight at all.

The marketing chief saved his most delicate recommendation for last: The brewery should do whatever it took to end the boycotts. The average person's perception of the Adolph Coors Company was negative, Rechholtz wrote, and that was going to kill them.

The company was about to enter Maryland, North and South Dakota, Minnesota, Wisconsin, Oregon, Kentucky, West Virginia, Pennsylvania, and Ohio. All had large unionized populations, and places like Pennsylvania and Ohio had huge ones.

Down the road were states like Michigan and New York, Rechholtz wrote, where an antiunion reputation would be fatal.

Beyond the unions were the ethnic minorities, the women, the environmentalists, and the gays. It was time for Coors to give all of them what they wanted, Rechholtz wrote. There was no shame in doing so. After all, a happier, more diverse workforce and a better environmental record made the company stronger, too.

The family had heard all this advice before, of course. But only from shareholders, hecklers in the trade press, and the Nichols crew—none of whose opinion meant a damn to Bill and Joe. Now, though, the advice was coming from Bob Rechholtz, who by his respect for family hierarchy had won a limited entrée. The Coorses were not inclined to tune him out.

"This is strong stuff," Peter said when he read it.

"Dangerous for me to write, I know," Rechholtz said. "But if the company doesn't change course, I don't have a future here anyway. Coors won't exist."

"Let me work on my father and uncle," Peter said.

Soon afterward, the board called a meeting to review bad news. After the brewery's brief season of optimism, sales were running almost 5 percent lower than the year before, owing at least in part, in all probability, to the newly energized boycotts. Then had come Bill's notorious speech, only a few weeks ago. Things were only likely to get worse. Max Goodwin turned to Peter.

"It's time to end the boycotts," he said.

Peter smiled.

"If you think you can do it, Peter, go ahead."

Bill sat like a chastened schoolboy. Joe was quiet, too. Goodwin told Peter to work on the most serious of the peripheral boycotts first: those of the blacks and Hispanics. Having settled those would put the company in a better position when it came time to talk to the AFL-CIO, he said.

Rechholtz found himself unsurprised by the family's rollover. They were at heart smart and decent people, he felt, and this was the only move to make. He never knew whether his white paper had tipped the scales.

Fred Rasheed, the NAACP's national director of economic development, was in his office in Washington when the call came from Bill Coors. Rasheed, an elegant and cheerful veteran of the civil rights movement, was intrigued. These were dark days for the NAACP and for blacks in general. The Reagan administration was, in many activists' view, demonizing African Americans with its War on Drugs, unraveling the social safety net on which many blacks depended, and openly hostile toward affirmative action. To see so prominent an enemy as Bill Coors approaching the trenches with a white flag was appealing.

Rasheed and NAACP president Benjamin Hooks received Bill Coors and his public relations chief, John McCarty. Bill apologized for the offensive comments he'd made. His words, he added, were taken out of context. Then he fell silent; Rasheed got the impression he'd been told not to talk too much, lest he put his foot in his mouth again. McCarty, smooth and jovial, did most of the jawing. What would it take, he wanted to know, for the organized black boycott to be dropped?

"We've done some checking," Rasheed said. "You have more blacks working at the plant than you used to, but hardly any in management. No black vice presidents. No blacks on the board."

McCarty blanched. "This meeting was, uh, really just for you to meet Bill, and hear his apology," McCarty said. "Any next stage should be handled by Peter."

Rasheed marveled that McCarty might have hoped Bill's apology was going to do it. The Coorses, he saw at once, were new at dealing civilly with public interest groups. He would enjoy, Rasheed thought, teaching them the ways of the world.

Rasheed insisted that a Coors family member be present at any future meeting. They arranged one for a few weeks hence, in Los Angeles. This time Peter led the Coors delegation. Rasheed showed up with a cadre of NAACP officials. They sat across the table from each other and started to talk.

Rasheed was impressed with Peter's calm. He didn't seem happy, but neither was he defensive or nervous. He made no apologies for his father or uncle and mouthed no platitudes about brotherly love. He was there to smooth feathers for the sake of business.

Rasheed told him that Coors would have to meet specific hiring and promotion quotas if it wanted to end the black boycott. Peter's eyebrows went up. "I don't know," he said.

"Well, we're not adjourning this meeting until you *do* know," Rasheed said.

Peter paled. No way, at this point, could he walk out on the NAACP.

In the end, he signed an agreement to negotiate a covenant. Watching Peter hunched over the paper, Rasheed had the sense he didn't know what he was getting himself into.

Now that he knew he had a win in the works, Rasheed organized a coalition of Operation Push, the National Black Newspaper Publishers Association, and several smaller black groups to make the win as big as possible and give everybody in the beleaguered movement a lift.

Ready when you are, Rasheed told Peter.

Peter sent John Meadows, a broad-shouldered, mild-mannered PR professional. Meadows was from Detroit, which turned out to be a plus in the talks; he had done business before with African Americans. He understood the principle of enlightened self-interest and always thought before he spoke.

Meadows tried to get more out of the blacks than a simple end to the boycott. The benefits Coors paid to blacks, he said, would be pegged to blacks' consumption. "The more blacks buy and drink Coors," he told Rasheed, "the more they get from Coors."

"That's not how it works," Rasheed countered. As a Muslim, he didn't drink and considered alcohol a scourge on his people. "We're in a position to end the boycott of your product. But we're not going to encourage our people to drink."

Rasheed broke off the talks and turned up the heat. "We are saying to Coors, 'We, the black community, do not want your money with strings attached,'" an NAACP official told the *Rocky Mountain News*.

Coors gave in. Ironically, Joe Coors had spent his life fighting affirmative action and special consideration for minority groups. On the national stage, at least, he'd been wildly successful. The Reagan years were the beginning of the end for affirmative action. Inside government and out, employers were freer now to hire and promote without regard to past discrimination—just as Joe had intended. But the fight had made Joe's own company a target. Now, to deflect boycotts, he was being forced to become a paragon of affirmative action.

Meadows—over the course of six meetings—agreed to an extraordinary list of demands touching every aspect of Coors operations and striking in their numerical specificity. Because 5 percent of the metropolitan Denver population was black, Meadows committed 5 percent of production jobs to black applicants. Coors would hire one black vice president and nineteen black mid-level managers. The company would include blacks "at all levels of its corporate structure" including the board of directors. Coors would also assign twenty planned distributorships to blacks, buy at least $4 million worth of goods annually from black vendors, invest 8 percent of its cash and pension fund in black-owned banks, buy 8 percent of its coverage from black insurers, direct almost $9 million to black-oriented advertising, and earmark half a million dollars in donations for black causes. The covenant, over five years, would effectively tell the Coorses how to spend $325 million. To ensure compliance, Coors would submit to audits quarterly the first year and semiannually thereafter.

It was, by any standard, an enormous list of concessions for a corporation to make, and especially so for a corporation as obsessed with family control as the Adolph Coors Company. All the coalition had to do in return was "help understanding of Coors within the black community."

The AFL-CIO begged the NAACP not to shatter boycott solidarity by making a separate peace with Coors.

Rasheed argued the case for the covenant to Benjamin Hooks. "Look," he said. "We can't forgo more than three hundred million dollars in opportunities just to support the unions. Remember, the unions have their own history of discrimination."

Hooks gave Rasheed the nod and Rasheed—who didn't drink—was photographed shaking Peter's hand and holding a bottle of Coors. The shortest but most recently newsworthy of the campaigns against Coors was officially over.

Next came the Hispanics. Their boycott was, in Coors's home state at least, the longest-running of all. Peter made a couple of overtures. But his request to create an exhibit at the annual conference of the National

Council of La Raza was rebuffed. His effort to buy an ad in La Raza's magazine was equally fruitless. La Raza was the largest of the national Hispanic organizations, and none of its savvy leaders was about to let Coors chip away at the boycott through meaningless public relations gestures. But Raul Yzaguirre, La Raza's president, had always believed the boycott should have an objective, a path to a cease-fire and declaration of victory. Yzaguirre, a barrel-chested Mexican American with a broad, rugged face, decided to take Peter's peace feelers at face value.

Like Rasheed, he formed a coalition to negotiate. Cubans and Puerto Ricans, the Hispanic Chamber of Commerce, even the American G.I. Forum—which had long since compromised with the Coorses and ended its boycott—participated. Yzaguirre insisted that Peter Coors himself attend the talks.

Peter endured a good deal of shouting.

Yzaguirre sat across the table, amazed at Peter's control. A furious chicano activist shoved his face against Peter's, screaming about discrimination, spittle flying, and Peter met his eyes with an expression so calm it seemed Zen. "I will not apologize for or defend my father or my uncle," he kept saying. "I am not them, and I refuse to be judged by the past. I am here in good faith to do business with you."

Peter wasn't willing to ladle out benefits this time without return commitments. "It's always gimme-gimme-gimme with these people," he muttered to an aide in a moment of frustration.

In the end, the Hispanics got a deal similar to the blacks'—a five-year commitment involving hiring, promotion, procurement, distributorships, banking, and generous donations to Hispanic causes. But their agreement depended on consumption; if Hispanic market share went up, Coors would do more for them. The preamble noted "the principle that a corporation should reward every segment of its consumers, the lifeline of its existence, with a fair and reasonable portion of the benefits it has at its disposal." Neither Adolph Coors the founder, his son, nor his grandsons would have conceived such a principle. The duty of a corporation, in the Coors tradition, was nothing more or less than to make a good product and sell it at a fair price. But this was generation four and times had changed. Five weeks after signing the covenant with the blacks, Peter gave his signature to the Hispanics.

While watching Peter sign, Yzaguirre got the impression that Peter was personally relieved—not just that Hispanics would stop vilifying his family's beer, but that his company was finally going to operate under principles he could be proud of.

If so, the Adolph Coors Company paid a high price for Peter's peace of mind. His uncle Bill's "intellectual capacity" speech had cost the brewery control of a cool $650 million. Worse, the covenants dangerously misled the brewery. They were promulgated on the idea that the boycott was directed at Coors's personnel policies. Fix those, the covenants implied, and the boycott goes away.

But this was 1984, seven years after the strike and the start of the boycotts. Most of the people eschewing Coors couldn't even remember the casus belli, beyond some vague sense that Coors had broken its union or dissed minorities. By the middle of the Reagan years, that hardly made Coors unique. David Sickler had achieved his objective; the company had become a stand-in for Reaganism. Joe Coors had wanted to personify the conservative movement and by financing its revolution he'd gotten his wish.

In the wake of Peter's victories, MALDEF, the Hispanic group to which Bill had been trying to give a thousand dollars, once again refused donations from Coors and denounced the covenants because of the Coorses' "enunciated political views." Coors could have named Cesar Chavez chairman of the board, and it wouldn't have mitigated the family's creation of the Heritage Foundation, its opposition to affirmative action and low-cost legal services for the poor, its support for candidates who wanted immigration cut off and English as the country's official language. Peter Coors was named "man of the year" by the Mexican American Foundation, but San Antonio Mayor Henry Cisneros canceled his speech at the foundation's conference in protest.

Looking for black causes to support as part of the black covenant, Coors offered to sponsor an annual event in Jackson, Mississippi, honoring Medgar Evers, but it blew up in their faces. "I would hate to think that Coors can abuse us and then appease us by supporting black causes," the state NAACP director said as he called for a reintensification of the black boycott.

Coors had become the paragon of a workplace offering opportunity to women, with more women overall, and especially in technical and supervisory positions, than the average American corporation. Yet at precisely the moment the black and Hispanic coalitions were choosing to focus on Coors's corporate conduct, the National Organization for Women was voting explicitly to ignore it and join the boycott. Joe had bankrolled institutions and candidates that were feminism's sworn enemies, and NOW wanted to punish him for it. (Bill's comment to *Life* magazine around then, that he supported ERA "but a woman's place is in the beauty parlor," didn't help, either.)

The president of the Oregon AFL-CIO preached militantly that the boycott was not about Coors's labor practices. "The primary concern to me and to the members of the Oregon AFL-CIO is the ideology that follows Coors beer wherever it is sold," he said. Peter had believed, as he'd promised away control of more than half a billion dollars, that things were about to get better. He was wrong.

The same summer that Peter signed the covenants, as the Democrats were preparing to nominate the first woman vice presidential candidate in U.S. history, the largest deliberative body in the world heard a resolution to boycott Coors. For the eighty-five-hundred-member assembly of the National Education Association even to consider voting to boycott set off a panic at Coors. The NEA, the country's biggest teachers' union with more than a million and a half members, was independent of the AFL-CIO; if teachers joined the boycott, it would be a terrifying metastasis for Coors. Radicalized teachers might not only reject Coors themselves but might poison the minds of a generation of future beer drinkers.

Letters from Coors to every member of the NEA executive board only made the teachers angry. When the NEA executive board met in September—a full seven years after the strike and just as Peter was winding up the black and Hispanic covenants—the country's biggest union voted to join the Coors boycott.

Bill and Joe Coors found themselves in a familiar corner of confused frustration. Their brewery was aswarm with Visigoths, making commercials that Adolph Coors, Jr., would have been embarrassed to watch, let alone produce. Torrents of family money were pouring out the door in a feverish attempt to mutate their regional, quality-conscious brewery into something neither Bill and Joe, their father, nor their grandfather had ever wanted: a flashy, bloated, "national brand." A mob of minority special interest groups was telling the family whom to hire, whom to promote, and how to manage the brewery. And now schoolteachers—a group with no conceivable beef against the Adolph Coors Company—were boycotting. Surely the world was adrift from its moorings.

Bill and Joe reacted the way they often had before when pressed against the wall: They turned on their employees. Just as they had after the 1957 strike; when Ad was kidnapped in 1960; and again in the dark year of 1976, when they first experienced reverses, Bill and Joe became convinced their workers were "disloyal." Once again, they became obsessed with the idea that their "family" of employees was engaged in all manner of nefarious behavior. This time, the crime they suspected was drug abuse.

It was an odd choice of misbehavior on which to fixate. Nobody loathed the idea of prohibiting intoxicants more than the grandsons of Adolph Coors. Bill in later years would tell one associate that he was in favor of legalizing drugs. By instinct and upbringing, the Coors brothers shared the sentiments of an earlier Republican, Abraham Lincoln. "A prohibition law," Lincoln once said, "strikes a blow at the very principles upon which our government was founded."

But this wasn't 1860, when candidate Lincoln was responding to the infant temperance movement; or 1916, when prohibitionists put Adolph Coors out of the beer business. It was 1984. The country was panicked over the appearance of crack cocaine and the War on Drugs was a centerpiece of Ronald Reagan's domestic agenda. The Coorses' attitudes about drugs were therefore complicated. Philosophically, they disliked government policing individuals' leisure habits. But Reagan was their hero, and a friend of the family. Illegal drugs evidenced a disrespect for social order. And drugs were associated with groups—blacks, Hispanics, hippies—whose political agenda stood opposed to the Coorses'.

Also, there did seem to be illegal drugs in the brewery. Managers were reporting to security that workers were coming stoned to work and buying drugs from each other on the job. Bill and Joe Coors were not the only executives in the country worried about drug use in their companies.

The Coors brothers, however, took their antidrug campaign to the edge of the law and, allegedly, well beyond it. According to their own security chief, who ran their antidrug operation, the Adolph Coors Company hired a convicted arsonist and suspected killer to man a secret undercover squad, donated large sums to the local district attorney to get the criminals deputized, carried investigations far off company grounds, wangled access to technology and records usually reserved for police, illegally wiretapped employees' phones, laundered money through its lawyer's office to keep the project hidden "from some smart-ass reporter," used the investigations to harass a political opponent, and "loaned" a security officer to work undercover drug cases unrelated to Coors.

The convoluted tale can be pieced together from evidence and depositions compiled for two lawsuits. One was filed by the security chief against the brewery. Coors says it fired David Floyd because he had an affair with a subordinate, developed a speed habit, and couldn't account for company funds. Floyd says he was fired to cover up the company's embarrassing "Gestapo" tactics. And what Floyd refused to describe, he implied, was even worse. In more than eight hours of testimony involving unlicensed guns, unauthorized cocaine buys, illegal wiretaps, and the possible bribery of a district attorney, Floyd pleaded the Fifth Amendment only once: when asked if he'd ever conducted "undercover investigations with respect to labor unions."

The Colorado Supreme Court threw out Floyd's case in January 1999—because, it said, Floyd willingly participated in the illegal acts he alleged.

The second lawsuit was brought against Coors's outside law firm by a Golden bar owner named Ken Mueller. Mueller almost lost his liquor license because the Coors's law firm—which was also representing Mueller at the time—secretly helped Floyd set up drug stings in his bar. Coors's law firm paid Mueller an undisclosed sum to settle the conflict-of-interest lawsuit.

David Floyd—stout, slow-speaking, and frog-eyed—was a former Iowa sheriff's deputy who was hired as a Coors security officer shortly before the 1977 strike. In 1984, around the time the NEA was voting to join the boycott, Floyd was investigating reports of drug dealing in the plant and needed some cash to set up a buy-bust sting. Rather than go through normal petty-cash channels at the brewery, his boss took Floyd for a ride across town to the offices of Golden's most influential lawyer, Leo Bradley.

Bradley, a big man with heavy eyebrows and an imposing air, had been the Coors family's personal lawyer and the brewery's primary counsel for decades. Zealously loyal to the Coors family, Bradley had, according to deposition testimony, ordered his lawyers to serve as bartenders at the Coors booth at the annual state fair, and had once reprimanded a subordinate for ordering a scotch-and-water before a dinner meeting. "You're here on Coors business," Bradley had snapped. "You should know enough to order a Coors beer." Floyd had met Bradley on several occasions.

This day, though, Floyd and his boss didn't drive all the way to Bradley's office. They stopped a few blocks short. Floyd's boss got out, told Floyd to wait, and disappeared. A few minutes later, he returned and threw an envelope of cash into Floyd's lap.

It worked this way, Floyd's boss told him. Bradley gave them the cash, and then billed it to the brewery as a legal expense.

Why not get the money through regular channels at the brewery? Floyd wanted to know.

The brewery had union issues, his boss told him, and didn't want the employees to think they were being spied on or that the security department was a Gestapo organization. Floyd testified that his boss told him they used to get the cash directly from Joe Coors, but this worked better.

Floyd's investigations occasionally led him off brewery property into surrounding communities. Not being a sworn law enforcement officer, Floyd was no more sanctioned to buy and sell drugs than any private citizen. But he did so, with the knowledge of local police departments, as part of joint investigations. He was Coors's man, after all, and Coors was the biggest employer and taxpayer around. Technicalities were ignored.

Now that the Adolph Coors Company was buying drugs on the street, the market was bigger and the number of drug dealers lurking in Golden began growing to meet the demand. Ken Mueller, owner of Shotgun Annie's bar in downtown Golden, noticed the sudden increase in drug dealing in the streets and alleys surrounding his business. He called the police to complain, but because the police were helping Coors arrange a lot of the drug deals he was reporting, they couldn't help him.

Everything about Mueller clashed with the culture of the brewery that dominated Golden. The trim, restrained, conservative, and thoroughly western men of Coors saw in Mueller a hugely overweight interloper from Chicago who spoke loudly, held liberal views, and disrespected both his adopted hometown and the Adolph Coors Company. Mueller, who also owned a big dance hall in Denver, groused publicly as a beer retailer about Coors's inept marketing. When the police failed to clean up the drug dealing, Mueller began ridiculing them in the press, and even led a couple of noisy demonstrations to the police department building. Mueller says that in retaliation, Golden police officers harassed him—unscrewing his light bulbs and then issuing him tickets for inadequate lighting, roughing up customers, and towing their cars. Floyd's police friends convinced Floyd—wrongly, he later learned—that Mueller was a Chicago-Mafia pimp and drug dealer. So Floyd, now chief of Coors Security, decided to kill two birds with one stone and set up his drug deals in Shotgun Annie's. "It was a war, almost," Floyd says about the targeting of Mueller.

"Keep up the good work," Coors's lawyer, Leo Bradley, told Floyd one afternoon. "We have to rid Golden of this vermin." Floyd and Bradley talked about Mueller's liberal politics and penchant for noisy criticism. They agreed he was a "scourge of the community." According to Floyd, Bradley called Mueller "a round, fat fucker." (Bradley, who declined to be interviewed for this book, was not asked about this quote in his deposition.)

One afternoon, Mueller was having his hair cut by Frank Leek, who used to cut old Mr. Coors's hair. Leek was now the only Democrat on the Golden city council and a political ally of Mueller's. Leek told Mueller the city was getting ready to revoke his liquor license because of drug dealing at Shotgun Annie's. Mueller heaved himself out of the chair and with the hair on one side of his head shorter than on the other, he walked up the street to see his lawyer—a partner in Leo Bradley's law firm.

Mueller's lawyer knew nothing about Coors's drug investigations because Bradley kept them a secret from his partners. The lawyer also knew nothing about Bradley encouraging Floyd to "rid Golden" of his client. He declined to represent Mueller in the liquor-license matter because he knew a lawyer with more experience in such matters. But he did continue as Mueller's retained attorney while Bradley, the head of his law firm, secretly supported Floyd's campaign against Mueller. This alleged conflict of interest became the basis of Mueller's lawsuit against the firm. Mueller still knew nothing about the role of Coors or local police in his troubles.

In his deposition, Leo Bradley did not deny that his law firm advanced money to Coors for the drug investigations, or that one of its lawyers was representing Ken Mueller while the firm was simultaneously helping Coors conduct the drug buys that endangered Mueller's liquor license. But Bradley testified that he believed his law firm "absolutely" did nothing improper, that advancing money to clients was standard practice for his firm, and that he believed he had no obligation to inform Ken Mueller of his alleged conflict of interest.

As Mueller was scrambling to defend his license, a scandal erupted in the Golden Police Department. Narcotics were missing from the evidence locker. In the turmoil, both the police chief and the city attorney were fired. What happened next showed Mueller how incestuous Golden was. Needing an interim police chief and city attorney, the town chose Coors's security chief and Coors's outside lawyer: David Floyd and Leo Bradley. In terms of law enforcement, the company town and the company were now one.

By this time, Floyd's drug investigations had descended into a quagmire of nightmarish legal liability. Floyd later made the following allegations in court findings: Two of the people Floyd had hired to make his buy-busts had long criminal records; one had been convicted of burning down a police station and was even believed by police, according to Floyd's testimony, to have committed at least one murder. Their salaries had not been reported to the Internal Revenue Service. Coors Security had opened confidential personnel files that included psychologists' notes. Coors had bent or possibly broken laws by gaining access to the files of the nearby Westminster Police Department, the FBI, and the National Crime Information Center. Coors had persuaded the Jefferson County Sheriff's Office to sign a waiver letting Coors buy electronic eavesdropping equipment normally available only to police departments. With it, Coors had produced more than a hundred illegal wiretap recordings without benefit of police authority or a search warrant—and then gave the recordings to police.

Coors's investigators were also buying—and in at least two cases, using—illegal drugs without the protection of a badge. As far as the law was concerned, they were no different from any other citizen. Their drug buys were felonies. So Coors arranged to have four of its security men deputized. Floyd's attorney told the court that in Jefferson County, deputizations are supposed to be approved by all four sitting judges. But this was Coors territory and these were Coors security men. Their deputizations were signed by a single judge, who later refused to testify about the matter. In his lawsuit, Floyd presented a photocopy of a $7,500 check from Coors to the district attorney's forfeiture fund, and record of an additional $5,300 payment. These, he alleged, were payoffs for the deputizations. The district attorney, when asked about it for this book, said he remembered nothing.

Coors's extralegal activities spread even beyond Colorado. By this time, Coors had built a packaging plant on its Virginia land. Coors Security officer Sandra Justice, a robust bleach blond who enjoyed shooting machine guns on weekends, was sent as an undercover agent to investigate drug dealing there. She flew east on the corporate jet with Bill Coors and discussed her assignment with him. Justice quickly determined the Virginia plant had no drug problem. But she stayed on at the request of local police to set up drug stings in surrounding towns. "I was the hottest commodity in the county," she remembered. "A single woman with a functional car, all her own teeth, and a fridge full of beer." She illegally obtained a driver's license under a phony name, carried an unlicensed gun, bought and snorted cocaine, and surreptitiously videotaped "friends" doing deals in her apartment—all on the Coors payroll. Finally, someone cut the brake lines on her car and nearly killed her. More than a hundred Virginians were arrested as a result of her work. None had any association with Coors.

One of Leo Bradley's young associates learned of the law firm's role in the unsavory drug investigations and was shocked not only that his firm was "violating the code of professional responsibility" but also at the amount the firm had fronted the investigations: more than a quarter million dollars. The associate wrote a strongly worded memo warning Coors and his own bosses that—according to the associate's testimony—they risked all manner of legal trouble. The response of Floyd's boss was to order him to "bury" the investigations "so some smart-ass reporter . . . won't find it." They continued financing the operation through Leo Bradley's law firm to protect it by attorney-client privilege.

Not long after, Floyd went into a personal tailspin. Working sixteen-hour days without a break, he contracted mononucleosis. His boss—one of Coors's fit, straight-arrow middle managers—ordered him to lose weight and stop smoking. Floyd got hooked on diet pills, and when those ran out, he started using security-department petty cash to buy street speed. He staggered into Ken Mueller's dance hall one night, mumbled an apology, and later spilled to Mueller the whole story of Coors's involvement in the drug stings. Floyd ended up in a hospital and rehabilitation center. Coors fired him for failing to account for more than $100,000 in company funds and for having an affair with Sandra Justice.

Floyd owned up to petty theft but claimed he legitimately spent and accounted for the big money. As for having an affair, he claimed to have evidence that plenty of top Coors executives and family members had done likewise without being fired. He said he was prepared to name names. The night before his lawyer filed the suit, someone broke into his office and pried open all the locked file cabinets. Nothing was taken. Worried about such an eventuality, the lawyer had stored the Floyd files in another lawyer's office. He filed Floyd's suit on schedule in May 1994.

Golden was a small town. By 1994, Bill divorced Phyllis, and the Jefferson County district judge who threw out Floyd's suit against Coors was the same one who would perform the wedding of Bill and his third wife, Rita Bass, just three weeks later. The judge—Bass's "old family friend," according to the *Denver Post*—had to void her opinion and recuse herself from Floyd's case. A second Jefferson County judge stepped in and affirmed the dismissal. No reasonable person, both judges ruled, could find Coors's behavior sufficiently "outrageous" to warrant a lawsuit.

Floyd appealed, and the Colorado Court of Appeals found his suit indeed had sufficient merit to go forward. But in January 1999, the Colorado Supreme Court sided with Coors and the lawsuit died. The court said that Floyd had not been fired for refusing to break the law; he had gone along willingly, so his lawsuit was invalid.

It took one of Coors's few women executives to put a stop to the wild West drug squad Coors had fielded for seven years. In 1991, Coors chief counsel Caroline Turner sent her superiors a sheaf of Leo Bradley's bills and said she wouldn't pay them because "they are not legal services." She also suggested that Bradley's firm write them off "since they share some blame in this costly problem."

In seven years, the Coors undercover drug squad yielded only a handful of minor arrests in Colorado. Perhaps its biggest achievement was to add a quarter million dollars to the demand for drugs in Jefferson County. In the entire history of the investigations, Coors Security never participated in a buy-sell transaction that it didn't set up itself.

Back in the autumn of 1984, David Floyd's drug investigations were just beginning. Few in the company knew about them, and they hadn't yet mutated into the dreadful legal problem they would one day become. The company's main focus was relieving itself of the boycotts that were dragging down sales. The black and Hispanic boycotts had been "settled." But the NEA had just voted to boycott. So it came to pass one day that the telephone rang on the desk of Barbara Yentzer, a young official at NEA headquarters in Washington. The caller identified herself as Nancy Williams.

It took Yentzer a moment. "Oh," she finally said, "from Denver."

Yentzer had recently transferred to Washington from the NEA's Denver office. Williams, a Coors public relations officer, had often attended NOW meetings in Denver, begging the group not to join the boycott. Yentzer had liked Williams and had felt a little sorry for her, as she futilely waved her list of Coors employment achievements. "How are you?" Yentzer now asked.

"*I'm* fine," Williams said. "But the company is upset about the NEA boycott. Is there any way to undo this?"

"Lord," Yentzer said. "I don't think so." But they talked a while and Yentzer found herself promising Williams she'd speak to her boss, NEA general counsel Bob Chanin.

Tall, patrician, and voluble, Chanin shared with Yentzer a taste for tough issues and tricky choices. It didn't take long for them to talk each other into meeting face-to-face with the dreaded Coorses.

John Meadows and Nancy Williams met them at the brewery, listed Coors's impressive personnel reforms, and asked what the company could do to end the NEA boycott.

"Nothing," Chanin told them. "You have to settle your differences with the AFL-CIO first."

Meadows rolled his eyes.

"Just what *are* your differences with the AFL-CIO?" Chanin asked.

Meadows stared blankly.

"The issues," Chanin pressed. "What does the AFL-CIO want?"

Meadows thought a long moment. "I don't know," he said finally. "We haven't had any contact with them for eight years."

"You don't *know*?" Chanin asked, flabbergasted. "You've been under a boycott for eight years and you don't know what they *want*?"

Meadows laughed sheepishly. "That's damn funny, isn't it? You'd better come meet Peter."

Peter explained that the old complaints were moot; Coors had cleaned up its act. "The real issue," Peter told Chanin, "is that we're nonunion."

That was part of it, Chanin thought. He'd done some checking. Coors's California market share was down to 14 percent from a high of more than half. Even in Colorado, Coors was down from a half to only a fifth of the market. After a good 1983, 1984 was shaping up to be a clunker. It appeared that Coors generally enjoyed a flurry of sales when it first moved into a state. Then, hobbled by the boycott and swamped by the superior marketing firepower of Anheuser-Busch, Coors sales flagged.

"Do you want to begin a dialogue with the AFL-CIO?" Chanin asked.

"Jeez . . ." Peter said.

"It can't hurt to talk."

Peter laughed. "Well, that's never been my uncle's philosophy," he said.

"How about your father?" Chanin asked.

The smile left Peter's face. "His neither," he said softly.

Peter indicated, in a half whisper, that he'd like to begin talks with the AFL-CIO. He was, after all, under orders from the board to "fix it with everybody." Chanin called Larry Gold, his counterpart at the big labor federation, and offered to broker talks.

In a series of furtive phone calls, both sides told Chanin they were adamant that talks be kept secret. Chanin reserved a meeting room in one of the huge anonymous hotels surrounding Chicago's O'Hare Airport, halfway between Colorado and Washington, D.C.

Expanding into state after state while trying out new products and packages was a logistical ordeal. The fifty gigantic kettles in the brewhouse—copper cylinders thirty feet across and two stories tall—had to be rotated among products with Swiss precision. If the balance got out of whack and the brewery ended up with, say, too much Killian's and too little Light, the Killian's would go stale and be thrown out while brand-new distributors would have insufficient Light with which to wage price wars against Anheuser-Busch.

It wasn't only the kettles that required close timing. The malthouse had to be in sync with the brewhouse because each beer used a different roast of malt. The barley farmers, in turn, had to match the pace of the malthouse. On the other end of the line, packaging rotated feverishly among Coors Banquet, Coors Light, Killian's, Herman Joseph's, and Extra Gold; among bar bottles, no-return bottles, quarts, twelve-ounce cans, sixteen-ounce cans, six-packs, twelve-packs, cases, kegs, half kegs, Memorial Day promotions, Independence Day promotions, Labor Day promotions. . . .

This was the hell that marketing had wrought. A glitch anywhere could knock the whole plant out of kilter and often did. Moreover, shipping beer from Colorado to, say, Cleveland, was enormously expensive.

A-B and Miller had breweries scattered all over the country to split up the work of making and packaging myriad products. The Virginia plant didn't yet exist; Coors's single brewery was squeezed between Bob

Rechholtz's doctrine of "critical mass," which required complex marketing and expansion to all fifty states, and Bill Coors's Victorian insistence on monitoring all of the company's brewing from his armchair in Golden.

Rechholtz, eager to take advantage of the national economies of scale that Coors had been denied for so long, created ads, in-store displays, and promotions to appeal to all 250 million Americans at once. He didn't notice that Anheuser-Busch, having gone national much earlier, had by this time learned to take the opposite tack. A-B was carving the country into geographical markets, submarkets, and sub-submarkets. Texas, for example, is culturally different from Vermont. But even within Texas, A-B had learned, Dallas is different from Houston. San Antonio Hispanics are different from Galveston Hispanics. The permutations were endless. Budweiser ran national ads, but it also helped each of its 950 distributors tailor displays, holiday promotions, and TV and radio spots to its own unique market.

Coors, on the other hand, was tone-deaf to cultural and geographic differences. When the company moved into New York, for example, it tried marketing to Hispanics using the song "La Bamba," which is Mexican. New York's Caribbean Hispanics found the ad foreign—if not downright offensive—*The Wall Street Journal* reported.

Because of vastly increased marketing and shipping costs, Coors was earning less than before Rechholtz had arrived. But volume was way up, and Rechholtz kept insisting that volume was more important near-term than profit.

They had to build a national customer base, he kept telling the board. He promised them that the payoff would come.

The board decided that Rechholtz's marketing people needed their own office building, and began constructing a stylish, five-story steel-and-glass tower across Clear Creek from the brewery. To production workers, the new building was "snob hill," a fancy palace for the new elite—and more depressing evidence that the Visigoths were not only inside the gates, but were running the show. For the marketers, the building was Elba—a distant exile. The brewery was the seat of power; being removed to a distance reminded the marketers that the family viewed them as a foul necessity, like a sewage plant. Divergent attitudes about the new building weren't improved when the board decided, halfway through construction, to postpone completion until profits picked up. To the old-timers, this was proof that the company couldn't really afford it. To the marketers, the delay was churlish punishment for not delivering profits fast enough. In general, everything about the new building exacerbated hostility between the traditional culture of Coors and the newfangled marketers the company needed. Rechholtz remembered Bill's welcoming lecture, warning him that he'd have to make the company accept marketing. This gift of a building was exactly the wrong thing to do.

The company was in environmental trouble, too. Workers in the can plant reported that the water in the drinking fountains had an "off taste." Solvents from the plant, which the company had surreptitiously dumped years before, had made their way into the drinking-water well under the plant. Coors made the same decision it had made when it first discovered water contamination in 1981: The company kept quiet.

Around this same time, Colorado health officials were trying to get someone to pay attention to evidence they'd found that the area immediately downstream from Coors had double the national average of low-birthweight babies and childhood cancer. A state toxicologist later told a newspaper that Ann Gorsuch's EPA had been informed about the anomalies, "but apparently [there was] no follow up."

Meanwhile, the local EPA office, faced with a separate Coors problem, extended a questionable waiver to Coors. Under an agreement that dated back to the Carter years, the brewery was to have made its last toxic-waste delivery to the Lowery landfill—an approved toxic dump—in November 1981. For reasons never made clear, Thorton Field—the former Coors attorney and toxic-waste-industry lobbyist who headed toxic-waste enforcement under EPA chief Ann Gorsuch—signed a waiver letting Coors make an additional toxic delivery to Lowery months later. By the time the story broke, Field had been demoted for having "imprudent conversations with interest groups." Defending Field, another EPA official dismissed the issues as nothing but a minor "stink" raised by "some people." Then it was revealed that this official's wife worked in Coors's lobbying office in Washington, D.C. The story, carried nationally, did the brewery no good. (Though Coors's sway over Colorado is great, the brewery is rarely accused of outright bribery. "Coloradans don't need to be bought," says the Denver historian Phil Goodstein. "They kowtow to rich people for free.")

It seemed the company could do nothing right. Back in the marketing world, Rechholtz had overcome the family's resistance to entering the $700 million "cooler" business dominated by Gallo's Bartles and Jaymes. But Coors, unwilling to dabble in wine, made a monumental gaffe. It hustled out a fruit-flavored beer called Colorado Chiller without taste-testing, without market surveys, without focus groups—in short, without any of the customary spadework.

Rechholtz's people explained this failing as trusting in their "guts." In part, though, everybody at Coors knew Bill was appalled—stricken, really—at the idea of producing a sugar-sweetened, artificially colored beer. Every molecule of his brewer's body resented it, and he let Chiller go forward with all the enthusiasm of a man signing a consent form to have his malignant testicles removed. Marketing was torn between knowing they needed an entry in the cooler market and lacking the heart and courage to spend a nickel more of Bill's money on it than was necessary. So Chiller was a compound calamity. The product itself was execrable— brilliant chartreuse, cloyingly sweet, and smelling like skunk. The bottle was the same ugly brown as an ordinary beer bottle, with a label so stark and unadorned it might have been designed by the Agriculture Department. The ads—hideous penguin puppets shivering in a North Pole bar—were both annoying and counterintuitive; they inspired desire for a hot drink, not a cold one. Coors killed Chiller even before all the distributors received it. It was the perfect failure—doomed because deep down, Bill Coors, and by extension the culture of Coors, wanted it to fail. To succeed at candy-colored, fruit-flavored beer would have been apostasy.

Again, the timing of the failure was wretched. Coors was about to enter New England, six relatively liberal states as far removed as possible—without leaving the United States—from Coors's traditional western territory. The marketing people were fiercely reviving Ad's 1959 argument that retailers should be allowed to place Coors unrefrigerated on the dry shelf. Three quarters of all beer purchases are made on impulse, they argued. The beer has to be out where the customer can grab it. Bill, though, was firm; Coors beer is unpasteurized and must be kept cold. The brewery had been cold-filtering beer for almost two decades and Bill knew this process rendered it almost as stable as pasteurized beer. But almost wasn't enough. The customer must taste Coors at its peak, Bill insisted.

Having less to do around the brewery, Bill had gotten into the habit of wandering through supermarkets in the Denver area, checking date codes. When he found stale beer, he made an angry call—usually from a parking lot pay phone—demanding the distributor come that day and pull the old beer.

Into the chaos at Coors, John Murphy of Miller Brewing dropped a bombshell. He released Miller's first unpasteurized beer—Miller Genuine

Draft—and built an entire ad campaign around its cold-filter process. Coors had never used cold-filtering as a unique selling proposition. In fact, the only time the public had heard about it was when the AFL-CIO used it as a cudgel, convincing the California and Oregon legislatures that unpasteurized beer was unhealthy. Now the Coorses could do nothing but watch agape as John Murphy danced off with what should have been their ad campaign. Murphy had no qualms about letting Genuine Draft be sold from the dry shelf, and on the strength of its "cold-filtered" ads, Miller Genuine Draft sold more beer in its first year than any other new beer brand in history.

It was late spring of 1985. Bill and Joe were sixty-nine and sixty-eight years old, respectively. That they were out of their depth was embarrassingly evident. Bill was still beloved around the brewery and by many people in Golden and Denver. Joe, stiffer and more reserved, was liked and respected by many people inside and outside of Coors. But to even their biggest boosters, it was clear that it was time for them to step aside and let the next generation take over.

The oldest son, Joe Jr., was not a contender for the presidency. He was still in quasi-exile at one of the ceramics division's subsidiaries in Oregon, and wasn't expected back anytime soon. After attending that year's Cornell commencement, Joe had flown straight from New York to Portland to pay his eldest son a surprise visit. He'd found Joe Jr. not at his desk but out on the company lawn taking practice shots with a pitching wedge. Joe was livid.

Jeff and Peter had a few more secret lunches at Rolling Hills Country Club and decided to make a direct pitch to Dad and Uncle Bill. Adolph Jr. had taken over the brewery from his father when he was thirty-nine—exactly Peter's age, and Jeff was older. It was true that Dad and Uncle Bill hadn't taken over the brewery until their father died. But the brewing industry was stable then, and Adolph Jr. had been well equipped to run the brewery until he died. He'd left behind a business in 1970 that was bigger, but fundamentally identical to the one he'd inherited in 1923. The industry now, though, would be unrecognizable to him. And it was growing increasingly so to his sons.

Dad and Uncle Bill grew up in the old world, Peter told Jeff. We grew up in this one.

Coors quietly announced a "reshuffling." Bill and Joe were no longer presidents. They moved upstairs. Bill became chairman and CEO, Joe vice chairman and chief operating officer.

The positions to which they named Peter and Jeff would not have made sense to anyone who didn't know the family's tradition. For the past four years, the quiet, scientific Jeff had been in charge of operations and technical affairs, while the more gregarious Peter had headed sales and marketing. Peter would have been the obvious choice for president, given the ascendance of marketing in the industry. But Jeff was the older son, so he became president. Peter, who had little engineering experience, was named chief of the brewing division. Though titles had never meant much at the Adolph Coors Company, these assignments would ultimately wreak havoc.

But in the meantime, a fresh wind of positive change blew through the brewery. Bill and Joe had always dismissed computers as "distracting toys"; now they were being unpacked on every clerical worker's desk. The marketing department made its much-delayed move to "snob hill." Gary Naifeh, the fireball Texan, launched a raunchy and hugely popular Halloween campaign featuring "Elvira, Mistress of the Dark," a leggy, buxom vampiress with teased-out black hair, Addams Family makeup, and a clingy black gown. The company announced plans for the $70 million packaging plant in Virginia—the one Sandra Justice would soon investigate—to take pressure off the overworked Golden brewery.

As he moved into the new office building, Rechholtz gave his marketing team a much-needed pep talk. "If we can market watery beer brewed by right-wing weirdos—who are held responsible for every plague and pox known to mankind—we're doing one hell of a job of marketing."

Rechholtz's strategy had boosted sales 7 percent since 1983, against 2 percent for the industry as a whole. True, he conceded, earnings were down because of the costs of expansion. True, he conceded, the company was now spending three times as much on ads as it earned in profit. But he'd warned the Coorses profits would suffer near-term. They must build volume, he continued to urge. They must reach critical mass. They must become a national brewer.

19

Someone
Else's Ass

Eight days after assuming the presidency of the Coors brewing division, Peter Coors walked into an O'Hare Airport hotel conference room and shook the hand of Bill's "self-appointed executioner," Tom Donahue, the third-ranking official of the AFL-CIO.

Donahue didn't look like the blunt, cigar-chewing labor bosses of yore. His only trait that recalled labor roots was a broad New York accent. Otherwise, he was as smooth and urbane as a corporate CEO. He believed in procapitalist, nonconfrontational "business unionism." He opposed most strikes. And as far as Donahue was concerned, the beef with Coors was not ideological, but tied to the company's treatment of its workers.

Nor did Donahue, at fifty-six, feel like the dragon-slayer Bill had envisioned. His entire union career had been one of encroaching defeat. He'd been an assistant secretary of labor in the Johnson administration, when unions were welcome at the tables of power. But he'd become George Meany's executive assistant in 1973, the eve of labor's steepest-ever decline in membership and influence. Shortly before Reagan moved into the White House, Donahue had been elected secretary-treasurer under AFL-CIO president Lane Kirkland. From that post, he'd witnessed the PATCO debacle, the hardening of government's attitude toward unions, and the collapse of labor's clout. Every year of Donahue's tenure, the labor federation had lost a million members. Those who remained had little fighting spirit. Not long before the O'Hare meeting, a *New York Times* poll found more than half of those living *in union households* believed unions had too much influence. Donahue went into the talks with Peter badly needing something he could call a victory.

Peter introduced John Meadows and a red-faced, red-haired man whose Irish-sounding name Donahue didn't catch but who, it seemed to Donahue, was there to demonstrate that Coors hired Irish Catholics like Donahue. The man said not a word all evening. For half an hour, the men stood chatting awkwardly. John Meadows finally got tired of standing and sat down. Everybody followed suit and the talks began.

Donahue opened by describing his misconception of the boycott, which he shared with the Coorses. "It has nothing to do with your family's politics or any issue larger than how you treat your workers," he said. As far as official AFL-CIO policy was concerned, that was true. And Donahue wanted to believe that the labor federation had the power to turn boycotts on and off like a light bulb.

Peter was delighted to hear Donahue's characterization of the boycott. If the AFL-CIO could stop it, all Coors had to do was satisfy the AFL-CIO. That would be painful, philosophically taxing, and sure to cause titanic arguments with Dad and Uncle Bill. But it was possible. Coors had the capacity, Peter and Tom Donahue believed, to end the biggest and most intractable of the boycotts.

What Donahue wanted from Coors was an agreement of "neutrality," a commitment that Coors would not oppose an organizing drive, hire a professional union buster, or threaten workers to induce them to reject a union. Under the law, a union shop had to be created by a vote of the workers. So Donahue could not himself request a contract. Neutrality was the most he could ask.

Such was the state of the labor movement in 1984 that the AFL-CIO was asking Coors to do little more than obey the law. Federal labor law forbade threatening or firing workers for union activity, forbade offering raises shortly before union votes, forbade exerting any kind of undue pressure. But Ronald Reagan's presidency saw itself as a corrective to what it viewed as the overzealous Labor Department of earlier Democratic administrations. Reagan's Labor Department was reluctant to pry into a businessman's relations with his own workers. During this moratorium on enforcement of labor laws, an entire industry of "labor consultants" had coalesced, expert at probing the limits of the government's willingness to enforce the law. Often, the smartest way to bust a union was simply to break laws freely and crush the union like a bug. Even if the company was unlucky enough to merit Labor Department attention and be found guilty years later, it would only have to pay a fine equal to a fraction of the value of a union-free shop. This is what Donahue wanted Coors to agree not to do.

"I'm going to have a hard time selling neutrality to my father and uncle," Peter said. "They believe neutrality is selling the farm. They feel strongly about unions."

"That's obvious," Donahue said.

They talked until eleven that night, committing to nothing but further talks. Donahue had booked a room at the hotel. Peter told him he planned to fly back to Golden. "You can't measure the worth of a Lear jet by the cost of an airline ticket," he said with a wink, "but by the ability to sleep in your own bed."

Lowell Sund, the soft-spoken former board member, tried to keep his retirement promise to "keep an eye on Peter." Peter, though, was rarely at his desk. He was often on the road, taking distributors to dinner and on hunting trips. He loved showing up in the field to surprise and give pep talks to the sales force, and holding powwows with Rechholtz and the marketers. It seemed to Sund that Peter was behaving more like a junior marketing executive than head of a gigantic brewing division. Peter had no discernible interest in water rights, real estate, or any of the other dry but crucial functions of a large brewery. He left those aspects unattended, or to be handled by underlings. Poor Peter, Sund thought. He was running away from the brewery.

This was the era of management best-sellers, and Peter scrutinized them in search of the magic formula that would revive the company: *Theory Z, In Search of Excellence, The One Minute Manager, High Output Management,* and anything by Peter Drucker. Every couple of months, it seemed, Peter carried a different management bible under his arm, quoting it eagerly, planning yet another reorganization to maximize efficiency. A few months later, under the sway of the next management guru, Peter would be waving a different book, espousing a whole new plan.

His big brother Jeff, on the other hand, stuck to one book. Jeff's

Christian faith, acquired during his courtship of Lis, had deepened as he matured. He'd built a chapel behind the locked gate of what was, for the Coorses, an uncommonly ostentatious estate. He prayed often and found his love of the Lord ruling more and more of his business and personal life.

Much of what went on at the brewery bothered Jeff deeply. It had begun with Art Stone's jingles and country music ads. Jeff took contemporary music seriously, and believed it to be, as did many born-again Christians, Satan's language. According to the Bible, Satan had begun as one of God's angels, Lucifer, with the special task of providing music in heaven, but when God had expelled him for trying to usurp his authority, Lucifer had taken with him the power of music. Modern music, lascivious in rhythm, salacious in lyric, was evidence to Jeff of Satan's growing strength in the world. The businessman in Jeff recognized the need for popular music in Coors advertising, but the Christian in him recoiled.

Jeff could barely look at the Halloween promotions using "Elvira, Mistress of the Dark." They stirred in him a powerful revulsion, even fear.

On an even more fundamental level, the very fact that the family company was a purveyor of alcohol presented an even greater and more paradoxical moral dilemma for Jeff. The brewery was running a "drink in moderation" campaign, which served as a reminder that beer can cause drunkenness. The book of Galatians listed drunkenness alongside murder, idolatry, adultery, and other vices that keep a sinner from inheriting the Kingdom of Heaven. For a Christian as devout as Jeff, manufacturing a means toward drunkenness created a moral dilemma that would take him years to resolve.

In the meantime, Jeff tried to ignore his qualms. He was Jeffrey Coors, after all, great-grandson of Adolph Coors and president of the Adolph Coors Company. There was no room in his life for Christian doubt about the morality of alcohol.

He had to cope with more immediate stresses, too. Jeff was a scientist and an engineer, quiet and careful, at home in the world of tangible problems and quantifiable solutions. And he was a second son. Like Uncle Bill, he'd never expected to run the entire corporation, with its vagaries of personnel, finance, marketing, and planning. He did his best. And he prayed hard.

Peter couldn't get Dad and Uncle Bill to agree to Tom Donahue's conditions.

"Neutrality?" Joe asked, incredulous. "We are *not* neutral about unions and we can talk to our employees any way we choose."

Months passed and Peter couldn't bring himself to call Tom Donahue.

In the meantime, he worked hard to make the covenants with Hispanics and African Americans pay off. Coors had spent only about a quarter of the money promised for Hispanic-oriented ads, and already that had put Coors among the top ten Hispanic advertisers in the country. Hispanics now made up almost 9 percent of Coors's sales, up from less than 6 percent when the covenant was signed.

Coors was doing less well with the African-American organizations that had signed what was known within the company as the black covenant. The brewery still hadn't named its first black vice president, and Fred Rasheed was turning the screws. "You're not living up to your commitments," he told Peter in an icy phone call.

"We are making a good faith effort to find qualified candidates," Peter said. "But anyone fit to be our vice president is already vice president at another company."

"Don't give me that 'we can't find qualified applicants' line," Rasheed said. "If you do not live up to your end of the bargain, we will not feel obliged to live up to ours."

On other fronts, the boycott was worsening. A third of the bars in Seattle refused to serve Coors. The student government of the University of Massachusetts at Amherst had barred Coors from campus. The Boston city council had passed a resolution supporting the boycott. Detroit's fire department refused to accept a thousand smoke alarms donated by Coors. Customers in focus groups told Coors marketers that no matter how attractive the product or the commercial, they'd never buy Coors because of the family's politics. Mothers Against Drunk Driving, already furious at Coors for turning Halloween into a beer holiday, capitalized on the company's soiled reputation by using Coors bottles in its posters to represent alcohol in general. Gays were newly infuriated when Coors said it wouldn't allow homosexual employees to work in the brewhouse or in packaging because of "public perception" regarding AIDS. The South Dakota Farmers Union even joined the queue, boycotting because the brewery's boasts of "select barley strains" allegedly maligned barley farmers who didn't grow for Coors.

As if all that wasn't enough to turn off customers, a Dallas jury made Coors pay half a million dollars to a man who'd claimed to find a headless mouse in a bottle of Herman Joseph. Bill was sputtering. He knew every inch of the production line and there was no way, he said, a mouse could get squeezed into a bottle. But after a four-day trial, the jury decided Coors had exhibited "conscious or known indifference to the safety of its customers." The phrase made it into boycott leaflets along with photos of the mouse in the bottle; a significant number of women told Coors researchers they'd never put a bottle of Coors to their lips again.

This was the moment Bob Rechholtz had set aside to enter Michigan, one of the most heavily unionized states in the country. Not only was the Wolverine State unionized; it was battered and angry. Detroit was missing out on the Reagan boom. Successive energy crises, foreign competition, and lack of automaker foresight had driven the region's economy to its nadir. Unemployment in the area had risen nearly 20 percent as plants closed. The *Houston Post* was almost as popular as the *Detroit Free Press* for the "Help Wanted" ads that idled car workers scrutinized desperately. Local businesses, starved of blue-collar customers, were folding. Detroit's cauldron of rage and anxiety might have been a good environment into which to introduce a beer, but not with Joe Coors's name on the can.

Coors barreled into Michigan with a heavy-caliber barrage of slick ads and enticing discounts. But like America in Vietnam, the company underestimated the ability of poor but well-organized guerrillas to cripple a fire-breathing behemoth.

David Sickler flew to Michigan to meet with Owen Bieber, president of the United Auto Workers. "I have a lot of guys sitting around doing nothing," Bieber told him. "What do you need?"

Sickler and Bieber deployed squads of idled autoworkers to picket bars, liquor stores, and restaurants. Not only had Reagan left heavily Democratic Detroit out of his boom, he'd also made a hard time harder by cutting aid to the cities. For men with nothing to do all day but wring their hands, the boycott against a friend of Ronald Reagan became a satisfying reason to get out of bed. It didn't take much, either, to convince business owners to forswear Coors, not when they could serve their customers good alternatives. Michigan remained ferociously loyal to its homegrown, union-made beer: Stroh's.

Sickler didn't drive Coors out of Michigan altogether, but he fought the brewery to a draw. Coors sold barely enough beer there to pay for the expansion. As he prepared to fly back to Los Angeles, Sickler paid another call on Owen Bieber, to say thanks.

"Thank *you*," Bieber said, warmly shaking his hand. "Look, boy. The way we've had the shit kicked out of us, I can't tell you how good it felt to kick someone else's ass for a change."

Muzak flowed over guests shedding furs in the Imperial Ballroom of the Fairmont Hotel in Washington, D.C. In gowns and tuxedos, smiling couples made their way to seats at dozens of round tables. Gigantic blowups of Coors family members ranged the walls. From above the long dais beamed a twelve-by-fifteen-foot photograph of Joe. The members of the Colorado Association of Commerce and Industry were assembling to roast the conservative movement's senior financier.

Joe's wife Holly, spare and energetic, flitted around the room, greeting friends and nervously assuring that every detail was just so for her husband's finest moment. When the lights dimmed, Holly spoke first, presenting a slide-and-home-movie show of "Highlights of My Life with Joe"—including their courtship on Nantucket, the wedding, their years in Golden, their adventures in Washington. Then came the roasters.

Unfortunately, Joe's quiet, straightlaced life yielded little humorous grist. And Holly had insisted on vetting all ten roasters' remarks, lest Joe be embarrassed. Speaker after speaker tried to find something funny yet inoffensive to say about Joe. The best was "He was born with his clothes on." But the remark was ad-libbed, not in the text Holly had approved, and she let it be known she was unhappy about it.

But Holly's displeasure faded when the lights darkened again, and everyone was reminded that—humorless rube though he may be—Joe Coors was still one of the most influential conservatives in America. There, on a huge-screen TV, appeared the President of the United States, Ronald Wilson Reagan.

"Those of the liberal persuasion . . . think of themselves as Santa Claus," Reagan said. "Well, Joe has spent much time and resources opening up the eyes of the American people to the fact that, while the federal Santa may bring a few gifts, he leaves with all the silverware." Finally, there was laughter.

Reagan spoke of the advice Joe had given him over the years. "The most recent was about this gizmo I have to wear in my ear these days," Reagan said. "He advised me, if I have trouble hearing, I should wear it in my right ear. That's Joe for you. He never wants to hear from the left."

Joe rocked with laughter, Holly hugging his arm and beaming at the screen.

"Joe, I know you've taken a lot of ribbing about how far to the right you are on the political spectrum, but we know you're really a moderate at heart," Reagan said. Then, after a perfect comic pause, "Sure. Anyone who buys that should have no trouble believing the one about you having a complex because you're too short. . . ."

"Here's to Joe Coors," Reagan concluded. "The best in the west!" He delivered a mock military salute. The room erupted with cheers.

Holly was ecstatic with gratitude. For her, Ronald Reagan was a figure of magical proportions—part president, part matinee idol, part saint, part crush object.

After the roasting, Holly continued her long-standing correspondence with him. She wrote dozens of notes on the letterheads of her myriad Reagan-promoting organizations. Some were pecked out on her cursive typewriter, others she scrawled in her loopy hand. All gushed with a schoolgirl's enthusiasm:

Please hang tough on the budget and taxes! You are in the driver's seat and Tip O'Neill is just trying to make it hot for you. We are with you 100%! You are the only one who can save America from the financial catastrophe of what would happen with people like Tip, Teddy and their ilk if they were in control!

> Gratefully,
> Holly

You are the greatest president this country has ever known and I thank God that He saved you for all of us these days and His purposes. Thank you. We love you.

> Always,
> Holly

It was a brave and wonderful thing for you to do to take the first steps to remove us from UNESCO. It was the *right* thing to do, and I congratulate you for your honorable stand.

> Sincerely,
> Holly

Reagan answered every one of Holly's letters, usually scribbling them by hand to be typed onto White House stationery. Their affection was mutual. A typical note read:

> Thanks for the pat on the back. Even presidents occasionally need to be told that they "done good." Nancy and I send our warmest wishes for a happy and healthy new year to you and Joe.
>
> Sincerely,
Ron

Holly kept a vigil for any disloyalty she might detect in others. She scolded the director of the Peace Corps—whose budget Reagan had nearly halved on the recommendation of the Heritage Foundation—for giving a speech that failed to "extol the accomplishments of this administration and particularly the greatest president of this century, Ronald Reagan."

"We have discussed this before," Holly wrote, "and quite frankly I do not feel you give him the tribute due. He has provided the very climate for free enterprise revival for which the Peace Corps depends." Reagan rewarded Holly by appointing her ambassador to the Americas. She welcomed the chance to "work with the women of Latin America on their problems" and ever after used the title "ambassador."

After the roast, and a couple of weeks after his sons Peter and Jeff took over the brewery, Joe Coors paid a call on William Casey, director of the Central Intelligence Agency. Casey had run Reagan's 1980 campaign and although he was the kind of eastern-establishment "liberal" Joe had tried to keep out of the administration, the two men were friendly. Joe met Casey in the Old Executive Office Building next to the White House and asked if there was anything he could do to help the anti-Sandinista rebels in Nicaragua.

"The guy to see," Casey said, "is Oliver North."

Joe knew North from anticommunist and conservative gatherings, but didn't know what the Marine officer was doing for the President. Casey told him he was handling assistance for the Contras and Joe walked immediately across the White House lawn to North's basement office.

Lieutenant Colonel North greeted Joe warmly. "Oh, there's lots you can do," he said. He pushed a brochure across his desk, showing an airplane made by Maule Air, Inc., in Miami that could take off and land at tiny airstrips. "Our guys need one of these in the worst way," North told Joe.

Joe looked at the price: $65,000.

Okay, he said.

North wanted the donation made quietly. Congress had explicitly banned aid to the Contras. He asked Joe to wire the money to an account in the Credit Suisse bank in Switzerland—the same account North established to channel to the Contras secret proceeds from illegal missile sales to Iran. Joe had one condition: He didn't want the plane used to haul weapons, but only for "humanitarian" purposes. North said he understood completely, and shook Joe's hand.

John Recca liked to say, with a mysterious flick of his dark eyebrows, that his Italian-American family in Modesto, California, had been "friendly" with the Gallo wine family ever since Prohibition. Recca, dark and wiry with a dashing mustache, managed one of Gallo's brands and frequently sat in on board meetings with Ernest Gallo himself.

Ernest was about Bill Coors's age, but unlike Bill, Ernest enjoyed selling his product as much as he liked making it. He was up on every price promotion run by every competitor in Laramie, Wyoming, or Rome, Georgia. He knew to the penny what it cost to truck a thousand cases of Gallo across upstate New York. He knew which Virginia county was about to rescind a blue law and let wine be sold on Sunday. The old man would gather Recca and the other managers and quiz them on how their brands were doing in various cities. "Hooston," he'd say in his heavy Italian accent, and when he was satisfied with results there, "Meeami." If a manager blamed a distributor for poor sales and Ernest accepted the explanation, he would push a button on the speakerphone and chew out the distributor right away, with all the brand managers listening. It was brutal but effective. "Plan your work," was the Gallo maxim, "and work your plan."

Recca enjoyed Gallo, but in beverage marketing in the 1980s it was best to broaden one's résumé. Recca was intrigued by an offer from Bob Rechholtz at Coors. He'd never worked for a brewery. And the parallels between the companies—each owned by old families—were comforting. Recca said he'd think about it.

Rechholtz called again and again. Coors really wanted Recca, and that in itself was appealing to a boy from Modesto. Finally, Recca agreed to move to Golden with the assignment of reviving the bottled-water idea.

What was missing in Golden, Recca quickly realized, was a sense of urgency. Coors seemed happy to let him tinker with water products indefinitely. Recca had also expected a family company like Gallo, where the patriarch was a fully involved player. For a family company, Coors seemed strangely to be lacking the day-to-day family element. Bill Coors shook Recca's hand only once, and Peter was barely visible behind a fog of divisional managers, directors, and vice presidents. The few times Peter attended meetings, he seemed shallow and distracted. Once, the bottled-water team was presenting an analysis of why Colorado Chiller had failed and was doing a good job, Recca thought, of confronting the company's mistakes. Suddenly, Peter blurted, *"The One Minute Manager* says a problem only exists if there is a difference between what is actually happening and what you desire to be happening."

Recca's people exchanged glances, perplexed.

So? Recca wanted to ask.

After a respectful silence, the conversation resumed, and not long after, Peter excused himself from the meeting.

In contrast with the lean machine that was Gallo, Coors seemed to Recca a ponderous elephant of a company, choking on layers of useless middle managers. He walked through the public relations department and had to repress a chuckle. There must have been two hundred people there, an entire university of white, black, male, female, Hispanic, gay, Jewish, Catholic, Muslim, Protestant, and Hindu spokespeople—a face for every conceivable boycott challenge.

Gallo had also had its share of image problems, confronting a whopper of a boycott by the United Farm Workers in the 1960s and '70s. But Gallo had never hired more than a handful of mouthpieces to respond. It seemed to Recca that Ernest knew instinctively how to handle the boycott, by keeping a low profile and avoiding provocative comments.

Ambivalence was paralyzing Coors, Recca thought. In one corner was Bob Rechholtz, feverishly whipping the company to expand into every state. In the other was family tradition, refusing to let distributors and retailers display beer on the easy-to-reach dry shelves. Neither fighter could deliver a knockout blow. The result was a bloody mess.

In states like Illinois and Connecticut, Coors was using distributors who'd been handling other brands for years. To begin selling Coors they'd had to build refrigerated warehouses and stock Coors only in the refrigerator. All this for a barely profitable product with 4 or 5 percent market share.

This new generation of distributors rebelled as consistently as the old.

They begged for new products. They wheedled advertising support. But most of all, they pleaded to be allowed to display Coors on the dry shelf.

Peter loved to extemporize on the importance of distributors. He was fascinated by the example of Frito-Lay described in *In Search of Excellence*. The snack company had a 99.5 percent success rate in getting its products to stores on time. "They go by the motto 'Service to Sales,'" Peter told his people. "Frito-Lay lives for its distributors."

But Peter couldn't give his own distributors the thing they wanted most: permission to stock beer on the dry shelf. Nor could Jeff. As a brewing engineer, Jeff knew modern methods meant that cold-filtered Coors would do about as well as any of the other beers on the dry shelf. Had he been president of any other brewery he'd have been authorized to give the nod. But Bill refused to allow it. He was still irritated by the way Miller Genuine Draft swiped credit for cold-filtering. But mostly, he couldn't bear the thought of his beer sitting at room temperature.

Coors belatedly began running ads boasting of its own cold-filtering technique. It was bad enough that Coors looked like it was imitating Miller Genuine Draft instead of the other way around. But right in the middle of the Coors campaign, somebody in advertising made a colossal mistake. In one of his sudden inspirations, Gary Naifeh had by this time swung again from the legal-drinking-age market to the slightly older beer drinker, and in so doing had shifted from tits-and-ass ads to sober, quiet pitches by the handsome actor Mark Harmon. They clashed with the va-voom Halloween campaign featuring Elvira in a way that would have made the consistent-strategy-obsessed Nichols blanch, but as commercials they were popular. The Harmon campaign was going well until Rechholtz's people shot an ad with the actor standing in front of a dry shelf full of unrefrigerated Coors. So lax and undisciplined was the demoralized company that nobody caught the mistake—neither the ad producers, the brand managers, Naifeh, nor Rechholtz.

Bill Coors caught it, though, while home watching television. And every Coors distributor caught it. They descended on the brewery with machetes. Why was the company spending itself into the poorhouse on refrigerated warehouses and trucks? they wanted to know. Why were we crippling ourselves by hiding the beer in the coolbox? Why were we suffering this way if we were going to show Coors being sold warm on television?

Ironically, the fiasco converted Bill. He agreed to let Coors be displayed warm—for two weeks per can, no longer! Coors still had to be shipped cold and stored cold at the distributors'. But now the six-packs could claim their place on the eye-catching mid-store dry shelves. It had taken an embarrassing blunder, but Coors had shed another of its millstones and was inching forward.

By now it was early summer of 1987. Three years had elapsed since Peter's first conversation with Thomas Donahue at the AFL-CIO—three years in which the Michigan debacle had unfolded and Peter had anxiously prepared to begin selling Coors in the union strongholds of New York, New Jersey, and Pennsylvania. The company was moving into New York now and Joe still hadn't budged on neutrality. In the last three years, Coors had bought the optioned Virginia land and announced plans to build a packaging plant. The AFL-CIO had quickly placed a new condition on Coors: Build the Virginia plant with union labor. The company couldn't very well act in good faith toward organized labor, Donahue argued, while launching an enormous construction project with nonunion workers. On the phone from Ithaca, New York, where he was attending Cornell's commencement, Dad had flown into a rage at the very idea, to say nothing of the labor federation's attempt to twist his arm. Once again, Joe had ordered Peter to stop talking to the enemy.

But now that Bill and Joe had given ground on their no-dry-shelf rule, it was possible they'd give a little ground here, too.

Peter liked to start each day with a long run through Golden. He'd jog up his long driveway, under the full-size American flag streaming from the flagpole, turn right and right again, and lope along the shore of one of the brewery's artificial lakes. To his left would rise the tall barley silos of the malthouse and behind them, the brewery's bright cloud of steam. The air would be rich with the roasty smell of toasting malt.

Peter would often turn left on Tenth Street, which followed the bank of Clear Creek opposite the brewery. To Peter's left, the plant's buildings would gleam in the slanted morning sunlight: can plant, bottle factory, malthouse, brewery, can and bottle lines—more than a mile of solid factory. Often, the morning shift would just be coming on as Peter ran by.

One morning in June, Peter crossed Green Street on his run, turned up Crawford, and was presented with a perfect nightmare. Attached to a bungalow that used to be a real estate office was an enormous banner: TEAMSTERS COORS ORGANIZING OFFICE. Somehow, Peter kept his legs running, past brawny men in windbreakers moving file cabinets and desks through the door. One of them noticed him and they all dropped what they were doing to run to the curb and shout obscenities at his back, middle fingers raised.

Teamsters! Just when things were starting to look up. It had been ten years since the strike. The company was a paragon of good pay, benefits, and affirmative-action policies—yet the boycott was stronger than ever and a whole new union was about to pick a fight.

Tom Donahue, too, got word that Teamsters were sniffing around the Coors brewery. To lose Coors to Teamsters, of all people, would be ignominy. Donahue needed an agreement with Coors more urgently than ever, and not just because of the Teamsters. Organized labor had had a hard three years, too. Union membership plummeted to fewer than seventeen million Americans, down nearly a quarter since 1980. The AFL-CIO was sliding toward irrelevance.

Donahue had been keeping his talks with Coors secret from all but his superiors. Now he felt he owed a call to David Sickler, who had worked his heart out on the boycott for a decade.

When Donahue phoned the office in Los Angeles, he learned a friend in the Seafarer's union had wangled Sickler and his wife berths on a freighter to Hawaii—Sickler's first vacation in the ten years since the Coors strike. It took Donahue days to track him down. Finally, Sickler called from a beachside pay phone on Maui.

"We've been approached by Pete Coors," Donahue said. "What should we be asking for?"

Standing in his sandy bare feet and wolfing a cigarette, Sickler understood at once that the boycott was ending. He was surprised to find he felt okay about it. Sickler hadn't achieved his goal of destroying the Adolph Coors Company. But he recognized the moment as one in which the AFL-CIO could declare a victory, and that was the important thing. It helped that Sickler admired and trusted Tom Donahue; if Donahue thought ending the boycott was the right thing to do, that carried a lot of weight with Sickler.

"The boycott has made Coors a better employer," Sickler said.

"No argument there. We're pushing for union labor on their new brewery and neutrality in any organizing drive."

"Those are the two things I'd ask for," Sickler said. They talked a few minutes more and Sickler hung up the phone, knowing his ten-year battle against Coors was coming to an end.

Shaken by the sight of Teamsters handbilling the brewery gates, Peter tried again with the elders. They refused both neutrality and the idea of building the Virginia plant with union labor. Peter begged: Let unions build the plant, and when they're finished, they'll be gone. Let the unions talk to our employees without interference; we treat our people so well they're sure to vote no. But Bill and Joe wouldn't hear of it.

The talks between Peter and Donahue became an open secret. After Donahue talked to Sickler, rumors cascaded through the AFL-CIO and reached Coors workers in Golden. In a memo to department heads, Peter and Jeff acknowledged, "We have been working to find a way to remove the boycott." But they made clear Joe's caveats. "Occasionally there is speculation that the family or upper management desires our employees to be organized so the boycott will be lifted," the memo read. "You need not speculate further. We will continue to resist union efforts."

Coors fought the Teamsters hard, giving raises and, in a newsletter, instructing supervisors to "remind [your subordinates] that signing a union authorization card is like signing a blank check or a power of attorney." The Teamsters complained that raises during a union drive were illegal and they forced Coors to retract the falsehoods in the newsletter. But unbound by a neutrality agreement, Coors kept fighting.

It was at precisely this time that David Floyd hired the ex-cons for his drug squad, started illegally wiretapping employees, and shifted the secret surveillance of employees into high gear.

Peter, restrained from settling with the unions, searched feverishly for ways to take command and make his family business perform. Lean staff, well led—that was the Frito-Lay secret, according to the authors of *In Search of Excellence,* and Peter tried their tricks. He held "leadership meetings" of his senior staff. He tried "quality circles" and pep talks for the workers. He even handed out five-dollar bills to those brave enough to disagree with him. And he kept a stream of new marketers coming, people from such successful consumer-products companies as Head Skis, Philip Morris, and 7UP. All were struck by the flabbiness of Coors, which showed even in Peter's up-to-the-minute efforts. The "leadership meetings," which by definition were to be small and tight, often bloated to more than a hundred people. The new blood wasn't replacing the old, but was simply being added. It seemed to the newcomers that a job at Coors was a sinecure for life. The problem with this place, they told each other, was that nobody worried about getting fired.

Around this time, Peter decided he needed to get away, and took his twelve-year-old son bass fishing in Tennessee. Drifting among lily pads in the molten August heat far from Golden, Peter finally found the courage to defy his father. Peter had put too much effort into his talks with Donahue. It was crazy to deny the brewery the chance to rid itself of the boycott, when all Donahue wanted in return was temporary union labor in Virginia and for Coors to obey the law in Colorado. Peter didn't want a union at the Golden brewery any more than his father did. But he was confident that the company now treated its workers so well they'd reject an organizing drive. Tom Donahue got a surprise call from Peter asking him to fly to Nashville for a talk. The breakthrough was so unexpected that when Donahue flew down to Nashville and was driven out to the house where Peter was fishing, he found Peter still by the lakeside, reeking of fish and ajingle with lures.

Things moved quickly. Avoiding the word "neutrality," the Adolph Coors Company nevertheless promised to "assure its employees of their right to form, join or assist labor organizations, or to refrain from doing so, without suffering penalty." The company also agreed to build the Virginia plant with union labor. In return, the AFL-CIO promised to call off the boycott and "use its best efforts" to notify not only its member unions, but all nonfederation unions, including the NEA, that its boycott was over.

Peter flew to Washington a couple of weeks later to stand beside AFL-CIO president Lane Kirkland and, in front of the television cameras, sign the agreement.

"Mr. Kirkland," a reporter shouted as soon as the paper was signed. "Will you now drink Coors beer?"

"No," Kirkland said, and Peter felt the floor drop out from under him. "I only buy union-made products," Kirkland continued. "When a union represents the workers at Coors, I'll drink their beer."

All Peter could do was make the most of it. The Coors company newspaper splashed a gigantic headline across its front page: IT'S OVER!!!

But the announcement of the AFL-CIO agreement only seemed to make the boycott flare up again. Black and Hispanic groups that hadn't signed on to the earlier covenants held press conferences to denounce the settlement. The gays went ballistic. The Teamsters angrily declared themselves stabbed in the back. Even within the AFL-CIO, everybody took pains to say that all that had changed was that the official boycott was over. Coors was still the only nonunion mass-produced beer in the country. Trade unionists might not be boycotting Coors anymore, but neither were they going to drink it until its label bore a union bug. A television news crew cornered David Sickler and asked if they could film him drinking a Coors now that the boycott was over. "You get within ten feet of me with a can of Coors," he snapped, "and you're going to have to go to the hospital to have it removed."

Bill made it clear that Peter's agreement with the AFL-CIO did not signal a shift in politics for the Coors family, either. "Will we keep quiet?" he asked rhetorically when the *Los Angeles Times* called about the agreement. "Don't bet on it. Taking part in politics is a duty." The battle lines remained drawn.

Peter's hair, dark and shiny a few years ago, had gone wispy white. Everything was so confusing! He'd reach out to solve a problem, and as he touched it the problem would change shape. Settling the boycott only seemed to revive it. Selling more and more beer earned the company less and less money. And now, out of nowhere, a mediocre import called Corona was achieving the cult status Coors had once enjoyed. Corona wasn't even considered special in Mexico, yet in just a couple of months it had rocketed to become the number-two U.S. import after Heineken. What's more, it was sold in clear bottles, which meant Corona either added preservatives or the beer spoiled quickly. But beer drinkers had shown they didn't know or care—or perhaps they even preferred clear glass. Miller's colossus, Genuine Draft, came in clear bottles, too. All Peter knew was that Corona had come out of nowhere to blow past Herman Joseph's and Killian's. Yet another mediocre beer was sweeping away his family's excellent brews, and Peter hadn't a clue as to why.

The Halloween campaign was a bright spot. It extended by a couple of months the peak beer-drinking season, and made it easy to move beer left over from the summer rush. The "Elvira, Mistress of the Dark" ads were eye-catching and popular. Coors had 150,000 lifesize cardboard Elviras manufactured to stand in beer aisles. They were so strikingly sexy that retailers fought each other for them.

Then one afternoon, Bob Rechholtz told Gary Naifeh, the excitable Texan, to kill the Elvira campaign. "Now."

"What?"

"This comes from the top," Rechholtz said. "Jeff doesn't like it."

"Jeff doesn't *like* it?" Naifeh screeched. "It sells beer!"

"Don't ask, just do it," said Rechholtz, who achieved his limited success by not challenging the family's deep-seated beliefs too directly.

Naifeh banged on Peter's door.

"I don't see anything wrong with Elvira," Peter said listlessly. "But it's not worth fighting over."

Naifeh had a lifesize Elvira standing in the marketing department, and he called one of the company's artists to see if they could make it less offensive. They created a paste-on panel to send to the retailers that, if matched properly to the original, put a new top on Elvira and showed less cleavage.

Cleavage, Rechholtz told Naifeh, was not the problem for Jeff.

"Then what is?" Naifeh cried, clutching his beloved two-dimensional sex-goddess.

Rechholtz leaned in close to Naifeh. "Jeff thinks it's satanic."

"What!"

"Shh," Rechholtz hissed. "Satanic. A message from the devil. Get rid of her."

Just when Peter thought the boycott settlement would help improve the brewery's image, *Financial World* magazine put Coors on its list of the "ten worst managed companies in America." Peter could dismiss the magazine's primary criticism—that Coors wouldn't borrow money to market aggressively—because he knew it wasn't exactly fair. Even without borrowing, Coors was spending more per barrel on marketing than any other brewer—a mind-boggling turn of events for Peter, who only ten years earlier had been struggling with the smallest per-barrel ad budget in the business. Also, Peter knew *Financial World* institutionally took the side of shareholders, and Rechholtz's "critical mass" strategy had come at the short-term expense of Coors shareholders. Rechholtz had warned the family to expect that. But to *Financial World*, Coors was the embodiment of corporate arrogance. The article led with a hypothetical quote, which the author said typified the attitude of lousy companies: "If you don't like the way we run this company, sell your stock."

Financial World took a second swing at Coors a few issues later, harshly profiling its forty-year-old chief financial officer. The article spooled out two thousand words on why Coors was financially dead in the water, shot down the CFO's excuses, sneered at his Pollyanna optimism, and finally quoted him snapping: "I'm laying out our strategy. You and the financial community have to decide if you want to invest in it." In other words, if you don't like the way we run this company, sell your stock. Wall Street took Coors up on its offer: Twelve years after going public, Coors's share price was lower than where it had started.

In the fall, Peter convened a leadership meeting for senior executives and their wives at Keystone ski resort to hear a management guru talk about "Building Meaningful Relationships" in and out of work. He also hoped to plan, finally, for a subpremium beer. These low-end beers, selling for fifty to seventy-five cents less a six-pack than the regular "premiums," held almost a quarter of the market. They were a huge and growing arena in which Coors was unrepresented. Bill and Joe had long refused to consider putting their name on a "cheap" beer.

Peter, usually receptive to strategies for convincing the elders, was subdued throughout the meetings. He seemed distracted and morose. He excused himself during one Meaningful Relationship seminar to take a phone call and when he returned, his eyes were wet.

"The brewery is going to make an announcement today, and I want you to hear it first," he said. "My parents are splitting up."

Joe and Holly? Coors marketers were a difficult group to surprise, but this news hit them like a tsunami. Holly and Joe were the most straightlaced people imaginable! They were pillars of traditional family values! They were the perfect couple!

The full story was even more shocking. Joe had owned up to why he'd so ardently attended Cornell commencements the past thirteen years: He'd been trysting with a woman he loved. Joe had been betraying Holly since the early 1970s—since the days of TVN and his fight to get on the public television board. Now, he was leaving Holly and moving with his longtime lover to a million-dollar vineyard in northern California. He would soon retire from active management. For Joe Coors, the embodiment of moral strictness, to have cheated for so long was unbelievable. And to run off to California! Leaving the brewery! The Coors execs wouldn't have been more surprised if Joe had confessed to being a Soviet spy.

Holly, atilt with grief and humiliation, showed up at the Teamsters organizing office one morning, shook hands with the startled men in windbreakers, and urged them to "go beat the shit out of those sons of bitches up there."

Jeff, floored by the depth of his father's sin, prayed fiercely.

Joe Jr., banished for a decade and denied company leadership because he'd broken a family rule, found bittersweet vindication in his father's confession. Dad's holier-than-thou act had been a sham and Joe Jr. took the opportunity to rise from his obscure subsidiary job. A few weeks after his father left for California, Joe Jr. became president of the ceramics subsidiary.

Peter, devastated by the news, let the company sink into a year of mishaps. He allowed Gary Naifeh to change the Coors Banquet can from its distinctive creamy yellow—used for almost a century—to beige, and the logo from blue to black. Banquet's core customers, thinking the beer had changed, screamed blue murder and Peter had to backtrack—an expensive embarrassment. A copycat in Florida stuffed a mouse into a can of Banquet. Peter fought him in court instead of quietly paying a settlement. That the man was sent to prison for attempted fraud was small consolation for nationally broadcast images of a slimy dead mouse curled in the bottom of a can of Coors. Peter's younger brother Grover, working across the creek at one of the technology subsidiaries, sank a bundle into mass-producing photovoltaic cells that unrolled like paper towels. "Who are we going to sell these to?" an aide asked the excitable young Coors. "Don't worry about it," Grover replied. "People will buy them. They're so *neat!*" The project failed.

By the first quarter of 1989 the Adolph Coors Company was reporting its worst results ever. It wasn't just a matter of falling profits this time; Coors had actually lost money for the first time since going public. The only good news, from Peter's perspective, was that the company had whipped the Teamsters three-to-one in an organizing vote.

Then, as though clutching a reed and pulling himself out of a raging torrent, Peter found a way simultaneously to revive the company and put his indelible mark upon it.

20

The Second Smartest
Thing to Do

The Stroh family ran the nation's oldest continuously operating brewery. Bernhard Stroh had opened a small brewhouse in Detroit in 1850 and by the late 1980s Stroh's was the country's third biggest brewer after Anheuser-Busch and Miller. Stroh's was a distant third, to be sure—it had only 10 percent of the market against Miller's 22 and A-B's 42. Right behind Stroh's was Coors, with almost 9 percent in 1989. Peter Stroh, president of his family's brewery, was sixty-two, closer in age to Peter Coors's father than to Peter. The two Peters liked each other, if from a respectful distance. Both were scions of German-American brewing families more interested in making a good beer at a decent profit than in driving competitors out of business. The Strohs were as proud of the fire-brewing method they'd developed in 1912—heating the kettles with flame instead of steam—as the Coorses were of their cold-filtering. The Strohs and the Coorses recognized in each other a longing for the old days. Moreover, they shared a belief that it was precisely their longing that made them strong. That set them above their peers. And that would once again prove endearing to customers.

In the meantime, both were in the same kind of trouble. Neither was close to critical mass.

Sold only in the eastern United States, Stroh's various brands didn't add up to close to 15 percent of the national market. Peter Stroh's strategy had been to buy existing brands; New York's Schaefer Brewing Company and then Milwaukee's Schlitz. He borrowed a pile of money for the acquisitions, but the only acquired brand worth a damn was Schlitz Malt Liquor, which held almost half of the small but high-priced malt liquor market.

Overall, Stroh's was stalled.

One day in 1989, Peter Stroh called Peter Coors with a suggestion. They were each operating as half of a strong corporation, he said. Coors had a light beer that was doing well, and a superpremium—Killian's—that had potential. But Coors didn't have a malt liquor or a subpremium. Stroh's, on the other hand, had a light beer that hardly sold and no superpremium. But they had a great-selling subpremium in Old Milwaukee. And they had Schlitz Malt Liquor.

Coors was strong out west; Schlitz was strong back east. Separately, both companies were each stuck at a 10 share or below. Together, they would have a full range of products and an 18 share—within striking distance of Miller.

Why didn't they merge, Stroh suggested. Coors should buy Stroh's and create one big national brewer.

The idea thrilled Peter. Coors and Stroh's were made for each other. And acquisition was the slick, expedient, modern way to expand. Wall Street analysts didn't think much of Coors's plodding attempts to manufacture new products. But mergers and acquisitions titillated those guys. In a single, bold stroke, Peter could double the size of the company, fill gaps in the product line, and more then double market share, garnering instant "critical mass." It was a strategy for the 1980s. By acquiring Stroh's, Peter could make the Adolph Coors Company his own. He could bequeath the next generation a truly up-to-date corporation.

In late September 1989, while the world was watching East Germans pour into Czechoslovakia as the Iron Curtain tore, Peter convened a press conference in a corner of the company cafeteria to announce that he was buying the Stroh's Brewing Company for $425 million. Peter had agreed to take aboard almost all of Stroh's—not only its five breweries, two can plants, and fifteen brands of beer, but also the $300 million in debt that Stroh's had acquired in buying Schaefer and Schlitz. Coors would also swallow its legendary aversion to unions, Peter told the dumbfounded reporters, and respect Stroh's labor contracts.

Wall Street was delighted. The financial press welcomed Coors into the fold with an eruption of praise. "A new force in the brewing business," one analyst crowed. "The second-smartest thing Coors could have done," another said with a laugh. "The smartest thing would have been to acquire Miller." *USA Today* said the acquisition would "launch Coors into a neck-and-neck battle for the number-two position with Miller." For several days after the press conference, Peter basked in the first praise the company had earned from the financial community since going public fourteen years earlier. Coors's share price jumped a dollar and a half overnight; not enough to push it over its IPO price, but a welcome improvement. After the sting of the *Financial World* articles, Peter finally felt on top of his game.

One analyst called the merger "a change in Coors's overall culture," and Peter and Jeff frankly acknowledged the family was swallowing a bitter pill, violating the founder's no-debt rule. "It's a little scary," Jeff said. "We all have a problem with it," Peter added. "We've shocked a lot of people."

Not least, apparently, Uncle Bill. Noticeably absent from the press conference and from the jubilant coverage was the grand old man of the Adolph Coors Company, William Coors. When pressed, Coors's public relations people said cryptically that Bill had left the country—and that they didn't know where or for how long. Nobody asked what Joe thought; he was off in California—the dark side of the moon—with his new fiancée. Hammered at the press conference with questions about what his uncle Bill thought of so radical a move, Peter pointedly said, "Jeff and I are running the business."

If so, they had a sudden and unexplained change of heart later that fall. Coors abruptly announced that Bill Coors was reassuming the role of president, ousting Jeffrey. Then came an equally terse press release saying Coors was backing out of the deal with Stroh's. The big purchase about which everybody had been so excited was off.

The Coors family had always been secretive, but the silence surrounding this decision was complete. Nonfamily board members were in the dark. So were corporate officers. Stroh was equally silent.

Coors executives and investors on Wall Street could only surmise why such a sweet deal had been canceled. Bill wouldn't take on debt, they speculated. Or Bill wouldn't acquire inferior breweries. Perhaps Bill had balked at the union contracts. Or maybe he couldn't stand compromising

the "Brewed with Rocky Mountain Spring Water" slogan. Had Bill origi-
nally given his assent and then changed his mind? Or had Peter struck
the Stroh's deal without telling him, and suffered a countercoup?

Wall Street was disappointed—not only that the deal that would have
modernized Coors was off, but that the Colorado brewers had reverted
to their imperious, whim-driven, secretive ways.

Jeff went to Hawaii and stayed six months on what the public relations
department called a "stress leave." In Jeff's brief tenure as president, the
company had all but foundered. And when he and Peter had tried to
reverse the decline by merging with Stroh's, Uncle Bill had slapped Jeff
aside, metaphorically sending him to bed without supper.

But that wasn't the worst of Jeff's anxieties. Something deeper gnawed
at Jeffrey Coors. Do not be drunk with wine, Ephesians commanded.
Drunkenness was a sin. Was it not a sin, then, to manufacture beer? To
aide and abet the drunken? True enough, Jesus' first miracle was to turn
water into wine. And First Corinthians does exhort us to serve wherein
we are called. But wine is a mocker, says Proverbs 20:1, and strong drink
a brawler. Given the sexual and even satanic overtones of modern beer
marketing, the brewing industry seemed no place for a Christian.

In Hawaii, Jeff decided that he could no longer reconcile brewing with
his Christian faith. When he returned, it was to one of the outgrowths of
the old Porcelain plant across Clear Creek.

Joe Jr. was across the creek, too, at Porcelain. Even by Coors standards,
Joe Jr. was plainspoken. More than once, he had conceded to colleagues
that he wasn't up to the management jobs his birthright had held for
him. Like his brother Peter, he forced management books on his staff,
but unlike Peter he didn't read many himself. "I can't read every book
someone recommends," he told his assistant Bev Obenchain. "I might get
influenced by them." Similarly, he told her he had to leave the office
early every day—to play golf—because "whoever presents an idea to me
at four, four-thirty in the afternoon is going to get what he wants." He
was, he freely admitted, a "golf bum." He kept a suit in the office for
rare occasions, and otherwise lived in pastel pants and polo shirts.

Like Grover's, Joe Jr.'s subsidiary was a shambles. Coors Ceramics—
formerly Coors Porcelain—had no idea how much its products cost to
make, so it couldn't price its wares intelligently. At times it charged too
little and cut its margins, and at other times it charged too much and

lost business. Without diligent cost accounting, Coors Ceramics could no longer compete for government contracts. Joe Jr. could no more keep his mind on corporate details now than he had been able to on his homework forty years earlier. At one point he took six months off to learn to pilot helicopters, and thereafter enjoyed clattering down onto the Coors Ceramics lawn, scattering pedestrians and leaving the machine in everybody's way.

Meanwhile, Peter soldiered on. If he felt cheated of his chance to rocket the family business toward the twenty-first century with his bold financial stroke, he complained to nobody. He rescued a nugget from the collapsed Stroh's deal, agreeing to buy Stroh's brewery in Memphis for $50 million. Neither Coors nor Coors Light would be brewed there, but several coming experimental brands, including nonalcohol Cutter and the spiced Blue Moon ales, could be manufactured there without risking the core brands' Rocky Mountain Spring Water slogan.

Also at this time Peter opened the Virginia plant. Coors continued brewing Coors and Coors Light in Golden, but then, instead of finishing beer earmarked for the East Coast with Colorado water, Coors shipped it in tank cars to the Virginia plant, where it was mixed with local water before bottling. Bill would not have agreed to such a thing had the water back east been ordinary. But Coors's Virginia plant, on the slope of some of the Southeast's highest mountains, enjoyed superb water. The Virginia plant not only relieved pressure on Golden, it was good for the beer. It shortened by days the beer's trip to East Coast customers. Peter also finally brought a subpremium—Keystone—to market, and it was an even bigger first-year seller than Miller Genuine Draft had been.

Peter continued his leadership meetings and kept trying on management styles from the business-shelf best-sellers. He brought in a high-priced management consultant and created an elite strategy team, the "Red Lions of December," complete with their own logo-printed T-shirts. He established a "customer satisfaction program" that viewed internal departments as "customers" of each other—another Frito-Lay trick he'd picked up from *In Search of Excellence*. Like Joe Jr., he put his people through sensitivity training, diversity training, and confrontation training. He continued encouraging executives to disagree with him without fear.

But Coors still hadn't learned how to nurture fleeting good news into long-term growth. After the initial Keystone excitement died down, the old pessimism descended on the brewery. Now that expansion through merger had been ruled out, the company was likely looking forward to a long holding action. Decline appeared inexorable. Keystone helped the bottom line a little, but Anheuser-Busch and Miller were too big and too mean to be held at bay just by brewing good beer.

What did it mean anymore to be a Coors? The brewery Peter had inherited was not the brewery his forebears had enjoyed running. Gone were the days of intimate friendships with the workers, pride in holding 60 percent market shares, and the unwavering affection of the public. Among many Americans, Coors was now a dirty word. Maybe, in the long run, Dad had done the brewery a favor by disappearing with his mistress to California. He wasn't in the boardroom seconding Uncle Bill's stubborn opinions.

Uncle Bill, though, was very much around, clinging, Ahablike, to a dream of the old world—of unblinkingly loyal German-speaking workers, of neighborhood customers drinking local beer because it tasted good. Bill was seventy-six years old. His adherence to careful diet, exercise, and meditation rendered him fit as a man half his age. As his dream of the good old days sank below the waves of modern commerce, Uncle Bill seemed perversely determined to drag the company down with it.

Peter Coors may not have been the best leader of men. But he was no fool. He could see what was wrong with his family's business: Ambivalence was killing it. Stuck between nostalgia and pragmatism, the brewery was dying in limbo. No matter how many marketing brains Peter recruited, they couldn't make significant progress in a company that treated them like invaders. More than a decade after Uncle Bill had agreed to hire the first real marketer, he still couldn't accept their presence. That first marketer, Art Stone, had preached that the taste and knack for marketing had to come from the very top. In the years since, Peter had read the books of countless management pundits, who had all said the same thing. Marketing couldn't be grafted onto a corporation that was institutionally hostile to it. With Bill back at the helm, the question seemed to be, Which would pass away first, he or the brewery?

Unlike Bill, the Adolph Coors Company was obese. The company had had its share of problems with its employees, but according to Coors family mythology, its devotion to employees was complete; the paternalist relationship between owner and worker was as tightly woven into the brewery's fiber as Clear Creek or the aluminum can. Adolph the founder had kept the business going during Prohibition, his grandsons remembered, just to keep his people employed. The founder's son, "the old gent" Adolph Jr., had known every worker by name. And everybody remembered how Bill used to play piano at the workers' retirement parties.

Coors was more than a business; it was a family and a culture that cherished its members. At the dawn of the 1990s, this translated into a perilous excess of help. Drifting around the plant were people Joe and Bill had hired forty years earlier; they were dead weight on the payroll and, worse, they kept the company mired in the past. Some of them were people Peter had played with as a boy—or whose *children* Peter had played with as a boy. It would have taken a harder heart than Peter's to fire them. The problem wasn't entirely family friends and neighbors, either. As Peter lurched from one new management technique to another, he added adiposal layers of middle management that he never found the nerve to thin.

In his darkest moments, Peter felt that the deadest weight on the Adolph Coors Company was himself. What else could explain the paradox of Coors throwing more money per barrel at marketing than any other brewer with so little result? Peter had told John Nichols long before that he didn't believe he had the smarts or experience to make it outside of Coors. Left unsaid was that if he wasn't fit to run another corporation, he wasn't fit to run Coors, and that he had the job only because of his family name.

But if he lacked a genius for marketing and the personality of a battlefield commander, perhaps Peter had the next best thing. He began mulling a radical idea.

Gary Naifeh, the hyperactive Texan who was known around the marketing department as the Preacher, was feeling desperate. Coors was going to ruin. Despite four years of hard work by John Recca, the bottled water product had died for lack of family interest and Recca had moved on to Hiram Walker. The Stroh's deal was mysteriously canceled. Clunkers like Herman Joseph's were kept alive by the financial equivalent of heart-lung machines.

Then August Busch III delivered an insult that Naifeh took personally. Bud Light blatantly stole Naifeh's slogan for Coors Light—"It Won't Slow You Down"—spinning it as "It Won't Let You Down." Naifeh wanted to sue them, but nobody at Coors seemed able to rally the enthusiasm for a good street fight.

Naifeh decided to do something about it. He set out to make a commercial so provocative, so directly aimed at Anheuser-Busch, that A-B would have to respond, which in turn, he hoped, would provoke some fire-in-the-belly at Coors. The commercial, produced by Foote, Cone and Belding, posed the question, Where is your beer born? It juxtaposed scenes of burbling Rocky Mountain streams with those of the Missouri River slogging through industrial St. Louis. The implication was obvious: Coors was brewed with the nation's purest water and Budweiser with factory waste. Naifeh brought the commercial to Bob Rechholtz and then to the full board of directors, and everybody liked it. Naifeh was thrilled. But then they directed him to run it in New York, Chicago, Los Angeles—every place but St. Louis.

Typical, Naifeh thought. To make a hard-hitting commercial and then balk at showing it in Augie Busch's hometown. Unforgivably timid. Did the Coorses really think the people at Anheuser-Busch wouldn't see it if it wasn't run in St. Louis? Did they think it would make Augie Busch less angry? The whole point is to make him angry! To hell with it, Naifeh figured. Without asking advice or permission, he called Foote, Cone and Belding and ordered them to run a "roadblock," to air the commercial simultaneously on all three networks, during the evening news—in St. Louis.

The commercial ran on a Sunday and on Monday it was the talk of the Coors brewery. A knot of marketing people huddled over coffee cups in the cafeteria, wondering aloud who would be so stupid. Naifeh, walking past, marched over and said, "I did it. When Augie Busch is angry he makes mistakes. We have him right where we want him." Then he stormed off, leaving the marketers shrugging.

August Busch III certainly got angry. He flew in his private jet to Denver and summoned Peter to meet him at the airport. Augie didn't even disembark, but made Peter come aboard to be castigated. What filtered out to the marketing department was that Busch was simply livid and swore revenge.

Nobody knew how far he'd go. Nobody dreamed he'd cut straight for the heart of Coors's identity.

Busch filed a complaint with the Federal Trade Commission, saying the slogan Coors had been using for more than a hundred years— "Brewed with Rocky Mountain Spring Water"—was a lie. Coors shipped concentrate to Virginia, where it was mixed with water that rose far from the Rocky Mountains, Busch argued.

Coors countered by saying that only a beer concentrate was shipped east, and besides, all of it was *brewed* with Rocky Mountain spring water. Some of it is later *blended* with Virginia water.

Sorry, the federal regulators said. Coors could use the old slogan only for beer that was packaged in Golden.

Running two simultaneous slogans—for beer packaged in the East and the West—was out of the question. The company founded by Adolph Coors—who moved to Golden to avail himself of the water—could no longer boast of the attribute that made its beer special. "Brewed with Rocky Mountain Spring Water" was taken off all the labels.

Naifeh was mortified. "You should have fired me as soon as I did it," he told Bob Rechholtz. Naifeh hadn't been disciplined at the time of the ad but expected the ax to fall now.

Rechholtz simply waved him out of his office and told him to forget it. To Naifeh, Rechholtz appeared amazingly sanguine about the loss of the company's age-old slogan. Yet even stranger, the family reacted the same way. That which was most precious was taken from them, thought Naifeh, yet nobody cried, nobody complained, nobody disputed the ruling. Soon after, Naifeh left to hawk Taco Bell for PepsiCo.

From his perch at Taco Bell, Naifeh could see why Coors had refrained from squawking about a ruling on its water.

Someone squealed.

An anonymous caller to the Colorado Department of Health said Coors had been concealing serious contamination of its groundwater going back at least to 1981. Coors finally fessed up: It had known that its famous spring water was polluted and had hushed it up for nine years.

The Environmental Protection Agency offered to settle for a million-dollar fine—petty cash—but Peter put up a fight. As he saw it, he'd confess to the violations rather than put the Health Department through the expense of an investigation. That should earn him some consideration. Also, if he could negotiate a lower fine, the problem would appear less serious to consumers. The EPA already had ranked Coors "Colorado's worst polluter" for 1990.

Peter ultimately agreed to pay a quarter-million-dollar criminal fine plus a $400,000 civil settlement, the bulk of which was to be spent on a bike path along Clear Creek. "[We are] outraged," the regional director of the National Toxics Campaign told the *Rocky Mountain News*. "Coors gets away with paying—for polluting public water supplies—a fraction of what they normally spend on advertising what good environmental citizens they are."

Once again, Coors was compelled to mobilize its army of "corporate communications specialists" for a massive counterattack. It launched a $40 million literacy campaign and something called Clean Water 2000. It touted Peter's chairmanship of Ducks Unlimited and a new, high-tech process the company had developed to clean up the chemicals it had spilled. Most important of all, Peter agreed to step in at the eleventh hour and commit $30 million to help build a baseball stadium in Denver. His was the last piece of financing to fall into place, and it gave Denver the clout to win a National League franchise, in a squeaker, over St. Petersburg, Florida. By timing his offer at the last possible minute, Peter not only became Denver's white knight, but at a bargain-basement price. As Denver's baseball savior, he garnered the right to name the stadium Coors Field.

Would that a baseball stadium could have solved Coors's real problems. The pollution charges and resulting PR dustup were but irritations. The problem at Coors wasn't lack of sales. The company was selling more beer than ever, thanks to Coors Light. The problem was that Coors was selling more beer but making less money. Back in the good old days, Coors had earned almost thirty cents for every dollar's worth of beer sold. Now it earned little more than a penny—about a sixth the industry average. In fact, the more Coors brewed, the less money it seemed to make. Bob Rechholtz had spent some $2 billion on marketing in his decade-long tenure, and the company was in a deeper hole than when he started. From 1983—the start of Rechholtz's "critical mass" strategy—Coors was selling a third more beer but earning, in constant dollars, a quarter as much. Market share had risen to almost 10 percent, but it hadn't done the bottom line any good.

Accusations flew like bullets at the O.K. Corral. "If we hadn't pursued critical mass," Bob Rechholtz said in his own defense, "Coors might be out of business altogether." Sure, his detractors argued. But what if we'd done it *right*? What if we hadn't gone out of the way to offend customers? What if we'd let distributors use the dry shelf from the start? What if we'd positioned Coors Light properly so it didn't kill off our flagship brand? What if we'd opened breweries back east to increase our capacity and ship less expensively? What if we'd reacted faster and saved our money on duds like Herman Joseph's and Chiller? What if we'd fielded products to fill every market niche, instead of standing on the sidelines like wallflowers at a prom? What if we'd patiently built upon a clearly articulated strategy, and coordinated all our advertising and promotion materials, instead of stabbing wildly in the dark for quick fixes? In short, what if we'd acted like a sober twentieth-century corporation instead of a gargantuan nineteenth-century mom-and-pop store?

Bill had said at the beginning of the eighties that his business plan was "survival." And survival was all he got.

These were Golden's darkest days.

Nineteen ninety-one had been bad; 1992 was terrifying. First quarter earnings fell 88 percent from the dismal first quarter of the year before, to little more than three quarters of a million dollars.

Coors's long-term financial performance was embarrassing. The family would have been richer if it had closed the brewery in the early 1980s and put its money into an ordinary passbook account. Every now and then potential buyers appeared in the mist to offer a lifeboat. Seagram's. Coca-Cola. The Australian brewer Foster's. Bill sent them away. As long as he had breath in his body, Bill was determined to keep his brewery afloat and in the family.

Awash in crisis, Peter cried, "Mayday!" and began heaving assets and people over the side. First to go was the corporate jet that let him sleep in his own bed. Then he started doing the unthinkable for Coors—issuing pink slips. Some fifty people were shown the door—tiny cuts, considering that the company had almost seven thousand employees—and these first to go were mostly newcomers. Still, it was excruciating for Peter. He had no idea how to decide who should go. Almost everybody put in a good day's work. Should the choice be strictly functional? Or should he consider which of the potential layoffs had families?

As the firings began, Peter was noticeably absent from the brewery. He no longer shared a beer with other executives on Thursday night, was rarely seen drawing himself a cup of coffee in the cafeteria. He even stopped kicking around ideas with his marketers, part of his job he'd always loved. Peter had begun appearing in commercials, so his workers could see him every night on television standing in the snow "somewhere near Golden, Colorado" pitching the beer. But they rarely laid eyes on him in the flesh. When they did, they told each other he looked ashamed.

Next to go was much of the vertical integration of which the Coorses had always been so proud. Adolph the founder had built his own malting operation and icehouse, and as the company grew, the Coorses had mined their own coal, drilled their own gas, and built their own power plant, can plant, and bottle factory. They had created their own ad agency, construction company, and insurance company—in part because when the company was young Denver hadn't offered such services.

But this was 1992. Denver had grown up. It would be cheaper, Peter realized, to outsource a lot of operations. One by one he shed them, and hundreds of bricklayers, roustabouts, and actuaries who'd drawn a Coors check their entire lives found themselves working for someone else. Or not working at all.

The ax fell next on the nonbeer businesses. The Ceramics shop had grown into a group of high-tech companies that made everything from metal-foil detergent boxes to panels for bulletproof vests. But even with Jeff, Grover, and Joe Jr. running the technology companies, they were considered an afterthought, and their personnel a farm team for the brewery. They also put Joe Jr. and Jeff in an awkward position; running subsidiaries dominated by the brewery made them effectively subordinate to their younger brother, Peter, and that rankled. The nonbeer businesses were, at best, lackluster performers. They might do better on their own.

In December 1992, the family announced it was spinning off the non-beer companies into ACX Corporation, which, like the brewery, was to be mostly owned and entirely controlled by the Coors family. The brewery would continue on its own, as The Coors Brewing Company. Wall Street liked the idea, though it hardly did backflips. Smith, Barney's analyst sniffed that the spinoff "certainly [isn't] enough to change our neutral investment stance." Coors remained a go-nowhere investment. The outsourcing and the spinoff only nibbled at the edges of the real problem they were intended to address—the embarrassing corpulence of the brewery's payroll.

The awful truth began to dawn across the Golden valley: A massacre was coming.

After all that Peter's great-grandfather had done to keep paychecks flowing during Prohibition, the idea of firing good workers because of external pressures was as antithetical as making substandard beer. On the other hand, Peter knew that if he didn't do it, the entire brewery might come crashing down. Then everybody would be out of a job. It was a classic Hobson's choice, like deciding to amputate a gangrenous limb to save a patient.

Which was not a job one did oneself. If saving the Coors Brewing Company meant firing folks, Peter was going to find someone else to do it.

Of course, it wasn't just firing that had to be done. Rechholtz's idea of sacrificing everything for critical mass might have been the only path to take in the early eighties, but under Peter's leadership it plainly hadn't worked. Peter didn't have what it took to turn the Coors Brewing Company into the first-rate marketer it needed to become. But he did have something that would prove equally useful: humility. Peter's father and uncle had been oblivious to the moment when they went from being assets of the corporation to liabilities. Peter was not going to repeat their mistake.

At a leadership meeting in the fall of 1992, Peter told his astonished marketers that he was planning to hire a new president and chief operating officer—an outsider—to manage the family brewery. For the first time, he said, someone not named Coors would run the company. "A lot of things have to be done that I don't have the stomach to do," Peter said, alluding to the impending layoffs. With the disarming candor for which the Coorses were famous, he added that the company needed new leadership "and I'm not smart enough."

A wave of relief passed among the workers, and admiration for Peter's self-effacing grasp of reality. If only the old men had done the same thing years earlier.

The question quickly became, Who will the family choose? Would it be a beer man? Was there even a beer man out there worth hiring who would take on such a task?

The past two decades had been shouting a simple lesson into Coors's ear: that the modern beer industry was about image, and narrow-minded devotion to product was lethally outdated. When Philip Morris first had transformed the brewing industry with Miller Lite seventeen years earlier, Bill had refused to see the changes. The hotshot marketers at Miller and Anheuser-Busch were to him nothing but Visigoths—loud brutes in fancy ties tearing down the temples of quality and erecting false idols in their place. They had no roots, no loyalties, no core, Bill and Joe concluded, and so, they concluded, the Visigoths had no future.

They were wrong, of course. Peter—then but a stalk of a boy—was seduced. When he began talking of inviting the Visigoths inside the walls of the Golden brewery, Bill and Joe refused. Then, to humor the boy, they had bought him one as a toy—the out-of-his-depth Lee Shelton—and then, in the late 1970s, one thing had led to another. Peter clamored for more and more marketing firepower. Bill and Joe were compelled to go along. In light of the strike, the boycott, and the combined ravages of A-B and Miller, they knew the brewery was in a kind of trouble they couldn't handle themselves. But they gave with one hand and took away with the other. They let the Visigoth Art Stone inside the walls, but gave him little money or authority. On a whim born of momentary desperation, they hired the arch-Visigoth John Nichols, but after Nichols offended them with his impertinent disregard for authority and tradition, they clamped down. Afterward, only marketers from the beer industry were allowed inside the gates, the Coors brothers wanting to have it both ways. Bob Rechholtz was trusted because, though a marketer, he was quiet, respectful, and a beer man. When Rechholtz told the brothers to lay bales of money upon the altar of "going national," they did so, and they even put Rechholtz on the board—a marketer, to sit among giants who had brewed beer and made cans alongside their father.

Bill and Joe had believed they were making the necessary accommodations to the modern ways of doing business. But as Rechholtz could have told them, they never really did. Bill and Joe—and after Joe's departure, Bill alone—had remained stuck in the old world. Nobody who fully accepted the exigencies of the modern marketplace would have waited so long to make peace with the unions. Nobody wholeheartedly eager to compete would have insisted on serving the entire nation from a single brewery. No beer executive who understood the market principle of image over product would have held on to Herman Joseph's while failing to field a light beer, a malt liquor, and a subpremium. And no beer company serious about competing in the 1980s and '90s would have backed out of the Stroh's deal, or allowed itself to be led for so long by a septuagenarian brewing engineer and a nephew who'd never worked outside the family business. The industry belonged to the Visigoths now. The cigarette marketers at Philip Morris had stormed Milwaukee, seized an honorable brewery, and turned it into the industry trendsetter with slick imagery. August Busch III had gone Miller one better. He'd not only hired a swarm of Visigoths, he'd also became one himself, in so doing doubling the size of his family's corporation.

Peter Coors would never be a Visigoth. He had neither the training, the experience, nor the taste for blood. And as the past seventeen years had demonstrated, he wasn't fit to command Visigoths, either. To command Visigoths one must be one.

On February 8, 1993, Peter announced he was hiring a man named Leo Kiely to be president and chief operating officer of Coors Brewing Company. Peter would stay on as CEO, he said, to "build relationships with . . . the financial community, legislators, and our customers." He would, in other words, go back to taking people to dinner for a living. Bill would remain chairman. But day-to-day operation of Adolph Coors's brewery would be in the hands of Kiely, a man as yet unknown in the brewing industry.

Kiely had been president of Frito-Lay, the PepsiCo subsidiary Peter had read so much about in *In Search of Excellence*. After graduating Harvard and earning his M.B.A. at Wharton, Kiely had worked for Wilson Sporting Goods and then for a division of 7UP. He had moved to Frito-Lay as vice president of brand management around the time Bob Rechholtz had joined Coors. Until wooed by Peter, Kiely—beefy and gregarious beside the slim, shy Coorses—had never thought about beer in his life, except as a drink to go with Chee·tos. He had no brewing experience, no friends in the industry, no feel for the craft or history of brewing. And though it pained Bill Coors, none of that mattered. What Kiely knew—and knew well—was how to dangle brightly colored, low-priced consumer products before people and get them to bite.

This, 120 years after Adolph Coors had founded the Golden brewery, was what the company needed. There would be no more striving for critical mass either. Kiely's mission was a hard run for the immediate dollar. "I am here," he told reporters, "for the stockholder."

The long war against the Visigoths was over. Command of the Coors brewery was theirs.

Epilogue

The Coors story ends there. The company still exists, of course, but it is now, in most respects, just another big corporation. Much of what made it the brewing industry's idiosyncratic anachronism has been stripped away.

Four months after taking charge, Leo Kiely announced he intended to reduce Coors's payroll by almost 70 percent—through outsourcing, early retirement, incentives, and firings. "You have to be competitive," Kiely told an industry magazine, "and you have to give a fair return to your banker." That a president of Adolph Coors's brewery planned to offload two thirds of his employees to please a banker was a powerful signal that times had changed.

An unusually large portion of Coors's workers had never worked anywhere but Coors. Many were Golden High School graduates. The idea of leaving Coors, even with Kiely's incentives, terrified them. Some went running to Bill—who had been to many of them more like a workplace uncle than a boss—and pleaded, often in tears, for their jobs. Surely, Bill still called the shots, they thought, just as he had when Peter was president.

But one of Peter's main reasons for hiring Kiely was that Kiely couldn't be bullied by Bill. When old brewery workers came weeping to Bill, he backed away muttering about changing times. Unable to endure the pain of Kiely's cuts, Bill finally left his beloved brewery. He moved his office across Clear Creek to ACX. For the first time since World War I, Bill roamed the Coors brewery no more.

Bill's brother Joe sold the vineyard and moved with his new wife to a subdivision near Palm Springs. In 1997, he suffered a mild heart attack and shortly thereafter, at age eighty-one, he read the Sinner's Prayer and became a born-again Christian. "If I die before you," he told his big brother, "I'll be waiting for you in heaven."

The lucky workers allowed to stay at Coors were sent to "financial reality" courses on company time in which they were taught in Sesame Street terms about the rigors of competition, the imperatives of stockholders, and the importance of cash flow. Duly educated, they then experienced an "adjustment" of their "compensation package" that effectively cut their pay and froze their pensions.

His "critical mass" strategy abandoned, Bob Rechholtz retired from Coors and was replaced not by a beer man but by a marketer who had worked for Tropicana and Kellogg.

Brewhouse employees—the elite of Coors's blue-collar workforce—began to notice sharp young M.B.A.s in neckties sniffing around the kettles. Production meetings, theretofore run by brewers, now were chaired by marketers in suits who had never before been inside a brewery.

Frito Banditos, the old-timers called them.

The Frito Banditos had two obsessions: volume and color—moving lots of beer out the door, and making sure its color is right. Noticeably absent from their short list of concerns was flavor: Aging was cut by a quarter, and in summer to as little as half. The brewery, rushed to produce and short on expertise, began experiencing "clean breaks"—incidents of contamination that required recall. Old-timers protested to the Frito Banditos that Coors was going to end up having to pasteurize its beer. At one particularly contentious meeting, in which the men in coveralls leapt to their feet shouting at the Banditos, a plant supervisor brought the session to a close by barking, "Get used to it. Sales and marketing is running this ship."

And running it well, according to Kiely's new standard. After a rocky first few years, return on equity—negative 6 percent when he was hired—was up over 11 percent in 1997. After more than a century of no debt, the company's debt was up to 19 percent of its equity. Wall Street was pleased enough to let Kiely ride the historic bull market. In 1998, Coors's share price climbed to the mid-50s, double where it was when Kiely had come on board. Kiely was too good a businessman to make the Schlitz mistake and let product quality suffer too long. He eventually heard the workers' concerns, stopped cutting corners, and reduced the incidence of clean breaks. In 1996, Coors won a gold and four silver medals at the Great American Beer Festival. Whatever one thinks about the Coors family's politics, it's hard to deny that they make excellent beer.

But Coors's employees, the "family" of workers of which Bill Coors was so affectionately proud, suffered more reverses. Many longtime workers earning close to twenty dollars an hour were replaced with eight-dollar-an-hour Manpower temps. Coors even did away with one of its most beloved and idiosyncratic perks: free beer on the job. The company, no longer self-insured and newly fearful of liability, viewed beer not as Adolph Coors's sacred elixir but as an abusable substance in a factory. Drinking was limited to two cups at the end of the shift. To drink beer in Adolph Coors's brewery any other time was now a firing offense. On top of the layoffs, the pay cuts, and the sudden hegemony of the Frito Banditos, it was insulting to have to sneak the fruits of their labor in furtive gulps like bothersome teenagers instead of respected adults. This wasn't what Coors was all about!

The workers beseeched Bill and Peter to take the company back from the Frito Banditos. An anonymous group published a one-issue underground newspaper called *Incite!* that sought not to unionize Coors workers but to return them to the plantation days of Bill's paternalistic rule. Published "in the hopes that Bill and Peter Coors see the abuse they are suffering at the hands of the 'Chee·tos gang,'" *Incite!* complained about the replacement of experienced brewers with temps, slipshod shortcuts in production, and beer contamination.

If Bill and Peter saw *Incite!* they never responded. In fact, they had all but vaporized. Bill never came to the brewery anymore, and Peter was there as little as possible, slipping in and out at odd hours in his green Jeep Cherokee to avoid being buttonholed by aggrieved workers. Even the Christmas party was abandoned, and "Winterfest"—the special beer Bill had brewed annually for it—was mass-produced and niche-marketed as a seasonal superpremium.

It was enough to make some brewery workers start thinking again of the unthinkable: a union. They figured organized labor would jump at the chance to reorganize Joe Coors's brewery. But neither the Teamsters nor the United Auto Workers appreciated the symbolism of reorganizing one of the country's most legendarily antiunion companies. Their attempts were halfhearted at best. Coors remained the only nonunion mass-produced beer in the country.

Coors held on to another characteristic from the pre-Kiely days: The family remained committed to turning the country politically rightward. The Coorses created a new foundation named for nearby Castle Rock to lavish some $2 million a year on Heritage, the Mountain States Legal Foundation, A Christian Ministry in the National Parks, and other organizations that "promote a better understanding of the free enterprise system," "help ensure a limited role for government," and "uphold traditional Judeo-Christian values."

Though Joe retired from the political battlefield after revealing his betrayal, ex-wife Holly and second son Jeff continued to carry his ideological sword. Both joined the Council for National Policy, a secretive conservative strategy group whose membership reads like a Who's Who of the Christian Right—Pat Robertson, Ralph Reed, Phyllis Schlafly—and whose agenda would do away with public education, environmental regulation, and abortion rights. With Jeffrey as chair, Paul Weyrich's Free Congress Foundation filed a brief in a 1995 Hawaii Supreme Court case against same-sex marriage calling it "repugnant to the laws of nature and nature's God."

At the same time, though, Jeff voted with the rest of the Coors Brewing Company board to become one of the first companies in the country to extend health benefits to the partners of gay employees. The brewery also bought the NAACP $10,000 worth of computers and sponsored the U.S. Hispanic Chamber of Commerce annual convention in Denver.

It was by such gestures that the family begged to be judged.

"Why do some people consider it a sin to be a conservative?" Bill asked in the opening words of his 1998 self-published family history. At age eighty-three, a quarter century after his family became famously political, Bill still viewed the boycott as an unprovoked attack. He always wanted credit for having the courage to be "a good citizen," and for doing his "duty" by involving himself in politics. But it is only courageous to take an extreme and vocal stand because doing so invites consequences. In Bill's case, the consequences were vast communities of alienated potential customers. For many people, granting health benefits to a handful of gay employees' partners is less significant than giving $150,000 a year to the Free Congress Foundation, which supports candidates who consider homosexuality "an infamous crime against nature." For many people, finally naming a Mexican American to the board of directors is out-weighed by enthusiastic support for the Heritage Foundation, which backs anti-immigration and English-only initiatives. For many people, a black company vice president does not counterbalance millions given to fight affirmative action, welfare, and civil-rights enforcement. Although bludgeoned into becoming more progressive within the walls of its brewery, the Coors family has chosen to remain committed on the national level to reversing the racial, sexual, environmental, and social revolutions of the twentieth century. Millions of people who feel themselves beneficiaries of those revolutions continue to choose from the dozens of other beers on the market.

In 1998, the AFL-CIO threw a gala in Los Angeles to honor David Sickler, now fifty-four, who was retiring from running the federation's southern California office. "How many of you drink Coors beer?" a speaker asked the four hundred people in attendance. Not a single hand was raised.

Official or not, the Coors boycott continues, helping to keep the company from reaching its "critical mass" dream of a 15 percent market share. Ironically, the more efficient Leo Kiely makes the company—the more profit Coors earns on every barrel it sells—the more the lingering boycott hurts. Every bottle not sold takes a bigger chunk out of the bottom line. Committed to restoring the past, the Coors family finds itself trapped in its own hellish version of it. At the Hispanic conference he sponsored in 1996, Peter Coors was practically booed off the stage.

"Is there any possibility that history will change?" he implored the jeering crowd. "What do we have to do to move on?"

List of Interviews

George Abbott: 6 May 1997
Adrienne Anderson: 21 May 1997
David Anderson: 16 January 1997, 20 January 1997
Carol Andreas: 22 July 1996
Jane Arthur: 4 February 1997
Dale Atkins: 20 March 1997
Allan Baird: 16 October 1997, 18 October 1997
Everett Barnhardt: 18 March 1997
Brad Beckham: 14 January 1998
Chuck Bennett: 23 February 1998
Steve Bieringer: 14 May 1997
Virgil Boatwright: 21 February 1997
Jim Brown: 24 February 1997
Robert Burgess: 17 January 1997
John Carbaugh: 6 February 1998
Bob Chanin: 1 June 1997
Andy Cirkelis: 7 October 1997, 18 October 1997
Virginia Collbran: 27 January 1997
James Coors (E-mail): 9 May 1997, 29 May 1997, 31 May 1997, 8 September 1997, 10 September 1997
Jeffrey Coors: 13 August 1997
Joseph Coors, Jr.: 13 August 1997
Peter Coors: 27 May 1997, 13 August 1997, 14 April 1998 (E-mail), 19 February 1999 (E-mail)
Phyllis Coors: 2 April 1997, 9 June 1998
William Coors: 13 August 1997
Bo Cottrell: 15 October 1997
Ray Cuzzort: 14 January 1997

Jim Davies: 31 March 1997, 2 April 1997
Michael Deaver: 1 June 1997
Jack Debell: 14 March 1997
Kenneth DeBey: 27 February 1997, 2 September 1997, 9 September 1997
Raymond Delgatto: 25 March 1997
John DeVore: 13 October 1997
Ed Donaghy: 2 May 1997
Thomas Donahue: 4 June 1997
David Edgar: 5 January 1998
Al Ehrbar: 11 December 1997
Dick Franklin: 20 May 1997
Calvin Fulenwider, Jr.: 23 May 1997
Charles Gates: 7 November 1997
Thomas Geoghegan: 18 June 1997
Nita Gonzalez: 9 April 1997
Phil Goodstein: 2 January 1997
Max Goodwin: 14 April 1997
JoAnn Greenberg: 18 March 1997
Caren Griffin: 28 February 1997
Chuck Hahn: 26 January 1998
Harris Hamlin: 14 April 1997
Eric Hammersmark: 9 April 1997
Jack Hawkins: 9 April 1997
Bob Henson: 3 December 1997
Roy Hernandez: 13 November 1997
Bill Himmelman: 16 April 1997
Bill Holbrook: 12 September 1997, 9 October 1997, 3 February 1998
Ron Holtry: 27 May 1997, 14 October 1997
Philip Hufford: 1 December 1997
Swanee Hunt: 19 March 1997
Charles Isaac: 10 April 1997, 21 April 1997
Paul Jacobs: 13 October 1997
Kevin Johnson: 2 October 1997
Don Jorgenson: 19 February 1997
Sandra Justice: 12 March 1997, 19 March 1997
Sander Karp: 21 May 1997
Gerry Kaveny: 12 November 1997
John Kerr: 1 April 1997, 2 April 1997
Alan Kistler: 15 December 1997
Charles Klare: 30 May 1997
Jay Kopplin: 11 December 1997, 15 January 1998, 25 February 1998
William Kostka: 3 March 1977
Dick Kreck: 17 February 1997

Craig Kuhl: 20 March 1997
Nick Kurko: 23 September 1997
Frank Leek: 28 January 1998
Cindy Leeper: 20 November 1997
Lisa LeMaster: 22 May 1997
Martin Jay Levitt: 8 August 1997
Jeff Lieb: 7 August 1997
Mel Linn: 14 October 1997
Dennis Long: 16 October 1997
Tom Looby: 1 December 1997
James Lucier: 15 February 1998
Daniel Lynch: 18 February 1997
Allan Maraynes: 29 May 1997
William Marlin: 2 December 1997
Gerald Maykuth: 8 September 1997, 10 September 1997
Fritz Maytag: 15 May 1997
Doris McGowan: 9 January 1997
Mark McNamar: 3 April 1997, 2 October 1997, 16 October 1997
Don Mielke: 26 March 1997, 14 November 1997
Bill Moomey: 4 April 1997
Scott Moore: 14 July 1996
Ken Mueller: 18 November 1997, 22 December 1997
Mary Murphy: 20 February 1997
Gary Naifeh: 13 May 1997, 26 February 1998
Jay Nelson: 5 November 1996, 13 November 1996, 10 October 1997
John Neu: 16 April 1997
John Nichols: 3 April 1997, 22 May 1997, 19 September 1997, 23 September 1997, 30 September 1997, 12 April 1998 (E-mail), 29 April 1998 (E-mail), 13 October 1998 (E-mail), 22 October 1998 (E-mail)
Mary Ann Nichols: 30 September 1997
Tony Noblett: 5 March 1997
Lyn Nofziger: 3 June 1997
Pat Nolan: 14 November 1997
Beverley Obenchain: 6 November 1997
Mark Obmascik: 2 April 1997
Daniel O'Brien: 16 February 1998
Warren Ost: 21 February 1997
Erlinda Padilla: 31 October 1997
Charles Papazian: 6 February 1998, 21 December 1998 (E-mail)
Ron Parker: 17 March 1997
Cindy Parmenter: 17 December 1997
Jay Dee Patrick: 7 October 1997
Chuck Patterson: 21 January 1998

[List of Interviews]

Fred Rasheed: 29 May 1997

James Raymond: 11 June 1997

John Recca: 14 March 1997, 10 April 1997

Robert Rechholtz: 11 June 1997, 9 December 1997

Dan Ritchie: 19 May 1997

Richard Roberts: 5 May 1997

Clifford Rock: 1 May 1997, 19 May 1997, 21 October 1997

Gil Rodriguez: 22 March 1997

Bill Roehl: 15 October 1997

Tony Rollins: 2 June 1997

Herrick Roth: 22 May 1997

Richard Rothstein: 7 January 1998

Edward Rozek: 10 February 1997

Charlie Russell: 20 March 1997

Bob Schieffer: 17 October 1997, 17 November 1997

Gary Schmitz: 22 November 1996

Ron Seaman: 2 December 1997, 11 December 1997

John Seligman: 15 October 1997

Scott Service: 6 October 1997, 8 October 1997

Lee Shelton: 24 March 1997, 8 September 1997, 22 February 1999

David Sickler: 24 April 1997, 3 November 1997, 23 December 1997, 29
August 1998 (E-mail), 6 November 1998 (E-mail), 5 January 1999
(E-mail)

James Silverthorn: 11 February 1997, 4 September 1997, 9 September 1997

June Smith: 16 February 1998, 17 February 1998 (E-mail)

Frank Solis: 7 October 1997

Jerry Steinman: 26 February 1997

Morgan Steinmetz: 25 September 1997

Jim Stokes: 19 November 1997

Arthur Stone: 13 March 1997, 25 March 1997, 28 March 1997, 21 February
1999, 22 February 1999

Lowell Sund: 17 April 1997, 21 October 1997, 10 November 1997, 17 November 1997

Dale "Buzz" Sweat: 17 March 1997

Eugene Tardy: 26 February 1997, 13 March 1997, 21 January 1998

Steven Toler: 14 November 1997

Gary Truitt: 18 February 1998, 20 February 1998

Ben Tucker: 18 April 1997, 2 October 1997, 15 October 1997

Urvashi Vaid: 17 April 1997

Fred Vierra: 29 December 1997, 23 November 1998

Richard Viguerie: 17 October 1997, 9 January 1998

Howard Wallace: 13 July 1997

Mike Wallace: 10 April 1997

[List of Interviews]

Bob Weinberg: 3 March 1997
Paul Weissman: 4 March 1997
Charles Z. Wick: 7 April 1997
Barbara J. Yentzer: 1 June 1997
Raul Yzaguirre: 4 June 1997

Acknowledgments

Among the myths that guide the Coors family is a belief that the press is out to get them. "They won't talk to you," their spokesman told me. "They've been burned too many times."

In truth, the Coors family and their company have been coddled by the press to a remarkable degree. My years as a business reporter taught me the difference between hostile, neutral, and sympathetic coverage. The Coorses, having enjoyed decades of the latter in the mainstream and trade press, and in such television coverage as the *60 Minutes* segment, have little about which to complain. Regardless, the Coorses largely hide behind the wall of "no comment" demanded by the founder and his son.

So I have little for which to thank them. I enjoyed one short meeting with Peter, and then one two-hour session in the Queen Anne mansion with Peter, Bill, Joe Jr., and Jeff. I spent the bulk of both meetings trying to convince them to be interviewed. They refused, and put the word out to their friends and employees to do likewise.

But many talked anyway; in all, more than 150 people agreed to be interviewed, and I am indebted to all of them.

When I asked Bill Coors if he would walk me through his brewery to explain the massive factory he built, he told me it would do me no good. "You wouldn't understand it," he said plainly. (Peter graciously countermanded his uncle and permitted a VIP tour. Many thanks to him, and to Tina Gustafson for conducting the tour.)

The Coorses allowed company spokesman Joe Fuentes to answer questions of factual detail, and he did his best under trying circumstances. Thank you, Joe.

This is the second book that Cate Sewell, an archivist at the Ronald

[Acknowledgments]

Reagan Presidential Library, has helped me research. Cate knows where the good stuff is buried and how to match it to the project at hand. Many thanks to her, and her colleagues Mike Duggan and Steve Branch.

Jay Nelson was my first interview for this book. On the verge of retiring as Smith, Barney's beverage-industry analyst to write a novel, he understood my needs as both a researcher and a storyteller. Stan Oliner of the Colorado Historical Society not only bent rules and worked overtime to help me; he also bought lunch. Kristin Bloomer took time away from earning a Ph.D. to do considerable library-burrowing. In addition to sharing his experiences at Coors, Lowell Sund helped with biblical questions. Scott Moore, professor of political science at Colorado State University, came up with the idea of this book in the first place. Carlos Arevalo-Flores stepped in at just the right moment with just the right help.

Henry Ferris, my editor at William Morrow, radiated encouragement throughout and helped fill a lot of narrative potholes. David Falk's copy editing was sublime. It is furthermore my great fortune to be represented by Kris Dahl at International Creative Management, an elegant combination of cheerleader and drill sergeant who knows what sells and how to sell it.

As always, Bill Chaloupka—professor of political science and environmental studies at the University of Montana—was a fount of ideas, recommendations, inspiration, and criticism. I'd be nowhere without him.

When college students ask me how to become a writer, my stock response is, "First of all, marry my wife." For without Margaret Knox I'd have no writing career at all. Her help goes way beyond debriefing and coaching my research, her months of tough and graceful line editing, and her full-time care of our daughter, Rosa. Above all, Margaret keeps the intellectual amperage of our marriage cranked high, and the household as rich in language and ideas as it is in love and play and romance. Would that I could thank her enough.

Bibliography

Aldrich, Nelson W., Jr. *Old Money: The Mythology of America's Upper Classes.* New York: Alfred A. Knopf, 1988.

Anderson, Martin. *Revolution: The Reagan Legacy.* Stanford, Calif.: Hoover Institution Press, 1988.

Athearn, Robert G. *The Coloradans.* Albuquerque: University of New Mexico Press, 1976.

Baker, James H., and LeRoy Hafen, eds. *History of Colorado.* Vol. V. Denver, 1927.

Banham, Russ. *Coors: A Rocky Mountain Legend.* Lyme, Conn.: Greenwich Publishing Group, 1998.

Baucom, Donald R. *The Origins of SDI.* Lawrence: University Press of Kansas, 1992.

Bellant, Russ. *The Coors Connection: How Coors Family Philanthropy Undermines Democratic Pluralism.* Boston: South End Press, 1988.

Bradlee, Ben, Jr. *Guts and Glory: The Rise and Fall of Oliver North.* New York: Donald I. Fine, 1988.

Broad, William. *Teller's War: The Top-Secret Story Behind the Star Wars Deception.* New York: Simon & Schuster, 1992.

Brooks, Thomas R. *Toil and Trouble: A History of American Labor.* 2nd ed. New York: Delta, 1971.

Burgess, Robert J. *Silver Bullets: A Soldier's Story of How Coors Bombed in the Beer Wars.* New York: St. Martin's Press, 1993.

Cannon, Lou. *President Reagan: The Role of a Lifetime.* New York: Simon & Schuster, 1991.

———. *Reagan.* New York: G. P. Putnam's Sons, 1982.

Chaloupka, William. *Everybody Knows: Cynicism in America.* Minneapolis: University of Minnesota Press, 1999.

[Bibliography]

Conny, Beth Mende. *A Catalyst for Change: The Pioneering of the Aluminum Can.* Adolph Coors Co., 1990.

Conway, Flo, and Jim Siegelman. *Holy Terror: The Fundamentalist War on America's Freedoms in Religion, Politics and Our Private Lives.* Garden City, N.Y.: Doubleday, 1982.

Coors: A Report on the Company's Environmental Policies and Practices. New York: The Council on Economic Priorities, Corporate Environmental Data Clearinghouse, 1992.

Crawford, Alan. *Thunder on the Right: The "New Right" and the Politics of Resentment.* New York: Pantheon Books, 1980.

Dorset, Lyle W., and Michael McCarthy. *The Queen City: A History of Denver.* Boulder, Colo.: Pruett Publishing Co., 1977.

Foster, Mark S. *Henry M. Porter: Rocky Mountain Empire Builder.* Niwot, Colo.: University Press of Colorado, 1991.

Garreau, Joel. *The Nine Nations of North America.* New York: Avon, 1981.

Goldwater, Barry. *The Conscience of a Conservative.* Shepherdsville, Ky: Victor Publishing Co., 1960.

Gottfried, Paul, and Thomas Fleming. *The Conservative Movement.* Boston: Twayne Publishers, 1988.

Hernon, Peter, and Terry Ganey. *Under the Influence: The Unauthorized Story of the Anheuser-Busch Dynasty.* New York: Simon & Schuster, 1991.

Hutchinson, John. *The Imperfect Union: A History of Corruption in American Trade Unions.* New York: Dutton, 1972.

James, Ronald A. *Our Own Generation: The Tumultuous Years.* Boulder: University of Colorado, 1979.

Judis, John B. *William F. Buckley, Jr.: Patron Saint of the Conservatives.* New York: Simon & Schuster, 1988.

Kirk, Russell. *The Conservative Mind, from Burke to Santayana.* Chicago: Henry Regnery Co., 1953.

Kluger, Richard. *Ashes to Ashes: America's Hundred-Year Cigarette War, the Public Health, and the Unabashed Triumph of Philip Morris.* New York: Alfred A. Knopf, 1996.

Knight, Harold V. *Working in Colorado: A Brief History of the Colorado Labor Movement.* Boulder: University of Colorado, 1971.

Kostka, William. *The Pre-Prohibition History of Adolph Coors Co., 1873–1933.* Adolph Coors Company, 1973.

Lakoff, Sanford, and Herbert F. York. *A Shield in Space? Techology, Politics and the Strategic Defense Initiative.* Berkeley: University of California Press, 1989.

Leonard, Thomas, Cynthia Crippen, and Marc Aronson. *Day by Day: The Seventies.* Vols. 1 and 2. New York: Facts on File, 1988.

Limerick, Patricia. *The Legacy of Conquest: The Unbroken Past of the American West.* New York: Norton, 1987.

Martin, William. *With God on Our Side: The Rise of the Religious Right in America.* New York: Broadway Books, 1996.

Meltzer, Ellen, and Marc Aronson. *Day by Day: The Eighties.* Vols. 1 and 2. New York: Facts on File, 1995.

Nash, George H. *The Conservative Intellectual Movement in America Since 1945.* New York: Basic Books, 1976.

Nelson, Douglas, and Thomas Parker. *Day by Day: The Sixties,* Vols. 1 and 2. New York: Facts on File, 1983.

Piven, Francis Fox, and Richard A. Cloward. *The New Class War: Reagan's Attack on the Welfare State and Its Consequences.* New York: Pantheon, 1982.

Public Papers of the Presidents of the United States: Ronald Reagan 1986. Washington: Office of Federal Register, 1988.

Robinson, Archie. *George Meany and His Times.* New York: Simon & Schuster, 1981.

Ronzio, Richard, ed. *The 1967 Denver Westerners Brand Book.* Vol. XXIII, *The Westerners.* Denver, 1968.

Rusher, William A. *The Rise of the Right.* New York: William Morrow, 1984.

Schieffer, Bob, and Gary Paul Gates. *The Acting President.* New York: E. P. Dutton, 1989.

Smith, Gregg. *Beer: A History of Suds and Civilization from Mesopotamia to Microbreweries.* New York: Avon, 1995.

Smolla, Rodney A. *Jerry Falwell v. Larry Flynt.* New York: St. Martin's Press, 1988.

Stanley, Thomas J., and William D. Danko. *The Millionaire Next Door: The Surprising Secrets of America's Wealthy.* Atlanta: Longstreet Press, 1996.

Van Munching, Philip. *Beer Blast: The Inside Story of the Brewing Industry's Bizarre Battles for Your Money.* New York: Times Business, 1997.

Von Damm, Helene. *At Reagan's Side: Twenty Years in the Political Mainstream.* New York: Doubleday, 1989.

Wallace, Mike, and Gary Paul Gates. *Close Encounters.* New York: William Morrow, 1984.

Watt, James. *The Courage of a Conservative.* New York: Simon & Schuster, 1985.

West, Ray, ed. *Rocky Mountain Cities.* New York: Norton, 1949.

Whitford, David. *Playing Hardball: The High-Stakes Battle for Baseball's New Franchises.* New York: Doubleday, 1993.

Williams, H. Page. *Do Yourself a Favor: Love Your Wife.* South Plainfield, N.J.: Bridge Publishing, 1971.

Williams, Roy O. *Preparing Your Family to Manage Wealth.* Marina, Calif.: Monterey Pacific Institute, 1992.

[Bibliography]

Zieger, Robert H. *American Workers, American Unions, 1920–1985*. Baltimore: Johns Hopkins University Press, 1986.

Zinn, Howard. *A People's History of the United States: 1492–Present*. New York: HarperCollins, 1995.

Index

[*Index*]